Isaac Daniel Stewart
Utah in America

Val D. Rust

DORRANCE
PUBLISHING CO
EST. 1920
PITTSBURGH, PENNSYLVANIA 15238

Dorrance Publishing Co
585 Alpha Drive
Suite 103
Pittsburgh, PA 15238
Visit our website at www.dorrancebookstore.com

ISBN: 979-8-88729-213-7
eISBN: 979-8-88729-713-2

To Liz and Shannon,
special daughters of a great man

Contents

Introduction vii

PART I: Polio and Its Aftermath 1
  1. Elder Stewart Gets Polio 3
  2. The Family Learns Elder Stewart Has Polio 17
  3. Rehabilitation in California 27

PART II: The Early Life of Dan Stewart 43
  4. Young Danny 45
  5. Elder Stewart 47
  6. A Summer of Depression 75
  7. Poli Sci and Marriage 91
  8. Attending Law School 109

PART III: Dan the Lawyer and Professor 121
  9. The Justice Department 123
  10. Professor Stewart 135
  11. Jones Waldo 149

PART IV: Utah Supreme Court 167
  12. Utah Supreme Court in Crisis 169
  13. The Transformation Begins 183
  14. Matheson's Legacy 197

PART V: The Justice and his Pen 209

   15. U.S. Constitution 211

   16. Utah Constitution 221

   17. Common Law 233

   18. Expert Witnesses 243

   19. Evidence 251

   20. Utah's Heritage of Evil 263

   21. Church and State 277

   22. Dissent 287

Part VI: Life Space 301

   23. Mountain of the Lord's House 303

   24. Dinner and Discussion 313

   25. Legacy and Death 325

Bibliography 343

Index 367

INTRODUCTION

Dan Stewart began serving on the Utah Supreme Court at a time when state leaders were assessing their place in the United States. By 1976, local sentiment against national norms had reached a point where Utah Senator Jake Garn, Dan Stewart's former classmate at East High School, could say, "I don't think it's anybody's damn business what we do in the state of Utah."[1] He was talking about protests by conservationists against building a major coal-burning power plant near Kanab. And Justice Albert H. Ellett, whom Dan Stewart later replaced on the Utah Supreme Court, went even further, claiming that the federal government, particularly the U.S. Supreme Court, was robbing Utahns of their God-given rights: "We are like galley slaves, chained to our oars by a power from which we cannot free ourselves."[2]

Garn and Ellett, as well as most other Utah leaders, rejected intrusion on their sovereignty by outsiders, claiming that norms of American society did not hold for them. Justice Ellett even declared that the Bill of Rights did not apply to Utah.[3] One consequence was that critics in and out of the state scorned the Utah Legislature and Supreme Court as backwater, provincial institutions.[4] Some legal experts even suggested that the Utah Supreme Court

---

[1] Salt Lake Tribune, April 19, 1976.

[2] Utah Supreme Court, "Dyett V. Turner," in *439 P2d 266* (1968).

[3] Ibid.

of the 1950s, 60s, and 70s had become a laughing stock in the law schools of America.[5]

This is an intimate account of Isaac Daniel Stewart, but his story is also a record of a critical transitional era in Utah. In every historical period, incidents come and go, but a biography gives the reader a personal glimpse of how one major figure in that drama responds to events and contributes to the social and cultural developments taking place. We explore the dramatic shift in Utah's relationship with America through one man. Dan Stewart resisted separation from the larger American society. At a time when most Utah leaders openly displayed isolationism and partisanship, Dan Stewart was able to remain a devoted member of his church and the local social and political culture, and, at the same time, commit himself to the demands of loyal American citizenship. In 1979, when he was appointed to the Utah Supreme Court, he insisted that his decisions coincide with the U.S. Constitution and federal laws.

It is difficult to create an overall sketch of Dan Stewart's judicial rulings. He was assigned the cases he would review, and so he had no control over what they were. No single event, court case, or opinion made by Stewart changed the course of Utah history, but the cumulative effect of his participation was part of a thought and values revolution taking place in the state. To be sure, Stewart's voice in the struggle to restore relations with the country was not alone; however, the consequences of his influence rippled through social reality until dramatic change could be found in the connections between Utah and the rest of America. These vindicated his faith in the democratic idea of America. Stewart was privileged to be the first of several prominent Utah Supreme Court justices, including Gordon R. Hall, Richard C. Howe, Dallin Oaks, Christine Durham, and Michael Zimmerman. In the 1980s and '90s, these justices turned the Utah Supreme Court into an acclaimed and model American institution.

Stewart developed his strong allegiance to the U.S. early in life. This was strengthened, soon after the war, when he was a missionary in West Ger-

---

[4] Grace Lichtenstein, "Utah's Conservative Court Is Center of Duspute over Rulings," *The New York Times* (Nov. 30, 1975).

[5] Greg Orme, "Interview at the Sheraton Park Motel in Park City, Utah " (Sept. 10, 2019).

many. While he was preaching about Mormonism, he became a student of German culture and literature, learning to appreciate the dangers of political excesses, and the trauma Germans had experienced during World War II.

While working with the Justice Department, and as a practicing lawyer, Stewart dedicated himself to antitrust issues, challenging attempts on the part of businesses to reduce competition and establish monopolies. He also resisted those entrepreneurs who took advantage of fragile landscape and deserts for immediate financial gain.

As a university professor, Stewart successfully pushed for clarification and implementation of rules related to hearsay evidence, memory, and witnesses in the courts.

After he was appointed to the Utah Supreme Court, he argued for the complete separation of church and state. He challenged attempts on the part of fellow justices to take a middle-ground approach to church/state issues. He believed that, despite the long tradition of Mormon dominance in Utah, both the state and the church would be stronger, if separation were maintained.[6]

Even while arguing the importance of the rule of law, and the awareness that those who break the law suffer its consequences, Justice Stewart extolled civil disobedience as, at times, a necessary vehicle to achieve justice. He argued that Blacks and other minorities were justified to engage in non-violent civil disobedience.[7]

Dan demanded that women be treated equally in the workplace. In his view, the law allowed women the right to terminate pregnancy, but if the woman chose to have a baby, he argued that the state should be a supporting partner with new mothers in terms of financial assistance and released time from work. He also demanded that women earn the right to be with their children. For Stewart, children's rights were as important as the mother's rights.

In criminal cases, Justice Stewart advocated holding capital punishment in check. He did this even when the Utah Supreme Court was asked to consider

---

[6] Utah Supreme Court, "Society of Separatists V. Whitehead, 870 P.2d 916," (Dec. 10, 1993).

[7] I. Daniel Stewart, "The Rule of Law and the Dilemma of Minorities," *Dialogue: A Journal of Mormon Thought* III, no. 4 (1968).

heinous cases such as the so-called Hi Fi murders in Ogden.[8] He also advocated that the courts provide a safety net for those of the mentally ill who do evil. His court briefs demanded that the prison system treat prisoners humanely. He may be the only state supreme court justice ever to appear at a state prison probation hearing for an inmate.

Some issues Dan Stewart was known for, were of interest primarily to the legal community. Among the many legal contributions he made had to do with clarifying the U.S. and Utah Constitutions. He was also known for his concern that common law be recognized as a part of Utah's heritage, especially the laws that were established in the Mormon courts prior to Utah becoming a state. He was a specialist in rules of evidence. He was an early critic of the unquestioned value of eye-witness testimony. He argued that special evidentiary consideration be given to people with impaired mental capacity who break the law. He demanded that the testimony of young people required special protections. He was a strong advocate for the use of specialist testimony, including psychologists and social workers.

His arguments were measured and well-stated, sometimes brilliant. His written work was straightforward and analytic; although, when he was dissenting from other's briefs, his language was creative and colorful, at times, caustic. His preparedness was legendary, indicating an unmatched mind and work ethic.

All of this came from a man who spent more than fifty years of his adult life in a wheelchair, mostly as a paraplegic and later as a quadriplegic. He contracted polio while serving in West Germany as a Mormon missionary. He was confined for months in an iron lung, struggling just to breathe, paralyzed from his chest down, with limited use of his arms and shoulders. He had restricted lung capacity. But he refused to allow polio's tragic, debilitating consequences to curb his unbreakable perseverance, his dreams, and his aspirations.

After spending almost two years in California and Utah hospitals, learning to breathe and hold a pencil, Dan re-entered the University of Utah. He studied political science under Professor Francis Wormuth, and ultimately gave the valedictory address to his graduating class. He excelled at the Uni-

[8] Beverly DeVoy, "Hi Fi Evidence Unpacked," *Deseret News* Aug. 9, 1992.

versity of Utah law school, graduating number one in his class as well as serving as the Editor-in-Chief of the *Utah Law Review*.

He was given a coveted position as a law clerk for the Department of Justice in Washington, D.C., writing U.S. Supreme Court anti-trust briefs. On returning to Utah, he established a reputation as an outstanding professor of law at the University of Utah. He went into private practice for eight years as a partner in a prominent Salt Lake City law firm in the field of antitrust litigation. Finally, Stewart spent twenty-one years on the Utah Supreme Court.

Dan grew up in what is generally considered to be a posh part of Salt Lake City and Utah. But at the age of twelve, his father died of a heart attack, and the financial challenges that followed colored his perspective about life. He quietly and resourcefully found afternoon and summer jobs, earning money to help keep the family afloat. Fortunately, he was both physically and mentally gifted. Dan was an all-star athlete in football.

He also immersed himself in classical literature of the West. He read works that usually only professional researchers tackle. While a student, he began the lifelong practice of subscribing to, and reading, national journals and newspapers. In addition, he was active in the Mormon tradition of ongoing discussion groups that explored national and global issues, including globalization, faith, race, gender, and poverty. He was an ardent fan of the Utah mountains and red rock area, believing that these were places where God Himself would spend His time.

The book is divided into twenty-five chapters. Each chapter is relatively brief and focuses on a specific aspect of Dan Stewart's life. The chapters are arranged into six sections. In the first section Dan Stewart is stricken with polio and spends two years in the hospital and rehabilitation. The second section provides a chronology of Stewart's early life. The third section deals with his life as a lawyer and a law professor. Section Four discusses the Utah Supreme Court during the last half of the twentieth century. The fifth section is the longest and deals with the time Stewart was a justice of the Utah Supreme Court. The final section deals with a couple of issues that carry through Dan's entire life. The final chapter deals with his legacy and death.

This book contains a quintessential Utah and American tale that spans almost seven decades. Extended Stewart family members have written about early family members. Dan's mother dictated a brief account of her own life.[9] And toward the end of Dan's life, he dictated his own life story to a child-hood friend and companion. In telling his own story, Dan had no great store of documents to guide his personal account,[10] so his personal story is informal and incomplete. Fortunately, for this story I have been able to gain access to extensive records and clippings kept by the Stewart family.

I have also interviewed scores of Dan's family members, friends, and colleagues. This narrative might provide an appropriate story of a Mormon Utah boy who encountered great tragedies in life, but who ultimately accomplished great things. Dan Stewart's life story not only helps us understand and appreciate his accomplishments, but it enlightens us about the recent history of Utah and its storied relationship with the United States.

---

[9] Orabelle Iverson Stewart, "Memories of Orabelle Iverson Stewart," (Salt Lake City: Private manuscript, Dec. 5, 1966).

[10] I. Daniel Stewart, "A Life: Dictated to Richard G. Ellis," (Salt Lake City, Utah: Draft Manuscript, 2002).

PART I:

POLIO AND ITS AFTERMATH

1. Elder Stewart Gets Polio

It was early Sunday evening in Freiburg, West Germany, and Elder Daniel Stewart was exhausted. He and the other Mormon missionaries had said goodbye to the last of about forty Saints gathered for the opening ceremonies of a new church building. It was in a residential area of town and was really a renovated family residence. Now, the missionaries were setting out to share an evening meal at a local restaurant. All nine, who had been assigned to the city were there.[11]

Missionaries usually travel in pairs, formally called "companions," but tonight it was an odd number, because Elder Erich Kirchhoefer had just been released and later that week was traveling home. The dinner was hosted by West German Mission President, Kenneth B. Dyer, and his wife. The missionaries rarely went to a restaurant that had tablecloths and the occasion allowed them to choose something from the bottom of the menu, such as *Sauerbraten* with potato dumplings, or a *Wiener Schnitzel*; these were too expensive when the missionaries paid for the meal themselves.

Elder Stewart was feeling over-tired; he had felt so for some months. For some time, he had complained in his journal of being "entirely pooped," "worn out," and "lifeless."[12] That morning, just outside Bern, Switzerland,

---

[11] Elders Erich Kirchhoefer, Karl Swan, Peter Freeman, Larry Bean, Gary Fogg, William Peterson, and Daniel Stewart, in addition to Sisters Beck and Grebow.

[12] I. Daniel Stewart, "Missionary Journal " (Hand-written in West Germany 1953-1955).

he and the other missionaries had risen early enough to catch a 5:00 A.M. train. They had spent the prior day serving in the new Bern Mormon temple. On the train back to Freiburg, he had begun to feel pains in his lower back, but it was little more than an annoyance.

When they arrived at Basel, they transferred to a train going north to Germany. In less than an hour they were in Freiburg, and they only had to transfer once on the streetcar before arriving near the new chapel. The opening ceremonies had already begun; nevertheless, President Dyer invited Elder Stewart to speak. At first, Elder Stewart was prompted to tell him he was not feeling well, but instead he decided to address the congregation. Having arrived in Freiburg the previous Thursday, he did not yet know those in attendance, but his reputation for speaking a flawless German had preceded him. He spoke freely and fluently about the restoration of the gospel of Jesus Christ.

By the time the missionaries arrived at the restaurant, Elder Stewart was in real pain. He "couldn't remain sitting but standing brought no relief either."[13] As he stretched his arms above his body, he commented to young Elder Gary Fogg, "My back is killing me." Fogg suggested, "You might have a slipped disk."[14]

But Elder Stewart was skeptical. He had played football all through high school and even at the University of Utah. He had never had a slipped disk, but now he was wobbly, worn out, and bone tired, and he was not able to eat much. He whispered to his companion, Elder Winfried Peterson, "Perhaps the two of us should leave early, so I can just go to bed and sleep it off."

The restaurant was on the edge of the old town, not far from the new chapel. Freiburg is an historically important city, known for its Medieval cathedral and Renaissance university. As they rode their bikes, they could see the *Martinstor*, with its arched entrance and high watchtower; the city was once fortified by a solid wall. The gate now served as one entrance to the old town, with a sprawling, charming, inner-city pedestrian zone.

---

[13] After he returned home and completed his rehabilitation, he wrote a brief account of this in his diary. See *Addendum*, Missionary Journal (Salt Lake City, Utah: Handwritten undated).

[14] Gary Fogg, "Missionary Journal," (West German Mission: Hand-Written Diary, 1955-1958). Jan 23, 1956.

The winter weather was unseasonably warm, and the brief bicycle ride was exhilarating. But when arriving at the new chapel on *Weierhofstraße*, Elder Stewart struggled up the stairs. The washroom and toilet were just off the landing on the second floor, where the recreation hall was located. He stepped into the washroom and gazed at himself in a mirror placed over the sink. What he usually saw was a tall, trim young man with broad, strong shoulders that his worn and threadbare suit could not mask.

He recognized his dark hair and slightly stern, chiseled face that usually communicated the message, "I am in charge," not just because he was tall and strong, but also because of his strength of face was showing pain, stress, and tension. Elder Stewart quickly washed his hands and went back out to the landing and slowly stumbled further up the stairs to the third floor, which the elders called "the attic." There were two large, partially finished rooms under a sloping ceiling, with dormer windows projecting horizontally beyond a pitched roof. Among the four beds in the far room, he sought out his own. Elder Stewart had arrived from Munich four days earlier, and he was reminded that seniority meant little in that environment.

The only cot remaining for him was old and in disrepair. The steel metal frame and springs were in decent condition, but the mattress was hard and lumpy. He took his suit off, hung it in the closest wooden wardrobe. Slipping out of his worn shoes, he climbed into bed. He fell immediately into a deep but unsettled sleep, and he did not hear when the other five elders quietly came into the attic and prepared for bed.

In his sleep, Elder Stewart felt he was careening here and there, each turn shooting pains through his body. He awakened from time to time, and he tried to sit or stand. He even tried to sleep on the floor, but he found "no alleviation from the intense pain."[15] During one episode of fitful sleep, he suddenly realized that Elder Bean was touching his arm, saying it was 2:30 in the morning, and Stewart's "moaning and rolling" woke up all the other elders. "What's the matter?"[16] "I don't know. I feel excruciating pain all over my body."

---

[15] Stewart, *Addendum*.

[16] Lawrence Bean, "Missionary Journal," (West German Mission: Hand Written Diary, 1954-1956). Jan. 23, 1956.

Elder Bean, who just that weekend had been set apart as the new Freiburg branch president, suggested they give Elder Stewart a blessing.[17] Giving blessings are common among Mormons, and every elder quickly learns how to perform the ordinance. Elder Bean got a container of "consecrated oil" from a small cabinet and placed a drop of its oil on the elder's forehead. Then, placing his hands lightly on Elder Stewart's head, he intoned: "Elder Isaac Daniel Stewart, through the authority of the Holy Melchizedek Priesthood, which I hold, I anoint you with this oil, which has been consecrated for the healing of the sick and afflicted. I do this in the name of Jesus Christ, Amen."

The missionaries then gathered around Elder Stewart, each placing one hand on his head and the other on the shoulder of the elder standing in front of him. Elder Peterson, Stewart's missionary companion, "sealed the anointing" and gave him the blessing. It is common in the church to say that the blessing is given as the Spirit directs, but it usually follows a pattern. Elder Peterson would surely have said, "The Lord is pleased with you and the work that you are performing as a missionary."

Then he would have reminded Elder Stewart, "You belong to a special community that will support you through every trial and test that you face." He might also have said, "Elder Stewart, you are recognized and revered among the missionaries. We all know and appreciate your special gifts and talents."

He then would have blessed him, saying, "Elder Stewart, we bless you that you will be comforted, that your pains will soon go away, and that you will have the courage and fortitude to face whatever difficulties you will encounter." Finally, he would have reminded his companion, "Elder Stewart, the Lord has a special mission for you." And he would have concluded the blessing telling Elder Stewart that he was in the Lord's hands, and "His will be done."

It is not uncommon that those being blessed find some relief, and Elder Stewart soon relaxed and went to sleep. The other elders withdrew into the front room of the attic to decide what to do next. They concluded that as soon as daylight came, Elders Karl Swan and Peter Freeman would ride their bikes to the home of brother Karl Becker, the first councilor in the branch

---

[17] Stewart, *Addendum*.

presidency. He was the only member in the branch who owned a car, a small Opel, and would be able to transport Elder Stewart to a hospital.[18]

Before the sun was up, early Monday morning, January 23, 1956, Elders Swan and Freeman were on their way. They woke brother Becker and explained the situation. As Becker was dressing, he suggested they should take Elder Stewart to St. Joseph's Hospital, because it was only three blocks away from the branch house. The Elders had heard that the Catholic Church focused on the welfare of its own members. Just three weeks earlier an LDS man had "fallen from a scaffolding, mortally injured," and the hospital refused to admit him.[19] Becker agreed that the Catholic hospital gave priority to its own members, but there was no way they would turn an American away.

He told them Catholics in Freiburg feel deeply indebted to Americans for the help they gave following the war. Even though the hospital suffered only minor damage, the *Amis* repaired the buildings. However, in 1940, the old town had been destroyed, when the Germans, on a bombing mission, believed they had crossed the French border and mistakenly bombed their own city. The Cathedral and Catholic Church administrative offices in the old town, had sustained great damage, but the *Amis* had completely restored these buildings. "They won't turn you away."[20]

After parking on the street next to the branch house, the missionaries found that Elder Stewart had already dressed, even though he was weak and in bad shape. They helped him down the stairs and into the car. Elder Peterson traveled with Elder Stewart.

Brother Becker turned on to *Wölfinstraße* and drove west two blocks before turning left on *Habsburgerstraße*. After only one block, the car came to St. Joseph's Hospital. Brother Becker had already explained that a better option probably would have been the famous Albert-Ludwig's University Clinic; however, he would have found it necessary to travel another three blocks past St. Josephs then turn right, skirt the old town, travel under the

---

18 Erich Kirchhoefer, "Interview at His Syracuse, Utah Home," (Feb. 21, 2018).

19 Stewart, "Memories of Orabelle Iverson Stewart."

20 Kirchhoefer, "Interview at His Syracuse, Utah Home."

railroad tracks, and drive another several blocks on *Breisacherstraße*, before coming to the University Clinic.

He reminded them that if Elder Stewart goes into the hospital, St. Josephs will be convenient for the missionaries. "We should go to St. Josephs." He drove up to the Emergency Entrance, and with great efficiency, Elder Stewart was quickly checked in. An attending physician asked him what was wrong. Elder Stewart explained, "The past few days had been stressful, and I might just be worn out." "Tell me what you have been doing."

He explained that he was an American missionary for the Mormon Church and had spent the past twenty-seven months in West Germany. He had been working in Munich, but last Thursday, he was transferred to Freiburg.[21] Friday morning, he participated in a major workshop for missionaries with leadership responsibilities. He attended because he had been assigned to oversee the work of about a dozen Mormon missionaries serving in the state of *Baden Württemberg*. The leadership session lasted about five hours, then everyone left for the train station to travel to Bern, Switzerland, where a new Mormon temple had recently been dedicated.

Arriving in Zollikofen, just outside Bern, the missionaries were housed in private homes within walking distance of the temple. Early the next morning, Saturday, from 7:00 A.M.to 3:00 P.M., they attended temple sessions and did "ordinance work." Although these sessions were wearing, it was such a privilege to go to the temple that everyone felt invigorated and energized. That evening, the missionaries went shopping in Bern. He wished to buy a Swiss Omega watch to take home to his mother.

"I called to the other Freiburg elders: 'Fellows, come with me.'" It was Saturday evening, after hours, and all the stores were closed, but we went to a jewelry shop and rapped on the door. The manager was still there and opened, and I said, 'I apologize, but I am only in Bern tonight, and I need an Omega watch.'

"I have what you need." "Kindly show me your ladies' watches." The manager placed a folder on the counter. After looking through it, I said, "I'll

---

[21] Kenneth B. Dyer, "West German Mission Records," (Church History Library: West German Mission Headquarters, 1955-1956).

take this one, and laid the money on the counter. We rushed back to Zolli-kofen and went to bed "[22] Early the next morning they were up to catch a 5:00 o'clock train; they wanted to be back in Freiburg, about 100 miles distant, in time to participate in the formal opening of a new church building on *Weierhofstraße*. He spoke at the meeting, and afterward, they all went to dinner, and he had felt ill ever since. [23]

The doctor agreed that Elder Stewart might just be worn down, or he might be suffering from lumbago, or some other muscle problem related to the lower back. He suggested that Elder Stewart return home, and if he later felt worse, he should return. Brother Becker drove the two missionaries back to the branch house, and Elder Stewart rested for the remainder of the day. Later in the afternoon, his condition took a dive, and the elders asked themselves what they might do. Elder Bean suggested: "Perhaps it's the cot. None of us wanted to sleep in that thing. It's bad, and he deserves something better."

Elder Fogg was the newest member of the group of six. The others told him to trade with Elder Stewart. Without changing the sheets or other bedding, Elder Fogg got out of his nice bed, and Elder Stewart was assisted to the better cot. However, the pain did not go away, and the other elders shifted uneasily around him.

Everyone spent another bad night. For Elder Stewart, the night was "a sleepless horror."[24] By morning, he complained, "My leg is very stiff. I can hardly bend it."[25] Elders Swan and Freeman were off again to Brother Becker's, and Elder Stewart was a second time in the Emergency Clinic of St. Joseph's. A different attending physician asked Elder Stewart to describe how he was feeling.

---

[22] His mother had written about this incident. It is found in: Stewart, "Memories of Orabelle Iverson Stewart."

[23] Karl Swan, "Interview at His Home in Roy, Utah, ," (Feb. 21, 2018); Fogg, "Missionary Journal."

[24] Stewart, "Memories of Orabelle Iverson Stewart."

[25] Gary Fogg, Fogg, "Missionary Journal." Jan 24,1956.

"It is difficult for me to breathe." "And I have trouble swallowing; it feels like there is a rock in my throat." "And I have difficulty moving my limbs." "And my back hurts." "And I have a terrible headache."[26]

The physician decided to take several tests to identify, if he could, what was causing all these problems. They drew urine, blood, and saliva samples. Until the tests were diagnosed, he would remain in the clinic. Elder Stewart felt a sense of disquiet. He knew something was wrong. Two days earlier, while in the Bern Temple, he had obtained permission to go off to one of the small "sealing rooms to pray and meditate about taking on the responsibility of lecturing throughout West Germany." He expected to be rewarded with a feeling that he was going to do a good job, but he later wrote in his diary, "I felt no peace enter my heart, as I usually experienced after supplicating the Lord." He had the impression that something was wrong, the "disquieting impression that something harmful would befall me."[27]

Brother Becker brought Elder Peterson back to the branch house, so that Peterson could explain to the other elders what was going on. His plan was to return to the clinic in the afternoon. Mormon missionaries are a disciplined lot; they all fell into their daily routine. Early that morning Elder Bean spent an hour with Elder Fogg working on his German grammar, then the two were off knocking on doors in the neighborhood around the new church building, they knocked on many doors, a typical approach at that time, and they were invited in a few houses.

Since Elder Fogg was a new missionary, he was only able to give a door approach. That is, he would introduce the missionaries and ask if they might come in and deliver a brief message. His introduction usually included a comment that they were the American missionaries. The elders found that the people they met were usually attracted to them as Americans as much as

---

[26] These are typical complaints of those who get polio. See, for example, Peg Kehret, *Small Steps: The Year I Got Polio* (Chicago: Albert Whitman & Co., 1996); Noreen Linduska, *My Polio Past* (Chicago, Illinois: Pelligrini & Cudahy, 1947); Fred Davis, *Passage through Crisis: Polio Victims and Their Families* (Indianapolis, Indiana: Bobbs-Merrill Co., 1963); Charles H. Andrews, *No Time for Tears* (Garden City, New York: Doubleday and Co., 1951); Turnley Walker, *Rise up and Walk* (New York: E. P. Dutton & Co., 1950).

[27] Stewart, *Addendum*.

they were church missionaries. Elder Bean explained that the Mormon Church had just opened a building that had been purchased, reconstructed, and furnished, and the German neighbors were welcome to drop by at any time. The missionaries also left a brief spiritual message and a brochure about the church.

Elder Bean suggested to Elder Fogg that he wanted to work on membership materials with Elder Kirchhoefer, so why didn't Elder Fogg use that free time to go back to the clinic with Elder Peterson and be with Elder Stewart. Bean was the new branch president, and he felt the need to work on the branch membership lists, identifying the people who held "callings" in the various organizations of the branch. He also wanted to go through the financial accounts showing who was donating money.

Elder Fogg was happy to go to the hospital, but he found that Elder Stewart, who had been feeling better in the morning, was feeling much worse as the day progressed. Both his legs and one arm were stiff and difficult to manage. By that evening, the doctors had been able to diagnose the situation. They announced: "The tests indicate that he has POLIO."[28]

The missionaries were shocked and questioned the results of the tests. They also complained in their journals that German doctors were objectively cold and didn't pull any punches in describing the condition of their patients. It was not encouraging for these young, forward-looking, optimistic Americans. However, reality soon set in and Elders Peterson and Fogg quickly contacted the other missionaries.

They also called President Dyer, who had returned to the mission headquarters in Frankfurt a/M. The president told them he would notify the Stewart family in Salt Lake City, via church headquarters, and come to Freiburg as soon as possible. Elder Peterson also announced, "I want to stay in the clinic with my companion as long as he is there. I know my way around a hospital because I worked there for three years."

The missionaries talked among themselves and confessed that, even though they were frightened of polio, they did not know much about it. With

---

[28] More specifically, he was diagnosed as having bulbar polio, the kind that attacks the central nervous system. See "A Life: Dictated to Richard G. Ellis."

today's electronic technology, it would have been simple for the missionaries to find information, but at that time they had limited access. Fortunately, Elders Swan and Freeman regularly visited the *Amerikahaus* (America House) in the old town to read *Time, Newsweek*, and the *New York Herald Tribune*.[29]

It was their way of remaining in contact with their beloved America. The purpose of the *Amerikahaus* was to disseminate information about democracy to the Germans. They knew its library contained a wide range of materials, and the next morning, Wednesday, the two were there when it opened, and they found several reference materials about polio.

Almost all those infected with the polio virus experienced only minor symptoms, such as fever, headache, diarrhea, but in a small number of cases, the cells leave the gastrointestinal tract and invade the spinal cord and motor area of the cerebral cortex.[30] In these cases, the motor neurons of the human are destroyed, which leads to paralysis. This is what was happening to Elder Stewart.

Polio is a disease of "countries blessed with unusually good sanitation facilities and hygienic standards."[31] In poorer environments, children were exposed regularly to the virus. When they are babies, they are protected, because they temporarily inherit immunity from their mothers. Over time they lose this immunity, but at the same time repeated exposure to infections stimulate their own immunity. Of course, during this period many suffer from attacks of the disease. Therefore, polio has been synonymous with "infantile paralysis." Most children in poor environments quickly develop immune systems that save them by suppressing any severe infection.[32] In wealthy areas, little children are not extensively exposed to the virus and so they fail to develop an immunity.

West Germany is a highly developed country. Consequently, at the time, many Germans were contracting the disease. In 1952, 10,259 new cases were diagnosed, 5,081 the next year, 3,980 the year after that, and 4,156 in

---

[29] Swan, "Interview at His Home in Roy, Utah, ." Feb. 21, 2018.

[30] Elizabeth Kenny, *Infantile Paralysis and Cerebral Diplegia* (Sydney, Australia: Angus & Robertson Limited, 1937).

[31] Roland H. Berg, *Polio and Its Problems* (Philadelphia: J. B. Lippincott Co., 1948).

[32] Ibid.

1955.[33] In 1956, even though Jonas Salk had already developed a vaccine for the disease,[34] it would not become readily available in West Germany until the early sixties. Unfortunately, Dan Stewart's social background failed to expose him to the virus when he was young, and he was not immune when it invaded his body.

The general incubation period for polio is about a week, but this can occur in as little as four days and as long as 34 days.[35] In other words, Dan Stewart could have been infected after he had arrived in Freiburg, but he was most likely infected before he left Munich or during the train trip to his new workstation.

At noon that Wednesday, the missionaries began a twenty-four hour fast. None of them ate any food nor drank water nor other liquid during the fast. This sacrifice brought the missionaries together in a common bond and focused their attention on the welfare of their brother in the gospel. It was a humbling time for all.

The doctors recommended that anyone who had close contact with Dan Stewart should be "vaccinated" with *gamma globulin*, to boost immunity against the polio virus. This was very expensive for the elders, seventy German Marks a shot (about seventeen dollars), but even though these shots were painful, given in the butt, the six were happy to get them. Elder Freeman, the newest missionary, was so frightened he passed out while in the nursing room, and they carried him to an empty bed on a stretcher.[36]

That same afternoon, about 4:00 P.M., President Dyer arrived from mission headquarters in Frankfurt a/M. He generally showed kind, warm eyes, a pleasant smile, and thinning wavy hair, but now he looked drawn, gaunt,

---

[33] K.-J. Rentzsch, "Incidence Rates of Poliomyelitis in Germany," *Post-Polio Health International* (2017).

[34] Katherine Krohn, *Jonas Salk and the Polio Vaccine* (Mankato, Minn.: Capstone Press, 2007).

[35] Roland Berg claims the infection might be present in the stools for as long as twelve weeks, before it manifests itself. See Berg, *Polio and Its Problems*.

[36] Karl Swan, *Missionary Journal* (West German Mission: Hand Written Diary, 1953-1955).

and tired. He also had a bad cold, but he explained that his priority was to be with Elder Stewart.[37] He said that he had always recognized the courage of the elder, who was hard driving and possessed an indomitable will that would carry him through this ordeal.

He also assured the missionaries that Elder Stewart need not worry about paying for the costs of German medical care. The church assumed responsibility for his care and stood behind his every expense. When Dyer arrived at St. Josephs, he found Elder Stewart to be depressed and dejected, and his body temperature was up; this wasn't a good sign. Elder Stewart complained that he had difficulty breathing.

That night Stewart's condition worsened. He found it even more difficult to breathe. Elder Peterson sensed that Elder's condition might be fatal. The clinical staff were doing whatever they could to make him comfortable, but no heroic measures were being taken to keep him alive. In good Catholic tradition, the staff even sent a telephone message to President Dyer, asking him to come and administer the sacramental last rites. "They thought Danny could no longer live."[38] In spite of this, Elder Stewart continued to survive. He refused to die.[39] He later told the other missionaries he was a loyal American and refused to die in a foreign country.

Finally, the next morning, when the medical doctors realized Elder Stewart was still alive, their attitude changed. The clinic had two iron lungs at its disposal, large bulky boxes that encased the entire body, except the head. These were the only two in all of the state of *Baden Württemberg*. Each iron lung had a bellows that exerted a push/pull force on the chest forcing it to expand and contract in the same way a breathing person expands and contracts the lungs. They placed Elder Stewart in the one unoccupied iron lung and began to treat him in a much different manner.

The next day, Friday, the missionaries began a second fast. That afternoon, they held a prayer circle. They all knelt, and each person said a per-

---

[37] Ibid.

[38] Stewart, "Memories of Orabelle Iverson Stewart."

[39] Mary Louise Holbrook, "Interview at the Dan Stewart Family Home in Salt Lake City," (June 7, 2019).

sonal but public prayer. Later, Elder Peterson went to the clinic to be with his companion. His presence during the night seemed to comfort Elder Stewart, even though his temperature was rising, and he was in a great deal of pain and discomfort.

2. THE FAMILY LEARNS
ELDER STEWART HAS POLIO

On Friday, the day after Elder Stewart took the train from Munich to Freiburg, and four days before he came down with polio, his mother returned home from her sales job at Boyd Park Jewelers, in downtown Salt Lake City. She was tired and the house on Butler Avenue was a mess. After a quick dinner, she began to clean. It was midnight before she finished, and she was physically and mentally exhausted.

Orabelle told herself, "Get to bed and sleep fast." She changed into her night dress, kneeled, and said a quiet prayer. For the next several hours, she restlessly lay in her bed, not able to drop off. Finally, as dawn was just beginning to break, she suddenly felt she was not alone.

She turned over and opened her eyes: "There stood my Danny. He looked terrible and very sad. He stood looking down at me for several seconds, even minutes."[40] Orabelle, ordinarily sensible and clear-headed, began to doubt herself. Perhaps she was dreaming, or even ill.

However, her every instinct told her: "Something is radically wrong. I arose, got on my knees, and prayed." It was Saturday morning, and she was

---

[40] Most of the following account is taken from: Stewart, "Memories of Orabelle Iverson Stewart."

scheduled to work; as the time drew near to catch the bus, she remained immobile. "I still could not dress or do anything." Soon, her youngest daughter, seventeen-year-old Carolyn, came bounding up the stairs. She burst into her mother's bedroom and happily announced, "Good morning, mother."

Carolyn found her mother in a state of "quiescence and distress." She quietly put her arms around her and kissed her. Orabelle relished this daily ritual. Her friend, Emily Smith Stewart, often described Carolyn as "a double dose of soda pop." "Mom, what is wrong?" "I don't know, dear, but something is very wrong with Danny. Something is terribly wrong."

Orabelle was worn out, but when the jewelry shop opened that morning, she was at her workstation. Her family was on a strict budget, and she felt she had no choice but to be there. Five years earlier, when her husband had a sudden heart attack and died, her family of four daughters and one son was left in a precarious financial position.

While Danny was on his Mormon mission, the family was expected to pay for his expenses, but the family's only income was from Orabelle's meagre salary at Boyd Park Jewelers. Even though she was stressed almost to the breaking point, Orabelle could not afford to put her job in jeopardy, and, somehow, on that Saturday, she made it through the day. As the store neared closing time, she remembered she had accepted an invitation to attend the Utah Symphony in the Salt Lake Tabernacle that evening. When she returned home after work, she went to her room and collapsed on the bed. At dinner time, the whole family, sensing that she was in distress, urged her to go to the concert.

"You never go anyplace for fun, and it would be such a treat for you." So, she went. The Utah Symphony, conducted by Maurice Abravanel, had a fine reputation and the program was Rachmaninoff, and Shostakovich. The dome-shaped Salt Lake Tabernacle was reputed to have the best possible acoustics, but Orabelle "disliked every moment of it." During the intermission, three female members of her local Mormon Ward, her church congregation, came by and asked about Danny. He had been their "block teacher,"[41]

---

[41] Formally known as a "ward teacher" and now called a "home teacher." It was the block teacher's task to visit them at least once a month and leave a brief spiritual mes-

crippled in his arms and legs, and died as a young man. While in her teens, Kathleen Barber, another classmate, contracted the disease and passed away. Myrna Nielson and Jeanine Anderson were confined to wheelchairs for many years.[45] All of Spanish Fork was in a state of shock. Some of the town's businesses shut down, as was the movie theater and the city swimming pool.[46]

In Salem, just south of Spanish Fork, the mayor advised young people to stop jumping into Salem Pond, as was their habit when the weather was hot. When Kenneth Taylor, in Payson, just south of Salem, contracted polio, the town fathers considered cancelling its summer Sunday evening band concerts in the park. The young people were so shaken by the disease that family members often chose not to tell them why they were sick. Kenneth Taylor often said, "The doctor came every day, but I didn't know I had polio."[47] Everyone else knew.

In Joseph, Sevier County, the town council prohibited young people from swimming in the irrigation ditches and canals during the month of August. In Ogden, some doctors advised parents to have their young children take naps every afternoon, so they would not become too tired and susceptible to viruses. In Salt Lake City, the swimming pools were closed during the summer, and kids were not permitted to go to the movies.[48] Officials warned everyone to avoid the Jordon River. Consequently, when Danny came down with polio, family members were so traumatized that they were almost frantic. And Orabelle did not have the money to go to her son in West Germany.

Dr. Preston Iverson, Danny's uncle and Orabelle's brother, was living in New York City. He was a highly qualified professor of medicine and a

---

[45] Bonnie Lee Crabb Pinegar, "Interview in Her Salt Lake City Home," (On File with the Author Sept. 26, 2018). Lynn Rowe, "Interview in His Home in Orem, Utah " (June 8, 2018).

[46] "Interview in His Home in Orem, Utah ".

[47] Nedra Taylor Hanks, "Telephone Interview at Her Home in Salem, Utah," (Oct. 2, 2018).

[48] Harold A. Decker, "Everett L. Cooley Oral History Project, 1983-2014," ed. America West Center University of Utah (Salt Lake City, Utah: Special Collections Library, June 26, 2010).

prominent plastic surgeon. The family reasoned that he could assist them. They contacted him, and he quickly agreed to fly to West Germany and make sure Elder Stewart was in good care. On Monday, January 30, 1956, less than a week after Danny had been diagnosed with polio, Dr. Iverson arrived in Freiburg. He found his nephew in the isolation ward of St. Joseph's Catholic Hospital and quickly learned that originally the medical personnel had failed to determine the seriousness of Elder Stewart's condition and had sent him home.

Dr. Iverson rightly complained to the family that "the care he was receiving in Germany was not the proper care."[49] However, he was aware that his nephew had the good fortune to be in Freiburg, the home of the world-famous Albert-Ludwig's University Medical Center.[50] If St. Joseph's proved to be inadequate, Dr. Iverson was confident he could call on their services. In some respects, Elder Stewart had been fortunate to be at the Catholic facility. The only two iron lungs in the state of *Baden Württemberg* were there.

Americans, such as Dr. Iverson, were often tempted to misjudge the quality of health care in Europe, thinking everything was superior in the U.S. In fact, at the time, medicine was advancing more rapidly in Europe than in America, which was just beginning its medical research tradition. In contrast, in 1930, the Max Planck Institute for Medical Research had been established in Heidelberg, and in spite of the Nazi period, research was on the cutting edge of the health sciences. And at the Medical Center of Freiburg University, several scientists had been awarded the Nobel Prize for chemistry and medicine.[51]

Dr. Iverson was in daily communications via telephone with the family in Salt Lake City; he soon let them know that Danny was receiving appropriate professional care. A few days later, when Dr. Iverson returned to America, he was satisfied that they were doing everything they could for the

[49] Mary Louise Holbrook, "Interview at Her Home in Salt Lake City,," (Feb. 22, 2018).

[50] Founded in 1457, during the Habsburg Dynasty, it was, at the time, rated second only to the University of Vienna.

[51] These prizes had gone to Harmann Staudinger (1953), Hans Adolf Krebs (1953), Georg von Hevesy (1943), Hans Spemann (1935), Adolf Otto Reinhold Windaus (1928), and Heinrich Otto Wieland (1927).

young man. And he was especially reassured with the way Mission President, Kenneth B. Dyer, was handling the situation.

Dyer was a remarkable mission president. Whereas too many presidents saw themselves as harsh standard bearers of the gospel, Dyer was primarily concerned with the welfare and well-being of the missionaries. He was neither a sophisticated analyzer of the scriptures nor was he worried about how small points of doctrine are to be interpreted. He was a businessman and a manager, who brought those skills into his missionary world. He recognized that missionary service is hard work and wanted the young men and women to have a positive, enjoyable stay in West Germany.[52]

He oversaw the Mormon Church in the country, which included the religious units of the church for U.S. servicemen and women. And he got to know the key military personnel. His managerial skills were valuable in working with them. Four months before Elder Stewart got polio, one of his senior missionaries had a mental breakdown, which included deep depression and delusions that he was Jesus Christ. He ordained his companion as an "Apostle" and cast out the devil from his quarters.[53] In late October 1955, that missionary was sent home for treatment, and Dyer arranged with the U.S. Military to fly him home from the Landstuhl Military Air Base.[54]

When Elder Stewart was stable enough to go home, Dyer knew exactly what to do. The process was facilitated on the American side by Emily Smith Stewart, daughter of former Mormon Church President, George Albert Smith, and a close friend of the Stewart family. She appealed to another Stewart family friend and neighbor, Utah Senator Wallace F. Bennett, whose son, Robert, was a close buddy and classmate of Elder Stewart.

Bennett contacted the Secretary of Defense, Charles Erwin Wilson, and requested that the U. S. military fly Elder Stewart home. That request facilitated the efforts of President Dyer in making formal arrangements.

[52] LeRoy Faerber, "Interview at His Home in Murray, Utah, ," (Feb. 20, 2018).

[53] Kenneth B. Dyer, "West German Mission Quarterly Report," (Salt Lake City: Church History Library, Dec. 30, 1955).

[54] That missionary subsequently recovered and went on to have a highly productive life. He was a professor of business at Brigham Young University and the University of Utah, and he returned four times to Germany to teach business for the U.S. Military.

Ultimately, the flight costs home were to be covered by the National Foundation for Infantile Paralysis. Emily Smith Stewart had worked with the Foundation, particularly on its "March of Dimes" campaign, and she was crucial in making the cost-free arrangements.

In 1938, President Franklyn Delano Roosevelt had created the Foundation, a non-partisan association of scientists and volunteers to help fund polio victims and its March of Dimes campaign. It used cheerful and confident slogans, poster children, and short films, showing famous people, such as Ernest Borgnine, Mia Farrow, Alan Alda, Mickey Rooney, all of whom had suffered from the disease. They were joined by the likes of Judy Garland singing "The Trolley Song," and Frank Sinatra, "I wonder Who's Kissing Her Now," in West Coast fund-raising extravaganzas. The campaigns were highly successful, and the white house was flooded with millions upon millions of dimes, which were used to pay for the treatment of patients and the development of specialized equipment.[55]

Even though various versions of the iron lung had been developed as early as 1832, the machine that Elder Stewart was confined to had been recently developed with March of Dimes money. Emily Smith Stewart took the lead in arranging for Elder Stewart to be sent from Landstuhl, West Germany, to Downey, California, where he would be placed in the renowned *Rancho Los Amigos National Rehabilitation Center*.

In West Germany, soon after World War II ended, the U.S. Department of Defense set up the Landstuhl Regional Medical Center and Air Force Military Base. Landstuhl was a little village near Kaiserslautern, but it quickly became the site of the largest medical center outside the U.S., serving as a treatment station for wounded American soldiers, as well as an evacuation unit for the U.S. military.[56]

It was located less than 175 miles north of Freiburg; a vehicle would only require about three hours to travel there, almost all the way on the *Autobahn*.

---

[55] David M. Oshinsky, *Polio: An American Story* (New York: Oxford University Press, 2005).

[56] Today, it continues to serve as an evacuation unit for soldiers wounded in Iraq, Afghanistan, Ethiopia, etc.

However, at St. Joseph's Hospital, Elder Stewart was still in critical condition, and he would remain there until he was well enough to travel. The missionaries, and others who knew him, made regular visits to the hospital making certain their fellow missionary understood how much he meant to them.

Finally, on March 9, 1956, in his iron lung, Elder Stewart was released from St. Joseph's. A U.S. Military plane flew him from Freiburg to Landstuhl, where he continued to be visited by President Dyer and other missionaries.[57] At the time, Elders George Jarvis and C. Dean Larsen were working in Kaiserslautern, just a few miles from Landstuhl. President Dyer contacted them, and they rushed to Elder Stewart's side. They found it frightening to see their fellow missionary in an iron lung. They found a man with an ashen face and someone who had difficulty talking. They gave him a blessing. These young men did not know what to say. They were afraid to promise more than God was going to give them, and ended up making a prophetic promise:

"We bless you that you will soon arrive in America." Elder Stewart whispered, "Thank you." He was clearly frightened at the prospect of flying home in an iron lung.[58] It would have been easy for him to disbelieve any positive future, and to declare that he had no faith in what was to come; however, he never lost his faith in his God and what the future would bring. Whatever his future life would be, Germany would remain a vital part of him. Two days later, Elder Stewart left for America.

---

[57] Dyer, "West German Mission Records."

[58] C. Dean Larsen, "Interview at His Home in Salt Lake City, ," (June 6, 2018).

3. Rehabilitation in California

On March 15, 1956, encased in his iron lung, Elder Daniel Stewart began an arduous and life-threatening trip from Landstuhl Military Air Base, in West Germany, to the United States. He was loaded into a C-118, a military version of the Douglas DC-6 commercial airliner, powered by four piston-driven propeller engines. It was especially equipped for carrying cargo as well as transporting medical patients. A group of military personnel, including three doctors, four nurses, and four technicians, headed by Captain Walter Weiss, were on the flight. Elder Stewart was accompanied by Elder Winfried Peterson, his missionary companion in Freiburg.

Six weeks earlier, the weather had been warm for that time of year, but during the first week of February, it turned bitter cold. When the C-118 took off, a monster storm, with hurricane-force winds, was swirling across the Atlantic Ocean. Cargo ships were being ripped and torn as they sought safe haven. The largest luxury liner in the world, the "RMS Queen Elizabeth,"[59] on its way from Southampton to New York, was so pounded and pelted, that 150 passengers were injured. And on the East Coast a blinding, swirling sixteen-inch snowstorm swept across the state of New York, throwing the state into disarray.[60]

---

[59] RMS = Royal Mail Service

[60] "16-Inch Snow Hits State, Snarls Traffic," *The Glens Falls Post-Star* March 17, 1956.

The C-118 was scheduled to make fuel stops in London, Newfoundland, Nova Scotia, and New Jersey. But the weather over the Atlantic was reaching catastrophic conditions, and before the plane arrived in London, it was forced to return to Landstuhl. Four times that day, the C-118 took off, and four times the storm forced it to return.

All the while, Elder Stewart was in his iron lung, being cared for by the medical team. Finally, the next day, the military plane was rerouted south, then west over Portugal, on to the Azores and Bahamas, and finally north to McGuire Air Force Base in New Jersey. All along the way, the plane showed signs of minor engine difficulty.

The Stewart family knew that Danny, as he was known to all, was scheduled to fly to New Jersey, then on to California.[61] His mother was aware of the horrific weather conditions over the Atlantic and spent every possible moment on her knees praying.[62] While at Bennion Jewelers,[63] she occasionally went into the Silver Room, where she could kneel in prayer. She was almost frantic, but as she prayed, a "peaceful feeling" would come over her. After work, she hurried home, closed herself in her bedroom, and resumed praying.

At midnight, Friday night, more than forty hours after the first C-118 take-off, the telephone rang at the Stewart home. Orabelle was so exhausted she felt she could not answer it. She finally lifted the receiver from its cradle but was too frightened to speak. The man on the line heard her breathe, and asked: "Is this the Stewart residence? Could this be Mrs. Stewart? This is the United Press."

Her immediate thought was, "He is going to tell me that Danny and the iron lung are at the bottom of the Atlantic." "Have you a son being flown in an iron lung from Germany?" "Yes!" "The United Press has just learned that they have landed in New Jersey."

---

[61] Most of the following account is taken from Stewart, "Memories of Orabelle Iverson Stewart."

[62] "Hundreds Die as 2 Storms Cripple East," *Deseret News* March 19, 1956.

[63] In 1952, the shop was sold, and the name was changed from Boyd Park Jewelers to Bennion Jewelers.

Orabelle was so overcome she could barely say: "What wonderful news that is. That is perfectly marvelous to hear." She spent the rest of the night in prayer, thanking her Heavenly Father for this blessing. The next morning, at 8:00 A.M., the Associated Press called, giving her the same news.[64]

When the C-118 finally landed at Randolph Air Force Base in Texas, Dan and the iron lung were immediately transferred to a waiting C-131, part of the 173rd Air Evacuation Squadron, and flown on to March Air Force Base near San Bernardino, California. The plane landed at 2:30 A.M., where a special truck from the *Rancho Los Amigos National Rehabilitation Center* was waiting to transport him to Downey.

A normal ambulance was not large enough to carry an iron lung, so the Rehabilitation Center had constructed its own truck with wooden sides and a canvas top. The iron lung was bolted in place. A gasoline generator supplied the electricity needed to keep the respirator and suction apparatus running. A nurse was with Dan, and the back of the truck was open, so those in a *Rancho Los Amigos* car following behind could see what was happening.[65]

When the truck arrived in Downey, the entire campus was blazing with lights, and the night staff gathered around the truck. They were curious who the celebrity was. He certainly had pull in Washington, D.C. They were informed the patient was "a young man, a very long, handsome young man, who was brought into the hospital very, very ill. He is not expected to live."[66]

Even though, in 1888, *Rancho Los Amigos* had been established as a general medical facility, by the late 1940s and early 50s. when polio epidemics often struck Southern California,[67] the Los Angeles County Health Department converted the facility to a rehabilitation center, mainly for polio

---

[64] The above account was drawn mainly from Stewart, "Memories of Orabelle Iverson Stewart."

[65] Colleen Aair Fliedner, *Centennial: Rancho Los Amigos Medical Center: 1888-1988* (Downey, CA: Rancho Los Amogos Medical Center, 1990).

[66] Stewart, "Memories of Orabelle Iverson Stewart."

[67] Geraldine B. Edwards, William H. Clark, and Robert M. Drake, *Polyomyelitis in California During the Pre-Vaccine Period* (Sacramento, CA: California State Department of Public Health, 198).

victims. By 1956, it was the largest such center in the U.S., serving thousands of patients each year.

As soon as Orabelle was informed that Danny had arrived in California, she was off to the Rio Grande Train Station to catch an overnighter to Los Angeles. Two brothers, Frank and Paul, lived in Southern California. They picked her up at Union Station, and they drove the car directly to *Rancho Los Amigos*.

The night before, the brothers had driven to the facility, and they were shocked at what they found. The sight of one iron lung, with the patient's head sticking out of one end, was disconcerting enough, but to see 120 iron lungs cramped into a single hall, shrouded by heavy curtains hanging from ceiling to floor, left a terrifying impression. With the help of an attending nurse, the two men quickly found Danny. He was lethargic from the long trip, almost in a coma, and his cramped muscles were causing terrible misery.

Frank and Paul were worried about the effect the sight would have on Danny's mother. They described the hall where he was located and cautiously told her, "Now don't be surprised or disappointed, but you will not recognize him; he looks so bad." She told herself, "They can't fool me. I would know Danny anywhere."

After arriving and locating the hall, and the aisle where her brothers told her Danny had been placed, she recalled: "I walked slowly up and down the double rows of iron lungs searching for my long, muscular Daniel. I walked clear to the end of the room, dismayed at having not even recognized him, and retread my steps."

She knew she wouldn't see her son, the football player, tennis player, or cornet player. However, she knew there was an essential Dan Stewart. a son of God, whose divine essence could never be destroyed. "Then I saw my dear, dark-haired six-foot-three-inch lad." Then reality began to set in: "All he could move were his lips and eye lids."

After twenty-nine long months, her joy at finally seeing her son cushioned the shock at finding him in such precarious condition. The sight of his mother lifted Danny's spirits as nothing else could have. The nurse cautioned them that they should not stay long. He had just completed a grueling and wearing 9,000-mile trip, and the Center had not yet begun his treatment. He had a long and difficult road to travel, but the nurse assured the Stewart brothers and sister that the staff members would do everything in their power to keep him alive. She promised nothing more.

The next day, Orabelle and a close friend, Sharee Wilcox, visited Westwood and spoke with the President of the Mormon Los Angeles Temple, Benjamin L. Bowring, and his counselors. Her brother, Paul Iverson, was a prominent lawyer in town. He was the lead attorney in the law firm, *Iverson, Yoakum, Papiano, and Hatch*, and he had done, without cost to the church, all the legal work related to the church property between Santa Monica Boulevard and Ohio Avenue, where the Temple, the chapel, the visitor's center, the genealogical library, and patron lodgings are located.[68] Paul had put Sharee in touch with President Bowring. Only a week earlier, the temple had been dedicated and stood at the top of a broad, sloping hill facing south. After giving Orabelle a blessing, the temple presidency drove the thirty miles to Downey to give Danny a blessing as well.

In the beginning, there were always setbacks. One day, Orabelle arrived at *Rancho Los Amigos* to find that a neglectful nurse had turned Danny's iron lung pulse in such a way that it was working against, rather than for, his own breathing rhythm, He told his mother that the iron lung was killing him. He whispered. "Something is wrong. I cannot breathe." Orabelle was appalled and quickly called for assistance.

Soon, Orabelle had to return to Salt Lake to continue her job at Bennion Jewelers. Upon arriving home, she found a letter from the secretary of the West German Mission, John D. Woodward, informing her that the missionaries had been able to sell her son's bike for $10.00. A check was enclosed in the letter.[69]

---

[68] Saundra Stewart, "Telephone Interview with Her in Los Angeles," (Oct. 16, 2019).

[69] John D. Woodward, "Letter to Orabelle Stewart " (Frankfurt a/M, West Germany March 16, 1957).

A family friend of the Stewarts, Emily Smith Stewart, had been wise to request that Danny be placed at *Rancho Los Amigos*. Four years previously, the hospital had formally been transformed into a rehabilitation center, and already it had the reputation for being the best such center in America. In 1952, soon after arriving, Robert Thomas, an energetic, capable young man, assumed the duties of Director of *Rancho Los Amigos*,[70] and he declared that he would take the Center in a new direction.

He proposed that the *National Foundation for Infantile Paralysis* assist him in transforming the hospital from a long-term chronic care facility to a rehabilitation center. The Foundation promised him the support he requested, but the medical staff at *Rancho Los Amigos* was cautious and reluctant to make the change. After all, Robert Thomas was not a medical doctor, but a hospital administrator.

Thomas proposed, for example, that polio patients be taken out of their iron lungs for a short time each day and be put on a "rocking bed." Patients were to lie on the bed, while it rocked like a teeter totter. When the patients' feet were high, the intestines fall down and push air out of the lungs. When the head was high, the intestines fall away, and the chest pulls air into the lungs. The seesaw or up-and-down motion of the diaphragm forced air into and out of the lungs. Even though the rocking bed had been used in England since 1932, it was not known in America. A trial was to be undertaken, but the nursing and medical staff remained skeptical. Fearing the worst, as the patient was removed from a respirator, they all crowded around. However, they soon recognized that the patient was delighted to get out of the iron lung and that after being placed on the rocking bed, managed quite well. This one incident helped the staff come to terms with the changes Thomas was recommending.[71]

In 1955, Thomas brought Dr. Geraldine Perry to the facility. She was a recent graduate of the Medical School at the University of California, San Francisco; a few months later she was assigned to be Dan's primary caregiver. She had an unusual background; before medical school she had served for

---

[70] He had been the Director of the Los Angeles County General Hospital.

[71] Fliedner, *Centennial: Rancho Los Amigos Medical Center: 1888-1988.*

six years in the military as a physical therapist. She was, therefore, open to a broad range of input from nurses, psychologists, but especially physical therapists, all of whom had an intimate knowledge of the needs of patients like Dan Stewart.[72]

She recognized that Dan Stewart was handicapped. This was a label he never attached to himself, nor were synonyms, such as "invalid," "crippled," "paralyzed," less painful and damaging to the ear. They all suggested that Dan had a condition that markedly restricted his ability physically to function. Even when it was apparent that Dan was handicapped, he rarely mentioned it. The closest he came was when he, occasionally told a friend, "I couldn't see myself as handicapped."[73]

In this regard, Dan's behavior was not unusual. Even Franklyn D. Roosevelt attempted to demonstrate that he was "normal," that he had the physical strength to take on himself the burden of the presidency of the United States. When Roosevelt was inaugurated, he demanded that he walk with a slow, swaying gait to the Senate Chamber, using braces that locked the knees in place. He stood through the entire proceedings, then walked out to the Capitol building's East Plaza, where 100,000 people waited and watched.[74]

The first steps of Dan's treatment were a "hot pack" practice developed by Sister Elizabeth Kenny,[75] a physical therapist in New South Wales, Australia. *Rancho Los Amigos* had been engaging in this procedure since World War II, long before Dr. Perry arrived, but she quickly decided to continue using the hot pack practice.

Dr. Perry explained to Dan that his muscles had gone into spasms and tightened like a knot. The Kenny method was intended to help his remaining

---

[72] E.g., Jacquelin Perry, "The Contribution of the Physical Therapist to Medicine," *Journal of American Physical Therapy Association* 45, no. 11 (November, 1965); "Responsibilities in Patient Care: The Need for Nonprofessional Assistants in Physical Therapy," *Journal of American Physical Therapy Association* 46, no. 3 (1966).

[73] Mary Louise Stewart Holbrook, "Interview at the Dan Stewart Family Home in Salt Lake City," (June 7, 2019).

[74] James Tobin, *The Man He Became: How Fdr Defied Polio to Win the Presidency* (New York: Simon & Schuster, 2013).

[75] "Sister" is an Australian military label, not a religious designation.

useful muscles relax and be stretched back to normal. At *Rancho Los Amigos*, the first stage of the so-called "Kenny method" lasted for two weeks and consisted of applying hot, moist packs on Dan every hour for twelve hours a day.[76] The packs were supposed to soften his muscles and make them pliable, and also to relieved him of the terrible pain his tightly knotted muscles were causing.

The physical therapists measured Dan's entire body—neck, shoulders, arms, hands, mid-section, upper and lower legs, and feet, and cut three sets of coverings—wool, plastic, and cotton—that met these measurements. The wool coverings were placed in a pressure cooker and steamed until they were very hot. Then they were run through a wringer to press out the excess water. The therapist wrapped Dan's bare skin in the wool coverings, then wrapped him in the plastic coverings, and finally, pinned the cotton coverings in place to hold everything together. The searing temperature of the wool coverings was so scalding hot that Dan felt like crying out, but he remained stoic and silent. He came to hate the smell of wet wool.

But after a few minutes, the hot packs cooled off and Dan's taut muscles would relax and he would temporarily be pain free.[77] For an hour, he remained in the hot pack, then the therapist renewed the process—twelve times a day. After two weeks, the therapists began the second stage of the Kenny method. They reduced the number of hot pack procedures on his body, but also began to "re-educate" his muscles. That is, the hot packs relaxed the muscles to the point that the therapist could stretch and massage them.

Dr. Perry explained to Dan that she was engaged in "rehabilitation," rather than custodial care, not to cure him, but to salvage whatever muscular residuals the medical staff was able to find in his body. A task of the physical therapist, who knew the body, was to find those muscles that could be rehabilitated, and work with them.

Sister Kenny had little professional training, and when she began her polio treatments in the Australian Outback, she assumed the muscles of patients

---

[76] Fliedner, *Centennial: Rancho Los Amigos Medical Center: 1888-1988.* A supplement to this account is found in Oshinsky, *Polio: An American Story.*

[77] A nice account of this procedure is found in Kehret, *Small Steps: The Year I Got Polio.*

had gone into spasms. In contrast, the medical profession claimed polio was a disease of the central nervous system. Her muscle re-education program seemed to be amazingly helpful, and since Dr. Perry was more interested in results than in theory, she embraced the Kenny method.

Dr. Perry was especially committed to getting Dan out of the "forced re-cumbency of the tank respirators."[78] She soon had him out of his iron lung for extended periods and was helping him straighten his neck and back, so that he might make the most of his rehabilitation routine. After only four months, Dan was free of the iron lung, although he continued to use the chest respirator, except for about eight hours during the day, when he was allowed to breathe on his own. Each day his own breathing time was increased just a little, although there were emotional and physical setbacks.[79]

On July 8, one of Dan's major setbacks occurred. His "fever was so high they had packed him in ice and turned electric fans on him."[80] Staff members decided his life was over, and they pulled the curtains around his stall. They contacted Frederich Dellenbach, who was the local contact person for Mormons in the Clinic, asking him to get in touch with family members and inform them that if they wished to see Dan alive, they must come quickly.

The medical staff feared that he would not survive the night, and if he did, he would likely suffer cerebral hemorrhaging and his mind would never again be the same. They worked frantically to stabilize his condition. Dan's fortitude and mettle were manifested. He not only got through the night, but quickly got back to his rehabilitation routine, and suffered no permanent mental damage.

Just one week later, Dan's sister, Saundra, who was living in West Los Angeles, wrote a letter to Ed. Moreton, a Federal Heights friend of the family. At the time, he was in the Navy, and was stationed in San Francisco, would later travel to Los Angeles and the two would visit Dan.[81] In the letter, Sandra gives a detailed account of Dan's physical condition. Here is part of her account:

---

[78] Personal note by Dr. Perry, written in July, 1967.

[79] Saundra Stewart, "Letter to Edward Moreton," (July 16, 1956).

[80] Stewart, "Memories of Orabelle Iverson Stewart."

[81] Stewart, "Telephone Interview with Her in Los Angeles."

Danny has improved a great deal since he has been here. He has the use of his left hand and arm to a great degree. When he arrived, all he could do was move his left hand and wiggle his fingers. He uses his right hand but can't lift it because many of his muscles in the arm are still paralyzed.

Saundra then explains how he was able to get out of the iron lung and rely only on the respirator. She comments on his legs: "As for both legs, they are completely paralyzed, except for one or two muscles in his left leg that enable him to turn his leg out just a little when he is having water therapy."[82] Dr. Perry was becoming well-known for developing procedures to fuse vertebrae in the back and neck, to improve a patient's breathing,[83] but, as she explained to Dan, he was so ill that she was unable to perform such fusion procedures.

Rehabilitation at *Rancho Los Amigos* included getting Dan on a rocking bed before breakfast. This schedule not only facilitated ventilation for Dan, but it also allowed more complete physical therapy. He was also put on a portable chest respirator, two pieces of armor which encircled his chest and back. When Dan's school friend, Ashby Decker, visited him barely two months after Dan arrived at *Rancho Los Amigos*, Dan was already out of the iron lung and using a portable respirator.[84] He was even occasionally able to sit in a wheelchair. By July, he still had only the use of his left arm and both hands; however, he found it necessary to learn to write using his left hand."[85]

The rehabilitation treatment was intended, ultimately, to return patients to self-supporting status in their homes and communities. As far back as the early 1940s, this "self-help" rehabilitation program had returned many polio patients to their families. By 1945, about half of them had recovered to the

---

[82] "Letter to Edward Moreton."

[83] E.g., Alice L. Garrett, Jacquelin Perry, and V. L. Nickel, "Stabilization of the Collapsing Spine," *Journal of Bone and Neck Surgery* 43-A, no. 4 (1961); Jacquelin Perry and V. L. Nickel, "Total Cervical-Spine Fusion for Neck Paralysis," ibid.41, no. A (1959).

[84] Ashby was in the military, and had been assigned to visit Victorville, California, and took advantage of this trip to visit Dan. See Ashby Decker, "Telephone Interview at His Home in Salt Lake City " (April 14, 2018).

[85] Stewart, "Telephone Interview with Her in Los Angeles."

point that, within three months, they left the Center. Most of those remaining were discharged by the end of one year.[86] Of course, Dan's case was so severe that such information seemed remote and not relevant to him.

When he had arrived in Downey, he was in a state of total exhaustion, and it seemed to him that he was living a nightmare, in a horrible environment. With hundreds of people around him, he had felt alone. And he knew he was surrounded by a host of other lonely men, women, and children, each forced to conceal their feelings of isolation and pain. Whatever interaction he had with others demanded that he speak lightly of his condition, though everything was extremely arduous. He was on the edge of life itself. A lesser person might have looked into the future with dark, trembling fear; however, that was not Dan's style. He looked objectively at his condition, and he was hell-bent on conquering it.

As Dan talked with others in the clinic and discovered their lives and bouts with polio, he began to appreciate who they were and what their struggles were. He discovered that, in one respect, he was one of the fortunate patients, in that someone from his family or the local Mormon ward was dropping by all the time. Dan's mother was in Salt Lake City, as were most other members of his family; however, Saundra, Dan's younger sister, was living in Westwood, California, and she regularly took the bus to Downey to visit and comfort Dan. Her trip was less than thirty miles, but it required two transfers and so many stops that one way required about two hours.

Two sisters, Elsie and Evva Osborne, were members of the local ward, and lived near enough to visit Dan on a regular basis. They were from Salt Lake City. Evva made arrangements for Snelgrove's Ice Cream Parlor, the grandest in Utah, to pack ice cream in a dry ice container and ship it to Downey. Evva kept it in her refrigerator and each time she visited Dan, she brought some for him to eat.

Several times, two other young women, Lilo and Roswitte Baertle, visited Dan. They were converts from Munich and had been baptized just five months before Elder Stewart began to work in that city. Because they were

---

[86] Fliedner, *Centennial: Rancho Los Amigos Medical Center: 1888-1988.*

new members, Elder Stewart and his companion had often instructed them in the gospel. Like so many Mormon converts of that time, the Baertle sisters migrated to America, and joined their older sister, Isolde, also a recent convert, who was living in Southgate, California, near Downey.

Isolde's husband was the son of Friedrich Dellenbach, who had been called by his bishop to look after the Mormon patients at *Rancho Los Amigos*. Dellenback informed the hospital administrators that he was responsible for the Mormon patients. He gave them his contact information in case an emergency should arise. Dellenbach often dropped in see how Dan was doing, and after the two Baertle sisters arrived from West Germany, they also regularly called by and gave Dan an opportunity to speak German again.[87] Friends from Salt Lake City, including high school buddies, Dick Ellis and Ed Moreton; and the Stewart Lab School music teacher, Mr. Hawkins, made the trip to Downey to see Dan. After Ellis had spent hours getting to Downey on the bus, and had waited for visiting hours, he was embarrassed when he walked right past Dan and didn't even recognize him.[88]

Many patients received only occasional visitors, and some never saw any. Dan began to learn about those around him and talked with them about what they were going through, and he began to share his own feelings and trials. He soon discovered that the polio victims at *Rancho Los Amigos* published a newsletter, *The Weekly Breather*; he volunteered to write about the lives of his new friends.[89] In addition, the newsletter provided an opportunity for Dan to begin the arduous task of learning anew the physical act of writing, now with his left hand; it gave him practice in holding a pencil and putting his thoughts and experiences down on paper.

Polio victims often had peculiar habits and traits. A few resigned themselves to spending their lives as shut-ins or even became beggars. However, the vast majority tried to become a productive member of society. That is why the occupational therapy phase of rehabilitation was so crucial. And

---

[87] Lilo Schiel, "Interview at Her Home in St. George, Utah, ," (August 14, 2018).

[88] Stewart, "A Life: Dictated to Richard G. Ellis."

[89] According to the librarian at Rancho Los Amigos, someone as bright as Dan would surely have written for *The Weekly Breather*.

when he returned to Salt Lake City, he would discover that most Utah polio casualties he met, showed that same urgent need. Ken Rigtrip, whom Dan met as an outpatient at LDS Hospital, had contracted polio while in the army; he refused to allow that to impede his desire to study law, even though he would do it in a wheelchair.

Rigtrip eventually became a Utah judge. Michael P. Collins was five years old, when he contracted polio, but despite great physical impairment, he graduated from medical school and practiced medicine in Salt Lake Valley. Jonathan Hughes Horne, who contracted polio at the age of four, became an orthopedic surgeon. Ellen Elizabeth Hancock Jerominski became a nurse, and she dedicated her life to being a therapist for fellow polio victims. Dan discovered that a chemistry professor at the University of Utah, Jean Masheter, had contracted polio at the age of six, and had spent years in physical therapy before obtaining a PhD from UCLA. She then moved to Salt Lake City.[90]

Dan also noticed the many children in the clinic, and he sympathized with their plight. The early stages of the children's lives had been completely disrupted, and Dan began to appreciate that, for more than two decades, he had lived a full and productive life. Polio had exposed him to life-threatening trials and struggles, but he recognized that, for twenty-three years, he had been able to experience life in a way that the little ones in the clinic would never know. His early life experiences had given him a capacity for resilience, and this new challenge increased his resolve to do what others did not expect him to do. He would never give up.[91]

One of the girl scout leaders in Downey was a recently baptized Mormon, Sister Meaders. Once a month she would bring her girl scout troop to the clinic, and the girls would read to the little patients. At first the girls in the troop were shocked at the room that looked like a gym, with "rows and rows of these big machines that were rather noisy." The children in the iron

---

[90] Each of the people named above participated in interviews for the Oral History project. See "Everett L. Cooley Oral History Project, 1983-2014." In *University of Utah, America West Center*. Salt Lake City, Utah: Special Collections Library,

[91] Angela Duckworth, *Grit: The Power of Passion and Perserverance* (New York: Scribner, 2016).

lungs were "smiling and nodding their heads when they could." Each time the scout troop visited, Sister Maeders would drop by and say "hello" to Dan. One of the girls in the scout troop was Christine, sister Maeders' eleven-year-old daughter. Christine would eventually marry Dan's neighbor on Butler Avenue, George Durham.[92] In 1982, she would be the first female justice to be appointed to the Utah Supreme Court. She and Dan would serve together there until Dan retired in 1999.

Almost every day, Dan went to the occupational therapy hall. For Dan, this would more appropriately have been called "arts and crafts therapy." The room was equipped with materials for painting, building, molding, or weaving. Most of the activities were intended to get the patients to exercise their hands and fingers. Others were "diversional" in that they led to actual products, such as clay figures and sculptures. Still others were "pre-vocational," in that patients would make products useful in the economy, such as brooms, rugs, and candles. Some of the activities led to professional careers. Tony Auth was so gifted in drawing that he eventually became a political cartoonist for the Philadelphia Inquirer. C.M. Campbell became a specialist in making and selling miniature reproductions of covered wagons and oxen.[93]

The therapists also told Dan about accomplishments of other polio victims. Erich Stegmann, for example, a gifted German, had learned how to paint using a mouth-held brush. He became a famous artist. During World War II, Ray Mendoza, who was once at *Rancho Los Amigos*, became famous for designing posters for U.S. Defense Bonds. A whole group of Rancho documentary photographers worked closely with specialists, such as Alfred Benjamin, in producing award winning films.[94]

Dan remembered that during his days at Stewart School, he had played the cornet with the orchestra, and as a soloist. According to his sister Mary Louise, he "played badly," but enjoyed being part of the musical group.[95]

[92] Christine Durham, "Interview by Liz Stewart in Christine's Home in Salt Lake City," (June 7, 2017).

[93] Fliedner, *Centennial: Rancho Los Amigos Medical Center: 1888-1988.*

[94] Ibid.

[95] Mary Louise Holbrook, "Interview at Her Home in Salt Lake City,," (June 5, 2018).

Now, with a lung capacity of about thirty percent, he recognized that he had little prospect of again playing a wind instrument. He even had difficulty reading, though the staff brought books and helped him learn how to hold the books, turn the pages, and keep his place.

The occupational therapy center also concentrated on helping patients learn how to care for themselves. They learned how to feed, wash and clean themselves. But, for almost his entire stay in Downey, Dan remained dependent on therapists to help him shave, eat, or dress.[96]

Dan was unusual among patients in that he began, as soon as possible, a rigorous regime of physical exercise. Every day, with the approval of Dr. Perry, he did whatever he could "without becoming overly fatigued."[97] Recently, two swimming pools had been built at *Rancho Los Amigos*, and with the help of a therapist standing nearby, Dan engaged in daily water aerobics. He had been a good swimmer as a teenager, and relished being in the water, where his useless legs would float.

Water treatment had been practiced since the time of Franklyn D. Roosevelt. At Warm Springs, Georgia, Le Roy W. Hubbard set up a water therapy program for Roosevelt and others that he tested for an entire summer, and Hubbard concluded that almost all the patients in the experiment made significant improvement in muscle power and joint flexibility.[98] At *Rancho Los Amigos*, therapists helped Dan take advantage of the buoyancy and invigorating qualities of water to enhance his morale and improve his muscle and joint functions.

Dan did whatever lifting exercises he could manage. His lower extremities, including hips, knees and ankles, were non-ambulatory. They would remain so for the remainder of his life. His upper extremities were very weak, particularly his shoulders, but his elbows and hands were stronger. He insisted on engaging in exercises involving his entire upper body. Therapists

---

[96] Rancho Los Amigos Medical Center, "Outpatient Progress Notes on Issac Daniel Stewart " (Downey, California August 29, 1995).

[97] Ibid.

[98] Tobin, *The Man He Became: How Fdr Defied Polio to Win the Presidency*. The so-called "Hubbard Tanks" are named after him.

also encouraged him to get outdoors and enjoy the beauties of nature and the fresh air of the sprawling campus.

The culmination of rehabilitation was to help patients begin thinking about an appropriate vocation. While it was, at times, possible to return the patients to their pre-polio occupations, it was usually not possible, so the team would explore closely related occupations or jobs. For example, while it usually would not be possible to resume the role of auto mechanic, perhaps the patient could work as a cashier in an auto mechanic facility.

Dr. Perry's team began to explore with Dan how he might prepare himself to realize his professional dream. Dan would have to cope with being a polio victim for the remainder of his life. It was possible that he would never advance beyond sitting in a wheelchair.

At the end of the year, Dan's condition had stabilized to the point that he could, by and large, care for himself by shaving, washing his face and hands, and eating on his own. Dr. Perry advised him that his condition would continue to improve, but that he ought to consider finding an alternative site in Utah that would not place such a heavy travel burden on his family. On January 10, 1957, he formally terminated his stay in Downey, California, and took the train to Utah.

PART II:

THE EARLY LIFE OF DAN STEWART

4. Young Danny

While rehabilitating at *Rancho Los Amigos,* Dan learned that the polio victims there developed an insatiable desire to succeed. And now in Salt Lake City, he discovered that Utah polio victims showed that same urgent need. Ken Rigtrip, whom Dan met as an outpatient at LDS Hospital, had contracted polio while in the army, and he refused to allow that to impede his desire to study law, even though he would do it in a wheelchair. Rigtrip eventually became a Utah judge.

Dan would soon learn of other polio victims who strove to succeed. Michael P. Collins was five years old, when he contracted polio, but despite great physical impairment, he graduated from medical school and practiced medicine in Salt Lake Valley. Jonathan Hughes Horne, who contracted polio at the age of four, became an orthopedic surgeon. Ellen Elizabeth Hancock Jerominski became a nurse, and she dedicated her life to being therapist for fellow polio victims. Dan discovered that a chemistry professor at his university, Jean Masheter, had contracted polio at the age of six, and spent years in physical therapy before obtaining a PhD from UCLA and then moving to Utah.[99]

Dan felt the same urgent drive; however, he also recognized that he had felt that need even long before he contracted polio. Aspects of his early life

---

[99] Each of the people named above participated in interviews for the Oral History project. See "Everett L. Cooley Oral History Project, 1983-2014." In *University of Utah, America West Center.* Salt Lake City, Utah: Special Collections Library,

surely contributed to his high aspirations. He enjoyed all the trappings of social status. He attended the best schools Utah had to offer. His friends were from the East side of the city. Many of the social, political, economic, and intellectual elites of Utah lived in his neighborhood.

Mormon President, David O. McKay's residence was less than seven city blocks from his home. Significantly, he was also from the American West, with its tradition of personal initiative and responsibility.[100] In spite of such indicators, success would not be inevitable, but was the consequence of hard work, foresight, and risk.

Danny lived in a conservative, patriarchal society that seriously believed families were established by divine inspiration. Both at home and at church he was taught that he was a literal spirit child of a loving creator, and in Junior Sunday School he sang with gusto, "I Am a Child of God." Believing in God was neither dramatic nor unremarkable. For Danny, God was as real as New York City or a molecule.

They were givens in a divinely inspired, well-constructed universe. God provided clear and simple rules of life by which to live. He took for granted that he knew and should follow these rules. Danny didn't want to be bad. He wanted to be good. He loved singing the hymns: "Do What Is Right," or "Choose the Right, When the Choice Is Placed before You."

There was a patriarchal order in his Mormon family. At meals, his mother taught him, when he was the oldest male present, that he must take charge and designate who was to say the blessing on the food. And at night, when the family knelt to pray, if Danny's father was not there, his mother instructed him to choose who was to say the prayer. Even as a young boy, he learned to act in positions of authority.

When Danny was born, the Stewart family was living in an apartment building, located on Third South and 740 East. They were part-owners, sharing ownership with the Daniel Sr. family, The apartment was down off the hill, just west of the University of Utah. The building was sizeable, four stories high with about thirty units. The Stewart family lived on the bottom floor in a half basement that had windows looking out onto Third South.

---

[100] Friedrich Jackson Turner, *The Frontier in American History* (New York: Holt, 1920).

With a family of six, the Stewarts had some difficulty fitting into the cramped quarters. It had only one bedroom, so family members were sleeping in the living room. The father and son slept together in the basement.[101] It was here that Danny began to grow and mature. Those first years of his life went by uneventfully.

Even though his mother, Orabelle, as the apartment manager, insisted that her children respect the privacy of the renters, Danny was an affable and agreeable youngster. He quickly befriended those dwelling in the apartments and was in an out of their private domains, bringing joy and happiness into the building. Danny also turned the building into his private playhouse.

He imagined the corridors were filled with enemies fighting America during World War II. He would fly down the stairs; he was a fighter plane pilot. He turned the long corridors into his private racetrack and raced from one end to the other. His early life was filled with fun and play. He did not ask himself what his later life would be. He simply enjoyed the moment. He was intent on discovery. That was his reward for having fun, for engaging to the fullest in playful activity.

In a similar manner, Danny's father was always exploring new adventures, novel ways of encountering the world around him. He seemed to have his fingers in everything. He was the principal at Sumner, then at Hawthorne Primary Schools. Even though Hawthorne was not in an elite part of town, Daniel Sr. turned it into a school with a reputation for high academic excellence.

Although Orabelle formally managed the apartment building, Danny's father looked in almost every day to lend moral support. He owned a used-car lot and sold pre-owned autos. He owned two service stations, one on Fourth South near the Rio Grande Train Station, and the other on South Temple, near Second West. Whenever he had a little extra cash, he would ask himself how he could invest the money in some new venture.

Because the family seemed to be doing well, with prospects of living in some luxury, they bought a good-sized bungalow-style house on Butler Avenue, located just a few blocks away from the apartment building and right behind Kingsbury Hall on the President's Circle at the University of Utah.

[101] Holbrook, "Interview at the Dan Stewart Family Home in Salt Lake City."

The house was not pretentious, but it was large enough to accommodate a family of six. All four children were in finished bedrooms in the full-size basement.

In 1943, everything promptly changed. Danny's father had a sudden and fatal heart attack. This represented one of the decisive events in the Stewart household. While polio was a pivotal and momentous event in Dan's life, the significance of the death of his father, Isaac Daniel Sr., cannot be overstated. But Danny's upbringing prepared him for that moment, and he met the challenge with persistence and tenacity.

Danny's father's death placed a great burden on Orabelle. Isaac Daniel Sr. had gone into debt to invest in the many businesses he had acquired. Orabelle disposed of the service stations, and used-car dealership, and the Stewarts also sold the apartment building, Orabelle did not receive anything from its sale, but the children received one-third of the funds, which were formally dedicated to their education. Orabelle was barely able to hang on to their house.

She had only a vague idea how she was going to sustain their lives, so that the children could continue to have the advantages the Butler Avenue address provided. She started renting rooms in the basement to college students, meaning there was lots of cleaning and maintaining to do. She also found a cashier position at the University of Utah Union Building,[102] then later took a sales position at Boyd Park Jewelers, in downtown Salt Lake City.

The Federal Heights neighborhood where they lived, was generally regarded as "posh." Their neighbors were prominent businesspeople, doctors, lawyers, and university professors. G. Homer Durham, eventually Academic Vice President of the University of Utah, lived just across the street. U.S. District Judge Willis Ritter lived just down the street. That location promised to be ideal for the young children. They attended Sunday school, sacrament meeting, primary, and Mutual Improvement Association at University Ward, which had a distinct reputation among Mormons. If she could

---

[102] Stewart. Issac Daniel, "Interview at His Home in Salt Lake City, ," (Dec. 8, 1999).

keep the children in Federal Heights, she knew that they would associate with the best people and attend the best educational institutions.

She never told them they must do well in their classes. That was just what one did. She never praised them or admonished them when they brought their report cards home. Everyone, including the children, assumed the teacher would indicate that they did good work. When Isaac Daniel Sr. died, the children were already enrolled in the Stewart Laboratory School, reputed to be one of the best "progressive schools in America,"[103] and Orabelle was obsessed that they remain there. In fact, they had enrolled Danny in Stewart School, while they were living in the apartment building. Even though they lived outside its catchment area, he was allowed to enter because his great uncle had founded the school.

Stewart Laboratory School modeled itself after the ideas of John Dewey, where the child was reared to be independent, working out its own program of studies. Danny's teachers tried to help him be a "happy, useful, rational, and moral being."[104] Danny's friend, John Bennion, who also attended the Stewart Lab School, describes that environment: "These were often called 'fun schools' rather than rigorous academic institutions. But from my vantage, the lab school was really for bright kids, so they could just take off and do whatever they were inclined to, or anything they wanted to do."[105]

The actual program of the school stressed creative self-expression. It allowed Danny to do what he wanted to do. For some kids, such a curriculum was detrimental, for they didn't know what to do that would be to their advantage. However, Federal Heights kids generally would have succeeded in any environment. Even Danny felt his program was a bit boring and wished his superiors would assign him difficult tasks; however, he was bright enough to take appropriate initiative.

---

[103] John T. Wahlquist, *The Activity School* (Salt Lake City: University of Utah, Department of Elementary Education, 1936); Frances Gilroy Davis, "A History of the William M. Stewart School: 1890-1940" (University of Utah, 1940).

[104] Wahlquist, *The Activity School*.

[105] John Bennion, "Interview at His Home in Salt Lake City, ," (Oct. 25, 2017).

Besides, the Stewart School was on the University of Utah campus, which became the kids' playground. For example, the medical school was right next door, and it was exciting to go across the street and look in the windows to see if there was a cadaver anywhere. The kids had access to the university swimming pool and gym, located just a block away.

Danny could have continued attending the lab school through junior high, but he decided to enroll in Bryant Junior High, located near the old apartment building the Stewart family had owned. The school drew students from a broad spectrum of social classes in Salt Lake City. Danny was particularly interested in participating in inter-school sports programs, and Bryant provided just such an opportunity. Ashby Decker, the sports editor of the school newspaper, quickly recognized the physical talents of Danny and mentioned him several times in sports articles about tennis and basketball. He would later excel in football in high school and college, but that sport was not allowed in junior high.[106]

At Bryant Junior High, Danny took a rigorous set of courses, including Latin, English, and mathematics.[107] After finishing Bryant Junior High, Danny then attended East High. It had the well-deserved reputation of being the best public school in Utah. His graduating class of 1951 included future members of the United States Senate from Utah, Jake Garn (1974-1993) and Robert Bennett (1993-2010); a future member of the Mormon Church First Presidency, Henry B. Eyring; a member of the U.S. House of Representatives representing Utah, James V. Hansen, (1981-2003); and Eugene England, A Mormon writer and scholar, who established the prominent quarterly, *Dialogue: A Journal of Mormon Thought.*

Danny was active in extra-curricular activities. He was the East High delegate on a ten-day trip to Flathead Lake, Montana, sponsored by the American Red Cross, to orient young people for future service in the high

---

[106] Ashby Decker, "Interview at His Home in Salt Lake City, ," (Sept. 27, 2018).

[107] Bruce S. Jenkins, "Everett L. Cooley Oral History Project, 1983-2014.," ed. America West Center University of Utah (Salt Lake City, Utah: Special Collections Library, June 15, 1993).

schools they attended.[108] He was featured in a *Salt Lake Tribune* article that explained how the whole Stewart family helped clean the house, while maintaining their homework schedule. "The kids enjoy their work because each has a special duty of keeping his or her room clean plus odd jobs."

The article notes that "Danny even manages to work on the side."[109] And he was featured in a *Deseret News* article about teenage attitudes toward maintaining world peace. Danny found the prospect of world peace to be "grim," but ultimately concluded that the technological advancements of the time dictated that "the future should be very promising."[110] As a senior he was a member of the school's "Service Committee." As a good Mormon boy, he was active in scouting, though he failed to earn his Eagle Scout badge.

At East High, Danny was known for his academic prowess. His program of study included physics, world history, civics, biology, geometry, Latin, commercial law, and English. He was also exposed to some great teachers. His Latin and history instructor, Miss Marion van Pelt, was especially engaging and interested in the students. She spoke often with the students about going on to college, stressing that the study of the humanities and social sciences ought to be seen as "a calling" rather than as something to become wealthy. He took American history from Hazel Whitcomb, and he had the reputation of dominating the daily discussions. His favorite teacher, was McKinley Oswald, who also served as the head football coach.[111]

As a reward for his secondary school academic performance, the University of Utah Committee on Scholarship Awards selected him to receive the Dr. Clarence Snow scholarship.[112] This scholarship did not provide a lot of money, but it had symbolic significance. There was a close connection between East

---

[108] "8 Students Lead on Red Cross Trip," *Deseret News* 1946.

[109] Ruth Strandquist, "Teenagers Can Sharethe Household Load," *Salt Lake Tribune* Feb. 2, 1951.

[110] Elaine Cannon, "Teensters Discuss World Peace Problems," *Deseret News* Jan. 2, 1049.

[111] George Jarvis, "Interview at the Church History Library in Salt Lake City, ," (January 28, 2019).

[112] A. Ray Olpin, "Letter from the Office of the President," (Salt Lake City: University of Utah, June 24, 1952).

High and the University of Utah. Their campuses were less than a mile apart, and even though almost all East High students went on to college, about two-thirds of all of them chose to go to the University of Utah.[113] and many of them became student leaders during their undergraduate years.

His lower division program at the "U of U" was, for Dan like attending a sumptuous banquet. There were so many delicious delicacies to partake of and no possibility of tasting everything on the table.[114] True to the experience of most freshmen, Dan did not do well his first quarter. Of course, he was on the football team, and his schedule was tight. In fact, of the five courses he took that first quarter, he received one C and two B's. He did better the rest of the year. In the second year, he received straight A's in all thirteen courses he took. During that first year, he was involved in general education courses. And he tasted of mathematics. physical sciences, technology, economics, political science, American history, and European history.

Danny had always been physically active. He lived less than a block away from Reservoir Park, where a city water storage facility had been covered over with lawns and trees. The Parks and Recreation Department also constructed several tennis courts on top of the large cement water storage tank. He played regularly on the courts and often entered age-competition contests. For example, the *Salt Lake Tribune* sponsored an annual tennis tournament, and when in high school, Danny beat his old high school buddy, Ashby Decker in the finals, at the Salt Lake Tennis Club.[115]

Danny played fullback on an East High varsity football team that usually competed for championship honors in the state's A-league, the highest level of play in Utah. His picture appeared regularly in the *Deseret News* and *Salt Lake Tribune* during football season.[116] He was so proficient in high school that, as a senior, he was selected to play in the Utah Shrine hospital all-star football game.[117] In 1951, as a freshman at the University of Utah, Danny

[113] Jenkins, "Everett L. Cooley Oral History Project, 1983-2014.."

[114] Liz Stewart, "Interview at Her Mother's Home in Salt Lake City, ," (June 6, 2018).

[115] Decker, "Interview at His Home in Salt Lake City, ."

[116] For example, "Talking It Over," *Deseret News* Oct.2, 11950.

played defensive half back, but toward the end of the season, he injured his back and was forced to retire from football.

Every young man in Salt Lake City enjoyed the mountains. In the winter, Danny and his buddies were often at Alta and Brighten testing their skills on the ski slopes. As he and his friends gathered between classes, someone would often suggest, "Hey, its beautiful out. Let's cut out and check out the quality of the snow." Most of the time, someone had a test, or was making a presentation in class, but that didn't stop the others from cutting class for the afternoon.

Socially, Danny had always been adept. At East High, male students often formed social cliques, depending on whether they played football, basketball, or baseball. Danny was part of a football clique, consisting of Dick Ellis, John Sherman, Paul Griffin, Larry Couch, and Ashby Decker. All through high school, they gathered every Sunday evening and attended sacrament meeting, the weekly worship service of the Mormon Church. Then they would go over to Larry's house, nearby on Sunnyside Avenue, and watch the *Colgate Comedy Hour*, staring Dean Martin and Jerry Lewis.[118]

At the time, almost all television sets were small little boxes, but Larry's parents had purchased a large, beautiful screen. Paul Griffin, claimed to be especially shy among girls, and he came up with the idea that the group form a "Be Mean to Girls" (BMG) anti-girl club, with a restricted membership and a formal set of by-laws. Its major intent was to refrain from dating and avoid contact with girls.[119] Such a scheme was futile.

While in high school, Danny bought an old 1941 Buick, the paint was chipping, and the tires were worn out. And it had a missing gear. One day, they drove up Emigration Canyon, and the engine gave out. They pushed the car until it got on a downhill road, and they coasted all the way to the Salt Lake Valley without the engine being on. Other times, they would test themselves to see how close they could come to running out of gas before

---

[117] Shrine Hospital, "All Star Football and Basketball," ed. Shrine Hospital (Salt Lake City, Utah August 15, 17, 18, 1951).

[118] Ashby Decker, "Interview at His Home in Salt Lake City ," (October 25, 2017).

[119] Paul Griffin, "Interview at His Home in Salt Lake City ," (October, 25, 1017).

the engine gave out. Sometimes they misjudged and would have to push the car a couple of miles before finding an open gas station.[120]

According to friends, the boys Danny ran with would often get into "philosophical talks," about how they felt about life. His friends later claimed Danny was such a deep thinker that he affected their lives much more than any of their teachers. He was on the East High debate team. He and his debate friends once debated a "girls' team," and they made the mistake of "ridiculing their arguments." The judge penalized them for not showing proper respect for young ladies.[121] His friends claimed Danny was "a fun-loving guy," who could have done anything he wanted. They found it odd that he chose the "stodgy profession of law."

In secondary school, Danny had the reputation of dating and socializing with the most popular girls at East High. One of his classmates claims that he always saw Danny socializing with "the most gorgeous girls" in the school.[122] One of these students, Barbara, a tall, graceful, slender young lady, even appeared in a "family picture" taken just before Danny's Mormon mission call to West Germany.

After Danny's father's death, he assumed the quiet role of the man of the house. Even though Danny was only twelve years old, when his father died, he felt it was he who must be the leader of the Stewart household. He was not yet able to be the primary bread winner, but while in his teens, more than one summer Danny worked for the Denver and Rio Grande Western Railroad (D&RGW), living in a boxcar; the crew repaired the rail bed throughout the mountain West, but they often worked on the line that ran up Spanish Fork Canyon past Thistle and into Price Canyon.[123]

One summer Danny worked on a drilling-rig. Another summer he drove a cement truck, though that didn't turn out so well; he took his girlfriend, Elaine Robbins, to the truck one evening and they became so involved in each other,

---

[120] Dick Ellis, "Interview at the Ellis Home in Salt Lake City," (sept. 21, 2018).

[121] Ibid.

[122] Dale Larson, "Interview at His Cottonwood, Utah Home," (Feb. 20, 2018).

[123] His school buddies, Paul Griffin, Paul Couch, and Dick Ellis, usually worked with him. See Decker, "Interview at His Home in Salt Lake City, ."

he forgot to keep the mixing drum turning. The cement hardened, and the next day, he spent several hours of hard manual labor cleaning it out.[124] He was eventually fired from that job, after he ran the cement truck into a ditch.[125]

During the school year, Danny always had after-school jobs. He mowed lawns, set pins in the local bowling alley on campus, and pumped gasoline. He even hauled garbage for neighbors. He would set up a large box on the back of his bicycle and go from house to house asking people if they wanted to dispose of anything.[126] They were often happy to give him things that proved to be of value, including classical books and long-play records.

His friends admired him for his skill in creating and finding jobs; they never realized that working was an absolute necessity for him. Danny was always acutely aware of his own personal secret. He was poor. Danny's early trials in dealing with never having enough money to pay for necessities like food or medical bills helped him develop the qualities of fortitude, endurance resilience and plain, old-fashioned grit that were to sustain him during the trials of his later life. His high level of intelligence served him well, but it was his passion and perseverance that made the difference in the success he was to achieve.[127]

In the fall of 1951, as a university freshman, Danny took part in the University of Utah fraternity and sorority rush, and he chose to join the Sigma Chi Fraternity. At that time, fraternity life symbolized a significant social distinction, and Sigma Chi's were the elite of the fraternity system. Younger students, such as C. Dean Larsen, recognized Danny as a leader of the fraternity, "one you looked up to."[128] He was only active during those freshman and sophomore years, but after he returned to school following his Mormon mission, he was never socially active again. However, many years later, at its 1994 Distinguished Alumni Banquet, his fraternity honored Dan Stewart for a distinguished career as a lawyer and judge.[129]

---

[124] Holbrook, "Interview at Her Home in Salt Lake City,."

[125] Decker, "Interview at His Home in Salt Lake City, ."

[126] Holbrook, "Interview at Her Home in Salt Lake City,."

[127] Duckworth, *Grit: The Power of Passion and Perserverance.*

[128] Larsen, "Interview at His Home in Salt Lake City, ."

5. Elder Stewart

On November 15, 1953, at age twenty-one, Elder Stewart arrived at West German Mission headquarters in Frankfurt am Main, where he was scheduled to remain for thirty months. At the time, he was one of about 2,500 full-time missionaries of the Mormon Church, most of whom served in the United States. The church decided where the missionaries were to serve, although there was rumor that young people from places like the exclusive Federal Heights neighborhood were usually sent to foreign missions, while most of those from small towns and working-class districts would go to places like Colorado, South Carolina, or Indiana.

The tradition was that the families would pay the missionary's expenses. In Danny's case, this placed a terrible burden on the Stewart family. Danny's bishop suggested that the family needed to find a solution, and two of his uncles volunteered to put up the funds for him.[130]

The missionaries received no formal training, either in the gospel or language. They spent a few days in orientation, but its purpose was mainly inspirational rather than instructional. The local wards were ready to help, should the family need financial assistance. There were always a small

---

[129] "Distinguished Alumni Banquet," (Salt Lake City Ft. Douglas Country Club: Sigma Chi Fraternity, May 12, 1994).

[130] Stewart, "A Life: Dictated to Richard G. Ellis."

number of female and retired missionaries, although in that day, relatively few were being called. Most, like Elder Stewart, were about twenty-one years old, when they arrived.

On November 1, 1953, Elder Stewart left Salt Lake City by train,[131] traveled by Pullman to New York, where he and a few other missionaries stayed at the Hotel Wellington. They toured the city for two days before embarking on an ocean voyage on the U.S.S. America. It took nine days of travel, with a fuel stop in Ireland, before they arrived in Bremerhaven, then they went by train to Bremen, then to Frankfurt am Main.

West German Mission President Kenneth B. Dyer met with the new elders at mission headquarters at 55 *Betinnastraße*. Dyer introduced himself and asked the new missionaries to tell something about themselves. Elder Stewart was tall, dignified and even a bit imposing, as he explained who he was. He mentioned that he spoke no German, but he clearly stood out as one having a commanding presence. He was obviously one born to be a leader.

President Dyer then told each of them where they were to begin their service, and who their first missionary companion would be. Elder Stewart was assigned to work in Heidelberg, a cosmopolitan city, with the country's oldest university (1386 AD). Elders worked in pairs, and he was to be a junior companion to Elder Herbert Ulstein, a German, who spoke no English.

President Dyer then reminded the new missionaries that they were among the first Mormon missionaries to be in Germany after World War II. They must take care to remain healthy. After seven years, Germans were still rebuilding their cities. Since the war, the water in the cities was not good and they should refrain from drinking too much of it. He explained that missionaries often were invited to eat with members, who warned their children that they cannot drink the water, even though missionaries usually request it.

"The water is bad for you. Most of the missionaries drink it because they come from America and are used to it." President Dyer suggested that they take the advice of the German parents: "The water is bad for you." And the alternative might be no better: "The milk is not pasteurized and might make you sick."

---

[131] "Handwritten Diary," (Salt Lake City, Utah: Personal, undated).

The assumption of church leaders was those missionaries going abroad would learn the language the way a native learns it. After arriving in Heidelberg, the two companions first communicated using hand signs, and by "making wild motions with their arms."[132] Like almost all new missionaries, Elder Stewart spent several hours each day studying the language. He always carried a small pocket- English/German-dictionary and was forever asking how to define and pronounce words being spoken. He would often stay up most of the night studying. When he got stumped, he would throw a pillow at Elder Ulstein, wake him up, and ask him the meaning of a word or how to pronounce a phrase. He revealed a sense of delight about learning something new, and always had a ready smile on his face. Ulstein later said that "he was the sharpest guy I had ever met on my mission."[133]

Every day the two companions spent about twelve hours studying, meeting with "contacts," associating with members, and traveling on their bikes and the streetcar. In the evenings, after returning to their rented room, they would eat a quick meal; then Elder Stewart would open his journal and record what the two of them had done.

While he was preparing to serve his mission, as did every other man or woman preparing to depart, Elder Stewart had gone to Zions Cooperative Mercantile Institution (ZCMI) and purchased a journal. They all looked the same. MISSIONARY JOURNAL was emblazoned on the hard, maroon cover, with a world map inside both the front and back covers. There were designated pages to record special events and dates, the location of his assignments, ordinances performed, and genealogical information. Missionaries usually scribbled a few lines at the end of the day, but Elder Stewart often wrote several pages, providing details of meetings, discussions, and readings. The last entry in his journal was on January 17, 1956, nine days before he was diagnosed with polio.

When he was a new missionary, Elder Stewart often wrote that he almost exploded with the desire to express his thoughts in German, and he noted that, at the time, he became "a little envious of those missionaries who labor

---

[132] Ibid.

[133] Herbert Ulstein, "Interview at His Bountiful, Utah Home," (Feb. 19, 2018).

in English-speaking countries." But his love for the German people quickly grew, and he expressed appreciation for living and serving in this "beautiful, romantic country."

Most of the time, the two companions were knocking on doors, a process known as tracting, and when someone answered the door, the missionaries would introduce themselves and ask if they might come in and deliver a brief spiritual message. On the first day, Elder Ulstein informed Elder Stewart that, at each door, he must say something in German. Every day they would knock on dozens of doors, so this gave him an opportunity to practice the few words that he knew. He first learned to say, in German: "Good day."[134] Then Elder Ulstein stepped in. After saying this at several doors, Elder Stewart then learned to say: "Good day. We are the missionaries."[135] Then Elder Ulstein again stepped in. After saying this at dozens of doors, his line became: "Good day. We are the missionaries, and we wish to visit with you."[136]

Then Elder Stewart began to elaborate a little, by saying. "We are the American missionaries of the Church of Jesus Christ," or "We have a brief message, and we wish to visit with you." Missionaries quickly learned that their identity as Americans was something special. In the minds of Germans, being a Mormon and an American were so closely linked that the elders did not hesitate to identify themselves as Americans, even when their companion was a German. At their age, they did not recognize the growing political tensions between the Utah Legislature and Utah Supreme Court and the federal government in Washington, D.C. They were proud of their American identity and exploited that identity, whenever they could.

Elder Stewart would say the same things dozens of times a day, and his German language learning had begun in earnest. Whereas most American missionaries required several months before they could speak well enough to give a message, Elder Stewart was doing so in a matter of weeks. Most missionaries in West Germany spoke what academics might call an

---

[134] *Guten Tag.*

[135] *Guten Tag. Wir sind die Missionare.*

[136] *Guten Tag. Wir sind die Missionare, und wir möchten Sie besuchen.*

American-Mormon-German, with its own unique words, pronunciations, and idioms, passed on from one missionary to the next. Elder Stewart defied this tradition and quickly learned to speak a beautiful, refined High German.

He soon gained the facility to follow the conversations of people the missionaries encountered. He had arrived in Germany about eight years after the end of World War II. Fortunately, Heidelberg was in the American Zone of Occupation, and when Elder Stewart arrived, the city had been largely restored to its prewar status. In the British and French Zones, these allies did not have the resources quickly to restore the bombed-out cities, so for many years, the rubble and destroyed buildings remained as constant reminders that Germany had recently been destroyed and humbled.

Regularly, the two missionaries ate lunch at small corner restaurants, where they tracted. These were frequented by German university students, who were curious to find an American eating there. Study abroad had not yet become popular, and the Germans marveled that a university student from the United States would be doing missionary work for a Christian church. They wondered even more that a political science student would do something like that. Elder Stewart found almost all the students knew philosophy and logic, and they constantly challenged his thinking.[137]

Less than four months after Elder Stewart arrived in Heidelberg, he recorded in his journal that he and his companion met a man, Herr J. Fiedler, who said that he was a member of the politically conservative Christian Democratic Party (CDU) and had once served as its Secretary General. Most missionaries would have launched into their prepared presentation, but Elder Stewart, was curious about German politics and knew enough German to ask: "As a member of the CDU, what is your notion of democracy?"

Fiedler responded by explaining that he believed the best political form "was an authoritative democracy wherein the authority would hear the opinions of the people and then make decisions." He explained that he was a conservative and argued that "liberalism eventually leads to Marxism, and something had to be done to stop this." The answer was with the Lutheran

---

[137] Stewart, "A Life: Dictated to Richard G. Ellis."

Church and other Christian churches. "When the people live the *Bible,* then we need have no fear of Marxism." Fiedler said he worried about living in Heidelberg, where a major university is found. The city is "a danger spot in Germany, because the university sponsors free thinking, such as liberalism, and this represents the seeds of communism."[138]

Always more prone toward contemplation than spontaneity, Elder Stewart wrote in his journal that he chose not to attempt an immediate response to Fiedler, and he complained that his German was too inadequate to respond. In addition, he confessed to himself that he was prone to consider seriously another man's point of view, that there were usually at least two sides of an argument, even when the other's point of view seemed dangerous and wrong. Then he reasoned with himself about what an appropriate rejoinder might have been, and what "obviously pertinent questions" were to be raised. He decided he might have asked, "What is the difference between 'authoritative democracy' and 'totalitarianism?'" or "Who chooses the authorities?" or "Should the authorities do what the people want?"

Elder Stewart worried about the scars the World War II had left on the German people. He recognized that he was just a young man and did not know much about Nazi Germany, the Jewish persecution, or the reason America entered the war. He listened when Elder Ulstein discussed the war with investigators, people interested in learning about the Mormon Church.

Barely a month after arriving in Heidelberg, Elder Stewart declared a growing sympathy for their viewpoint, and he wrote that "to the German layman the United States had no right to enter the war." The common man, who is not versed in world strategy, can only realize that Germany had virtually won the war, when the United States, for no good moral reason, entered the war to defeat the Germans and inflict upon them the horrible cruelties of a homeland war."[139] And after the war, the Germans had largely tried to atone for their Nazi sins.

Elder Stewart often talked with his companion about the war, and he discovered that his home and city had been "bombed and re-bombed and

[138] "Handwritten Diary."

[139] "Missionary Journal ". Dec. 15, 1953.

re-bombed." Ulstein told his companion that, as the bombers flew over, he would sometimes stand in the street, before running to a shelter, as the bombers flew over.

"There were so many, they blocked out the sun." Elder Stewart gained a "keyhole view of their awful fear, anxiety, and physical and mental suffering."[140] Elder Ulstein recounted that his father had been lost on the Russian front and was still missing. He was near tears as he explained to his companion soul-wrenching experiences of his family. Ulstein and his mother often came "near to starvation." Such accounts brought Elder Stewart close to his missionary companion, whom he found to be a "loveable character, always in a good mood, and easy to get along with. "

Elder Stewart remained in Heidelberg for more than five months before being transferred to Moers. There are striking cultural differences in various areas of Germany. Elder Stewart discovered that, when he was transferred, he usually required a couple of weeks to adjust to the way people spoke and to understand the local dialect. Heidelberg had represented a cosmopolitan high culture, while Moers was in Germany's industrial "coal pot." The people were Catholic and strictly working class; they spoke a crude German dialect.

He was fortunate to have been paired in Moers with Elder David Grotegut, from Spanish Fork, Utah, who was gifted in learning local dialects. Elder Grotegut helped Elder Stewart develop an ear, not only to hear, but to speak the rough, unrefined local tongue.[141]

In his diary, Elder Stewart expressed concern that the war had a different effect on the people of Moers than those in Heidelberg. He observed that many Moers residents had lost their religious faith: "Not infrequently, we meet people who say they believe in nothing more... . They had put their faith and trust in Hitler and when Hitler was crushed their future was crushed also. That meant that many of their hopes and dreams went down the drain along with Hitler."

---

[140] Ibid.

[141] David Grotegut, "Interview at His Home in Springville, Utah, ," (Feb. 22, 2018).

Elder Stewart wrote in his journal that Moers residents, by and large, had rejected the Catholic Church. He worried that these people confused the Catholic Church with belief in God and the *Bible*. Their negative sentiments against the church led them to reject their faith in God. Part of this loss had to do with the war. So many people believed that "if there were a God, he would not have allowed such a thing to take place." Elder Stewart believed the churches had failed to provide stable, "eternal" standards by which the people were to live, and that Catholic leaders had truly done a disservice to their members.

Elder Stewart observed that the Germans were accepting of the missionaries, but seldom converted. Most were indifferent to religion and did not allow it to direct their daily lives. They had gone through the rituals of baptism and catechism study, but the church did not serve as a guide to their daily lives.[142]

Yet another impression he gained while in Moers, was how much the Germans admired the Americans and how much they hated the Russians. He wrote in his journal, "I never cease to be astounded at how much respect the Germans seem to have." Former prisoners of war always commented on how well they were treated in the American prisoner of war camps. One man told Elder Stewart that "he was much healthier and fatter in the prison than he is now."

In contrast, millions of Prussian families had fled to escape the Russians and had settled in West Germany. Of course, Russians and other Soviet citizens had suffered terribly during the war; more than twenty-five million had lost their lives, but Elder Stewart believed this national tragedy did not excuse the Russians from the atrocities they committed. One refugee couple told "of a family, including the children, having their hands bound and pushed off a bridge into a river by the Russians. . . , of beating women before their husbands. . . , of gathering up the women and hauling them off to rape them. . . , of mass machine gunning of men."[143]

Even though he was still a junior companion in Moers, Elder Stewart was already considered to be an outstanding missionary; his language was improving by leaps and bounds. While tracting, he even met a professor, who

---

[142] Stewart, "A Life: Dictated to Richard G. Ellis."

[143] "Missionary Journal ".

agreed to listen to him read German and correct his pronunciation. His ambition was to speak in such a way that the Germans would not know he was an American.[144]

In some respects, Elder Stewart differed from the other "good" elders. He was absolutely inner-directed, though he was neither capricious nor flighty. In fact, his second companion in Moers, Wayne Kuehne, claimed that Elder Stewart "was the most organized person I had ever met."[145] Whereas most missionaries ran their lives according to a definite mission structure, Elder Stewart had his own internal clock and calendar. He would often stay up all night reading or studying, and sleep in all morning.

He paid no attention to the time missionaries were expected to spend studying, tracting, meeting investigators, consulting with members, and attending church meetings. Curiously, he consistently recorded how many so-called "cottage meetings" he and his companion held each day. Whereas most missionaries were happy to hold two or three meetings a day, Elder Stewart, often noted that he held eight to ten cottage meetings each day, and sometimes they would hold as many as seventeen or eighteen.[146]

Missionaries were expected to keep meticulous records about their day, and they would usually log more than eighty hours a week of formal missionary work. However, Elder Stewart's name rarely appeared on the regular notices sent out from mission headquarters, indicating who got on the honor roll for "working the most hours" or "baptizing the most people." He simply paid no attention to these conventions.

In August, while he was in Moers, his Salt Lake City girlfriend, Barbara, paid him a visit, which was against mission rules. Her parents had sent her to Europe to participate in a mini-*Grand Tour* of the main cities of England, France, Spain, Italy, and Germany. Barbara arrived in Moers from Italy and spent four days with him. Having been out less than a year, the suit he wore still showed some semblance of style and professionalism.

[144] "A Life: Dictated to Richard G. Ellis."

[145] Wayne Kuehne, "Interview at His Home in Orem, Utah, ," (Feb. 22, 2018).

[146] Stewart, "Missionary Journal ".

Elder Stewart left his companion at their apartment, and he took Barbara to what he called an "ice cream parlor" in Moers. Of course, there were no such parlors in West Germany, and it would surely have been a *Kneipe*, something like a British pub. They found themselves sitting near the "regular's table" where a group of beer-drinking Germans gathered, who obviously routinely visited the place, and were "sitting around a table playing guitars and singing German folk songs. It was quite romantic"[147] to hear *Muss I denn* or *Du, du liegst mir im Herzen.*

He noted in his journal that Barbara was more beautiful than ever, but he told himself he shouldn't think of that; he had committed himself to the Lord's work while in West Germany. When she pressed him to make a commitment, he insisted that to do so was not in the spirit of his mission. During these thirty months of his life, he had committed all his energy to missionary work.

However, he made a gesture of sorts by giving Barbara his *Sigma Chi* pin, but just before leaving, she gave it back to him. After she left, he confessed in his journal that he was so depressed that he felt he "had been shot in the stomach with a 12-gauge shotgun."[148] Even though he blamed mission rules on his inability to commit to her, there were also clear signs that other factors were coming into play. He wrote in his journal that he worried about the kind of mother she would be to his children. Would she raise them to be true members of Christ's gospel? A few months after Barbara left Moers, he wrote his mother complaining that he thought Barbara had always been motivated to attend church only because of social reasons, and that, for his sake, she was willing to try and gain a testimony of the gospel.[149] She really believed she loved him but giving his pin back to him freed her from ties that would bind her to him for the next two years.

Clearly, his missionary associates had enough trust in Elder Stewart that they did not report the incident of Barbara to President Dyer. And it would be a mistake to imply that their relationship was based on sexual promiscuity.

[147] "Letter Home to His Mother," (Moers, West Germany: Handwritten, Sept. 1, 1954).

[148] "Missionary Journal ". August 18, 1954.

[149] "Letter to His Mother," (Moers, West Germany: Personally written, August 1, 1954).

As so often happens in the life of Mormon missionaries, after Barbara returned home, she took her life in a different direction.

Another reason Elder Stewart may have been reluctant to commit himself to her, would likely have been that he was not yet able financially to support anyone. From the beginning of his mission, Elder Stewart worried about money. West Germany was still attempting to recover from the recent war, and its economy, though growing rapidly, was not yet competitive with the United States. Consequently, the dollar/German mark exchange rate greatly advantaged the American missionaries. However, such an advantage was not apparent to Elder Stewart.

Almost every letter he sent home made some reference to money. Apparently, early on, one payment from home was five days late. In his next letter he wrote: "*I must have my check by the first (FIRST) of every month. From now on send me $40 a month. However next time send me $20 additional in a separate check so that I can have a separate reserve.*"[150] Even though the exchange rate was more than four marks per dollar, which greatly advantaged the Americans, Elder Stewart knew that his family members were making great financial sacrifice to support him in West Germany.

Elder Kuehne recognized the dedication Elder Stewart was making to learn the German language, and he looked for someone to help his companion with his pronunciation. They found a young man who agreed to spend 2.5 hours a week with Elder Stewart, for a paltry 2.50 German marks (about $0.60). Elder Stewart soon reached such a proficiency that Germans often thought he was a local: "If I don't speak too much."

After serving in Moers for about five months, Elder Stewart was transferred to Düsseldorf, known generally as the German Paris, where he served as the senior companion to Elders John Karpowitz, and Don Williams. Karpowitz was an old friend from the University of Utah. Elder Stewart took his responsibility with junior companions seriously. He had four main tasks. First, he was expected to teach his junior companion, usually a new missionary, something about the doctrines and basic principles of the

---

[150] "Letter to His Mother," (Moers, West Germany: Handwritten, April 14, 1954).

Mormon Church. Most of the missionaries had grown up in the church and had learned its basic principles and doctrines, but they needed to learn how to state these doctrines in a clear and simple manner. The mission headquarters provided literature so this could be accomplished.

Second, Elder Stewart introduced the junior companion to the German language. Most of the new missionaries spoke no German at all, and the church had not yet instituted a language program for missionaries serving abroad. Every morning, after he and his companion had washed, dressed, and eaten breakfast, they sat down together and studied a textbook they purchased or inherited from another missionary.

Third, Elder Stewart helped the new missionary learn, in German, how to say a simple prayer, introduce himself, and give a brief message at the door where the missionaries were tracting. Elder Stewart had long ago demonstrated that he was an excellent teacher who helped his companions gain command of the language and the basic principles of the gospel.

Fourth, he helped the new elder memorize a series of lessons in German that would be given when the missionaries were fortunate enough to be invited into a home. These lessons consisted of a series of questions, such as, "Do you believe in God?" or "How many personages are in the Godhead?" The new missionary would also memorize the possible answers the investigator could give. The intent of the first lessons was to expose the Protestants or Catholics to what Mormons considered to be false doctrines and convince them that the Mormon Church contained God's true doctrines.

A fter four months in Düsseldorf, Elder Stewart was transferred to Kassel, where he worked with three different companions: Elders John P. Groscost, Ingo Zander, and LeRoy Faerber. It was here that Elder Stewart became a public figure. Whereas Mormon missionaries often held street meetings in the town square, Elder Stewart was not satisfied with that modest approach. He participated in a public forum at the *Amerika Haus*.[151]

He began putting advertisements in the local newspapers, the *Kasseler Zeitung* and the *Hessische Niedersächsische Allgemeine*, and had notices pasted on

[151] "Letter to Edward Moreton " (May 21, 1955).

advertisement boards about public lectures he was giving. Usually, the meetings were not heavily attended, but they were visible announcements that the Mormon Church was present in Kassel. The other missionaries often noted that Elder Stewart "was a deep thinker,"[152] an "intellectual type of person,"[153] who responded to questions from his small audiences by considering their inquiries. Even though the public lectures dealt with conventional topics, such as "Jesus Christ: You and the *Book of Mormon*," or "The Restoration of All Things."[154] Elder Stewart was not shy about raising his own questions, for instance, about the Mormon Church's racial policies, or Germany's shameful Nazi past. He even raised issues that were unfamiliar to typical Mormons, such as the positive relationship the Mormon Church had enjoyed with Nazism, citing the adoption, by Hitler, of the monthly fast Sunday, the assistance the Mormon Church gave to Germans seeking to document a clean, non-Jewish, genealogical past, and the dietary virtues Nazis saw in the Mormon Word of Wisdom.[155]

The one topic Elder Stewart always focused on was his belief that the Mormon church was the American Church. He had long-since learned that those investigating the church were usually as interested in America as they were religion. He would proudly proclaim to people in every gathering, that he represented the American religion and was there to share with them what that was. And he was not wrong in that assertion. Even one of the country's leading scholars, Harold Bloom, would one day write a book entitled "The American Religion."[156] And that religion, according to Bloom, was Joseph Smith's Mormon Church.

---

[152] Faerber, "Interview at His Home in Murray, Utah, ."

[153] Kirchhoefer, "Interview at His Syracuse, Utah Home."

[154] Stewart, "Missionary Journal ".

[155] See, e.g., David Conley Nelson, *Moroni and the Swastika: Mormons in Nazi Germany* (Norman, Oklahoma: University of Oklahoma Press, 2015); Gilbert Scharffs, *Mormonism in Germany* (Salt Lake City, Utah: Deseret Book Company, 1970). The basic arguments of recent books and articles are drawn from Dale Clark, "Mormonism in the New Germany," *Deseret News: Church Section* Dec. 9, 1933.

[156] Harold Bloom, *The American Religion: The Emergence of a Post-Christian Nation* (New York: Simon and Schuster, 1992).

In August 1955, Elder Stewart was transferred to Munich. He was the Supervising Elder for the missionary district, and he worked about three months with Elder Ralph Gisseman. By this time, he was a distinguished senior missionary and went public about his discomfort with the proselytizing plan he had been using. President Dyer had naively adopted, without change, the plan of the Great Lakes Mission, headquartered in Fort Wayne, Indiana. Elder Stewart complained that it was too negative in tone, and it was "too salesman like." He felt that the missionaries spent a good deal of time, at least in the first lessons, tearing down the Lutheran and Catholic religions.

Elder Stewart rejected the whole tone of the lessons and at a conference of missionaries in Bavaria he recommended a new approach be developed that emphasized the good things about Christianity in Germany. He suggested to the other missionaries that they tell Germans how valuable their Lutheran and Catholic experience had been and tell them that Mormons simply wanted to add to the strong religious foundation in the culture. He wanted missionaries to stress issues such as, "a person is a child of God," or that the family is the cornerstone of the gospel of Jesus Christ.[157]

In spite of his recommendations, he was not able to break away from the lesson structure he had worked under for his entire mission. He also wrote his own tract on the *Book of Mormon*, because he felt the ones being circulated by mission headquarters were "inadequate."[158] He did develop a presentation on the *Book of Mormon* and tried it out with mixed results.[159]

From time to time, Elder Stewart became thoughtful about his experience in West Germany. He describes in his journal how strong his testimony of the gospel was before coming to Europe, but as he looked back, he recognized that his testimony had been shallow. After more than two years, he dreaded the day when he would be released. It meant the close of the "most eventful, self-developing, and spiritual period of my life." He had come to love the mission field. It meant living a "higher type of life than I have ever lived previously. I can really say that I can feel the

---

[157] Stewart, "Handwritten Diary." December 28, 1955 and Jan. 7, 1956.

[158] "Letter to His Mother," (Munich, West Germany: Personally written, Oct. 10, 1955).

[159] "Handwritten Diary." Jan. 14, 1956.

spirit and influence of the Lord with me. I know that he will help me to accomplish righteous purposes... ."

On October 12, Elder Stewart's companion was transferred from Munich to another part of West Germany, and he began working with Don A. Stringham, a new elder, from Bountiful, Utah. In Frankfurt am Main, President Dyer had told Elder Stringham that he was being assigned to the best missionary in West Germany, and everybody he talked with told him he was "lucky to be with Elder Stewart." According to Stringham, this amazing senior companion was "a foot taller, ten times stronger, and smarter, and everything else."

He was mature and athletic. Almost no missionary did daily physical exercises, but every morning Dan Stewart insisted that Elder Stringham get down on the floor and engage in a vigorous workout. Then they would go out tracting, and, according to Stringham, "every time I opened my mouth, he corrected me. He could see how far behind I was, and he worked to help me catch up." Elder Stewart took Elder Stringham's language development in stride. The German word for raisins is *Rosinen,* and the word for razor is *Rasierer.* Elder Stewart laughed with gusto, when one morning Elder Stringham ordered milk and razors at the corner grocery store.[160]

Every day, during study time, Elder Stewart would read German literature, "not the church stuff that we all read," but the best of the German classics, including authors such as Johann Wolfgang von Goethe, Friedrich Schiller, and Heinrich Heine.[161] He found them particularly appealing because he found in American and British science a mechanistic description of reality, whereas certain Germans held firmly to the spiritual grounding of science. For them all nature and natural science serves God and spiritual ends.[162] And Goethe was especially vital to Elder Stewart. He rejected the old biological standard that forms or types are definite, constant, and unchanging. For Goethe, in anticipating evolution, they were always in the

---

[160] Don Stringham spoke at Stewart's funeral in 2005 and told this story.

[161] Don Stringham, "Interview at His Home in Salt Lake City, ," (Oct. 27, 2017).

[162] See for example, Ernst Cassirer, "Goethe and the Kantian Philosophy," in *Rousseau, Kant and Goethe* (New York: Harper and Row Publishers, 1945).

process of change, of becoming, of transforming themselves into something else.[163]

Elder Stewart believed his mission experience had been "the greatest experience of my life. I wouldn't trade it for anything. . . , and the experiences are too powerful for words and too profound for tears."[164] This statement does not diminish the fact that he had confronted difficult situations. About ten weeks before Elder Stewart contracted polio, he wrote of an incident in Landshut, a small city in Bavaria that he and his companion had visited. The town was so small, it suffered almost no allied bombing at the end of the war. Consequently, most of its houses were undamaged and were often in need of great repair. As the Supervising Elder, he and Elder Stringham spent the day with Elders Charles Dunn and Kenneth Hicken. He and Elder Dunn visited someone who was investigating the church, and he recorded in his journal the following:

I have never seen such abject poverty, filth, and depravity of the human mind as in Landshut. It is very black Catholic. We (Elder Dunn) and I went into one small room, which we reached after going through a couple of dark, musty, small passages. The stairs leading up to it were so steep that a person had to climb them almost as a ladder. There in this filthy hole sat a dirty, weathered up old lady. On the black coal stove were dirty pans and utensils and food was spilled all over. All kinds of rags and debris were strewn on the floor of wooden planks. This was the filthiest hole in which I have ever seen humans live.[165]

The Christmas holidays were special for Elder Stewart, particularly in Munich, the center of German Catholicism. During the holidays, Elders Stewart and Stringham reserved several evenings a week to participate in concerts, ballets and other celebrations. In early December they attended the operas *Hansel and Gretel* by Engelbert Humperdinck, and *Peter and the Wolf by* Sergei Prokofiev. Elder Stewart was particularly fond of the Prokofiev opera. They later attended the operettas, *Eine Nacht in Venedig* and *Vogelhändler.*

---

[163] *The Problem of Knowledge* (New Haven, Conn.: Yale University Press, 1950).

[164] Stewart, "Letter to Edward Moreton ".

[165] "Missionary Journal ". Nov. 5, 1955.

On December 21, they went to a concert of Christmas folk songs by the Munich Bach Choir, which sang J.S. Bach's best Christmas music in the *St. Markus Kirche.*[166] Elder Stewart heard music he doubted if Salt Lake City could ever replicate, and he rejoiced in absorbing the spirit of the South German culture. On Christmas the elders were in Füssen, near the *Hohenschwangau* castle, and they visited *Wieskirche,* with its inspiring Rokoko architecture and paintings, the most famous in Germany. The two elders were touched by the beauty and splendor of their adopted homeland. Right after the holidays, elders Stewart and Bennion went to the opera to experience Giacomo Puccini's *La Bohéme,* a love affair between a poor poet and a poorer seamstress in Paris.

That Christmas season, Elder Stewart wrote his Sigma Chi buddy, Ed. Moreton, who also lived in Federal Heights, and he suggested that the two of them go "cating" together as soon as he returned home.[167] Such a comment suggests that Elder Stewart had already broken off his romance with Barbara. And according to Elder Ben Bennion, his last companion in Munich, early in January Elder Stewart finally received a "Dear Dan" letter from Barbara. After more than two years, she notified him that she had been socially active and was now "pinned" to a fellow named Steve.[168] At the time, it is likely that Elder Stewart felt he had also moved on. He does not even mention her letter in his missionary journal.

On January 19, 1956, Elder Stewart was transferred from Munich to Freiburg. President Dyer had chosen him to spend the last three months of his mission touring West Germany and giving a series of lectures about the church. He had chosen well. Elder Stewart was an imposing person, who exhibited a presence and bearing that would raise the stature of the church in West Germany. At all times he showed a respect and even awe for Germans and their distinguished culture, but he was also poised and exuded a feeling that he knew what he was talking about. His family background was testimony that his pedigree was sound.

---

[166] Ibid.

[167] I. Daniel Stewart, "Christmas Postcard to Edward Moreton " (December, 1955).

[168] Lowell L. (Ben) Bennion, "Lnterview at His Home in Salt Lake City," (Sept. 9, 2019).

6. A Summer of Depression

Dan Stewart was finally home. He had spent two months at St. Joseph's, nine months at *Rancho Los Amigos*, and six months at LDS Hospital. Now he was in Salt Lake City on Butler Avenue. He found himself sitting in his backyard, under a blazing sun. A fence separated his backyard from that of neighbors living on Federal Way, and he could hear the children at play in the neighbor's yard. He also listened to the rustling of the leaves of the old apricot tree that promised another good crop.

It was nearing the end of June, and many of the apricots were already ripe on the tree. There was an old, poorly maintained single-car garage along the north side of the yard, shaded by a large aging elm tree. The small lawn, which he had so cared for as a young boy, was now cut and trimmed by a youngster who lived at the bottom of the hill. The boy likely didn't have to cut lawns, as Dan's case had been, to keep his family solvent. And the boy likely earned barely enough each week to buy a milkshake at the drug store across the street from President's Circle over on University Street.

The good family friend, Emily Stewart Smith, had already hired day workers to install a ramp from the front porch to the sidewalk out front.[169] Dan called to his sister, Mary Louise, to bring his old *Missionary Journal* out to him, and she promptly did so. Holding the journal in his hands, he saw

---

[169] Holbrook, "Interview at Her Home in Salt Lake City,."

that about a third of the 300 pages were unblemished. He turned to the last entry, then skipped several pages and began writing: "Salt Lake City, Utah. June 24, 1957." He skipped a line and continued:

It has now been a year and five months since my last entry. During this time my life has been profoundly altered, although the full extent of these changes I have yet to realize..., in a real sense the events of the last 17 months have been the acid test not only of the faith and conviction which I strength-ened, if not actually acquired while doing missionary work but also of my whole past life—my rearing, education—in short, of me.

After expressing a conviction that his mission had been worthwhile, he wanted to explain, if only to himself, what his present life was all about. He then went on to reflect on his physical condition:

No, I am not in the least bitter about the fact that this beautiful day should find me confined to a wheelchair, nor am I discouraged that I have spent so much time in one, although I do at times become discouraged about it. Perhaps the reason is that I want so much to get back in school, get my law degree & get married. This I can do and will do & must, in a wheelchair, but I certainly don't want to. Also, Barbara will be home from Europe on Wednesday, and although she is pinned to someone else, I still love her. If it weren't for this wheelchair, I would court her. Nevertheless, I shall get rid of the wheelchair, and feel that it will not be long before I will begin to leave it. [170]

Dan was clearly optimistic about the future of his life. He neither ex-pressed bitterness about his condition, nor had he altered his goals in life. He was anxious to get back to school and get his B.A. and law degrees. Most important, he still believed he would soon be out of his wheelchair and lead-ing a normal life. Even though Barbara was now "pinned" to someone else, he was looking forward to beginning his life anew with the woman he loved.

When elders left for the mission field, most did not leave a special girl behind, and those who did either eventually received a "Dear John" letter or the correspondence simply petered out, mainly because their lives were going in quite different directions. There were exceptions, in that the bond

[170] Stewart, *Addendum.*

between the two remained for the two-plus years the young man was away. Perhaps Dan and Barbara were the anomaly.

It is unclear how Barbara felt. She was a beautiful, attractive young woman, who had numerous suiters. She was in a sorority at the University of Utah, and every week she was going to a dance, a ball game, or a movie with a fellow student. Long before he contracted polio, she had distanced herself from Dan. There is no record that she ever visited *Rancho Los Amigos,* in the nine months he was in rehabilitation in Downey, California, and she was on holidays in Europe during much of the time he was at LDS Hospital. Clearly, she had moved on with her life.[171] That was not the case with Dan. He linked his relationship with his former life to his emotional bonds with Barbara. If one died, the other would surely follow.

When he was released from LDS Hospital, Dan still assumed he would one day get out of his wheelchair and once again live a normal life. At the time, post-polio syndrome was neither recognized as a clinical entity, nor seen as a problem.[172] Dan believed he could overcome the disease and never again regress to a state of muscle weakness and overuse.

During that summer, Dan continued to go back.to the clinic three times a week. Almost the entire first floor of the west wing of the hospital consisted of polio patients. The part of the West Wing, where the new patients resided was quarantined, and parents could only see their children through a plate glass window. The number of iron lungs was considerably smaller than at Downey, but their oppressive presence dominated the West Wing environment.

In 1951, for example, at the age of fifteen, Daniel L. Reilly contracted polio, and he was placed in the LDS Hospital. He had difficulty swallowing and could not breathe, so they placed him in an iron lung for about six weeks, until he was strong enough to breathe on his own. At the time, there were usually about four iron lungs in each of the large rooms, where the patients were located.

---

[171] Ironically, her life ended tragically. She died young from a severe muscular disease.

[172] Lauro S. Halstead and Gunnar Grimby, eds., *Post-Polio Syndrome* (Philadelphia: Hanley and Belfus, Inc., 1995). Preface.

Eventually, Reilly was placed in a bed near his iron lung and therapists would take him out of it during the day, if he could stand it. The sound of the compressors pushing and pulling air out of and into his lungs was oppressive. The therapists were able gradually to extend the time, until he was away from the iron lung for the whole day, and he only had to be placed in it at night, so he could relax and get some sleep.[173]

Dan was placed in a private room, away from the noise and commotion of the 570 other patients. Emily Smith Stewart likely pulled a few strings to get him into a private room. Dan believed this remarkable woman "could move mountains." There was a story about Emily meeting with President Ernest Wilkinson. He had a bone crushing grip, and after he applied it to her, she said, "Ernest, don't you ever do that again."

The next time she met him, he proudly applied his grip. "She hauled off and kicked him in the calf." She was a large woman, weighing about 300 pounds and she wore pointed shoes. Dan said, "I don't think he ever did that again to her."[174]

It was no longer necessary that he use the iron lung, and he continued to make progress. In Downey, at *Rancho Los Amigos National Rehabilitation Center*, he had even been able to rid himself of the artificial respirator and prior to departing for Salt Lake City, he could independently care for himself. And he was now in a facility that allowed his mother and sisters to visit with him on a regular basis.

The LDS Hospital had a reputation for having a staff of caring professionals. This professionalism extended all the way to the custodians and cooks. Those in the kitchen prepared great food; The cooks had been there for several years and took pride in preparing delicious, healthy meals.[175] But the hospital also had a strong reputation for the care it gave to its polio victims.

---

[173] Daniel L. Reilly, "Everett L. Cooley Oral History Project, 1983-2014," ed. America West Center University of Utah (Salt Lake City, Utah: Special Collections Library, Feb. 13, 2010).

[174] Stewart, "A Life: Dictated to Richard G. Ellis."

[175] Rowe, "Interview in His Home in Orem, Utah ".

Dan met a remarkable woman. Louise Lake had suffered polio and lost the use of her legs, but she dedicated herself to helping others who contracted polio. She taught Dan how to use the sliding board, which was the bridge between the wheelchair and the bed or a car seat.[176] That year, Louise Lake received the presidential award as the "Outstanding Handicapped American," and she attributed her progress to the treatment she was receiving at LDS Hospital.[177]

Dan had long been a keen chess player. As a young man, he played with his sisters, and he usually had difficulty finding friends, who were willing to challenge him. And at LDS Hospital he tested everyone in the wing, again with few takers. After returning home, he would invite young neighbors over, such as George Durham and teach them how to play chess. He would set up a game and ask the youngster "Now ponder, what's the best move, and what's the best move after that going to be from the opponent.?"[178] They claimed he was a good teacher.

The hospital had two requirements before doctors would release Dan. First, they demanded that he could sit, independently, in a wheelchair. At the time, wheelchairs were manually propelled, which posed great difficulty for someone who had little arm strength. Second, they insisted that Dan be able to use a stiff "slide board" that would be helpful in getting from his wheelchair to a regular chair, or in moving from his wheelchair into the seat of a car.

Casual and close friends would often drop by. George Durham, the young neighbor across the street, was often at the hospital to visit with Dan.[179] John Bennion, another neighbor in University Ward, was considering going on a mission. He had already received a call to go to West Germany, and he visited Dan in his private room, asking what he thought of the idea. Dan was unequivocal in his recommendation that he go. John suggested reasons for not

---

[176] Stewart, "A Life: Dictated to Richard G. Ellis."

[177] LDS Hospital, *A Tradition of Excellence* (Salt Lake City, Utah: LDS Hospital, 1980); ibid.

[178] George Durham, "Interview by Liz Stewart Whitney at His Home in Salt Lake City," (June 7, 2018).

[179] Christine M. Durham, "Interview by Liz Stewart in Christine's Home in Salt Lake City," (June 7, 2017).

going, such as his discomfort with the Mormon issue relating to Blacks and the priesthood. Dan simply suggested that John knew how to deal with such topics, and the church would allow him to say what he felt he needed to say.[180]

The Mormon Church has always wanted to satisfy the spiritual needs of its sick members. Fortunately, a Mormon meeting house was only a block away from LDS Hospital, and Dan would attend when he could. but when he was confined to his room, the Aaronic Priesthood would always bring the sacrament, blessed bread and water, to him.[181]

In March, one of his former missionary companions, Don Stringham, returned home. One of the first things Don did was to call on his old companion, and he resolved that he would do what he could to keep Dan company and help in any way he could. The polio clinic was almost like Fort Knox, in that a security guard was on each corridor and visitors had difficulty getting through this security. The guards wanted to know detailed information about a visitor.

"What is your relationship with Dan Stewart?" "Why are you here?" "Has the family given permission for you to come?" "Do you have any weapons on your person?" Don finally visited the chief administrator of the hospital and complained: "I was his missionary companion in Germany. He had such an impact on my life that I wish to do what I can for him. Please give me clearance to do this."[182]

Once he had formal approval to visit Dan, Don came two or three times a week for the rest of the time Dan was in the clinic. His visits were crucial. He served as a bridge to the outside world, talking about concerts, football games, the latest books, and who was doing what. Dan was becoming despondent about his future. He was discovering it would be necessary that he chart a new course of action, and he did not know quite how to begin. Don would take him out on the lawn of the hospital and as they ate sandwiches, Dan would explain his worries.

---

[180] John Bennion, "Interview in His Salt Lake City, Utah, Home," (June 6, 2018).

[181] Rowe, "Interview in His Home in Orem, Utah ".

[182] Don Stringham, "Interview at His Home in Salt Lake City " (June 4, 2018).

He reminded Don that prior to his LDS mission, he had been a student at the University of Utah, where he was the spectacular "big man on campus." Now, his physical disability prevented him from doing some of the basic physical, aesthetic, and social things he had enjoyed prior to his stay in West Germany. As Dan reviewed his life with Don, he wondered how his present physical condition would affect the choices he was going to make concerning his professional and social future.

On June 10, 1957, Dan was finally discharged from LDS Hospital, and he returned to his family home on Butler Avenue. He was expected to go back to the clinic three times a week for therapy. Every day at home, he spent at least an hour doing physical exercises.[183] According to Ken Rigtrup, Dan was always lifting a pair of small bar bells.[184] There was, at the time, great debate among professionals, some argued that physical exercise was detrimental to the well-being of polio victims, while others argued that carefully prescribed and supervised exercise could be beneficial. England was the first country to rely on orthopedic processes rather than exercise.

Specialists would prescribe casts and splints to immobilize limbs, on the theory that the muscles would thereby be preserved. This practice became common in the USA, but with negative results. Most American specialists argued that muscles were living tissues, and they would wither and die without exercise. Soon, physical exercise became regular practice among Americans.[185]

Dan was so determined that he was going to overcome his frailties, that he engaged in conditioning in whatever way he could. On his urging, the family installed a weight machine in the house, so he could lift weights heavier than the lighter bar bells. It may have been unwise practice to spend at least an hour a day exercising, but he was so intent on building up his body that this is what he did. Dan likely had almost no knowledge of the potential negative consequences of his personally designed training.

[183] Stewart, *Addendum*. E.g., On January 28, 1958, he wrote: Spent a couple of hours exercising."

[184] Ken Rigtrup, "Interview at His Home in Salt Lake City " (Sept. 28, 2018).

[185] Anne Carrington Gawne, "Strategies for Exercise Prescription in Post-Polio Patients," in *Post-Polio Syndrome*, ed. Lauro S. Halstead and Gunnar Grimby (Philadelphia: Hanley & Belfus, Inc., 1995). Berg, *Polio and Its Problems*.

In June of 1957, he made an assessment of the progress he had made. He sounded a bit clinical as he reviewed his own situation, stating that his condition was broadly in the "poor" to "poor plus" range. He admitted that he had a long road ahead of him:

Both legs are totally paralyzed except for a slight external rotation in the left leg. I have slight contractions in the glutes on both sides. This has come in about the last 11/2 months. My left arm and hand are in pretty good condition. I can lift 16 lbs. with my left biceps. The left shoulder is progressing and is in the poor to poor plus class. My right hand is in good shape, but I can't flex the elbow yet. The shoulder is about a poor minus or trace plus. Back is very weak—about a poor.[186]

After coming home, it was, at first, enough that he was on Butler Avenue, sleeping in one of the three bedrooms on the main floor. The family quickly installed a buzzer system in the house, so Dan could set off the alarm from any room. Dan's restless mind began demanding something more. His sister, Mary Louise, would see that he completed the daily crossword puzzle from the morning *Salt Lake Tribune*. She recruited everyone she could find to play chess with him.

He enjoyed going into the back yard in the middle of the afternoon, claiming he liked to work up a sweat. He attended church every Sunday, and regularly received visitors.[187] One guest was Edward Maryon, who would soon be the chair of the University of Utah Art Department. Maryon wanted to do a series of articles for the Mormon educational magazine, *The Instructor*, and he asked Dan to work with him on the series.

In the Mormon Church, every active male belongs to a "priesthood" group organized roughly according to age. When active men reach maturity, they usually serve as an elder through young adulthood. When Dan was released from the hospital, he was an elder in his local congregation, known as the University Ward. Those University Ward members met in a lovely building with a famous ceramic tile collage above the front entrance, depicting Christ ministering to the people.

[186] Stewart, *Addendum*. June 24, 1957.

[187] Holbrook, "Interview at the Dan Stewart Family Home in Salt Lake City."

Every Mormon adult is expected to accept a "calling" to do something in their ward as a leader, teacher, or secretary of an organization. Dan belonged to the elder's quorum in his ward. At the time, it was headed by John Bennion, who, when Dan contracted polio, was serving as a missionary in West Germany. Bennion's first counselor was Bob Bennett, who was the same age as Dan and was in his school class at East High. They immediately, called Dan to be the instructor in their weekly priesthood meetings. He already had a reputation for being a quality teacher, and they were delighted, because the Sunday gatherings promised to be well attended. They were not disappointed.

In an interview with John Bennion, who later served as the superintendent of Provo City School District and Salt Lake City School District, he explained that Dan was one of the few instructors he had ever known, who so motivated class members that they actively continued the discussion of the topic after the class had come to an end.[188] Dan's reputation was that he was an exceptional teacher, and for the remainder of his life, his church calling was almost always to be the instructor of the adult Sunday School class.

There is a great deal of formal teaching in the Mormon Church. Every organization has a teaching component, from primary, to young men's and women's organizations, to adult groups. As a lay organization, the teachers often are woefully unqualified and unprepared, and it is common for members to complain that the quality of teaching is not high. Consequently, Dan's reputation soon got around to the point that he was called to be the instructor of the adult Sunday School, so both men and women could attend.

He worked hard as he prepared for the classes. He would pay particular attention to issues on a given topic that he himself had not resolved. Then He would "go into the subject with a lot of intensity and try to learn the answer to some of those hard questions."[189] As he faced the class each Sunday, his gaze on class members was not so much friendly as it was stoic, just a bit detached, but reflecting an intensity that everyone noted.

[188] John Bennion, "Interview at His Home in Salt Lake City " (June 6, 2018).

[189] Stewart, "A Life: Dictated to Richard G. Ellis."

In 1967, Richard Poll published an essay using *Book of Mormon* imagery, contrasting "Iron Rod" Mormons with "Liahona" Mormons.[190] To those who did not consider themselves iron rod Mormons, the distinction was important, but to those who refused to question issues in the church, to claim that one was guided by a compass rather than holding fast to the word of God. Dan wished to clarify the distinction rather than resolve the issue.

The classes were always full, and some "visitors," belonging to other wards, often attended. One text assigned to Dan was *Christ's Ideals for Living*, authored by Obert C. Tanner, a philosophy professor at the University of Utah."[191] Written in 1955, it quickly became a favorite text for thoughtful LDS like Dan.

At the time, Dan teamed up with former Senator Wallace F. Bennett, in the class. Health in his life was never secure, and he found he would have to call Brother Bennett at the last minute: "Brother, I'm not feeling well right now. Do you think you could stand in for me?" "Of course, what is the topic?"

Dan's primary concern was Barbara. After returning home at Butler Avenue, his old girlfriend arrived back from her second European trip, and she dropped by. That first visit was not helpful. Barbara suggested that they go for a ride in her Jeep Cherokee, and he was embarrassed, when "she couldn't get his legs in the car."[192] The next entry into his journal addendum was July 23, 1957. He noted that he and Barbara had gone to a party hosted by Boyd and Ann Blackner. He got in and out of the car on a slide board: "It was humiliating."[193]

The evening of July 24, after celebrating Pioneer Day, with its glamorous parade down State Street, he went to a party at the home of Legrand and Mary Louise Holbrook. He had a good time. Legrand was already getting the reputation of giving Dan much of his free time. Legrand was a large man,

---

[190] Richard Poll, "What the Church Means to People Like Me," *Dialogue: A Journal of Mormon Thought* 2, no. 4 (1967).

[191] Ken and Kate Handley, "Interview at Their Home in Salt Lake City, ," (Sept. 24, 2018).

[192] Holbrook, "Interview at Her Home in Salt Lake City,."

[193] Stewart, *Addendum*.

with a large heart, and fun to be with. Everyone appreciated him for giving so much of his time to Dan. They soon became almost like brothers.[194]

Barbara was always in the background, but Dan was becoming increasingly uncomfortable with their relationship. In his journal, he recorded: "She doesn't know whether to act as my date, or just as a friend of the family, when we go out together." He thought she might respond warmly to his plan to go to law school, and when he next talked with her, he mentioned what he wanted to do. He was shocked to find that Barbara did not like the legal profession. She felt the law was nothing more than dirty politics.[195]

Dan's emotional state was spiraling down and down. It had not yet hit bottom, and every day he felt more and more despondent. He felt a sadness and hopelessness about the future of his life. When with the family, he tried to keep his feelings to himself; however, his sisters sensed something was tearing him up. They knew more than Dan realized. When Mary Louise was teaching at East Millcreek Elementary School, Barbara had done student teaching there, preparing to be a teacher. She and Mary Louise would talk from time to time, and it was clear to Mary Louise that Barbara had begun to move on with her life without Dan, even before he contracted polio.[196]

On July 25, Dan wrote:

I don't know of another time in my life when I have been so blue and depressed. I love Barbara deeply & I want her so much, but my sickness has put me in such a strange relationship. Sometimes I feel like my heart is being crushed and bruised by a huge mountain. It is utterly agonizing.

He wrote in his diary that he had never been so "dejected and depressed." The weight of his problems was almost "unbearable." This feeling of terrible and complete isolation lasted through the summer. If anything, it was worse than any depression he felt during formal rehabilitation.

---

[194] Shannon Stewart Clark, "Telephone Interview at Her Home in Corona Del Mar, Ca," (August 21, 2018).

[195] Saundra Stewart, "Interview at the Home of Marijana Benesh in Westwood, Ca," (Sept. 21, 2019).

[196] Holbrook, "Interview at the Dan Stewart Family Home in Salt Lake City."

Dan's conscious depression was focused on his relationship with Barbara. He believed she was the one who held his heart, and she would hold it forever. However, that relationship was clearly in trouble, but one might also speculate that his depression was more general. Until this time, his recent life had been taken up with rehabilitation and doctor's appointments.

He was finally just beginning to realize the permanent physical difficulties that he faced. He would be confined to a wheelchair for the rest of his life. Even though he was aware that his old self was dead, he was not yet to the point that he had constructed a new self-image. He had not yet completely cleansed himself of the old Dan. He was still in the purgatory of the desert and had not yet begun his assent up the mountain of rebirth.

The studies on the depression of polio victims is so mixed that it is difficult to draw any firm conclusions about Dan's emotional condition. It is even difficult to separate his physiological from his emotional states, except to conclude that depression is common among polio patients.[197]

There is a ritual in the Mormon community that returned missionaries give a "homecoming" speech in church. This usually happens within a couple of weeks after the missionary returns home, but in Dan's case, it did not happen until December 10, 1957, several months after he had been released from LDS Hospital. By this time, Dan's strength had returned to the point that he could speak for half an hour.[198] He was unable to stand at the pulpit, so they wheeled the wheelchair up on the stand and he sat sideways near the pulpit and used a hand-held microphone.

Part of the homecoming speaking ritual is to tell a story or two about something peculiar that happened, while the missionary was away. Dan did not disappoint the audience. He told of an hilarious experience in Heidelberg, where he began his mission. When he arrived in West Germany, he had no German language competence, and was learning German "on the job."

---

[197] Janet M. Liechty, "Psychosocial Issues and Post-Polio: A Literature Review of the Past Thirteen Years," in *Post Polio Syndrome*, ed. Lauro S. Halstead and Gunnar Grimby (Philadelphia: Hanley and Belfus, Inc., 1995).

[198] The Stewart family has a tape recording of the speech.

One of the branch members contacted the missionaries and asked them to bless a sick sister. Both missionaries participated in the blessing.

The first administers to a person by putting a drop of consecrated oil on the forehead and saying a brief prepared prayer. The second seals the anointing and gives a blessing, "as the Spirit directs." Elder Stewart's companion, Elder Ulstein, told him to go to a certain file where copies of ordinances were kept. Even though he did not speak the language, he could read the prepared prayer. When he started reading the blessing, his companion stopped him and told him he had pulled up the wrong blessing and he was ordaining the woman to the office of a Teacher in the Aaronic Priesthood.[199]

Dan explained to the congregation that he had been terribly sick when he got polio. The German doctors simply put him aside because they expected him to die. When he would not die, they finally began to treat him. Dan then launched on an abstract account of faith, discussing God's relationship with man, the law of consecration, and the principle of eternal progression. Dan thereafter refused to talk in public about his physical condition and always spoke only about general gospel principles. In the speech he did cite at length the popular account of Leo Tolstoy's positive impression of the American religion, Mormonism.

The popular version was spelled out by a distant relative of the Stewarts, LeGrand Richards,[200] who claimed Tolstoy was to have said: "If Mormonism is able to endure, unmodified, until it reaches the third and fourth generation, it is destined to become the greatest power the world has ever known."[201] Less than two weeks after his speech, Dan again wrote in his journal:

Dec. 21, 1957: I suppose that I must honestly say that I have rarely been so dejected and depressed. The weight of my problem is unbearable. To reflect for just an instance about the joys of past New Year's Eves is to feel insurmountable thrusts of a dagger in my heart.

---

[199] The Aaronic Priesthood has three offices: Deacon, Teacher, and Priest.

[200] LeGrand L. Richards, "Letter to Dan Stewart and His Wife," (August 27, 1982).

[201] Dan gave the standard Mormon version of Tolstoy, including: *A Marvelous Work and a Wonder* (Salt Lake City: Deseret Book, 1960). Inspection of actual accounts indicated Tolstoy never said such positive things. See, e.g., Leland A. Fetzer, "Tolstoy and Mormonism," *Dialogue: A Journal of Mormon Thought* 6, no. 1 (1971).

A month later, Jan. 28, he was at least beginning to understand that things were not going to work out in his relationship with Barbara. He wrote, "Sometimes I feel that I should break everything off so that she won't feel any obligations." He went on further, "Sometimes I just feel like telling her to go to hell and I've come damn close many times to doing it."

He and Barbara were clearly never alone together. They did see each other at fireside chats and classes. They had enrolled in an evening course at the university on the *Great Books of the Western World,* but her father had also enrolled, so he always sat with her in class. Dan found it curious that of all the topics in the series, including education, politics, honor, language, or fate, there was not a single work dealing with health or physical well-being. Dan was aware that Barbara was seeing another guy, Steve, but he was not clear how that relationship was going. In addition, he continued to worry about her religious commitment and emphasized, time and again, to those around him, how important God was in his life.

Dan was becoming reconciled to the end of his relationship with Barbara. In August, she married. He had not seen her for almost ten weeks, and the last time he saw her she had been "quite obnoxious." Dan had often mentioned that he was going to go to law school, and Barbara just as often said she did not like the legal profession.[202] Even though he knew, in his mind, that they would not be together, the weight of that reality was crushing the testimony of his heart.

Dan recognized anew the strength of the family milieu he found himself in. Even though his mother found it necessary to work all day, the *National Foundation for Infantile Paralysis* provided a nurse, who was with Dan when he was at home.[203] In addition, his sisters were always there for him. Even when he was in his teens, they had usually cooked the evening meal. Mary Louise, the oldest, set the model for the others, by planning and cooking nutritious menus. On special days, Mary Louise would try to prepare favorite dishes.

When Saundra turned sixteen, for example, Mary Louise prepared her favorite dinner of chicken a-la-king, carrot sticks, tossed salad, homemade

---

[202] Stewart, "Interview at the Home of Marijana Benesh in Westwood, Ca."

[203] Ibid.

rolls, and a birthday cake fit for a queen and topped with sixteen candles.[204] As Danny's sisters married and moved away, a younger sister would take over the chore. Danny never complained when Carolyn put too much salt in the pasta, or when she left the baking soda out of the biscuit dough. He was once featured in a *Salt Lake Tribune* article that explained how the whole Stewart family helped clean the house, while maintaining their homework schedule. "The kids enjoy their work because each has a special duty of keeping his or her room clean plus odd jobs." The article notes that "Danny even manages to work on the side."[205] While in high school, Danny would take on responsibilities in the kitchen, but especially in helping to clean the house. He was now unable to do most of the household chores, but all through his undergraduate years, Carolyn, the youngest, was always there preparing his evening meal.

---

[204] Holbrook, "Interview at the Dan Stewart Family Home in Salt Lake City."

[205] Ruth Stranquist, "Teenagers Can Share the Household Load," *Salt Lake Tribune* Feb. 2, 1951.

7. Poli Sci and Marriage

In the fall of 1957, Dan returned to the University of Utah. He had not been in school since 1953, and he was excited to again become a student. He was going to major in political science. It was a young social science field, having only been a formal program for a little more than a decade. While Dan had been off engaged in mortal survival, he knew that "poli sci" was exploding in terms of knowledge production.

However, Dan also recognized that he was grounded in the humanities as much as the social sciences, and humanists still showed greater reverence for the classics than most of those in the social and physical sciences. He recalled fondly the days and nights in West Germany, when he devoted hours to gaining an understanding of the humanistic literature of the Germans. He was confident that experience would serve him well as he got back into his undergraduate studies.

Dan was deeply grateful for his family. Almost all family events were taking place at the Butler Avenue home, so he could participate. For example, Mary Louise arranged to celebrate her four-year old son's birthday there. And Dan, as it was in the old days, was the "life of the party." Little Steve saw Dan sticking a carrot up his nose and turning his glasses upside down. Dan, ever playful at such times, enjoyed the occasion so much that he often began to choke from laughter, for lack of air in his lungs.[206]

---

[206] Steve Holbrook, "Interview at the Dan Stewart Home in Salt Lake City," (June 7, 2019).

The family would gather often at the Butler Avenue home. When they were together, one family ritual was to play "blow ball." Everyone would crowd around the living room table and place a ping pong ball on its smooth surface. The task was to keep the ball from falling off the table where someone was sitting. Often the yells and gasps would drown everything else out. And Dan did his part; he loved it. However, he had little lung capacity, and he was too often the victim of the play. He would blow, but no air came from his lungs. So, he would blow all the harder. Still no air came from his lungs, and the ping pong ball would often squirt past him, on to the floor. Then everyone would cheer. He was, again, the looser.[207]

A first major school hurdle Dan faced was how to get to his classes on campus. His old missionary friends and companions were arriving back from West Germany, and several of them were enrolled in school at the University of Utah. His former missionary companion, Don Stringham, offered to pick him up at his home on Butler Avenue. Don would park his car along the street in front of Dan's house, go up to the front door, where he and Dan would meet.

Don would then wheel him down the ramp and driveway to Stringham's car, lift him into the front seat, and place the wheelchair in the back seat. The drive to Orson Spencer Hall would take only a couple of minutes. Dan would carefully organize his class schedule, so he could remain on north campus and take one class after another, before one of his friends returned him home. When Don was unable to pick Dan up, he would invite a friend, who had a car, to do this. He was glad to do it.[208]

As an upper division student Dan launched into his political science major. He had decided for that major, long before he finished high school. As a boy, he was mowing a neighbor's lawn, when Professor Francis Wormuth walked by on his way to campus. While Danny thought of him mainly as a neighbor living down the street, Wormuth was generally considered to be

---

[207] Holbrook, "Interview at the Dan Stewart Family Home in Salt Lake City."

[208] Stringham, "Interview at His Home in Salt Lake City ". The author of this book was privileged to do this many times.

one of the distinguished faculty members of the university. He stopped and spent time chatting with Danny about his future studies.

Danny reasoned that he wished to join a profession that would give him status, prestige, and an important position in society. Wormuth agreed that these objectives were usually in the minds of people, when they were making decisions about what to major in. But he also suggested that such reasoning was immature and just a bit selfish. He said that Danny ought to consider going into something that provided a mechanism for him to express his ideals and bestow an avenue for Danny to help correct some of the defects that every social system exhibits.

Danny could make a difference in a world that tended to advantage those who prospered from the defects in society and neglected the "little guy." Wormuth suggested to Danny that he, himself, had gone into political science for those reasons, and he had never regretted that decision. Wormuth suggested that they chat about his decisions from time to time, and he went on up the hill toward the President's Circle.

On campus, the political science department was relatively young. In 1947, a small group of faculty members broke away from history to form a separate department. G. Homer Durham a neighbor of the Stewarts on Butler Avenue, was appointed the first political science department chair. He would later be elevated to the position of Academic Vice President of the university.

When Dan declared political science was his major, the department had about ten faculty members, including Francis Wormuth, Fern Schick, Ellsworth Weaver, and S. Grover Rich. Soon after he entered school, Wormuth dropped by his home and gave him some used political science books. He knew his handwriting skills were still very primitive. Dan noted, "I don't think you are going to be able to read my writing." "Yeah, I'll read it," and he did.[209]

All through the fifties, the new department was still trying to find its way and define its purpose and destiny.[210] According to Sterling McMurrin,

[209] Stewart, "A Life: Dictated to Richard G. Ellis."

[210] J. D. Williams, "Everett L. Cooley Oral History Project, 1983-2014," ed. University of

distinguished professor of philosophy: "Of all the faculty at the U, Francis Wormuth was the most brilliant,"[211] and in 1981 the Utah Academy of Arts and Sciences honored him as "one of Utah's greatest teachers and scholars."[212] Professors like Wormuth were certainly on the left side of the political spectrum. He was a scholar of classical and modern political systems, and a "thoughtful, extremely liberal" member of the faculty.[213]

In the early fifties, a young PhD, J. D. Williams, joined the faculty. Gus Bachman, the head of Salt Lake City's Chamber of Commerce, would likely have said J. D. Williams was more liberal than Wormuth. In fact, Bachman accused Williams of being "the only communist bishop in the LDS Church."[214] Dan's budding political philosophy resonated with Wormuth and Williams and stood in contrast to a growing number of positions both the Utah Legislature and the Utah Supreme Court was taking. These two institutions challenged many of the U.S. Supreme Court decisions being made in that day, such as state powers, freedom of speech, and conditions for employment.[215] There is a saying that "every young man dreams of social revolution." They are committed to a world driven by the ideas of Karl Marx and Friedrich Engels, and they argue for a future of socialism in America. However, as young people mature, they tend to grow out of that youthful fantasy and embrace a more tempered point of view. According to Irving Kristol, conservative American journalist: "Joining a radical movement when one is young is very much like falling in love when one is young."[216]

Utah America West Center (Salt Lake City, Utah: Special Collections Library, October 22, 1984).

[211] Edwin B. Firmage, "Everett L. Cooley Oral History Project, 1983-2014," (Salt Lake City, Utah: University of Utah America West Center, 2010).

[212] "F.D. Wormuth, U. Scholar, Dies," *Salt Lake Tribune* June 2, 1981.

[213] Robert and Dixie Huefner, "Interview in Their Home in Salt Lake City, ," (On File with the Author Sept. 24, 2018).

[214] Williams, "Everett L. Cooley Oral History Project, 1983-2014."

[215] These topics were discussed by Stewart in a paper he wrote for Wormuth. See I. Daniel Stewart, "Unconstitutional Conditions," ed. Instructor: F. W. Wormuth (Salt Lake City, Utah: University of Utah, Political Science Course 140, Spring, 1958).

[216] https://quotes.yourdictionary.com/author/irving-kristol/170708

So it was with Dan Stewart. Even as an undergraduate, Dan continued to be engaged in a humanistic curriculum, including a year-long study of the *Great Books of the Western World*. Earlier in the decade, this series of readings had been collected and published by scholars at the University of Chicago.[217] He also read social philosophy and German literature.

Dramatic political and legal events were taking place in America. *Brown vs. Board of Education* (1954) was a U.S. Supreme Court decision declaring that separate schools for black and white students were unconstitutional, and it led to an urgent attempt to integrate public school students. The so-called McCarthy era was winding down, after the U. S. Congress had voted to condemn Senator Joseph McCarthy for his conduct in an outrageous campaign against alleged communists in the U.S. government and military.

Even so, those who continued to back Joseph McCarthy, including Richard Nixon and Utah governor J. Bracken Lee, had little sympathy for anyone considered "liberal."[218] And thousands of Salt Lake City residents continued to flock to local high school auditoriums to hear the rantings of Robert Welch about greedy socialists, communists, and corrupt politicians, and what the John Birch Society was doing to expose them and thwart their international conspiracies.[219]

In a Socratic manner, Dan felt that class instructors exposed him, especially in the assigned readings, to all sides of political arguments. Political philosophy was hotly debated in his classes, although they rarely led to anger or hostility. Students took for granted that most issues could be argued from various points of view and generally respected students, who took the other side of an issue. According to Professor Daniel Dykstra, faculty promotions and tenure even took political sentiments into account. Though the University of Utah was generally considered to be a liberal in-

---

[217] Robert Hutchins and Mortimer Adler, eds., *Great Books of the Western World* (New York: Encyclopedia Britannica, 1952).

[218] Feuerlicht Roberta Strauss, *Joe Mccarthy and Mccarthyism: The Hate That Haunts America* (New York: McGraw Hill, 1972).

[219] George S. Benson, "Protecting Our Freedom," *Helper Utah Journal* Mar. 24, 1960.

stitution, the general climate was that a faculty member might be "too liberal, never too conservative,"[220] so Dan's budding moderate political philosophy was tested and criticized.

He had begun to formalize that philosophy while in West Germany
on a Mormon mission, where he found ample evidence of the devastating
consequences of a far-right political regime, and he sympathized with the
ideas of political figures such as Thomas Jefferson, Franklin D. Roosevelt,
and John F Kennedy, who advocated a strong American constitutional
democratic tradition. Dan's American history teacher at East High, Hazel
Whitcomb, had often stressed that America was an "exceptional" idea as
much as it was a place. Even so, Judge Thomas Greene would one day
claim that Dan's political philosophy was conservative, in-so-far as he
maintained a life-long respect and devotion to the rule of law and traditional institutions, including the court system, the federal government, and
state governments.[221]

The social science departments were housed in Orson Spencer Hall, a
large non-descript building on north campus next to the Union Building. It
contained many seminar rooms, thirty-three classrooms, and two large auditoriums, and almost all the political science courses were taught there. Dan
would spend almost all his time on campus in Orson Spencer Hall. When he
was not in class, he was able to take advantage of the building's many study
carrels, where he could rest, meditate, and do his homework.

Occasionally, Dan was frustrated to find a class he wished to take was
held in the temporary barracks near Fort Douglas, or down on South Campus; but in those classes available to him, he was always well-prepared, having read and reread the assigned readings. He was inclined to cite classical
documents, such as the *Magna Carta*, and authors, such as John Stewart Mill
and Charles Dickens, so his small library at home provided most of the literature he cited. His friends were always willing to pick up an article or a

---

[220] Daniel Dykstra, "Everett L. Cooley Oral History Project, 1983-2014," in *University of Utah, America West Center* (Salt Lake City, Utah: Special Collections Library, February 23, 1983).

[221] Thomas Greene, "Funeral Oration for I. Daniel Stewart," (June 23, 2005).

book in the university library, which was located on the President's Circle on south campus.

One of the remarkable events in Dan's life took place in the fall of his second year at school. He met his future wife. Dan's wife-to-be, Geraldine Elizabeth Bryan, had just graduated from the University of Utah with a PhD in psychology. That November, they were introduced at the home of Moroni Brown, where both had been invited to celebrate the birthday of Moroni's wife, Cherry. Dan had known the Browns since he was a young boy. They had lived in the same neighborhood and had attended the same Mormon ward. Moroni had served as Dan's priest quorum advisor through Dan's high school years. and he had long admired and respected the young man.

Moroni Brown was a psychology professor at the University of Utah. In 1954, he had taken Elizabeth on as one of his doctoral students, and for four years he had served as her advisor. They jointly published several research papers, and he chaired her dissertation committee.[222]

At the birthday celebration, Dan and Elizabeth were the only guests, who were not family members. Elizabeth glanced Dan's way but averted her eyes when his eyes reached her; she felt him looking at her. Dan saw a beautiful, trim, slender woman, of medium height, who wore her hair cut short. She soon looked directly at him with an open but shy charm. Her eyes had suddenly widened and glowed.

Dan returned the gaze so strongly that he would later have been able to sketch her face from memory. He concluded that she had been much around other young adults and was comfortable in their presence. At dinner the two sat next to each other and engaged in animated discussion. Her direct and welcoming gaze seemed to awaken something deep in him, a longing that he had suppressed for many months.

The fact that Dan was in a wheelchair seemed not to matter to her at all. He also discovered that she not only had completed her doctorate, but the School of Alcohol Studies had invited her to lecture, and the School of

---

[222] Elizabeth Bryan, "Psychological Characteristics of Adolescents in a Kindred Known to Have Facio-Scapula-Humeral Muscular Dystrophy" (University of Utah, 1958).

Medicine had asked her to be its chief psychologist in the Rehabilitation Center. She was also teaching graduate courses in psychology and education, not only at the University of Utah but at Utah State University and Brigham Young University. Their conversation continued during the lighting of the candles on the birthday cake and into the evening.

That birthday party was the beginning of a quick courtship between Dan and Elizabeth. Even though the end of the fall term was nearing, term papers were falling due, and Dan needed to prepare for exams, he and Elizabeth met daily in Orson Spencer Hall or the nearby Union Building, where they could get a snack, talk, and listen to each other's stories. One thing Dan discovered in Elizabeth was her belief that people who experience tragedies in life but remain emotionally stable, are grounded in something "bigger than they are."[223] He had come to recognize his own stability was grounded in a spiritual something inside him that was bigger than he was.

During the holidays, the Stewart family made a practice of attending several family and cultural events, On December 23, Elizabeth came to the Stewart family dinner, and on New Year's Eve, she also joined them at the *Nutcracker Suite Ballet* in Kingsbury Hall.[224] After the ballet, Dan accompanied Elizabeth to her small apartment on 1300 East, less than three blocks away from Dan's Butler Avenue home. She had organized a late New Year's Eve party, and had invited a few "stragglers" she knew, "who weren't connected with anything."[225] Dan was certainly a straggler, but Elizabeth had learned that he was clear-eyed in terms of his life objectives.

Two weeks later, on January 14, 1859, they celebrated Dan's birthday, and that evening he kissed her for the first time.[226] On January 20,

---

[223] "Troubles Also Produce Good, Conference Hears," *Ogden Standard-Examiner* April 25, 1959. Elizabeth gave a commencement address in the late 1970s, and she emphasized the importance of self-discipline and enduring human values. See Elizabeth Bryan Stewart, "Commencement Address," (Unpublished, Undated).

[224] Stewart, "Handwritten Diary."

[225] Elizabeth Bryan Stewart, "Interview at the Home of Shannon Stewart Clark in Newport Beach, California," (Sept. 18, 2017).

[226] Stewart, "Handwritten Diary."

she accompanied the Stewart family to the *Ballet Russe de Monte Carlo*. A couple of days later, even though they had known each other for only two months, he boldly suggested they consider marriage.

"Of course, he added, "we ought to wait a while." "How long would we wait?" "Perhaps for a year or so." Elizabeth's practical response: "Why wait? Let's do it before school starts next fall." Dan hesitated and asked, "What did you have in mind?"

"Moroni Brown introduced us with the idea that we would make a nice couple. He has known you since the time you were a boy, and I trust his judgment a lot. If we are going to get married, why not go just ahead and do it?"[227]

In March, Dan gave her a ring. When Orabelle saw it, she quietly reminded him that she worked at Bennions Jewelry Store, and she knew he could do better. In cool efficiency Dan asked Elizabeth, "Could you return the ring!" She was alarmed, asking herself "Why do you want the ring back?" But, of course, she only said, "Here it is." Several days later, Dan returned her ring, explaining, "The stone in this ring is of higher quality than in the first ring."

There were huge obstacles to overcome. For one thing, Dan did not have a job, and he was not likely to find one soon. Dan was completing his undergraduate degree, and he was slated to begin law school the next fall. This meant he would certainly not begin to work for another three years, and the possibility was always there that he might not be able to finish his degree program, which would leave him out on a limb with no place to go.

Elizabeth's father was critical of Dan, and even refused to speak to his daughter for several weeks. And when he did, he pressed her about finances: "How is he going to support you?" "I don't know," she responded, "but I am not worried about that." She told her dad, "He has scholarship money that provides the support he needs to stay in school," and "I am working, and we really don't need much to pay our expenses."[228]

"Dad, you must not worry about me and Dan. He is wise beyond his years. Everyone who knows him tells me he will be a great man. He is already well es-

---

[227] Stewart, "Interview at the Home of Shannon Stewart Clark in Newport Beach, California."

[228] Ibid.

tablished in the land of learning. He studies and remembers what he learns. He will go far, and I will be there with him as we, together, make our way."[229]

Second, for their entire married life, Dan would be confined to a wheelchair. Following his Mormon mission, he had never been ambulatory, even while using braces. On Feb. 10, 1958, he took his braces to the hospital and Mr. Hucko helped him "ambulate," when he was assisted. Two days later he went six feet by himself, on the parallel bars, while in braces. By April, he was "walking" about ninety feet while on the bars.[230]

It eventually became apparent that the braces were always going to be difficult to manage, and someone always had to be with him, lest he become unsteady and topple. So, he and Elizabeth stopped trying to fit him with braces, and he wore them only when he was in rehab. Instead, he continued to use a wheelchair, which worked out to be much better. Even so, it was manually operated, and he had to push it around by himself, which was hard.

Elizabeth's apparent indifference to Dan's physical condition, was likely associated with insights she had gained from her own research project. For several years, she had been investigating the life of an extended family in Southern Utah, near the Utah/Arizona border, suffering from a certain type of muscular dystrophy that caused progressive weakness and loss of muscle mass. She found that the attitudes of members of this Utah family differed from the reported attitudes of other families around the country suffering from the same disease.

Whereas researchers of those other families usually described them "as being very distressed and depressed," these Utah Mormon family members were upbeat, optimistic, and not at all depressed. They were neither nervous nor anxious, but they were actively engaged with their Mormon community working in a cooperative, constructive fashion.[231] Elizabeth devoted her PhD

---

[229] Ibid.

[230] Stewart, *Addendum*.

[231] Elizabeth Bryan Stewart, "Interview at the Home of Shannon Stewart Clark in Newport Beach, California, ," (Sept. 17, 2017).

dissertation to the study of the adolescents of this extended muscular-dystrophy Utah family.[232]

She had learned from her studies that happiness and joy are not dependent on physical well-being, and she took for granted that her marital success would not depend on Dan's physical condition, but he would be related to a strong community support system, as well as spiritual competence, emotional stability, and intellectual harmony. She reasoned that, in so many ways, hers was an "arranged marriage," not uncommon in certain parts of the world, and they have long provided the peace, security, and love found in successful marriages.

Third, Elizabeth was a Methodist, while Dan was a dedicated Mormon. For her parents, the third issue was paramount. Elizabeth had grown up a Methodist. Her father was angry that she would choose someone, whom he believed was not a legitimate Christian. He went to Sam Weller's bookstore and bought several anti-Mormon books. After reading them, he suggested to Elizabeth that she was deserting her family and culture. In fact, her mother and father stopped speaking to her, and, for several weeks, they refused to have anything to do with her.[233]

Dan had explained to Elizabeth that he wished to marry for "time and eternity" in the Mormon temple. She did not quite know what that meant, but it certainly meant she must join the Mormon Church. She was born in Pocatello, Idaho, where many Mormons lived. It was a small town and everyone knew everyone else, and the many Mormons she knew were good people. She was just a young girl when her dad lost his Union Pacific Railroad job in Pocatello. It was during the depression, and her dad had his teeth pulled. That one day off the job led to his dismissal,[234] so the family moved to Eli, then Pioche, Nevada, where the dad worked as an electrician.

In the previous century, Pioche had been a wild mining camp, and had a reputation of being the "baddest town in the West," made up of "thieves,

---

[232] Bryan, "Psychological Characteristics of Adolescents in a Kindred Known to Have Facio-Scapula-Humeral Muscular Dystrophy."

[233] Don Bryan, "Interview at the Little America Hotel in Salt Lake City, ," (Sept. 27, 2018).

[234] Stewart, "A Life: Dictated to Richard G. Ellis."

scoundrels, and murderers." Dozens of people died from knifings and shootings before anyone passed away from natural causes.[235] By the time the Bryan family moved there, Pioche had settled down, and had become a town with lawns, shrubs, tree-lined streets, and a place of historic, weathered scenery. And there were some nice people, including several LDS families. Elizabeth came to know many young Mormon boys and girls, and she respected their lifestyle.

She had even entertained investigating the church, with the prospect of joining, mainly because "she found the church to be so family oriented,"[236] but until Dan asked her to join, she had never taken the necessary steps, which included calling in a pair of local missionaries to explain to her the basic doctrines of this religion. When Dan asked her to marry him, Elizabeth finally had an incentive to act on her religious impulses, so she was willing to go along with his plan by joining the church. On January 30, 1959, barely two weeks after Dan had proposed marriage, Elizabeth was baptized, and the next day she was formally confirmed a member of the Church of Jesus Christ of Latter-day Saints. They planned to marry the next fall, just before Dan would enter law school.

The next spring, in 1959, Dan submitted his "senior thesis" research paper to the political science department, with the title of, "Republican Institutions in the Twentieth Century."[237] It was, in some respects, a romantic analysis of America and its unique position in the world. Even though he was a young man, he was familiar with the tension between political assimilation and autonomy that had taken place in his own state. Through the nineteenth century, Mormons had struggled to retain their political and religious autonomy, but after Utah gained statehood, the Mormon Church, hoping to assimilate into the American mainstream, deserted some of its traditions and practices that offended the rest of the country.[238]

---

[235] "Pioche ", (http://ghosttowns.com/states/nv/pioche.html June 18, 2018).

[236] Bryan, "Interview at the Little America Hotel in Salt Lake City, ."

[237] I. Daniel Stewart, "Republican Institutions in the Twentieth Century," (Salt Lake City, Utah: Political Science Department, 1959).

In Dan's senior thesis, he began by outlining how fruitful circumstances had led to the early development of "the most liberal institutions of the times." The country had achieved wonderful *laissez-faire* institutions characterized by a high degree of "federalism, checks and balances, judicial review, civilian supremacy over the military, political parties, and other important institutions... ." He maintained that American democracy was a "going concern." And he quoted Thoreau's motto: "That government is best which governs least."[239]

Dan then devoted most of the paper to an analysis of how American institutions had given way to a new political reality, characterized as highly compromised, suggesting that our democracy is no longer a given but may even have an end. He parroted many ideas being openly discussed in his home state. The democratic institutions that Dan characterized in early America were under threat, including sentiments, such as state's rights, and state judicial autonomy that continued to be championed by his own state.[240]

A s Dan prepared for graduation, he might have counted the many honors that he had received. He was invited to become a member of *Phi Beta Kappa*, the university's most prestigious academic honor society, *Phi Kappa Phi*, the oldest honorary society in the country, the Elbert D. Thomas Award, for the most outstanding political science student, and the Philo Sherman Bennet Essay Award, for the outstanding thesis written in the political science department. In addition, the Senior Class Council chose him to represent them by giving the valedictory address on graduation night. When the Council met to consider who would represent them, a name or two was tossed out, but when the chair, Bill Beers, suggested Dan Stewart, there was an immediate, spontaneous acclimation: "Dan is our guy."[241]

---

[238] Armand L. Mauss, *The Angel and the Beehive: The Mormon Struggle with Assimilation* (Urbana and Chicago: University of Illinois Press, 1994).

[239] Cited from Richard C. Snyder and Richard Carlton, *Roots of Political Behavior* (New York: American Book Co., 1949).

[240] Stewart, "Republican Institutions in the Twentieth Century."

[241] The author of this study happened to serve on that Senior Class Council.

In his valedictory speech,[242] Dan noted that the experience at the University of Utah was equipping many in his class eventually to move into positions of importance, as political leaders, executives in large corporations, medical doctors, engineers, and other professionals. He reminded his classmates that many of them were likely feeling free to voice their thoughts; however, almost all of them would be voicing the opinions of the majority and too many of them had been swayed by the military, mass media, government, or giant corporations into thinking what these institutions wanted the people to think.

Recalling his recent experience in West Germany, Dan pointed out that even under the tyrannical rule of Hitler, many Germans did not feel they had lost their right to dissent; however, they had been manipulated into thinking what Hitler wanted them to think. If the tyranny of the majority becomes pervasive enough, the possibility of dissent will be dampened.

Relying on the thinking of his old liberalism friend, John Stuart Mill, *On Liberty,* he argued that, recently, the U.S. government had taken steps that suppressed the ability of those in the minority to object to actions it was taking. Dan suggested such actions are inconsistent with the traditions of our country, and the students must dedicate themselves to a higher ideal than simple professional and economic success. He concluded that his fellow students in the graduating class of 1959 had a bright professional future, but they must never forget: "the hallmark of a free society is the right to dissent." And the hallmark of an educated man is "to listen to dissent."

In other words, Dan was idealistic about his educational mission, and he felt fortunate to be entering law school, where at least some of the faculty shared that idealism. According to Bruce Jenkins, Professor Herbert M. Schiller was just such a professor. He decried those who treated the law as a business, as a vocational trade.[243] He saw the law as one of the best ways to make a positive difference in the lives of people.

---

[242] I. Daniel Stewart, "The Right to Dissent," (Salt Lake City, Utah: Graduating Class of 1959 Valedictory Address, 1959).

[243] Jenkins, "Everett L. Cooley Oral History Project, 1983-2014.."

In September 1959, Dan Stewart was married in the Salt Lake Temple. It was a remarkable and memorable event, taking place about three and a half years after he had contracted polio, and a little more than a year after he had suffered a deep depression about the prospects of his post-rehabilitation life.

The Bryan family reluctantly had decided to give their blessing to the marriage. In August of that year, they had hosted a formal betrothal of Elizabeth at their home in Salt Lake City. Thirty close friends gathered around tables centered with pink carnations, and "ivy floating in brandy snifters."[244]

Because non-Mormons are not permitted in the temple, on Sept. 10, 1959, after the early morning marriage ceremony in the Salt Lake Temple, everyone, Mormon and non-Mormon alike, gathered at the chapel at Memory Grove, on the edge of City Creek, in a small canyon just East of the Utah State Capitol building, and they engaged in an informal "ring ceremony" intended to further bond the two.[245]

Because, in the temple, the member makes certain covenants and commitments, known as endowments, that require a special faith and dedication, usually, LDS officials require that a new convert be a member for a year before that person goes through the temple, Dan was able to convince those who signed his and Elizabeth's temple recommends that such a wait would not be necessary, and so she received her endowments.

In September 1959, when they were "sealed together" in marriage in the Salt Lake Temple, they made sacred covenants that they would remain faithful to each other not only through this life but into eternity. Such a commitment had significance to Dan. He assumed he would not have his deformed body in the afterlife, and he looked forward to the time when physical grief and pain are replaced by the pure joy that comes with an eternal physical body.

The evening following the early morning wedding, they gathered at a formal wedding reception at the Federal Heights ward house,[246] Don Stringham

---

[244] "Miss Bryan Reveals Troth," *Salt Lake Tribune* August 9, 1959

[245] Stewart, "Handwritten Diary."

[246] Don Stringham, "Interview at His Home in Salt Lake City, ," (Sept. 29, 2018).

was in the line with the two families. In attendance were all of Dan's old buddies and friends, including Ken and Kate Handley.

The next day the newlyweds celebrated their honeymoon, by traveling to Hot Lava Springs, Idaho, less than three hour's drive north of Salt Lake City, to celebrate their honeymoon. There the newlyweds could soak, splash, swim, and play in the naturally warm water. In August, less than a month before the wedding, Dan wrote in his journal that he was beginning a new life. He anticipated it would be "a life full of expectations of shared love, unbounded happiness, and of all the joys that life has to offer."

Thereafter, Elizabeth was happy with her "arranged marriage." It had not been a conventional courtship, but when Elizabeth held Dan in her arms, they often tenderly kissed one another on the lips. They clung to each other and exclaimed the joy that was theirs for finding each other, and she expressed the wonder she felt against his frail but masculine body. There was passion, and there was excitement. Polio has no effect on sexual organs, so "everything worked,"[247] even though it was necessary for Elizabeth to take charge of the physical aspects of their intimate sexual relationship.

Having already learned how to manage getting Dan in and out of her car, she was surely up to the challenge. There was contentment and a feeling that theirs was a special affection and a unique love. Dan had known beautiful women, and they also had shown affection and love toward him. That was all behind him, for Elizabeth was becoming his special partner, who, though not pretty such as one sees in a beauty contest, was more beautiful, in his eyes, than any other woman he had known.

Moroni Brown wanted to help the Stewarts get started, so he and Cherry converted their small, single-car garage into an apartment in Federal Heights, and they invited the newlyweds to stay there, asking them to pay only expenses. It was especially convenient, because the garage had no steps or elevated floor, and Dan could easily enter and exit the apartment with his wheelchair. Dan loved to listen to recorded classical music, and the Moroni Browns were ever being entertained by bombastic and triumphant music

247 Stewart, "Interview at Her Mother's Home in Salt Lake City, ."

such as "The 1812 Overture" by Peter Tchaikovsky, which commemorated the Russian victory over the French during the Napoleonic wars.[248]

Dan and Elizabeth would spend the rest of his life together. She determined that, as quickly as she could, she would work only half days. She established her own corporation but never worked full-time again. She considered her full-time job to be working as Dan's partner, and she was determined that she would be away for only four hours every day. The rest of her time, she was available for her devoted husband. Their life together would be a Mormon life, although both had perspectives that might be interpreted as unorthodox. The polio crisis only seems to have increased his testimony of the truthfulness of the church.[249]

Both of them accepted Jesus as the Christ. They took for granted that Christ's sacrifice was valid and in effect for all of God's children. They assumed the church was the restored gospel of Jesus Christ in these latter days. They believed in gifts of the spirit and in contemporary divine revelation. However, they took for granted that the church is run by human beings, who see God's revelations and truths through the darkest of lenses. And they insisted that reason go into their faith as much as feelings.[250]

---

[248] Holbrook, "Interview at the Dan Stewart Home in Salt Lake City."

[249] Dyer, "West German Mission Quarterly Report."

[250] Dan's declarations of faith during his LDS mission made this clear. See Stewart, "Missionary Journal ".

Chapter 8. Attending Law School

Prior to graduation with a bachelor's degree in political science, Dan Stewart had already taken the Law School Admission Test (LSAT), and he had formally applied to the law school at the University of Utah. When Dan applied, he had the good fortune that he was applying to an institution that enjoyed a relatively long tradition. In the early days of America, a person became a lawyer by "reading the law" and passing an examination.

It was only in the 1890s that the American Bar Association began pressing states to require students to attend law classes at the university. The University of Deseret, the predecessor of the University of Utah, had offered law courses as early as 1869, and in 1883 President John R. Park instituted a series of courses leading to a full-fledged Department of Law. Dan joined the program at the time accreditation was becoming a serious issue, and while he was in the program, the Utah State Legislature appropriated money for a new facility that would house the College of Law.

The University of Utah law school was in the upper floor of the Park Building, on the President's Circle. Named after John R. Park, whom Dan's great-grandfather, Isaac Mitton Stewart, had converted to the local faith, the building was, without question, the most beautiful on campus. Students could look out from classroom windows and see maple, elm, spruce, and cypress trees dotting the spectacular lawns filling the U that formed the President's Circle. The Park Building housed the Office of the President and other administrative offices.

With six beautiful Ionic columns framing the many steps of the front entrance, it is a magnificent structure, built of striking white granite; however, getting up the entrance represented a great challenge to Dan. Fortunately, the building had a back entrance, though it also had many steps. His fellow law students organized themselves into a help unit and saw to it that Dan was never without assistance in getting into the building, down the steps, and up the elevator to the classes on the upper floor. During the winter, with snow on the ground, students helped him from his car to the classroom. When he was not in class, Elizabeth was ever ready to help where she could.

Dan was idealistic about his educational mission. He found the students around him to be demanding and exceedingly liberal. They went out of their way to challenge authority. They even engaged in a "sit-in" and set fire to the ROTC building.[251] He believed he was fortunate to be entering a law school, where at least some of the faculty shared his idealism. According to Bruce Jenkins, Professor Herbert M. Schiller was just such a professor.

He decried those who treated the law as a business, as a vocational trade. Schiller always emphasized to his students that law ought to be viewed as "a calling," an "honorable profession."[252] Dan was not smitten with the study of the law, the way a pianist can fall passionately in love with a Steinway, Yamaha, or Bösendorfer grand piano, but he recognized that he was finally where he ought to be. He was in law school.

The University's law school would have been rated as a second- or even a third- tier institution, although it had regional significance, occasionally drawing talent from Montana, Wyoming, Nevada, Idaho, and New Mexico. The law program had recently begun to attract talented professors, particularly from Drake University in Des Moines, Iowa, including Daniel Dykstra, Bob Swenson, and Ronan Degnan. When Dan entered the law school, most of its

[251] "A Life: Dictated to Richard G. Ellis."

[252] Jenkins, "Everett L. Cooley Oral History Project, 1983-2014.."

faculty members, all Caucasian men, were beginning to publish actively in law journals, and this transition brought praise and concern.

The great public concern was that some professors were publishing ideas that many Utahns had begun to deem heretical, in that they might damage the ideals of the young Mormon students. During the 1950s there was a great deal of concern about academic freedom, and the central administration, headed by President A. Ray Olpin and Vice President G. Homer Durham, defended the rights of "faculty members to write and say what they honestly believed."[253] This controversy and its consequences contributed to the upgrading of the law school, although it remained a second-tier institution.

It was not difficult to be admitted to the university's law school. Bruce S. Jenkins, a law student in the 1950s, was a bit cynical about the admissions process. He was interviewed in 1993, and explained that "if you were warm, you know, and if you were at least ambulatory you would get in.... . I took no entrance exams, I simply applied."[254] Of course, Dan Stewart could not walk, but he still got in.

Even though, by every formal measure, Dan Stewart was qualified to enter the highest rated law schools in the country, it did not occur to him to apply to any other law school. According to his friend Don Stringham, Dan was a practical man. He spoke often about his desire to attend Harvard Law School, but recognized he had neither the money nor the physical capability of doing so. He had also recently married, and he, consequently, chose to continue his graduate education in Utah.[255]

The law school at Brigham Young University (BYU) had not yet been established, so the University of Utah served as the primary home for Mormon law students. Among Mormons outside Salt Lake City, the University of Utah had a negative reputation, seen as being too "secular." It seemed every academic who had a chip on his shoulder about the L.D.S. Church, appeared to gravitate to that institution and use it as a pulpit for complaints about Mormons.

---

[253] Dykstra, "Everett L. Cooley Oral History Project, 1983-2014."

[254] Jenkins, "Everett L. Cooley Oral History Project, 1983-2014.."

[255] Stringham, "Interview at His Home in Salt Lake City ".

To gain some perspective of the kind of student in the law school at the University of Utah, we shall look at Dan's own law school class. While forty students began law school with Dan, thirty-eight were men, and thirty-four graduated. An astounding nineteen of these students were from Salt Lake City. Eight others were from the rest of Utah, and only four were from out of state (The origin of one is unknown.). Stephen Hadley and Kenneth Rigtrup were from Idaho, while Alva Harris was from Montana and Billy Harris was from New Mexico. Seventeen, half of the graduating students, had received their bachelor's degree from the University of Utah.[256] In other words, in terms of its students, the law school was quite parochial.

The first year in law school was brutal. Its intent was to teach students to "think like a lawyer," but also to weed unqualified students out of the program. The curriculum of almost all law schools had become standard. Dan was expected to cover the fundamental concerns of law practice, including "civil procedure, constitutional law, contracts, criminal law, and procedure, property, and torts." He worked in groups that included advanced students, in writing exercises on legal problems. He prepared briefs, which must meet specific requirements, including paper size, typeface, and cover color,[257] and he argued moot lawsuits before the Moot Court Society and professors.[258]

One of the first pedagogical devices Dan was exposed to the so-called Socratic method, named after the classical Greek scholar. Socrates was an Athenian, who lived during the fourth century BC. He never wrote, and most of the accounts of the man come from his pupils, Plato and Xenophon. He would typically engage his students in a dialectical conversation about some claim the student or others had made. By asking for evidence, or challenging the assumptions the student had made, Socrates would stimulate critical thinking and help the student clarify his underlying assumptions and ideas.

---

[256] College of Law, "The University of Utah College of Law Introduces Its 1962 Graduating Class," (Undated).

[257] Jessica c. Van Buren, Mari J. F. Cheney, and Marsha C. Thomas, *Utah Legal Research* (Buffalo, New York: William S. Hein & Co., 2011).

[258] *Bulletin of the University of Utah College of Law*, (Salt Lake City, Utah: University of Utah, 1962).

The Socratic method had become standard in American law schools. Lawyers argue that it helps the student think quickly on his feet. Students are put on the spot and learn to be quick-witted and learn that there are usually several sides to a particular issue. Dan quickly learned to articulate whatever side he was expected to defend and argue. The method, at its best, involves a form of friendly argumentation, based on asking and answering questions related to a topic.

The professor would draw ideas out of class members regarding specific court decisions, and help the students clarify their underlying assumptions. Responsible professors tried to listen attentively to comments and thoughtful questions from the audience and respond responsibly and competently to their concerns. If he were a good instructor, he would, in a soft-spoken and respectful manner, built and maintained a reputation of asking questions that a typical teacher rarely asked. Of course, some professors would play games with the method, making the student look foolish, unprepared, or inadequate.

Students adopted various ways to cope. Some would treat the process like a game and refuse to take anything personally. Others would try to memorize the cases and their features, then regurgitate the information they had memorized, without really analyzing or comprehending the issues the case was raising. Dan was simply able to learn what was necessary and think as quickly as any other student.

Fourteen of the students in Dan's class were returned Mormon missionaries, and there were ongoing tensions between Mormon and non-Mormon students. Almost every day the Mormon students would hear complaints. "Here you are going 'home teaching,' when you ought to be preparing for tomorrow's classes." "You were the only person missing from our study group, because you think you need to attend church all day Sunday." "You feel you ought to be out helping some widow, when you really ought to be preparing for the exams."[259]

Some of the law faculty also complained that these and other LDS students were biased by "Mormon dogma and doctrine." However, scholars, such as Ronan Degnan, one of the non-Mormon law professors, observed

[259] Stringham, "Interview at His Home in Salt Lake City ".

that this bias, even if it existed, "didn't have any terrific visible or strong impact on the kind of product they had." To Degnan, the Mormons "were good students and they were well prepared academically."[260]

Dan Stewart was certainly a quality student. In fact, in 1983, two decades after Professor Degnan had completed a seven-year term on the Utah law faculty, an interviewer asked him to suggest the names of a couple of exceptional law students during his tenure in Salt Lake City. He replied: "Danny Stewart was one of the outstanding academic students at Utah, and in fact in my time of teaching" in the law schools at Drake, Utah, and UC Berkeley.[261] When Dan was later under review to return to the law school as a professor, potential colleagues at the University of Utah, Edgar Bodenheimer, Dan Dykstra, Fred Emery, and Bob Swenson voted for his return, saying "he was the best law student they had ever encountered."[262]

Dan's academic performance in law school was exemplary. In 1960, he was the first recipient of the Paul E. Iverson Scholarship in the College of Law. The *Order of the Coif*, the honor society for United States law schools, select students in the top ten percent of their class to be members, and the Order chose Dan to be a member. During his second year in law school, he served as the Case Notes Editor of the *Utah Law Review*. In each of the four issues of the journal, he oversaw the review of about half a dozen court decisions that seemed crucial to the Intermountain West.

Dan also prepared and published his first formal publication. It was found in the rather obscure Case Notes section of the *Utah Law Review* and dealt with the topic of the Burden of Proof in Summary Judgments of Utah court cases. He claimed that recent court cases in Utah had obfuscated the

---

[260] Ronan Degnan, "Everett L. Cooley Oral History Project, 1983-2014," ed. Edited by the University of Utah America West Center (Salt Lake City, Utah: Special Collections Library, March 1, 1983).

[261] Ibid.

[262] John J. Flynn, "Isaac Daniel Stewart: 1932-2005," in *Funeral Eulogy* (June 29, 2005).

issue of proofs that were necessary in making summary judgments of legal cases.[263] It was a fitting and apt article. Nobody was going to roll their eyes at his brashness for taking on a topic too big for a young student, nor would anyone accuse him of taking on an issue that was not appropriate for a first try at publishing.

In his third year, he served as the Editor-in-Chief. As is the case in university law reviews, the *Utah Law Review* was independently edited and published by students. Editorial staff members were determined by grade-point average. The Editor-in-Chief had the highest grade-point average in a student's class, an honor Dan Stewart richly deserved.

It is not surprising that the very first article in the first issue Dan edited had to do with a topic that occupied his legal mind for the remainder of his life: "Reflections on the Rule of Law."[264] Dan believed that the rule of law formed the foundation of our democracy. It is what holds Americans together as a civilization. He believed those who thumb their noses at the rule of law, are a threat to our society and must be held in check. In that issue, Dan also published his second formal article; it dealt with what is known in the courts as "limited appearance," which is used in civil procedure.

The defendant of a case disputes the liability he has suffered by the court seizing his assets. Dan declared that limited appearance had not received widespread acceptance, mainly because he felt attorneys had neglected to invoke it. While limited appearance has general application, Dan was concerned about its specific application in the confiscation of property. In Utah, the court obtains jurisdiction over the property of a defendant, if some connection can be found between the person's property and the subject matter of a lawsuit. However, Dan challenged this practice in that a person ought to be able to make a limited appearance. For example, if the property in question is a nonresident property, the state should not be able to obtain jurisdiction over that person's nonresident property.[265]

---

[263] I. Daniel Stewart, "Burden of Proof in Summary Judgment Left Uncertain in Utah," *Utah Law Review* 6, no. 3 (1960).

[264] Edgar Bodenheimer, "Reflections on the Rule of Law," ibid.8, no. 1 (1962).

[265] I. Daniel Stewart, "Limited Appearances," ibid.7 (1961).

During his time as the Editor-in-Chief of the *Utah Law Review*, Dan began to appreciate the importance of careful editing and text revision. He worked tirelessly with the other students, who were writing a review or editing an issue. He began to recognize that his schoolteachers and professors had never really taught him how to make revisions. As a student, he had usually finished his papers just before the deadline and had never had sufficient time to refine the paper before he handed it in.

The instructor had, typically, simply gone through his papers, marking and occasional typo or grammar mistake, and assigned a grade. Dan now faced the professional world and recognized that a skill he most needed had never been taught. The practice of editing and revision is common in most graduate programs, but it was not customary in school and undergraduate programs.

Another element missing from Dan's law training had to do with the Utah Constitution. There was no class in the entire curriculum that centered on it. Some might explain that the University of Utah saw itself as a regional university, catering to students from the entire Rocky Mountain states, and to train students concerning one state constitution would have been inappropriate. This neglect deprived law students, including Dan, from studying the legal tradition of the state.

At the time, Utahns were reacting against what had been a successful assimilation into the greater United States. When Utah became a state in 1896, its residents, mainly Mormons, had committed themselves to assimilation and becoming fully American. Sociologists confirmed how fully the assimilation process had become, not only in the way Latter-day Saints practiced their religion, but in secular and civil matters.[266] For example, having suffered through the great depress, in the 1930s, Mormons supported Roosevelt's New Deal, because it had communitarian overtones, and they saw the New Deal as a way of caring for the poor and disadvantaged.[267]

---

[266] Charles Y. Glock and Rodney Stark, *A Study of Religion in American Life* (Berkeley, California: Survey Research Center, University of California, 1964); Rodney Stark and Charles Y. Glock, *American Piety: The Nature of Religious Commitment* (Berkeley, California: University of California Press, 1968).

After World War II, Latter-day Saint leaders became increasingly concerned that, even though the church had achieved a certain level of respectability, members and leaders had also yearned to be known as a "peculiar and unique" religious group. After all, they were the "elect of God," chosen to inherit the blessings of the fulness of the gospel of Jesus Christ in these, the latter days.

A political consequence of wishing to be distinctive was the growing intent on the part of the those in the Utah State Legislature and in the Utah Supreme Court to separate themselves from mainstream thinking, in the name of states' rights and limited federal government. The State Legislature was dominated by rural Utahns, who resisted federal interference with their local interests, particularly federal attempts to regulate land that Washington considered to have scenic value.

Utah is blessed with some of the most distinctive, incredibly diverse, and beautiful landscapes in the world. Early observers had likened these wonders with the "elephantine structures of the Nile, the Grecian temples, the pagodas of China, the cathedrals of Western Europe... ."[268] And, to the consternation of Utah's leaders, federal authorities were intent on preserving these lands for future generations.

Locals considered federal efforts to preserve and protect Utah's canyonlands and fragile deserts to be an encroachment on their local privileges and rights. For example, Utah politicians were strongly against the federal "Utah Wilderness Act of 1984," national legislation, placing large tracts of public lands and natural resources, watershed areas, grazing lands, forests, etc., under federal protection.

Utahns had little interest in the federal government taking over their land, so outsiders could come in and enjoy the pristine landscapes and the "strange" peoples who lived there. In the early days of settlement, Mormons did not have time to find inspiration from the towering rocks, the magnificent

---

[267] Richard Bushman, "Mormonism and Politics: Are They Compatible?," (Key West, Florida: Biannual Faith Angle Conference on Religion, May 4, 2007).

[268] Clarence E. Dutton, *Tertiary History of the Grand Canyon District* (Tucson, AZ: University of Arizona Press, 2001).

landscapes, the flat-topped mesas, the sweeping vistas, and the ever-changing rock strata surrounding them. And now they resented the federal government's attempt to dictate what they should do.

Dan Stewart saw himself as Utah born and bred. And his self-perception was true insofar as his birth and upbringing were concerned; however, he had spent two years in West Germany, which taught him to avoid political extremes. He lived for a year in California when grit and resolve were his primary values. He was three years in Washington, D.C., where he had increased his commitment to work for the little guy. And for a decade, he had been affiliated with the University of Utah, which had the reputation of being one of the most "liberal" institutions in the state.

In so many ways, Dan outgrew his birthplace. He was ever at ease in the way he interacted with everyone, including elevator operators, taxi drivers, and store clerks, though he did not bother to develop a down-home style with the Utah vernacular, saying such things as: "Praise the Lard." "The farty harses were eatin carn in the barn." "I'm goin to swim acrost the crick in Harrican." But Dan became a critical observer of Utah's governmental institutions. However, through all of this, he maintained his allegiance to his childhood faith.

In this regard, Dan was much like other young Mormons who had become well-schooled. Researchers at Brigham Young University found that, unlike young people of most other faiths, highly educated Mormons were likely to attend church, pay a full tithing, and pray. Even though their political preferences often spanned the full political spectrum, they remained faithful and actively committed to the church.[269] Fortunately, before he graduated, Dan went out of his way to learn some of the legal traditions of his state and the Utah Constitution.

There was a long tradition that the best law firms of Salt Lake City automatically siphoned off the top twenty percent of the law-school graduates

---

[269] Stan L. Albrecht and Tim B. Heaton, "Secularization, Higher Education, and Religiosity," *Latter-day Saint Social Life: Social Research on the LDS Church and Its Members* (Provo, Utah: Brigham Young University Press, 1998).

from each graduating class at the University of Utah.[270] After Dan qualified to be a member of the bar associations of America, Utah, and Salt Lake County, he was shocked to find that, even though he was first in his class, he was not invited to apply for any open position at law firms in town, suggesting that his physical condition may have played a role.[271] In the West, it was not polite publicly to raise questions about a person's or a firm's motives; however, he quietly concluded that prominent law firms were simply not interested in taking a chance on damaged goods.

Consequently, Dan made application for clerkships at the Utah Supreme Court and at the Justice Department in Washington, D.C. He quickly received an invitation to serve as a clerk in the Utah State Capitol Building, under Edward Richard Callister, Jr., Associate Justice to the Utah Supreme Court. Callister had been appointed by Governor George Dewey Clyde, a conservative Republican. Dan's appointment was cut short, when he received notice that he had been appointed as a clerk for the Justice Department in Washington, D.C. Even though his Utah clerkship was to be for at least one year, Justice Callister generously encouraged him accept the Washington position.

Once the Stewarts had decided to move to Washington, Dan began to worry. He had no idea where they were going to live. He did not even know whether he could get into his office in the Justice Department. Elizabeth stepped into the situation. She had a PhD in psychology and understood his concerns. She advised him that the matters he was worried about were trivial. His only concern ought to be his work in the Department of Justice.

---

[270] These law firms included Chapman and Cutler LLP; Jackson Lewis, P.C.; Marcus Williams Young and Zimmermann, LLC; Parr Brown Gee and Loveless; and Jones Waldo PC,

[271] Stewart, "Interview at Her Mother's Home in Salt Lake City, ."

PART III:

DAN THE LAWYER AND PROFESSOR

9. The Justice Department

Before leaving Salt Lake City for the nation's capital, Dan contacted his old friends, Bob and Joyce Bennett, who were living in Arlington, Virginia. Bob served, at the time, as the chief-of-staff in the office of his father, Utah Senator Wallace F. Bennett. The Bennetts quickly found a suitable apartment in Arlington, Virginia, that was available on the ground floor in the Bennett's own neighborhood, with a sliding front door, and assured Dan and Elizabeth that everything would be ready when they arrived.

The move to Washington, D. C. was unreal. The family of three—baby Liz was about one year old—piled almost all their personal belongings into the old turquoise and white Oldsmobile. Elizabeth drove all the way. Dan sat in the passenger seat in the front, and Liz, born September 18, 1961, was confined to a crib that was wedged between piles of their belongings in the back seat and the roof of the car.

They drove more than 2,100 miles, mainly along interstate 80, one of the first interstate highways in the United States. Each late afternoon, they stopped along the way at an inexpensive motel showing a "vacancy" sign out front. Dan often reminisced, "We were dead broke in those days,"[272] so they looked for the least expensive places. The trip was so wearing that they usually drove only about five hours a day through Cheyenne, Omaha, Des

---

[272] I. Daniel Stewart, "Interview at His Salt Lake City Home," (Dec. 8, 1999).

Moines, near Chicago, Toledo, just south of Cleveland, and north of Pittsburgh. The only stops they made were to gas up, eat, and go to the bathroom. Elizabeth loved to drive fast. Despite that, the trip took more than nine days.

When finally arriving in Arlington after a long final day, in good Mormon fashion, they were greeted at the apartment by the Bennetts and another staff member of Senator Bennett's office, Chick Bradford, and his wife, Mary. They all celebrated by touring the small quarters that would serve as their home for the next three years. After their guests had helped them unload their car and departed, they put Liz to sleep, bathed, and fell into bed.

The next day, Elizabeth took Dan to the Justice Department Building on Pennsylvania Avenue. The back of the building faced the National Mall and was only a short block away from the National Gallery of Art. They had to go to the back of the building, because there were stairs at the front entrance. When Dan introduced himself to the clerks in the large marble edifice, there was a little stir about the fact that he was in a wheelchair. That moment of unease passed quickly, and he began to process the paperwork as a fellow in a special honors program. Although his division was on the third floor, he had no difficulty getting into his office; elevators were everywhere.

A decade earlier, the Justice Department had begun a special program, known formally as "The Attorney General's Recruitment Program for Honors Law Graduates," later shortened to "The Attorney General's Honors Program," which quickly become the premier entry-level initiative for lawyers in the country. It was open to young people, who had just completed law school and were in the top ten percent of their class. At the time, the number of candidates was somewhat limited, but it eventually attracted hundreds of applicants from every kind of law school.

Six clerks were selected each year. Dan joined Arthur Murphy from Fordham, George Kucik and Patrick M. Ryan from Villanova, and Michael Miller from Northwestern. Joel Hoffman from Yale had already been there for a year, but he became a member of the group. It never occurred to anyone to compare one fellow against another. From the beginning they all took for granted that everyone was highly capable but fortunate to be there.

They were all young and right out of law school. Their conversations were about what was happening in the nation's capital. This was an exhilarating time in America. John F. Kennedy was the youngest president in American history, and he brought an unprecedented vigor and optimism to the country.

His brother, Robert F. Kennedy, was the Attorney General in the Department of Justice, so his headquarters was in Dan's office building. The economy was actively expanding. The Peace Corps and Alliance for Progress stimulated young people to get involved in world affairs. Wage disparities between men and women were highlighted, leading to the Equal Pay Act of 1963, and civil rights was becoming a moral priority.

A year and three months after the Stewarts arrived, President Kennedy was shot in Texas, but the optimism and regard for possible change through government initiative remained high. None of the fellows was hostile to the government, nor to thoughtful government regulations. Nobody seemed to feel like he was an outsider. Even the one Republican in the group, Arthur Murphy, was from New York, which cast him as a political moderate.[273] Dan saw himself as expressly liberal, but he consciously demanded of himself that his legal decisions be based on demonstrable, objective facts.[274]

Dan and Elizabeth felt comfortable mixing with the other fellows, particularly those who, like themselves, had just married. They felt an immediate rapport with Joel Hoffman and his new wife, and they were often together for quiet weekend dinners. Arthur Murphy married soon after his arrival in Washington, and his new wife, Shannon, stayed with the Stewarts when she first arrived, until the Murphys could arrange for their own quarters. There was never any conflict in terms of political or religious values. The fellows all seemed compatible and comfortable with their social lives.

Dan and Elizabeth were fortunate to be in Washington at the time of Martin Luther King's "I Have a Dream" speech. It was delivered at the Lincoln Memorial to people calling for civil and economic rights. Dan was not

[273] Joel Hoffman, "Telephone Interview at His Home in New York City," (Sept. 19, 2018).

[274] Joe Smith, "Telephone Interview at His Home in Portland, Oregon " (August 30, 2018).

able to join the march on that day, which drew a quarter million people to the National Mall stretching out from the Lincoln Memorial, but he insisted that Elizabeth go across the Potomac River.

She listened to King's seventeen-minute speech, thought by many to be the greatest of the century.[275] Elizabeth was working three days a week at St. Elizabeth's Mental Hospital, where she was engaged in a post-doctoral psychotherapy training program.[276] Most of her clients turned out to be "ultra-violent criminals," who had been caught and incarcerated.[277]

Dan had the good fortune to be in the same division as one of his old law school professors, Ronan "Charles" Degnan. They often had lunch together. He shared with Dan that he worked on a few important law cases, such as the Philadelphia bank merger case. Dan continued to marvel that Degnan remained as "philosophical" as ever.[278]

The focus of the Stewarts' social life was with local members of the Mormon Church. Dan had always been committed to the church, and the young couple attended meetings on a regular basis. Dan sought out people of his own faith, who shared similar values. The Stewarts were never strait-laced about certain church practices. Elizabeth, who had grown up a Methodist, had only recently adopted the Word of Wisdom, the Mormon health code that prohibits smoking, drinking alcohol, coffee and tea. Dan never pressed her about total abstinence. He would even occasionally join her for a glass of wine or a lager Beer. When the Stewarts had company at their apartment, they kept a quality set of drinks of all kinds for their guests. On occasion, Dan drank coffee to sustain him during times when he was under pressure to meet a deadline.

Some of their values occasionally came into conflict with a church tenet, but the Stewarts never made an issue of them with their friends, both in and out

---

[275] Stewart, "Interview at the Home of Shannon Stewart Clark in Newport Beach, California, ."

[276] I. Daniel Stewart, "Letter to the Utah College of Law Alma Mater Office " (Salt Lake City, Utah June 2, 1963).

[277] Stewart, "A Life: Dictated to Richard G. Ellis."

[278] Stewart, "Letter to the Utah College of Law Alma Mater Office ".

of the church. One of their best church friends was Joe Smith, who had known the Stewart family in Federal Heights, although Joe's family had moved away when he was but seven years old. However, when the Stewarts arrived in Washington, he was attending George Washington University law school. He and his new wife would go out to dinner with the Stewarts every month or so.[279]

All four of them engaged in animated discussions. Both women were not shy about sharing their opinions about issues, such as race and feminism. In addition, from time to time, they attended the theatre and went on excursions to places like the Hill Cumorah and Williamsburg. The Smiths both agreed that Dan was smart, clever, and fun.[280]

The Stewarts had the good fortune to live close to the apartment of Bob and Joyce Bennett. They got together as often as they could, and they enjoyed sharing old stories about life in Federal Heights, East High School, and the University of Utah. One of their favorite stories was about the time Dan and Bob were finishing high school. In the summer of 1951, when the Korean War had just broken out, every male high school senior began to worry about being inducted into the U.S. military.

The athletic Dan Stewart was a likely candidate. He and his good buddy, Bob Bennett, were called in to take a physical exam, to determine if they were eligible for the draft. Of course, Dan was qualified in every way, while Bob came up short at every turn. Bob was too tall at 6'6," while Dan was a perfect 6'4." Bob was too skinny, while Dan was a perfect physical specimen. Bob could barely see the eye chart, while Dan had perfect vision. Bob had a hernia, while Dan was in peak physical condition. Of course, they both sailed through the intelligence exam. As fate would have it, unqualified Bob ended up going to Fort Ord in California for basic training, and he then became a chaplain in the military reserves,[281] while Dan, who qualified in every way, gained an exemption from the army, to go on a Mormon mission.

The Stewarts also established close friendships with Chick and Mary Bradford. He worked in Senator Bennett's office, and the young couple was

---

[279] Smith, "Telephone Interview at His Home in Portland, Oregon ".

[280] Ibid.

[281] Joyce Bennett, "Interview at Her Home in Salt Lake City,," (June 6, 2018).

pleased to associate with Dan and Elizabeth, who were always "good company" and "fun to be with." Washington was known as a theater town, and the foursome would regularly attend a performance at the Kennedy Center, Warner Theatre, or National Theatre.

Dan loved Shakespeare, and there were regular performances in these major theaters as well as the more intimate settings, such as the Shakespeare Theatre. Because Washington, D.C. was the nation's capital, no friendship was possible unless politics was a topic of discussion. Chick and Mary would one day be central players in the Equal Rights Amendment. It was always a central topic of conversation.[282]

Dan and Elizabeth realized that their Oldsmobile was not suitable for the Washington traffic and the necessity of Dan getting in and out of the car. It was clear that Washington demanded a certain status symbol, and in the case of automobiles, anything less than a Cadillac was inappropriate. They sold their old Oldsmobile and purchased a second-hand navy-blue Cadillac. The back seat was roomy and easy for Elizabeth to get the wheelchair in and out.

The professional program Dan was a part of in the Department of Justice was barely a decade old. In 1947, Harry S. Truman had signed the National Security Act into law, creating the Central Intelligence Agency (CIA). His intention was to create a non-partisan agency that would gather, process, and analyze national security information outside the U.S. The data it collected would be available to those in the government, particularly the military, to assist them in carrying out their global activities.

However, to Truman's dismay, the CIA quickly challenged his intent on approving the recognition of Israel as a Jewish state, thus politicizing its role. When Eisenhower took office in 1953, he took steps to depoliticize the Justice Department. One move he made was to establish a program that would bring the best and brightest law graduates into the Justice Department. A decade later, Dan Stewart was just such a recipient. In his group were different people, one from Chicago, others from the East coast. Joel was Jewish and from New York, while Dan was a Mormon kid from the West. Dan

282 Mary Bradford, "Telephone Interview at Her Arlington, Virginia, Home " (Feb. 1, 2019).

wondered, from time to time, if he had been selected for the program, be-cause his name, Isaac Daniel, sounded Jewish.[283]

The fellows were placed in the Appellate Section of the Anti-Trust Di-vision; it focused on preventing or slashing monopolies that would curb competition between businesses. For entry level positions, the pay was re-spectable, providing for grade 11 civil service pay and regular cost of living increases. Each fellow worked under a section and an assistant section chief, most of whom had been in the office for ten to twenty years. From the very beginning, their tasks were at the highest level, usually preparing briefs going to the federal courts of appeals or to the United States Supreme Court. Dan and his colleagues usually wrote the briefs used by the Solicitor General and his staff in a court of appeals or the Supreme Court;[284] however, Dan was occasionally able to argue, in person, a case in a federal court in Chi-cago or Washington.

The fellows were not doing start-up work. Their briefs were going to the highest courts in the country. It is a curious label for documents that are often thirty to fifty pages long. In addition, each was reviewed several times, line by line and word by word, by his section chief and assistant chief, and by the other fellows.

Their work schedule was hard and grueling. There was no time clock and no time sheets to fill out. No one cared if you came late or if you worked late into the night. Briefs were letterpress printed by the Government Printing Office. The fellows were the low men on the totem pole, so correcting the galley proofs fell to them, sometime without a lot of time between proofing time and the filing time. This often meant going to the Government Printing Office to read the proofs in the reading room and handing them directly to the printers.[285]

On occasion, in the middle of the night, after Dan had gone to bed, some-one in the office would call and insist that Elizabeth drive him to the printing

---

[283] I. Daniel Stewart, "Interview at His Home in Salt Lake City, ," (Dec. 8, 1999). Corrobo-rated by John Bates, "Interview at the Stewart Home in Salt Lake City," (Jan. 30, 2019).

[284] Stewart, "Letter to the Utah College of Law Alma Mater Office ".

[285] Hoffman, "Telephone Interview at His Home in New York City."

office so he could go through a brief. It was taken for granted that changes could be made right up until the last minute, as long as a change meant an improvement. Dan would have agreed with John Kenneth Galbraith, a Harvard economist, that when writing, there are some days "when the result is so bad that no fewer than five revisions are required." Galbraith points out that when he is "greatly inspired, only four revisions are needed."[286]

The fellows went even further than Galbraith. They would have argued, "It was common for us to revise a brief a dozen times or more before we were satisfied with the text."[287] Dan had joined a culture with shared norms and values absolutely suited to his inclinations. He was intent on succeeding, regardless of the personal costs in time and effort, just as the group was willing to do whatever was required to achieve its goals. Dan was so resilient that no setback was going to hinder his efforts, and the group was bent on finishing its tasks, and finishing them well, regardless of the challenges and hurdles they faced.

As a Law Review editor at the University of Utah, Dan had begun to engage in systematic revisions of drafts, but he never fully appreciated the importance of revisions, until he became a fellow in Washington, where he began to engage in multiple revisions of a text, particularly as it pertained to the law. It was obvious to him that briefs required extraordinary precision of thought and expression. Revisions were more than the proper placement of a comma, or the appropriate use of pronouns. Unclear writing always reflected unclear thought, and Dan knew that ideas and arguments required extensive refinement if he was successfully to argue his case.

This revision routine signaled a tradition that followed Dan Stewart through his entire career. As a professor, law associate, and Supreme Court justice, he had a notorious reputation for engaging in revisions of drafts right up until printing began. He was not alone in doing this; all the fellows made a practice of revising until the deadline, but Dan went even further than

---

[286] John Kenneth Galbraith, "Writing, Typing, and Economics," in *Writing in the Social Sciences*, ed. Joyce S. Steward and Marjorie Smelstor (Glenview, Ill.: Scott, Foresman and Co, 1984).

[287] Hoffman, "Telephone Interview at His Home in New York City."

most; through his entire career, Dan had a reputation for insisting on making twenty to thirty revisions of a single brief. Whereas journalists often sacrificed perfection in favor of meeting a deadline, Dan's work ethic remained, throughout his life, to aspire for excellence, even in the face of a deadline. His infatuation with rewriting went so far that one of his Utah Supreme Court clerks, David Gee, once found him editing a document he had already published.[288]

Most of the work done by the fellows involved anti-trust cases against parties who were charged with limiting free competition in the marketplace, such as a National Dairy Corporation price fixing case.[289] That corporation is, today, best known as Kraft Foods, a grocery manufacturing and processing conglomerate. The company began in 1903, when J. L. Kraft started purchasing cheese in Chicago's wholesale market and reselling it to local merchants. He and his brothers soon purchased a cheese factory and developed a process for pasteurizing cheese.

During World War I, they obtained several lucrative contracts with the military, and after the war, they began acquiring products, such as Miracle Whip. They also began internally to develop products such as Jell-O, Maxwell House Instant Coffee, Dream-Whip, Cool Whip, etc. And they expanded by merging with other companies, buying small companies, and going global, and eventually developed the reputation of doing everything they could to reduce competition and monopolize lines of food.

Such practices placed Kraft in the crosshairs of anti-trust enthusiasts, and the case that Dan Stewart worked on involved a processing plant in Kansas City, Missouri. National Dairy, as it was named at the time, attempted to undercut the local dairies in Kansas and Missouri, by selling its dairy goods at unreasonably low prices. By doing this, National Dairy attempted to destroy the local competition. Because the company operated

---

[288] David Gee, "Telephone Interview at His Home in Seattle, Washington," (July 16, 2020).

[289] U.S. Supreme Court, "United States V. National Dairy Products Corp. 372 U.S. 29 " (1963).

in many different localities, it could finance and subsidize a price war against small local dairies in one location.

These local dairies sued National Dairy, and the large firm argued at the District Court that the term "unreasonably low prices" was unconstitutionally vague, and it requested dismissal of the case, which the court supported. The case then went to the U.S. Eighth District Court of Appeals. and Dan Stewart and another attorney drafted the 250-page brief, outlining the position of the United States.[290]

On February 18, 1963, that court determined that the District Court was in error and ruled against National Dairy. The case then went to the U.S. Supreme Court, where comment was made that Dan's brief was of high quality, and their argument was sustained.[291] This case was highly publicized, and Dan's name became known in legal circles in Utah.

A second anti-trust example, where Dan Stewart was one of the appellees, was related to an appeal on the part of the American Society of Composers, Authors, and Publishers (ASCAP) against Metromedia, the owner of a chain of radio and television stations in New York State. In 1963, Metromedia applied for a so-called blanket license covering its ten radio stations, but that license proposal incorporated a markedly different method of computing royalties than was provided in previous ASCAP blanket licenses.

Since the 1940s, radio stations had paid a few cents to the publisher, author, or composer every time a piece was played. The fee was based on the so-called card rate, which indicated the maximum price that a station must pay but allowing discounts due to volume or other factors. The new royalty proposed by Metromedia would be based on the percentage of gross receipts of the station and other factors.

ASCAP rejected the new application and Metromedia filed a contempt motion against it. The District Court determined that ASCAP was not required to issue a special license of that kind, and Metromedia filed an appeal

---

[290] Hoffman, "Telephone Interview at His Home in New York City."; Stewart, "A Life: Dictated to Richard G. Ellis."

[291] "A Life: Dictated to Richard G. Ellis."

directly to the U.S. Supreme Court. Dan helped prepare a brief for the court; it subsequently dismissed the appeal "for want of jurisdiction."[292]

Several cases Dan was involved in were appeals from the Interstate Commerce Commission (ICC). The ICC was created in 1887 because of widespread agitation against the railroads. Rural areas, particularly in the West, had long complained that the railroads had abused their economic power to the detriment of state and city governments and other private transportation companies.

One case Dan was involved with was an appeal on the part of the ICC claiming that the New York, New Haven and Hartford Railroad Company had reduced its rail rates so far below other rail and trucking competitors that it could "fairly be said to threaten the industry." The ICC even suggested that the low rates posed a threat to the national defense. The rail company had reduced its rates in response to the new rates of a second company,

Sea-Land Service, Inc., which had converted four ships into crane-equipped trailer vessels, each capable of holding 226 truck trailers that could be mounted and demounted. With these ships, freight could be moved by highway trailers to a seaport. The trailers could then be lifted onto the ships, and when the ships reached their destination, the trailers would be off-loaded and hauled on highways to their destination. As a result, Sea-Land was able to provide efficient door-to-door delivery of goods.

In 1957, when Sea-Land Service inaugurated its new trailer shipping service, its performance was so efficient that its new land rates were generally five to seven- and one-half percent lower than the corresponding all-rail box-car rates. In response to these reduced rates, the New York, New Haven, and Hartford Railroad reduced its rail rates so they would be comparable with the rates of Sea-Land Service. In 1960, ICC assessed the matter and ruled that the new lower rail rates were "compensatory," meaning that they usually exceeded out of pocket costs. The ICC ruled that these reduced rates constituted "destructive competition," and continued use of the reduced rates were so low as to be hurtful of competition. It ruled that a more appropriate rate must be charged for the boxcar service.

---

[292] U.S. Supreme Court, "Metromedia Vs. American Society of Composers, Authors, and Publishers 382 U.S. 38," (1965).

The railroad brought action before a three judge District Court, seeking to have the ICC order set aside. In November 1961, the court ruled it would prohibit the imposition of a rate differential to protect the water carriers. Two years later, the issue came before the U.S. Supreme Court, and Dan was asked to help write a brief for the Justice Department. It reaffirmed that the ICC possessed the power to protect "all carriers from destructive competition," and it agreed with the District Court decision that lower rates be set aside. Further, it dismissed the claim that national defense was at risk.[293]

The kind of cases Dan was engaged in, while working with the Justice Department, provided a sound foundation for the kinds of legal cases that would engage his attention throughout his professional life. He was dedicated to the notion that the law is particularly critical for the little man, the members of society, who have traditionally been disadvantaged by social, economic, and political norms. Those struggling often came from lower-income backgrounds, and suffered from social exclusion, or have not had access to the economic opportunities that are taken for granted by those in the upper strata of society.

After three exhilarating years in Washington, D.C., the Stewarts decided it was time to return home. His tenure at the Justice Department was ending, and Dean Sam Thurman of the College of Law at the University of Utah, who had followed his progress in Washington, suggested he join the faculty. He waivered in his decision, thinking it might be good to go on to AT&T, where he had a job offer. Not long after that, Dan received news that his mother had breast cancer.[294] Everyone in the law school was delighted to receive his formal application to serve as an assistant professor at the University of Utah.

---

[293] U.S. District Court S.D. New York, "United States V. Atlantic Richfield Company and Sinclair Oil Corporation, 297 F. Supp. 1061," (1969).

[294] Stewart, "A Life: Dictated to Richard G. Ellis."

10. PROFESSOR STEWART

The Stewarts prepared to travel back to Utah, where Dan was a newly appointed assistant professor of law. When they left Washington, Elizabeth was pregnant, so she and Liz flew home. Dan stayed on for another month living with Joe Smith, while he finished up his work at the Justice Department. A friend agreed to drive him and the car back the entire 2,100 miles.[295]

Dan's contract required that he arrive at the university by July 1, even though teaching assignments began more than two months later. The time gave Dan a bit of breathing room to adjust himself. He was glad to be back in his beloved Rocky Mountains. Mount Olympus towered more than 9,000 feet above sea level and more than 5,000 feet above Salt Lake City and the valley floor, and the shady sides of the stark granite summits above Big and Little Cottonwood Canyons were still snow-capped.

The first order of business was to get Elizabeth through another pregnancy and prepare for the birth of their second daughter, Shannon.[296] The Stewarts looked for a place near LeGrand and Mary Louise Holbrook's home, and they soon bought a small red brick house with white trim, built in the middle of a large yard on the corner of 3900 South and 2600 East. It was located just below the 715 Belt Route so the drive past the mouth of

---

[295] Ibid.

[296] She was born on September 9, 1965.

Parley's Canyon to Foothill Drive and on to the university was relatively quick and easy.

There was a playhouse in the back yard, which was to serve for some time as the place of refuge for the two little girls. Mormon ward members built a ramp from the back door to the driveway, so that Dan would have smooth access to Elizabeth's car. She limited her work schedule so she could help Dan get to work and back.

Having lived all his life near a university, Dan was aware of the life of a professor. He knew that he was to be given precious time to withdraw, study, write, and meditate. Contemplation was a luxury few people enjoy, and good professors take time to think about concepts and ideas. At those times, Dan was alone, in isolation, and his wheelchair was not an encumbrance but served, in his mind's eye, as his private place of refuge, his place of quiet isolation, where he could freely reflect and compose his thoughts.

Dan's reputation as a writer and editor preceded him, and his friend, professor John Flynn, noted years after Dan left the university, that he and his colleagues "shamelessly exploited his willingness to read and edit our articles and speeches."[297] His colleagues' main difficulty was when they gave him their manuscript, they were never sure when they would get it back. Dan would take ownership of the document and subject it to several revisions before he would hand it back to them.

John Flynn recalled walking by Dan in the law library, and he noticed that Dan was struggling to remove a volume from the shelf. He sensed that Dan did not want any assistance. After he had removed the book and put it on his lap, he smiled at Flynn, and with a wink in his eye, he said a simple "thanks."[298] He knew his physical limitations, but he refused to compromise with the demands that life brought.

As a young man, Dan Stewart had dreams of being a great athlete, an independent student, and a competent lawyer. He recognized the limitations of his present physical condition, but he demanded of himself that he would continue to live in such a way that he would fight every step of

---

[297] Flynn, "Isaac Daniel Stewart: 1932-2005."

[298] Ibid.

his career with "perseverance" and "with a smile on his face and a wink in his eye."[299]

Thereafter, Flynn called Dan by his first name, "Isaac," not because the son of Abraham had been saved by Divine intervention, but because the Hebrew meaning of the word Isaac was "He who will laugh." Upon joining a group of people, Professor Stewart's wit and smile always lit up a crowded room.

When Dan arrived, the University of Utah was still general enough that it might have been called a teaching rather than a research institution. This meant that his primary task as a professor was to instruct. Dan's teaching load was considerable. Each term he taught several classes, and he was asked to teach new classes each year, which meant he had to develop new syllabi almost every term. Despite this, one of his students claimed, "I never saw him in an unprepared moment." He definitely "knew what he was talking about."[300] From 1965 to 1970, he taught many required courses, and so he was exposed to almost all the approximately 375 students in the five annual classes.

Classes for the new students introduced them to the way lawyers think. Dan would present a "fact situation" to the students, then he would ask, "What would you do?" After several students suggested what they would do, Dan would describe exactly what the lawyer had done. The readings were taken from the textbook, where the students would be exposed to classic cases of the law, and the good students quickly learned how to respond appropriately to his questions.[301] He demanded much of the students, but he always took the time to compliment a student, who did well. To those, who did not respond appropriately to his questions, he would say something that was neither condemning nor embarrassing, such as "Well, what you say is not false," but he would then suggest how the student might have responded more appropriately.[302]

---

[299] Ibid.

[300] Bates, "Interview at the Stewart Home in Salt Lake City."

[301] Anthony I. jr. Bentley, "Interview in His Salt Lake City Home," (June 5, 2019).

Each fall of the five years he was at the law school, Dan taught constitutional law to beginning students, focusing on the U.S. Constitution, and the laws that have developed out of it, including the allocation of power among branches, the nature and scope of judicial review, freedom of speech, the right to counsel, etc.

The law school faculty talked openly about being a regional university, serving the entire Mountain West. Consequently, almost no attention was given to the Utah Constitution, and there was certainly no seminar devoted to it. Contrary to the attitudes of those in the Utah Supreme Court and the Utah State Legislature, those in the university's law school were not bound to the growing attitude of alienation toward the federal government and U.S. Constitution.

Each fall term, Professor Stewart taught a second course, required of all beginning students: Federal and Utah Civil Procedure. This dealt with the process of civil litigation from the beginning of a lawsuit on to pleading, discovery, jurisdiction, the judge/jury systems, the trial process, and the final judgment.[303] Some students felt law school officials were using civil procedure to weed out marginally qualified students.

Dan chose not to participate in this ritual, and he went out of his way to assist students who were not doing well. Later in life, he reflected, "There's an enormous satisfaction in getting a good and proper result from someone whose deepest interests could be seriously damaged ... . Learning how to deal with people and their problems can be as exciting as law itself."[304] His students remember him as "always fair."[305] Professor Stewart sent at least one personal letter to a student, informing him he did not pass; he invited the student to retake the course, and, if he passed, his failing grade would not count against him.[306]

---

[302] Flynn, "Isaac Daniel Stewart: 1932-2005."

[303] "Bulletin of the College of Law," ed. University of Utah (Salt Lake City, Utah: University of Utah, 1977-78).

[304] Richard Ellis, "Interview of Dan Stewart at His Home in Salt Lake City, ," (Dec. 8, 1999).

[305] Bates, "Interview at the Stewart Home in Salt Lake City."

In the spring term, Dan taught courses in research and writing. The legal process is adversarial in nature, one side arguing for a defendant and another side arguing against. The skills necessary are not unlike those of the ancient sophists, who promised their clients they could successfully argue whatever side the client wished. In court cases, written legal briefs and filings are submitted by each side.

Whereas most university graduate programs claim to be scientific, law school research predates the scientific method and helps students learn how to identify court cases that support their point of view and write briefs and filings intended to persuade the court to rule in favor of the side a lawyer is arguing. The research courses Dan taught focused on the legal issues at play and analyzed the court cases that have supported a particular point of view.

Dan also taught advanced electives.[307] He was particularly concerned with the kind of evidence being admitted in court, and he regularly taught an elective on evidence. One of his former students, Steven G. Wood, recalled a compelling pedagogical experience in Professor Stewart's evidence course. Prior to a class session, Dan arranged for a group of other law students to rush suddenly into the classroom, go up to the front, cause a brief disturbance, then quickly leave.

As soon as they departed, Professor Stewart asked his students: "Write down in your journal what just happened. In a few minutes, I will quiz you on what you have written." When he saw that most of them were finished writing, he then posed a series of simple questions, asking them to read what they had written: "What just happened?" "How many men and women were there"? "What were they wearing?" "What did individual people do?" "How long were they in our classroom?"

The answers students had written down diverged wildly. Several students did not address many of the questions. Even the length of time they thought

---

[306] I. Daniel Stewart, "Letter to Mr. Morris Sorenson, Reno, Nevada," (Aug. 31. 1967).

[307] Some course he taught included: Federal Courts; Corporate Federal Income Tax; Regulated Industries.

the intruders were there differed dramatically. He then discussed how unreliable witness evidence may be and how frail is human recollection.[308]

Innovative pedagogy was a regular practice among law professors. They are exceptionally bright and often take pride in innovative teaching methods. On the first day of his constitutional history class, Professor Richard Aaron would bring a whole armful of books, folders, pamphlets, and documents into the class, and during the discussion, he would pick up a document here, and another there, just to let the students visualize how much reading was expected.

However, the professors were always concerned that students focus on the major issues they were to remember on topics. When Professor Denny Ingram, a colleague, wished the students to remember a particularly important point about tax law, he would get up on a table, wave his arms, and shout. Whenever Professor Richard Aaron wished to make a point that he wanted students to remember, he cited a little limerick poem by John Bytheway: "Inch by inch, life's a cinch; yard by yard, life's hard," meaning the students should not try to remember everything, but certainly the important things.[309]

In most of the courses Dan taught, he engaged in a typical Socratic approach, e.g., "What is evidence?" or "How reliable are eyewitness accounts?" But when the occasion called for it, he was not shy about lecturing. His teaching style, while demanding, was supportive. According to Neil Sabin, graduating class of 1970, "he was never jocular, and was always business-like."[310] He had little patience for "playing the game," of embarrassing, shaming, or calling out students who appeared to be unprepared.

Dan always spoke highly of people worthy of emulation. He praised the Dean of the Law School, Daniel Dykstra, who had already served as the academic vice president of the university, for exemplifying traits of "common

---

[308] Elizabeth Loftus, "Reconstructing Memory: The Incredible Eyewitness," *Psychology Today* 8 (1974)..

[309] Richard Aaron, "Interview at the College of Law, University of Utah, in Salt Lake City," (Feb. 1, 2019).

[310] Neil Sabin, "Interview at His Home in Lehi, Utah, ," (June 8, 2018).

decency, his integrity, and his honest concern and respect for his colleagues, students, and staff."[311]

Whereas, at good universities most academics are required to publish extensively in professional journals, law professors are not inclined to engage in this process. A few law professors, including Dan's colleague, Edwin B. Firmage,[312] did publish major works, but Dan chose not to take that path. His written work concentrated on legal briefs and filings.

Dan was not reticent about taking on issues that piqued his interest or touched his sense of right or wrong. There was a case before the Utah Supreme Court involving what Dan, John Flynn, and others on the faculty thought was illegal in that it involved a merger that was in violation of a U.S. Supreme Court mandate. The State was moving to dismiss a pending appeal to the U.S. Supreme Court. Dave Watkins and John Flynn wanted to ask Dan's advice concerning the case.

A day or two before the State was to file its motion to dismiss the appeal, the two met with Dan in his backyard and suggested they challenge the State's motion to dismiss the appeal. Watkins was uneasy about doing anything, because none of the three was a party to the appeal. The Supreme court had no rule permitting intervention by a couple of law professors.

Dan's response: "So what! There is a first time for everything, and besides, what the State is planning to do is illegal and violates the express order of the court."[313] Watkins was still reluctant, but finally agreed to do so, when Dan said, "It was time to go out and tip over a few trash cans with a couple of leprechauns." The three filed their objections by telegram

---

[311] Edward Imwinkelried, James Hogan, and Kevin Johnson, "In Memoriam: Daniel J. Dykstra," (Davis, California: UC Davis, 2000).

[312] For example, Edwin B. Firmage, *Ends and Means in Conflict* (Salt Lake City, Utah: Frederick William Reynolds Association, 1987); *An Abundant Life: The Memoirs of Hugh B. Brown* (Salt Lake City, Utah: Signature Books, 1988); Edwin B. Firmage and Richard C. Mangrum, *Zion in the Courts* (Champaign/Urbana, Illinois: University of Illinois Press, 2001); Edwin B. Firmage, Bernard G. Weiss, and John W. Welch, *Religion and Law: Biblical-Judaic and Islamic Perspectives* (Winona Lake: Eisenbrauns, 1990).

[313] Flynn, "Isaac Daniel Stewart: 1932-2005."

to the Utah Supreme Court. The court subsequently denied the State's motion to dismiss the case.[314]

On occasion, Dan engaged in writing that targeted the general public. In 1968, his old classmate from East High School, Eugene England, was the editor of a new journal, *Dialogue: A Journal of Mormon Thought*. England invited him to participate in a "Roundtable" focusing on the rule of law amid the turmoil and flagrant civil disobedience of Blacks during the 1960s. The other participants were Dallin H. Oaks, a professor of law at the University of Chicago, and Royal Shipp, a senior analyst in the Federal Bureau of the Budget in Washington, D.C. All three scholars demonstrated that they were well versed in the literature related to the tumult and agitation taking place. Their essays were laden with footnotes citing the literature of the time related to racial unrest and violence.

Reflective of that time, all three discussants were white, and there was not yet any concept of "implicit bias," or other measure suggesting that all whites and Mormons are, by definition, racists.[315] As he was growing up, Dan never knew a Black person, although he spent three years in Washington, D.C., and it was predominantly Black. Of the three, only Shipp described his personal feelings about recent current events, but his attitude likely mirrored that of the other two participants. Shipp explained that he was born in the small town of Joseph, Utah, and grew up in a "comfortable Western Mormon home."

As was the case with most Mormons in rural Utah, as Shipp progressed from childhood to adulthood, he experienced almost no personal contact with Blacks. He also confessed that he faced the particular onus of belonging to a religion that, at the time, explicitly discriminated against Blacks. Whereas almost every other young man in the church received the priesthood, the church, for reasons rooted in its history, did not allow Blacks to be so ordained.

---

[314] "Note to Dan Stewart at the Time of His Award at the University of Utah Sesquicentennial Founders' Day Celebration " (Salt Lake City, UtahFeb 24, 2000).

[315] Armand L. Mauss, "Priesthood Ban against Blacks in the Mormon Church," *Dialogue: A Journal of Mormon Thought* 14, no. 3 (1983).

The riots Shipp experienced in Washington, D.C., "scared and shocked" him. He was "bewildered," but he quickly resolved to do whatever he could "to ameliorate conditions which cause riots." And he wrote that he believed that of all groups, Mormons ought to be the most sympathetic with the riots and other illegal behaviors Blacks were engaged in, because Mormons had also been harshly persecuted by government officials and had responded by engaging in civil disobedience.

The papers of Oaks and Stewart focused directly and forcefully on the rule of law as it pertains to civil disobedience. Both authors were strong advocates of the rule of law, and they addressed the issue of the place of rebellion and lawless behavior, when a minority group faces a society so prejudiced that it has established laws to disadvantage that group at every turn. Both lauded the lawful public protests of Blacks, including marches, picketing, and sit-ins to publicize grievances.

However, Oaks and Stewart split, when they considered an appropriate response to Blacks, who openly and deliberately violated the law as they attempted to gain public sympathy and influence government policy. Oaks was adamant that lawlessness, contempt for public officials, and civil disobedience leads to a disrespect for law. He also argued that Blacks have a stake in the observance of law, claiming such restrained behavior leads to sympathy for their cause. Those in the majority insist that everyone obey the rule of law, and the only assurance Blacks have against the tyranny of the majority, is to obey the law and rely on the judicial process to rectify grievances.

Stewart, having read Oaks' manuscript before submitting his own, challenged his stand. Throughout his adult life, Stewart often cited John Stuart Mill's *On Liberty*.[316] Mill openly celebrates individuality and disdains conformity. and in the opening pages of Dan's argument, he cited, at length, Mill's claim that the majority in any society will usually fail to act with restraint when dealing with a minority group. The majority will more likely tyrannize the minority, and the only recourse the minority has, is consciously and deliberately to engage in disobedient and coercive behavior.

[316] John Stewart Mill, *On Liberty* (London: John S. Parker and Soy, West Strand, 1859).

Several years later, Shipp confessed that he sided strongly with Stewart's argument, and admired him for taking on Oaks, who would one day be a Utah Supreme Court justice, a Mormon apostle, and a member of the First Presidency of the LDS Church.[317] Both Stewart and Shipp pointed out that Mormons had engaged in civil disobedience for several decades, concerning the issue of polygamy. The church finally succumbed to the federal government's insistence that it change its policy, but only after federal officials formally disbanded the church, jailed polygamous offenders, and began confiscating Mormon Church property.

In other words, the Mormon minority lost in its struggle against the majority. Stewart emphasized that, until 1890, Mormons had placed a higher priority on ecclesiastical law than the law of the land. He agreed with Oaks that moral justification does not excuse anyone from legal justification, in that the law is binding on all, regardless of personal agreement; however, there are many people who believe some laws are not just, and they are willing to take the consequences of penalties rather than yield their deeply held convictions. Stewart claimed that federal officials appeared to place a higher value on order and stability than justice and progress, and he stressed that civil disobedience, in certain circumstances, poses less risk to the stability of the United States than docile obedience.

Even though Mormons lost their struggle against the federal government on the issue of polygamy, they gave up their position, in large part to gain statehood and integrate themselves into the broader American mainstream. And they have been successful in doing so. Unfortunately, Blacks have a more difficult challenge. The jury is still out about whether they will ever gain full equality in American society.

In addition to teaching and publishing, Professor Stewart was expected to engage in professional, university, and community service. Because he was in the College of Law, his campus service component was high. Some academic senate committees deal with disputes between administrators, professors, and students; and law faculty members were asked to engage in

---

[317] Royal Shipp, "Telephone Interview at His Washington, D.C. Home " (Nov. 7, 2018).

processes on campus that emulated, in many ways, the legal system in broader society. In addition, law professors were drawn into university administrations, because they knew the rules that govern professional behavior. While Dan was a professor, he was a member of important campus committees, and he served actively in them.[318]

Dan's view of community service included legal assistance to those who were unable to pay for these services. His major outlet for doing such service was the American Civil Liberties Union (ACLU). Many University of Utah law professors provided such service. The Utah ACLU had been organized in 1958, at a time when the McCarthy hearings had wound down, and the blossoming of the Civil Rights movement in America was taking place.

Spencer L. Kimball was the Dean of the University of Utah law school, and he was one of the co-founders of the Utah ACLU. Consequently, it was common that law professors were involved in cases, and they typically did this work without compensation. In fact, when Dan Stewart was on campus, his colleague, Bill Lockhart, was active and served as the President of the Board of the Utah ACLU in 1970/71.

In 1967/68, during the Vietnam war crisis, Professor Stewart served as the major attorney in hearings and lawsuits challenging the draft reclassification process in Utah. On October 26, 1967, the director of the National Selective Service issued a memorandum directing local draft boards to review the draft status of anyone protesting the Vietnam war.[319] In one case, Stewart represented Henry L. Dewey, a student, who was twenty-one years of age and in good standing at his university. He was slated to graduate in June 1969. He had recently been reclassified from a 2-S classification to 1-A,

---

[318] He was a member of the campus building committee that oversaw the physical development of the university. He was a legal advisor on residency, and a member of the Faculty Regulations Committee, the University Research Committee, and the Committee on Education of Minority Groups.[318] To take a single case in point, the University Research Committee supervised the expenditure of university monies for research on campus. It developed rules and guidelines for the kinds of "secret" research that university faculty could conduct and provided seed money to new faculty members to stimulate their research.

[319] "Protestors Sue to Block Hershey's Draft Directive," *Civil Liberties, Monthly Publication of the American Civil Liberties Union* Jan., 1968.

which would make him eligible to be drafted into the military. On Dec. 14, 1967, the hearing was before the Selective Service Local Board #22.[320] In another case that received publicity,[321] Stewart represented a student who had been victimized by the decision on the part of draft boards to reclassify him. Henry Lowell Huey was one of approximately thirty students in Washington, DC, New York, New Jersey, Washington, and Utah.[322] Huey, a University of Utah student, had been reclassified and Dan Stewart joined with G. Kenneth Handley in fighting his reclassification process.[323]

In Utah, a small number of ACLU local chapters were organized. These chapters had no formal relationship with the state and national organizations but provided a working home for professors and others to work on local issues. Dan was active with the Salt Lake County chapter, and even served as its president in the late 1960s. This Salt Lake County chapter organized local meetings to discuss issues, such as "The Right to Dissent in a Free Society" (March 16, 1969). People such as Dan would also serve, without pay, to defend people, who were under fire for their activist points of view.

For example, professors Stewart and Lockhart volunteered to defend a teacher in Salt Lake City, who had been under threat of being fired, because he was a member of a group that had been identified by the House Un-American Activities Committee as subversive. They attended a meeting organized by the School Board in a hall that was filled, and there was some murmuring as Stewart and Lockhart came down the aisle to their tables, prepared to make formal presentations. However, the meeting was consumed by parents, who mostly defended the behavior of the teacher and the quality of his classrooms and instruction. The very presence of Stewart and Lockhart was enough to ensure an open discussion and a positive outcome.[324]

---

[320] Number 22 Selective Service Local Board, "Minutes of Selective Service Local Board " (State of Utah Dec. 14, 1967).

[321] For example, "Protestors Sue to Block Hershey's Draft Directive."

[322] "Protestors Sue to Block Hershey's Draft Directive," *Civil Liberties* Jan. 1968.

[323] "Huey to Appeal Decision," *The Daily Utah Chronicle* March 4, 1968

[324] William Lockhart, "Interivew at His Home in Salt Lake City," (Sept. 26, 2018).

On the surface, serving as a professor of law appears to have been an ideal position for Dan. It was demanding but highly rewarding. Yet, in 1970, he chose to leave the university. Some lawyers argued that Dan was making a wise choice, that private practice was far more rewarding than a university appointment. These lawyers claimed major law firms constantly deal with cutting-edge issues that university professors rarely touch.[325] In addition, the financial rewards outside the university are usually much greater. Nevertheless, his colleagues were shocked and perplexed when he announced he was leaving.

Professor Richard Aaron asked him, "Why on earth would you go into law practice?" Aaron had been in law practice before joining the university; he believed Dan was taking a step backwards by electing to leave the academy and join a law firm. Aaron always maintained that law firms have a myopic view of legal practice. Lawyers in law firms usually fail to rise above specific issues. They can't see the forest for the trees.[326]

Dan's response, "I want to do some things that I can't do here."[327] He was a strong-willed person, who made decisions and no amount of arguing would change his mind. The reasons Dan was leaving the academy are complex and difficult. John Flynn had several conversations with him: "He told me he had to do so to provide for his family, because he did not know how long he would be around. He was deeply devoted to his family, and they to him."[328]

Dan's explanation to his friend and colleague was true, but a more complex and noteworthy explanation came from one of Dan's former law students, John Bates: "Dan was in a box at the U."[329] He was one of eight professors in the law school, some of whom had been there for many years. John Flynn was a senior colleague, who had carved out a particular specialization in antitrust litigation. He taught all the antitrust courses; he addressed all the academic issues at the University of Utah related to these matters.

---

[325] Stringham, "Interview at His Home in Salt Lake City ".

[326] Aaron, "Interview at the College of Law, University of Utah, in Salt Lake City."

[327] Ibid.

[328] Flynn, "Isaac Daniel Stewart: 1932-2005."

[329] Bates, "Interview at the Stewart Home in Salt Lake City."

Before becoming a professor, Dan had worked in the Antitrust Division of the Justice Department in Washington, and he decided he would devote his life to matters that prevented the development of monopolies and unfair business practices and encouraged cooperation between small businesses. He believed this was his true calling. The law school had been a wonderful place for him to grow and thrive, but it did not allow him to concentrate on that calling. Even though he would ever remain a scholar and an academic, he decided it was time to move on.

11. JONES WALDO

While teaching at the University of Utah, Dan Stewart began consulting for the Jones, Waldo, Holbrook, and McDonough law firm.[330] Established in 1875, the firm enjoyed a long-standing reputation. Many of its partners and associates moved on to take important positions as legislators, judges, and academicians. At least six associates were appointed to the bench of the Third District Court.[331]

Four became professors at the Universities of Utah, Texas Tech, and Weber State. They chaired important educational administration bodies, including the Utah Board of Education, or the Board of Regents of the University of Utah and Utah State University. They were politically active in both the Democratic and Republican Parties and ran for governor and the U.S. Senate. They gained important reputations for service work with groups such as Ballet West, the Utah Symphony, the Utah Food Bank and the Utah Community Service Council.[332] Following his tenure as the longest serving governor of Utah, Calvin Rampton chose to join Jones Waldo; he served for thirty years as the firm's president.

[330] Hereafter, "Jones Waldo."

[331] Lesley Lewis, William Bohling, Randall Skanchy, Barry Lawrence, Adam Mow, and Andrew Stone.

[332] Most of this information taken from https://www.utcourts.gov/judgesbios/showGallery.asp?dist=3&ct_type=D

The legal profession was, at the time, a small, insular group. Lawyers came to know most of the other attorneys in town. They followed each other's careers and knew who was doing what. For example, Professor Stewart had met Don Holbrook, a partner with Jones, Waldo, while he served as the *Editor-in-Chief* of the *Utah Law Review*, and sometime after he arrived back in Salt Lake City from Washington, D.C., Holbrook invited Dan to come to lunch at Lamb's Grill. Holbrook was a distinguished, well-groomed figure, who "walked around like he was an aristocrat." However, he was always gracious and socially adept.[333] At the time, Holbrook was chairing the Board of Regents of the University of Utah. Having graduated from its law school, he took a great interest in what was going on there.

Lamb's Grill was located right next to the Walker Bank Building on Second South and Main, next door to the Jones Waldo office. It had the reputation for being much the same as it was at the end of World War I. The restaurant reserved a large eight-seat table for Jones Waldo lawyers and their guests, who ate lunch and took breaks there. Dan knew Germans called such a table a *Stammtisch*, because it was reserved exclusively for a special group. The *Salt Lake Tribune* also had its own *Stammtisch* there.

The day Dan visited, other lawyers dropped by to say hello, and George Lamb, the owner, said "hi" as he circulated through the noon crowd. Holbrook even asked Dan if he would like to meet judge Willis Ritter, who, at the time, had been on the bench of the Tenth Circuit Court for fifteen years, and was eating at a different table.[334] Dan agreed, although he explained to Holbrook that Ritter was his neighbor on Butler Avenue, and he already knew him.

Holbrook pointed out to Professor Stewart that they had strong Democrats and Republicans at Jones Waldo, so they had two rules at the table. You don't talk politics, and you don't discuss the case you are working on. Otherwise, anything goes.

---

[333] Shannon Stewart Clark, "Interview at Her Home in Corona Del Mar, California," (May 22, 2019).

[334] Most of this account comes from Randon W. Wilson, "Interview at the Jones Waldo Law Firm in Salt Lake City," (Feb. 1, 2018).

Holbrook could have commented: "I understand you have been in Washington for some time." "Only three years." "Tell me what you were doing there." "Mainly, I wrote briefs for the Antitrust Division of the Justice Department. They were usually for Supreme Court cases." "I am aware of the National Dairy price fixing case you worked on."

"We were happy with the outcome of that case." "Professor Stewart, you may know that at Jones Waldo I handle most of our antitrust cases. Would you be interested in working with me on a case from time to time?"

Dan replied that he was just beginning his tenure at the university, and that when things settled down a bit, he might be able to help out. He did not yet realize that he would be shut out of antitrust issues at the law school, because his colleague, John Flynn, was the antitrust specialist. Dan had begun to build his career around antitrust issues, which resonated both with his moderate tendencies and the conservative environment where he was working.

Shortly after the lunch at Lamb's Grill, Holbrook asked Dan to work on an antitrust case involving mechanical contractors, who perform repairs, alterations, or installations for a building or other structure. He explained to Dan that most of the bids for mechanical contracts in Utah were funneled through a Mechanical Contractors Bid Depository, which processed sealed bids for available jobs. Even though the Depository was set up to encourage competitive free enterprise, Harold Christiansen claimed his firm, The Palmer-Christiansen Company, which dealt with construction for healthcare, had suffered because the rules set up by the Depository had been restrictive, forcing Christiansen to cease his affiliation with the Depository. Holbrook explained that the U.S. District Court D had ruled against Christiansen, who wanted to move the matter to the U.S. Supreme Court.[335] Dan responded that his experience working with the Supreme Court might help. Ultimately, the Supreme Court chose not to hear the appeal; however, the case allowed Stewart to work closely with Holbrook.

---

[335] US Court of Appeals Tenth Circuit, "Mchanical Contractors Bid Depository V. Christiansen, 352 F2d 817," (Nov. 15, 1965).

Holbrook was impressed with the briefs Stewart produced and asked him to work on another antitrust case involving the merger of two petroleum giants, Atlantic Richfield Company and Sinclair Oil Company. Both Stewart and Holbrook believed this merger would have substantial anti-competitive effects, and they joined together with attorneys David Meincoff and Donald Mullins of the Justice Department, as well as attorneys from other regions of the country, to argue before the Southern U.S. District Court of New York.[336]

There were other cases that Dan worked on, including an administrative law case,[337] where Dan argued that an injunction against a Utah insecticide firm placed no hardship on that firm, because it was allowed to continue to produce and market its pesticides while the issue wound its way through a cumbersome legal procedure. However, most of the cases that came to a firm never reached a judge's or jury's decision. They were settled or reconciled informally, usually by way of mediation.

In 1970, Don Holbrook suggested to Stewart that he consider coming to the firm full-time. Dan expressed concerns. He loved his work at the University of Utah, and it provided what appeared to be an ideal professional outlet for him. He would certainly earn more at Jones Waldo, but a major concern was related to the location of the law firm. The office was in the center of Salt Lake City, just two blocks south of Temple Square.

Swarms of tourists were a constant problem. LDS Church headquarters, just East of Temple Square, was also a source of congestion. At the time, people were driving up and down streets looking for parking spots. Dan Stewart worried that Elizabeth would be frustrated by the downtown traffic.

Holbrook was not deterred by Stewart's objections and persisted in his invitation for him to be an associate with Jones Waldo. It is a bit ironic that Holbrook a member of the Board of Regents of the University of Utah, would tell one of the university's star professors: "You could do better by leaving the university."

---

[336] York, "United States V. Atlantic Richfield Company and Sinclair Oil Corporation, 297 F. Supp. 1061."

[337] Tenth Circuit U.S. Court of Appeals, "Pax Company of Utah V. United States, 454 F2d 93," (Jan. 26, 1972).

After giving the matter serious consideration, Stewart decided it would be to his advantage to do just that. Neither he nor Holbrook was disappointed with the decision. The lawyers there had a lot of talent, and these colleagues quickly came to regard him as one of the most qualified and outstanding attorneys in the business. In fact, Holbrook later wrote, that Professor Stewart exhibited "the most amazing capacity for written expression of any lawyer I've ever worked with."[338] It was clear that "Don Holbrook was the reason Dan went to the Jones Waldo firm."[339]

One of the most memorable antitrust cases Jones Waldo ever engaged in was affectionately known as the *Cackling Acres Case*, pitting a California egg company, Olson Farms, against several small Utah egg companies. The case was especially significant for Dan Stewart. Judge Michael Murphy later observed that from the Olson case, "Dan was crowned king" among Utah lawyers.[340] The case undoubtedly contributed directly to Dan's appointment to the Utah Supreme Court, and it was significant for other associates at Jones Waldo.

The case came to the firm mainly through Randon Wilson, a Jones Waldo associate, whose father was a farmer connected with Highland Dairy in Murray, Utah. He and his father were well-known among farmer cooperatives, and when fourteen egg producers and distributors in the general Salt Lake City area joined together to sue Olson Farms, the Utah poultry group approached Randon Wilson and invited him and Jones Waldo to represent them. Because of Dan Stewart's expertise with antirust issues Wilson then invited him to take the lead in the case.[341] Communalism has strong roots in American traditions and is especially important in Utah. Its origins were religious in nature, but now found expression in all

---

[338] Cited in Richard Cameron Blake, "Tribute: Justice I. Daniel Stewart," *Utah Law Review* 2000, no. 1 (2000).

[339] Michael Murphy, "Interview at the U.S. Court of Appeals in Pasedina, California," (Feb. 1, 2018).

[340] Ibid. and this transition brought praise and conclusions.

[341] Wilson, "Interview at the Jones Waldo Law Firm in Salt Lake City." See Gossner v. Cache Valley Dairy Association, 307 F. Supp. 1090 (1970).

facets of society, so Dan and Randon were comfortable working with an association of farmers.[342]

The fourteen egg companies claimed Olson Farms was attempting to undercut them and monopolize the egg industry in Utah through fixing and depressing the prices paid to egg producers. In the view of the Utah farmers, this was clearly a violation of the Sherman Act, which protects competitors in business from harm by preserving a competitive marketplace. The local farmer's description of the case could have come straight out of a textbook on justice for the little guy. Even the name of the suit fit the mold.

Originally, this group of egg producers intended to list all fourteen company names in alphabetical order, but they decided to put Cackling Acres first, because the name suggested this case was "the little guys vs. the big guys."[343] And that identity with the little guy might have been extended to the jury members. When the jury was being impaneled, judge Anderson asked a diminutive Asian lady if she had an interest in eggs. She replied, "Oh yes, I often make egg-foo-yung."[344]

Dan explained in his lead opinion that in 1965, Olson Farms had moved into the state. It already owned half interest of another large egg firm, Oakdell Egg Farms, from Idaho, which had recently built a large egg production facility in Riverton, just south of Salt Lake City. The brief argued that the two large egg farms were intent on monopolizing egg production and distribution, and on running the small Utah farmers out of business.

Dan and his colleagues charged Olson with violations of the Sherman Act, the Robinson-Patman Act, and the antitrust laws of Utah. In essence, the plaintiffs claimed Olson Farms had conspired to depress prices paid to egg producers and to fix the wholesale price for eggs. They also claimed Olson had conspired with egg distributors to monopolize the distribution of eggs in the state.

After a ten-week trial, the case was submitted to a jury, which sided with Dan and his colleagues. The jury ruled in favor of four of the plaintiffs "on

---

[342] Randon Wilson built his entire career around informal associations of many kinds. See ibid.

[343] William Bohling, "Interview in Downtown Salt Lake City," (Feb 1, 2019).

[344] Ronald J. Ockey, "Letter to I. Daniel Stewart," (Jan. 11, 2000).

the basis of a restraint of trade violation." The remaining ten were awarded damages for a "conspiracy to monopolize violation." Damages for both awards came to a whopping $574,593.[345] The Olson case clearly established Dan as a first-class lawyer.

The case represented a remarkable outcome for Dan, in part, because it was the first jury trial he had ever conducted. According to observers, "Dan was magnificent in court: exceedingly well prepared (though somewhat tired from late nights), brimming with style and grace despite the 'pressure cooker' of trial, zealous in his pursuit of perfect representation of his client."[346]

The lead attorney for Olson was Harold G. Christensen, a highly venerated lawyer in Utah. Christensen's team included Dan's former colleague and friend at the University of Utah, John Flynn, who was sympathetic with antitrust issues, but who had the breadth of experience to understand there are always at least two sides to an issue. Olson's lawyers, decided to appeal the case to the Supreme Court. They had what they considered to be good grounds. The Olson Company was respected in California, and the case had been filed at the time when egg consumption had plummeted. In 1970, the National Heart Association had declared that cholesterol was responsible for heart disease, and that the consumption of eggs, which were high in cholesterol, placed a person at high risk for heart attack and stroke. Consequently, the sale of eggs plunged in both Utah and California. Olson lawyers claimed the egg industry could not survive unless it quickly improved its efficiency in every respect.

Clarence Dean Olson, the president of the company, was a respected egg farmer. He had served on the National Advisory Committee for the poultry industry, as President of the Pacific Egg and Poultry Association, and as the Director of the Pacific Egg Marketing Association. He rejected the claims of the American Heart Association that eggs were bad for human consumption. He was confident he was involved in a healthy, productive industry, a claim that has since proved to be well-founded. He later established the Dolco Packaging Company that produced the first foam egg cartons.

---

[345] "Cacklling Acres, Inc, Et Al. V. Olson Farms, Inc.," in *541 F. 2d 242* (U.S. Court of Appeals, Tenth Circuit).

[346] Blake, "Tribute: Justice I. Daniel Stewart."

Olson's lawyers claimed Utah's egg production and distribution industry, which had been a thriving and efficient business in the 1920s, had become stale and inefficient. The Olson Egg Company had a reputation for being well-planned and productive. The Olsons had figured out how to feed and house chickens efficiently. They pointed out that Utah chickens were still running loose, while California chickens were being caged in thousands of small cages arranged in tiers, where farmers could easily control feeding and remove manure. At the time, chickens "running loose" represented a poor farming technique. Dan protested that claim before the bench, "Judge, that is just plain air," and noted there are plenty of advantages of chickens grubbing freely for worms, bugs, sprouts, clover, and other foods rich in antioxidants, fatty acids, and vitamins.[347]

The Olson lawyers claimed that the California company was attempting to bring greater efficiency into a floundering Utah egg industry. They had developed poultry medicine and were mechanically gathering eggs. All the while, they claimed that Utah's producers had neither installed refrigeration equipment nor taken advantage of the fact that they were closer to the Midwest grain belt than California.

Dan and his team had, indeed, cast the Olsons as a big California firm that was trying to destroy honest, industrious, small Utah farms. In fact, the Olsons had strong Utah roots. The two brothers, who directed the company, were born in Utah, were good practicing Mormons, and had attended the University of Utah. The president of the company, Clarence Dean Olson, was an all-conference guard on the University of Utah football team and was serving as the bishop of his Mormon Westwood Ward. He had previously served as the mayor of Beverly Hills, and he was a long-time member and chair of the city's Planning Commission. Consequently, the brothers could easily claim that they had no ill feelings toward Utah.

In its brief to the Supreme Court, Dan and his colleagues argued that the Olson company had gone beyond the point of simply being efficient; rather that it had embarked on monopolizing the market by intentionally driving egg producers and dealers out of business. Dan located a former

347 Murphy, "Interview at the U.S. Court of Appeals in Pasedina, California."

Olson executive, who testified that Olson took steps to achieve market dominance, directing sellers and buyers to favor Olson eggs, to reduce competition by acquiring competitors, and buying competitors' eggs and keeping them off the market, thus establishing a monopoly. When Olson entered the Utah market in 1966, there were several hundred Utah producers of eggs. By 1971, half a decade later, there were only four, and Olson and his "co-conspirators" controlled seventy-two percent of the distribution of eggs.

The Olson case was significant to Dan's career and the careers of other associates at Jones Waldo. Randon Wilson spent the rest of his professional life working with informal associations and business cooperatives. Dan's former associate and friend at the University of Utah, who was on the other side of the "egg case," confessed that Dan was so "thoroughly prepared day in and day out" that "he would have won the case even if there had been less merit to the case." It was obvious to Flynn that Dan had the capacity to "turn a marginal case into a landslide win."[348] His arguments were well stated, sometimes brilliant. There was little poetry in his language. It was straightforward and analytic. His preparedness was legendary, indicating an unmatched work ethic. Richard Blake later wrote a tribute to Dan, including the following:

His tireless preparation, thoughtful analysis, and zeal for clients, set a standard. He expected much from himself and from those who worked with him. Often, they toiled into the night and early morning to develop an argument precisely and to find the 'right case' to support it. Despite the rigors of intense cases and hard work, Dan remained in good spirits and tried to keep his associates upbeat.[349]

While the egg case established Dan's reputation as an antitrust specialist and expert, it also presented a shadow side. Dan worked closely with Jones Waldo associate, Christopher "Kit" Burton. One of their clients, the Dairyman's Cooperative, began engaging in a number of mergers, and in the mid-1970s no-less than eight separate antitrust cases arose out of the

---

[348] Flynn, "Isaac Daniel Stewart: 1932-2005."

[349] Blake, "Tribute: Justice I. Daniel Stewart."

mergers. Dan and Kit found themselves fighting to defend the firm's actions, something "Dan did not particularly enjoy defending."[350] Dan did not want to have anything to do with them. The clients "were not nice people to work with." They were deliberately engaging in "unlawful conduct," and Dan didn't like it at all.

Dan Stewart was not only passionate about antitrust issues, but he was ardent about First Amendment matters that guarantee freedom of assembly, the press, religion, and speech. Don Holbrook asked Dan if he would be interested in working on a case involving a prisoner at the Santa Rita Jail in California, who had committed suicide. KQED, the public television station in Salt Lake City, had sought permission from the California County Sheriff Houchins to inspect and photograph the facility, to determine what the physical conditions of the prison were.

Houchins rejected the request, and this led to a legal struggle for the media to gain access to the prison.[351] KQED asked Jones Waldo to represent them, and the case went all the way to the Supreme Court, and Dan, the lead attorney, included news reports from California television and radio stations about conditions in the jail, and a psychiatrist report that prisoners were suffering because of conditions. Dan claimed Houchins restricted access to the jail, because he was attempting to hide conditions there. With two abstentions, the Supreme Court voted 4/3 in favor of Houchins. The majority claimed the media have "no special right" to the jail greater than that accorded the general public, and they remanded the case back to the District Court.

Dan worked at Jones Waldo through most of the 1970s. That decade, especially in the late 1970s, the practice of law was changing. It was almost no longer a profession but had become a "billable-hour factory."[352] Prior to that time, Jones Waldo never billed by the hour. Joe Jones, Don Holbrook and others looked at the cases they had taken on and billed the client according to the value of the work the firm had performed. When Dan joined Jones Waldo, it was part of a small legal community with quality lawyers

---

[350] Christopher "Kit" Burton, "Interview at His Home in Salt Lake City," (June 4, 2019).

[351] Houchins v. KQED, Inc. 438 U.S 1 (1978)

[352] Burton, "Interview at His Home in Salt Lake City."

who knew each other. Everyone took for granted that they could be civil with one another, whether the case was large or small, and resolve issues in a professional manner.

Things were changing. The law firms were growing and taking on more and more clients. The tradition was that cases were usually settled out of court. Then lawyers began to see the financial benefits to them of taking a case to court. They became committed to a course of action that was not always in the best interests of their clients.[353] Such developments were especially difficult for Dan Stewart. Everyone was working until late in the evening, and nobody thought of the toll it was taking on Dan. His work at Jones Waldo had worn him out. He was exhausted, and he knew he had to chart a different professional course. Dan recognized that he was a great burden on his family and friends. Elizabeth would never admit that caring for Dan was a burden:

"I loved him. Nothing you do for someone you love is a burden."[354] That is true in an abstract way, but the family members faced the daily tasks of life with a "man of the house" not able to handle chores that typically fell on the man's shoulders. He was constantly making requests of family members.

"Please get my briefcase."

"Where is my lunch? "

"Turn the water off."

"Could you turn that lamp on?"

"I need a pen."

"Could you turn the temperature down a bit?"

The requests go on and on.

"Empty the waste basket."

"Open the window." [355]

There had been an occasional sense of relief. One of the incentives of the family moving to Millicent Drive was because it had an unfinished basement.

---

[353] Alan Sullivan, "Interview in His Salt Lake City Law Office," (June 6, 2019).

[354] Stewart, "Interview at the Home of Shannon Stewart Clark in Newport Beach, California."

[355] Clark, "Handwritten Note to Val Rust."

Dan and Elizabeth hired dayworkers to finish a couple of rooms and create an outside basement entryway. They found renters who would be willing to care for the house, the large front and back yards, which required trimming, weeding, cutting grass, watering, etc. The renter would also fix the drain when they became clogged, replace the burned-out light fuses, and get the water heater replaced when it went out.

Once a week, the renter would take the garbage cans to the street, and every day would bring in the mail. He would regularly wash the many windows and occasionally vacuum the floor. The winters were particularly difficult. Stark, cold winds would flow down Emigration Canyon, dropping sleet and snow on the hillside where Millicent Drive was located. The renter would keep the sidewalk and driveway clear, so that Dan could navigate himself to the car without fear of slipping or sliding. Even so, at times during the winter, the falling snow drew a veil over the neighborhood, making it impossible to keep the driveway completely clear.[356]

The daily burden of dressing was a tremendous burden. Every morning, the Stewart family members got themselves dressed, made their beds, prepared and ate breakfast. Then they waited, waited, waited for Dan to get himself ready, so the day could move forward. He would consume more than two hours every morning washing, grooming, and dressing himself. The slightest setback represented another half hour delay. After rehabilitation, he never had full use of his arms and hands, so each of his daily chores was an excruciating, almost futile, activity.

The early morning was when Dan could best care for himself; however, it was also when he was grumpy. This usually meant that family members would leave him to himself to do the things he could manage, so they would not have to be near him. He had little problem shaving because he had access to an electric shaver. He would usually brush his own teeth, although it was a major task to get the toothpaste onto the toothbrush. He would also comb his own hair by dropping his head so he could reach the crown of his skull with his brush. He always wore contact lenses, which he would put in by himself.

---

[356] Clark and Whitney, "Conversation with Val Rust at the Family Home on Millicent Drive in Salt Lake City."

After he finished doing all the individual tasks he could manage, the caretakers would step in. Dan never took a bath or shower. Elizabeth helped him bathe on his bed, using towels and wash clothes. Dan would wash what he could, but she would scrub the parts of his body that were difficult for him to reach.

Dan allowed Elizabeth to lay out the clothes he was to wear for the day, but he demanded that he dress himself. Both he and Elizabeth always dressed in their Sunday best. Such attire was not unusual in downtown Salt Lake City. Those working at Church headquarters always wore dresses and suits, as did missionaries and volunteers on Temple Square. Those attending Temple sessions were always in nice dresses and suits. And professionals working in the city center dressed in the same way. .

Dan's wife dressed formally. Hers was a conservative glamour featuring conventional formal wear, and quality suits and knee-length skirts. She always wore silk hose and heels, and only wore slacks while she cleaned or cooked at home. The fashion of the day was the "hippie look," but she rejected such attire. Neither did she wear miniskirts or evening dresses. She also chose not to stand out in the public arena. She did not wear pearl earrings, necklaces, hats, chunky high heels or fitted blazers.

Elizabeth was never invasive when it came to the things Dan wore, but she was always in the background while Dan dressed. In the late 1960s and 70s creative individuality was the fashion mode. There were few rules that dictated how a person should dress. Cheap synthetic clothing was flooding the market, and the casual anti-conformist look was prevalent. That period also allowed Dan to be who he was. He demanded of himself that he dress more formally than most.

Dan would usually begin dressing while lying on the bed and pulling his slacks over his useless feet and legs. Even when doing this on the bed, he had difficulty raising his middle body so he could pull his pants up to his waist. At times, he allowed Elizabeth to step in when the process became too exhausting. His belt had already been strung through the trouser loops, so he needed only to buckle it in place.

He would then put on his socks. They were always loose fitting enough that his biggest challenge was to get the toes into the top of the socks, then slip them over the heal and up the bottom of the leg. Dan could barely reach his feet, let alone wriggle them into the shoes. He always wore dress shoes that had laces. They required the ability to tighten and tie the laces. The process of pulling the laces tight required practice and ingenuity, but that was nothing compared with knotting them. Dan would fumble several times before he succeeded.

Dan always wore white dress shirts. He could usually get his arms into the sleeves without great difficulty but buttoning the front and the cuffs required patience and greater finger dexterity than he was usually able to muster. He selected and tied his own tie. Tying his tie, usually a half Windsor knot, required great practice and patience. Even experienced dressers often start over more than once, before they have the tie positioned just right., and the process demands thumb and finger dexterity of both hands. As the day progressed and Dan tired, others would take over certain chores. In the evening, when he needed to shave, brush his teeth, or comb his hair, someone was likely there to help him do the job.

Kit Burton, an associate at Jones Walden, observed that Dan's physical condition was rarely fully appreciated by those within the legal community. Even Kit, who worked closely with Dan, initially saw his impairment as a slightly objectionable obstacle in getting cases resolved. While trying to appreciate the good work that Dan was accomplishing, he admitted he sometimes felt a slight sense of resentment to work with someone who had a "disability" and was "handicapped."

This was before the time the world was as responsive to the needs of the disabled as it is today. The "Americans with Disabilities Act" prohibits discrimination based on disability in employment, but it was not passed in Congress until 1990. Even the Civil Rights Act of 1964, which focused on race, religion, sex, and national origin, did not mention the disabled. Few provisions for transportation were made.

Buildings were not constructed with the handicapped in mind. Public accommodations made no provision for the disabled. Listening devices were not yet available. And it wasn't as though America was worse than other countries. In England, for example, young children with disabilities were placed in residential schools out in the country. No matter how healthy fresh air was, the real purpose of these schools was to make the children invisible to the rest of the population.

It was left to the personal sensitivities and sensibilities of those associating with Dan to assist him in whatever way they could. In mid-life, after he had finished school and worked for several years, every morning, Elizabeth dropped Dan off at the law office, where he spent eight years, named Jones Waldo, and picked him up at the end of the day, and even returned him to the office, when he needed to work in the evenings.

Those in the office tended to accept her presence as a given, and occasionally they treated her like she was part of the office furniture. She set her work schedule in such a way that she was always available. Even though she possessed a PhD and a law degree, she never worked more than twenty hours a week, so that she could devote time to Dan. Her contribution was monumental.

Jones Waldo attempted to deal with some problems Dan faced. "They even installed a bathroom in his office." By the early 1990s, Dan was using an electric wheelchair. While it facilitated moving from one place to another, it was bulky and difficult to manage in tight spots. In the office, when Dan would shift from the wheelchair to a regular office chair, the maneuver was delicate. It took greater upper body strength than Dan could manage.

The process of shifting his body demanded that he plant his arms on the arms of the wheelchair, shift his body, thrusting it forward, and land on the cushioned seat of the office chair. Shifting from office chair to wheelchair was also problematic. The chair usually had no arms, so Dan was unable to lift himself into the wheelchair. Someone would have to make certain the wheelchair wheels were locked in place, so it would not slip away. Once in place at the table, Dan required someone to place legal pads, pencils, pens, and special documents in place before work could commence.

When Dan's legal team had an appointment in court, it would take several days to prepare for the event. They had to account for the parking spaces they would occupy. It was especially hard to get him to Federal court. "With the curbs in Salt Lake, there was a lot of tilting him back and wedging the chair over the curb."[357]

According to Kit Burton, they needed to identify all the steps, stairs, and doorways they would have to negotiate. "We had to have two attorneys help us get to court, if we had a brief bag." They always identified the marshal and asked him to help, "because we had to go up about twelve steps to get into the courthouse."[358]

Once in the building, they would identify the courtroom where they were scheduled to meet, and they sought to find any special obstacles they might encounter. They had to make sure the doors were not locked, the aisles were not blocked. and the chairs and tables were in place.

What was Dan's response to all of this? He accepted it with great equanimity. He even seemed to enjoy the circus being played out around him. Fortunately, after he got over his early morning grumbles, Dan was inclined to be quite cheerful. He always enjoyed a good laugh, and sometimes, when things got a little too chaotic, he would begin to chuckle at the absurdity of it all. At times he would laugh to the point that his weakened muscles no longer functioned. He lost his breath and even stopped breathing, so that someone would have to step in, pat him on the back to get him breathing again, and help him return to his normal cheerful self.[359] With his subtle wit, "there was always that smile, twinkle in his eye and perseverance, perseverance, perseverance."[360]

Kit's attitude toward Dan changed only after Dan had left Jones Waldo for the Utah Supreme Court. Kit married Betsy, and she soon had a baby. They discovered that the boy, named Nick, had suffered a stroke while he was in utero.

The stroke "left him deaf, dumb, and blind." His right brain did not function. In addition, he was having about 150 severe seizures a day. The new parents were in shock, then depression set in, when specialists informed

---

[357] Burton, "Interview at His Home in Salt Lake City."

[358] Ibid.

[359] Holbrook, "Interview at the Dan Stewart Family Home in Salt Lake City."

[360] Flynn, "Isaac Daniel Stewart: 1932-2005."

them that Nick would not survive. He would not live. In those days, nobody talked about kids who were severely disabled. There was certainly no cure for Nick's condition. Such a situation was usually a source of shame for the parents. For Kit and Betsy, depression quickly turned to resolve. They decided their condition would be otherwise. Betsy already knew, "Nick was the light of my life."

Kit and Betsy discovered there was a community of activists with disabled children, and they joined that group. They heard story after story of parents who had no place to turn but themselves. They were told that they had a small window of time. In the first years of life, the brain is malleable, but by the time the infant is six years old, "the brain is set and would not improve." The parents reasoned they could train the left brain to take over many of the functions of the right brain, and they created a strict daily schedule of loving activity and training.

Kit Burton's infant child opened a new world for his parents. Kit began to appreciate what Dan Stewart had been going through. Dan's problems were no longer just an inconvenience; they were a source of genuine empathy and understanding. This got Kit "up close and personal" regarding the decisions Dan was making every day of life. He began to understand that when Dan had informed him that he was thinking of leaving Jones Waldo, Kit acknowledged that Dan had no other option. He was worn out. The stress of life in a top legal firm was taking its toll. Kit could see it. It was increasingly difficult for Dan to synchronize his life with that of Jones Waldo. That life would have been hard for anyone, but for Dan it was suicide. He decided he must get away from that environment, or he would not survive.

PART IV:

Utah Supreme Court

12. Utah Supreme Court in Crisis

After deciding to leave Jones Waldo, Dan Stewart considered various future professional options; some negative choices were obvious. He would never go into politics, as had his friends and classmates, Jake Garn and Bob Bennett. Dan loved to study politics and history, but he refused to engage in political action. He had never even bothered to run for a school office.

Dan would never be a part of Mormon Church governance, as were his other classmate, Henry Eyring, and law professor, Dallin Oaks. The only time he had taken on church leadership positions was while in the mission field. Dan would never choose a life as editor and literary critic, as had another classmate, Gene England. Dan sought a contemplative life. It did not include getting mixed up in the stress of publishing.

So what was he to do? He believed God's framework for human progress and stability, was the law, and legal work was his primary professional qualification. His uncle, Paul Iverson, lived in Los Angeles, and had recently invited Dan to join his prominent law firm, *Iverson, Yoakum, Papiano, and Hatch,* located *in* the city's financial district. The firm was well established, and Paul Iverson was a member of Commission 21, and associated with Los Angeles leaders, such as Edwin Pauley, Dorothy Chandler, Franklyn Murphy, Armand Hammer, J. Paul Getty, and Robert Ahmanson, who were intent on creating a city arts center, a world-class university, distinguished museums, and a global trade center that would transform a provincial city into to a dominating social/cultural empire.[361] Iverson assured Dan that he would be sensitive to his physical and energy limitations, and he promised Dan that he would be a part of that transformation. But Dan asked himself why he should jump from one hot plate, Jones Waldo, onto another.

Dan decided he would stay in Salt Lake City, and work in the legal system, with something like the Utah Bar Association, or as a judge. Dan easily saw himself working in any one of the many courts in the state. If he could find the appropriate thing to do, no day would be too long, no winter too cold.

Then, in 1978, he received a call from the Utah Bar Recommendation Committee, asking if Dan would be willing to have them send his name to the Governor of Utah, who had the power to appoint him to the Utah Supreme Court. Dan was aware that such an appointment meant a two-thirds cut in his salary, but he quickly said "yes." The very next day, Governor Matheson announced that he was appointing Dan Stewart to replace Justice Albert H. Ellett, who was retiring. [362]

When the call came to Dan, Scott Matheson had already served as governor for two years, and he would remain at the State Capitol until 1985. Two years older than Dan, Matheson had attended East High School and had completed a political science degree at the University of Utah. Rather than attend the University of Utah Law School, Matheson chose to get his law degree from Stanford. Having been a classmate of Dan in high school, and a fellow student in college, Matheson knew Dan and was familiar with his career. As was Dan, he was a Democrat in a Republican state.

Utah was dominated by Mormons. Throughout their early history in the West, Mormons faced a difficult choice: Should they assimilate with Americans, or should they retain their uniqueness?[363] They had long claimed to

---

[361] E.g., Margaret Leslie Davis, *The Culture Broker: Franklyn D. Murphy and the Transformation of Los Angeles* (Berkeley, CA: University of California Press, 2007).

[362] Stewart, "A Life: Dictated to Richard G. Ellis."

[363] Eugene E. Campbell, "Pioneers and Patriotism; Conflicting Loyalties," in *New Views of*

be different, to be God's chosen people. The Mormon Church held to radical theological stances that set it apart, including its commitment to an eventual theocracy, its communitarian doctrines, and its distinctively gendered theology.[364]

From the beginning of their stay in the Rocky Mountains, Mormons had been persecuted. During the 1850s and early 1860s. Johnston's Army, of the United States government, had occupied Salt Lake City. In addition, polygamy in the church had inspired three major national congressional laws: they outlawed polygamy, jailed Mormon authorities, seized all church assets, and eventually dissolved the church. LDS leaders finally gave up polygamy, revised their state constitution, gave up their own political party (*The People's Party*), and accommodated their lives to the point that, in 1896, Utah was admitted into the United States as the forty-fifth state.[365]

As early as 1903, President Joseph F. Smith had proclaimed that the church "does not engage in politics; its members belong to the political parties at their pleasure."[366] And since the 1930s, the Mormon Church had officially insisted that it was politically neutral, and only entered the world of politics when "moral issues" were at stake.

When Dan was considering leaving Jones Waldo, two major moral controversies had drawn the church into play. First, in the 1970s, the Equal Rights Amendment (ERA) proposed changing the U.S. Constitution and guaranteeing equal rights for women. It had been approved by the House of Representatives and Senate, but it needed to be ratified by thirty-eight state legislatures. Wide bipartisan support was shown, and thirty-five states quickly ratified the ERA. Soon some conservative women began to oppose the ERA. In 1975, Barbara B. Smith, the President of the LDS Relief Society, gave a talk declaring that she and other faithful Mormons, should be against the ERA. Otherwise, women would be required to serve in the military and

Mormon History, ed. Davis Bitton and Maureen Ursenbach Beecher (Salt Lake City, Utah: University of Utah Press, 1987).

[364] Ethan R. Yorgason, *Transformation of the Mormon Culture Region* (Urbana, Illinois: University of Illinois Press, 2003).

[365] Matthew Bowman, *The Mormon People: The Making of an American Faith* (New York: Random House, 2012).

[366] Joseph F. Smith, "Congress and the Mormons," *Improvement Era* (1903).

become policemen, and they would be discouraged from being ordinary housewives.[367] Other Mormon Church leaders quickly fell in line.

A small group of LDS women in the Washington, D.C. area, including Sonja Johnson, Maida Rust Withers, and Hazel Davis Rigby formed a group they called "Mormons for ERA." Even though the church became critical of their movement, some people in Salt Lake City, like Dan, became emotional allies of the Washington group. The Dinner and Discussion (D&D) group that Dan belonged to, discussed the ERA, and sided with the stand "Mormons for ERA" were taking. Both Dan and his wife spoke out in favor of the Equal Rights Amendment.

The second "moral issue" at the time, was the 1973 *Roe v. Wade* decision, when the U.S. Supreme Court affirmed a woman's constitutional right to have an abortion.[368] While the church had long declared "human life is a sacred gift of God," it had allowed members to have an abortion in "exceptional circumstances," such as pregnancy from rape or incest, when the life of the mother was at stake, or when the fetus was known to have severe defects. That policy did not change, but the church spoke out as forcefully as it could, that "elective abortion" was not a choice among faithful Mormon women.[369] Dan's position was predictable. While not disallowing the church its policy, he vigorously supported the U.S. Supreme Court decision, simply because it was now the law of the land. The rule of law required that *Roe v. Wade* was to be honored and respected.

The ERA and *Roe v. Wade* were issues being played out in Washington, D.C., but the problems Governor Matheson faced had to do with the Utah State Legislature and the Utah Supreme Court. Both were in a state of crisis. Reflecting the shift of the church away from becoming too tied to national interests, both had moved strongly away from their allegiance to the national government and stressed Utah's rights and interests. From 1946 to 1978, all

---

[367] Drawn from: Barbara B. Smith, "Frequently Asked Questions About the Proposed Equal Rights Amendment: A Closer Look," *Ensign* March (1980).

[368] U.S. Supreme Court, "Rowe V. Wade, 410 U.S. 113," (Jan. 22, 1973).

[369] https://www.churchofjesuschrist.org/study/manual/gospel-topics/abortion?lang=eng

the nine justices appointed to the Utah Supreme Court, except Robert LeRoy Tuckett, who belonged to no church, were Mormons, so the Court reflected the church's shifting attitudes away from federal policies and practices.[370]

The Utah Supreme Court actively resisted federal meddling in local issues. In a 1974 decision, during the reign of Calvin Rampton as Governor, in *State v. Winkle,* the Utah Supreme Court declared that "the rights and liberties of the Constitution of Utah are equal to and in some instances superior" to those of the U.S. Constitution.[371] Justice Albert H. Ellett voiced constant critique of the federal government for "arrogating to themselves more and more of the powers not only not granted but expressly forbidden them."[372] His convictions were so strong that he allowed them to be expressed in court cases he wrote. For example, in *Dyett v. Turner* Ellett complained that the U.S. Supreme Court had so departed from the U.S. Constitution that "the federal courts have arrogated unto themselves the powers and duties which rightfully belong to the state courts."[373]

A year later, Grace Lichtenstein published an article in the *New York Times,* giving a scathing account of Utah Supreme Court rulings. She claimed they failed to uphold the First and the Fourteenth Amendments to the U.S. Constitution.[374] The First Amendment to the U.S. Constitution, including freedom of religion, speech, and the press, was not questioned in America at large. However, Lichtenstein pointed out that the Utah Supreme Court had ruled that the First Amendment does not apply to Utah but only to the federal government.

The major First Amendment issue the Utah justices focused on, according to Lichtenstein, was to support the Mormon Church's policy that there are limitations on freedom of speech. If a church member is acting in an official

[370] Stephen W. Julien, "The Utah Supreme Court and Its Justices," *Utah Historical Quarterly* 44, no. 3, Summer (1976).

[371] "State V. Winkle, 528 P.2d 467," ed. Supreme Court of Utah (1974).

[372] J. Alen Crockett, "Remembering Justice A.H. Ellett," *Utah Historical Quarterly* 61, no. 3, Summer (1993).

[373] Court, "Dyett V. Turner." Ellett later wrote an autobiography titled: *Forty-Four Years as a Redneck Judge.*

[374] Lichtenstein, "Utah's Conservative Court Is Center of Duspute over Rulings."

capacity, that person should not contradict the official policies of the church. Rank-and-file members were also admonished that they should not overstep the boundaries the church placed on them. Lichtenstein also noted that the Utah Supreme Court justices wanted to make certain their behavior as justices was protected. For example, litigants had threatened to sue Justice Henriod for libel, and he wanted to protect himself from a suit.[375]

The Fourteenth Amendment gave equal protection and rights to former slaves, but later to women, immigrants, and now LGBTQs.[376] Lichtenstein indicated that the Utah Supreme Court defied the Fourteenth Amendment by ruling that women could not receive unemployment insurance for the last three months of pregnancy and the first six months following delivery. The Court argued that pregnancy was a woman's destiny, and so she could not claim protection of her individual rights.

The early days of the Mormon Church had spawned a society of strong, independent women. The best men were often away on missions proclaiming the restoration of the gospel, while the wife stayed at home and kept the businesses humming, maintained the ranches, harvested the crops, cared for the households, and raised the children. This independence later manifested itself in women like Dan Stewart's mother, Orabelle. When her husband died, she did not look to Washington or Salt Lake City for assistance, but she took on the task of survival by herself. Since the 1930s, the church had a generous welfare program, but Orabelle knew that was for the poor and those unable to care for themselves and it was not for people like herself. Even so, Mormon theology placed restrictions on women. The man formally "presided" over the family, including wife and children. However, the women insisted that men were not to "dictate" to the wife and children.[377]

Lichtenstein pointed out that outside observers of the Utah Supreme Court were in shock about the two decisions she had noted, concerning the First and Fourteenth Amendments. She noted that Professor Edward B. Firmage, of the University of Utah law school, just shook his head and suggested

---

[375] Ibid.

[376] lesbian, gay, bisexual, transgender, and queer

[377] Yorgason, *Transformation of the Mormon Culture Region*.

these decisions "demonstrated ignorance of over half a century to United States Supreme Court case law." She noted that Professor John Flynn, also from the University of Utah law school, suggested the Court was "out of touch with reality."[378] Dan's former colleague in the law school, Professor Arlo van Alstyne, would even judge the state legislature to be far worse than the Utah Supreme Court.[379] When Judge Greg Orme was a student at George Washington University Law School, he heard professors regularly comment that the Utah Supreme Court was the "laughingstock" of state supreme courts, for its disregard for the fourteenth, fifteenth, and sixteenth amendments to the U.S. Constitution.[380]

The criticisms were often dismissed by the Utah Supreme Court justices, because their critics were usually located at the University of Utah, one of the state's "liberal" institutions, and widely perceived by Mormons "as a hotbed of resistance."[381] Vernon B. Romney, a Republican and the state's Attorney General from 1969-1977, told Lichtenstein, "I guess some of us wouldn't want to be thought of as dumb, but I don't think the fount of all wisdom resides in Washington, D.C."[382]

Romney was a devoted member of the church, having served as a missionary and belonging to the prominent Romney family.[383] He believed, as did most Mormons, that the U.S. Constitution was divinely inspired, but would one day "hang by a thread as fine as a silk fiber," and it would be saved by diligent members of the church, including politicians in Utah like himself. He took for granted that Washington D.C. was full of corrupt politicians, who conspired to take away Americans' freedom and liberty.[384]

---

[378] Lichtenstein, "Utah's Conservative Court Is Center of Duspute over Rulings."

[379] Aaron, "Interview at the College of Law, University of Utah, in Salt Lake City."

[380] Orme, "Interview at the Sheraton Park Motel in Park City, Utah ".

[381] Richard Poll, "Utah and the Mormons: A Symbiotic Relationship," in *New Views of Mormon History*, ed. Davis Bitton and Maureen Ursenbach Beecher (Salt Lake City, Utah: University of Utah Press, 1987).

[382] Lichtenstein, "Utah's Conservative Court Is Center of Duspute over Rulings."

[383] George Romney was his cousin.

[384] The quotation is attributed to Joseph Smith just before his death, in his so-called "White Horse" prophecy.

During the 1970s, such an opinion about Washington, D.C., was challenged by academic specialists of Utah's political and legal systems, who were candidly blunt about the sad situation in Utah's government. Dan Stewart maintained a special file of "idiot cases" from the Utah Supreme Court. This file surely included the time he was on the Supreme Court, and likely would have contained a 1981 case involving a Michael Prows, who was injured while on the job, and requested compensation from the State Industrial Committee.

It turns out that Prows regularly engaged in "horseplay," by flipping rubber bands at others, and even flipping a piece of wood with the rubber band, pretending it was a play sword. Of course, others reciprocated in these pranks. Eventually, Prows was injured in his right eye by a play sword, and he requested that he be compensated for being "injured, while on the job." The Utah Supreme Court agreed that he should receive compensation, claiming that a certain amount of horseplay is always a part of the work environment.[385] The Court's decision was enough to elicit letters to newspapers decrying the verdicts justices such as D. Frank Wilkins and Richard J. Maughan had recently made. Such decisions had included the reversal of the conviction of a Vietnamese refugee, who had detained a seventeen-year-old girl against her will and setting aside the death sentence of someone convicted of murder by his peers.[386]

There are reasons why the reputation of the Utah Supreme Court was so retrograde. For instance, its poor reputation involved compensation. The Supreme Court justices had the lowest salary of any other comparable court in the nation. And even more astonishing, their pay was about half that of most justices of the peace in Utah. Consequently, it was difficult to attract the best legal minds to the Supreme Court.

The reputation that salaries were terrible had extended to the East coast. When news of Dan's appointment was made public, a colleague in Washington,

---

[385] Utah Supreme Court, "Prows V. Industrial Commission of Utah 610 P.2d 1362," (1980).

[386] For example, Kennard Jensen, "Letter to the Editor: 'Raps Wilkins Decisions'," *Desered News* July 28, 1981.

D.C., sent congratulations to him telling him he was aware that he had been working at Jones Waldo and involved in antitrust issues. He then wrote: "I hope you have found it sufficiently financially rewarding so that you can afford the luxury of being a judge."[387]

The reason for such low compensation can be traced, in part, back to the early period of government in Utah, which was controlled by the church. There is a Mormon tradition that people serve, without compensation, in whatever capacity the church feels is necessary. There is no professional clergy, and every worthy member is expected respond to a "call" to serve in some compacity. Consequently, concert pianists willingly play the organ in church services. Lawyers will do the legal work, without compensation, necessary to buy property for the church and build houses of worship. On Sunday, young girls will tend little children in the nursery.

In the early days of Utah, there was little separation between the spiritual and the temporal. When the saints migrated to the Great Basin to establish Zion, they set up their own court system, with its own "technical pleadings, rules of evidence, and pettifogging lawyers."[388] It was taken for granted that citizens would serve as judges, lawyers, and jurists with little or no compensation. Even with the establishment of territorial courts, they only served non-Mormons, while members of the church relied on church courts to settle differences. A vestige of that court system still exists in the church, but it now deals with membership issues, such as disfellowships and excommunications.

The tradition of serving without compensation also carried over to retirement pay. The retirement payments to the Utah Supreme Court justices were meager, close to being non-existent. Consequently, the judges refused to retire until long after their competence began to flag. In the 1970s, three of the justices were over 70 years old. Justice Ellett told a curious visitor, "If you're here to tell us we're a bunch of conservative old fogies, you're

---

[387] Robert B. Hummel, "Personal Letter to Dan Stewart," (Nov. 9, 1978).

[388] Firmage and Mangrum, *Zion in the Courts.*

right."[389] He was well-known for never scheduling hearings or organizing committee meetings.[390] According to Magleby and Peterson, Justice Ellett had long expressed the following opinion: The United States Supreme Court had far overstepped its constitutional bounds and was fast eroding the sovereignty of the states.

In reaching this conclusion, he relied upon his belief that the Fourteenth Amendment to the Constitution should be considered unconstitutional, having been ratified illegally and under duress.[391] There were, of course, highly competent lawyers, who agreed with Ellett. Dallin H. Oaks, former Law Professor and then President of Brigham Young University, claimed recent U.S. Supreme Court decisions, by what was known as the "Warren Court," had set "unfortunate precedents" in the courts of the land.[392]

Fortunately, Justice Ellett was going to retire, and Dan Stewart was slated to replace him. Stewart would also face financial difficulty when he was on the bench. For example, the judges had only part-time clerks or university law students, who were prone to engage in "sloppy research" and produce "poorly written opinions."

James Lowrie, of Jones Waldo, was fond of citing an example of the lax attitude of Utah Supreme Court justices. Duke Wahlquist, a judge on the Second District Court, based in Ogden, Utah, was once asked to sit on a Utah Supreme Court panel by delegation, and he was assigned to write an opinion. He took the assignment seriously, and he wrote an analysis of the case and how the court had come to a reasoned decision. It was a complex issue and Wahlquist required more than thirty pages to do the analysis. He submitted it to the Utah Supreme Court and the next day Justice Allan Crockett, a man of extraordinary memory, brought it back to Wahlquist. He had edited it down to six or seven pages, and all the analysis and reasoning

---

[389] Lichtenstein, "Utah's Conservative Court Is Center of Duspute over Rulings."

[390] James B. Lee, "Interview in His Home in Salt Lake City," (June 6, 2019).

[391] James E. Magleby and John M. Peterson, *Justices of the Utah Supreme Court: 1896 - 1996* (Salt Lake City, Utah: Quality Press, Inc. , 1997).

[392] Dallin H. Oaks, "The Beginning and the End of a Lawyer," *BYU Law Digital Commons* 2 (12.15.2009).

had been stripped out. Judge Crockett insulted Wahlquist by explaining, "We do not have enough budget to print something that long."[393]

Another of Utah's quality problems had long been the selection process for Supreme Court justices. In choosing a justice, the governor was not accountable to anyone. Such discretion hearkens back to the time Brigham Young almost single handedly ran the local government. Until the 1980s, the governor selected whomever he wished for the Utah Supreme Court.[394] There had always been a nominating committee to ensure that multiple candidates were available. However, when the earlier committees forwarded their nominees to the governor, he had the freedom to decide who was to be named. For example, in 1951, Governor J. Bracken Lee appointed his former campaign manager, F. Henri Henriod, to the Utah Supreme Court.[395]

In 1984, five years after Stewart became a justice, a strict process of review was finally established and it was included in the Utah Constitution, effective July 1, 1985.[396] An Appellate Judicial Nominating Commission was established to select candidates to fill vacancies for the Utah Supreme Court. The Commission was charged to nominate between five and seven people. Once they were selected, the Commission was mandated to invite written comments. These comments were reviewed and forwarded, with additional comments, to the Governor, who had thirty days to select the final nominee, who was then subject to Utah Senate approval. Candidates had to meet certain qualifications, such as being a resident, able to practice law, and be thirty, but not more than seventy-five years of age.

The above process was part of a larger reform activity that began in 1973. Prior to that time there was no court system in the state. There were trial courts maintained in each of the twenty-nine counties. In addition, there

---

[393] James Lowrie, "E-Mail to Shannon Stewart.," (June 12, 2019).

[394] Lee, "Interview in His Home in Salt Lake City."

[395] Magleby and Peterson, *Justices of the Utah Supreme Court: 1896 -1996.*

[396]

http://judicialselection.com/judicial_selection/reform_efforts/formal_changes_since_inception.cfm?state=UT

was a state-wide independent juvenile court. Some municipalities operated their own city courts. In addition, some municipalities and counties ran their own Justice of the Peace courts. Finally, the Utah Supreme Court was an appellate court for this collection of courts. It was a mess, and in 1973, the state began a series of reforms that would eventually create a state court system comprised of two appellate courts (Supreme Court and Court of Appeals), trial courts including district and juvenile courts, as well as justice courts located in each of eight judicial districts.[397]

When Matheson had approached Dan about the possibility of joining the court, Dan had expressed appreciation and a desire to serve, but he explained he was aware of the Court's weaknesses and shortcomings. In addition, he worried that he and his family could not survive on the salary it paid. Governor Matheson told Dan he was appointing him, because Dan was the kind of person to help "restore the integrity and honor" of the Court. Governor Matheson was aware that, for many years, the Court had been moribund, and he was attempting to bring it to "modern times." The governor explained to Dan that his appointment was a first step in his desire to restore the integrity of the Utah Supreme Court.

At the time, that appointment was almost entirely in the hands of Governor Scott Matheson. Fortunately, Matheson took the selection process seriously, He promised Dan that he would take steps to increase the income and retirement pay justices received. Dan Stewart's appointment was likely the most important Matheson was to make in the two terms he served.

In 1978, Governor Matheson proclaimed that he was appointing Dan Stewart to the Utah Supreme Court. In the formal announcement, the governor said he had "long been impressed with Mr. Stewart's background in constitutional law and civil procedures, as well as his strong academic record at the University of Utah."[398] Two days later, the *Salt Lake Tribune* wrote that Dan was an "ideal choice."[399]

---

[397] Cheryll L. May, *Utah Judicial Council History* (Salt Lake City, Utah: Utah Judicial Council, March, 1998).

[398] "S.L. Lawyer Named to Utah Top Court," *Deseret News,* Nov. 4, 1978.

[399] "An Ideal Choice," *Salt Lake Tribune* Nov. 6, 1978.

At the turn of the century, the *Salt Lake Tribune* would exclaim that "the appointment of justice Stewart to the Utah Supreme Court was a turning point for the court itself."[400] In 1981, Dallin H. Oaks was also appointed. Oaks believed he was appointed because he could more easily influence the "conservative" legislature to act on needed changes in the court system.[401] A year after Oaks appointment, Christine Durham would become the first woman Justice. Finally, two years later Michael Zimmerman would be appointed. Quickly, one of the worst state Supreme Courts would become one of the best.

---

[400] "A Great Jurist," *Salt Lake Tribune* May 2, 2000.

[401] Dallin H. Oaks, "Interview in the Church Office Building in Salt Lake City," (June 15, 2021).

13. THE TRANSFORMATION BEGINS

On the morning of Jan. 8, 1979, Dan Stewart and his family arrived early at the Utah State Capitol Building. An imposing structure, designed by German architect, Richard K. Kletting, and completed in 1916, the building served thereafter as the center of Utah's government. It is more opulent than most, having many granite columns, a high central rotunda, and about seventy long steps leading up the front of the building. The day was significant for both Dan and the state. It signaled the beginning of a change of quality change of the Utah Supreme Court.[402]

Dan stood out in any crowd. As he sat in his wheelchair, in his Sunday-best dark suit, it was apparent he was on the sundown side of his forties. Eight wearing years at Jones Waldo had destroyed any sense of physicality, but he looked like a man born to take charge, to command. It was a cold winter morning. Governor Matheson explained to the audience of family, friends, justices, office staff, and reporters that he expected Justice Stewart "to give years of respected service to his native state and its legal profession."[403]

And Dan would exceed the governor's best expectations. This was the first day of the court's transformation. By the end of the century, many legal

---

[402] Randy Dryer, "Interview with the Author in His Law Office at the University of Utah," (Sept. 9, 2019).

[403] "New Utah Justice Takes Oath ", *Salt Lake Tribune* January 9, 1979.

scholars considered the 1980s and 1990s as the "golden period for the Utah Supreme Court."[404] Dan Stewart sat on the bench throughout the dramatic change in the court's quality and stature. He was there for twenty-one years, serving with nine other justices, one third of the court's entire historical membership.[405]

On that day, Dan toured the State Capitol with his family. They began at the central rotunda that reached more than 250 feet above the floor. Dan directed the small group to look at the paintings on the walls depicting various historical periods in Utah. The state could make an uncommon claim: the Governor, the State Legislature, and the Utah Supreme Court were all housed in one building. The Governor's office was located on the north side, the legislature on the south side, and the Supreme Court on the east end.

One could walk straight east from the rotunda to the stairs leading up to the doors of the courtroom on the second floor. Of course, Justice Stewart would take the elevator. His office, as well as the offices of the other justices, were along a corridor around the outside of the courtroom. His own office, and the workstations of his clerks, were directly behind the courtroom. The building is located high on Capitol Hill, so Stewart could look out his office window and see his beloved "Ute Stadium," right next to Foothill Drive, on the East side of town.

As was common in public buildings of that period, the courtroom was ill equipped to deal with someone in a wheelchair. For several weeks Dan Stewart was required to locate himself below the raised bench where the justices sat. Finally, the court wardens got around to installing a small lift so that Dan could take his rightful place on the bench.[406]

By law, there were five members of the Utah Supreme Court: three Justices, an Associate Chief Justice, and a Chief Justice. Each member served a ten-year term that could be renewed. The last two years of a term, that justice was automatically designated the Chief Justice, although Dan requested

[404] Ray Rivera, "Robe Warriors Shaped a Golden Era," ibid. Jan. 31, 2000.

[405] Blake, "Tribute: Justice I. Daniel Stewart."

[406] Shannon Stewart Clark, "Telephone Interview at Her Home in Corona Del Mar, Ca," (Sept. 18, 2020).

that he never serve that high position. As the head of the state court system and as the liaison in charge of communicating with other state court systems, it would have been necessary to travel far more than he could manage.

Though Dan Stewart had never appeared before the Utah Supreme Court as a lawyer, he was ideally suited to serve.[407] For three years, he had worked in Washington, D.C., preparing briefs for the U.S. Supreme Court. For five years, he had been a professor, specializing in the U.S. Constitution, and teaching constitutional law, civil procedure, evidence, contracts, and criminal law. And for eight years, he had worked in a private law firm, gaining experience from the vantage point of a trial lawyer. Justice Gordon R. Hall, who had joined the Court two years before Justice Stewart, said: "When Dan arrived, he fit right in, as if he belonged there."[408]

Dan later wrote: "I felt prepared for the position."[409] The Utah Supreme Court is an appellate institution. All cases coming to it originate in one of eight district courts in the state. Salt Lake County is in the Third District and is obviously the busiest of the eight. Once a district court ruled on a case, loosing lawyers had the right to appeal the decision to the Utah Supreme Court.

Each justice was responsible for every fifth case that came before the court. There was no bickering for this or that case. When it was Dan's turn, he got whatever came up. This meant that Dan sometimes knew more than the lawyers about the laws related to a case; at other times, he was relatively ignorant of the relevant laws, and these cases provided valuable learning experience.

When a case was assigned to Stewart, he had access to all the briefs, evidence, and arguments from the district court. He was also assigned two clerks, who researched each assigned case and prepared memoranda for him, explaining the merits of each side. Justice Stewart treated the clerks with respect and honor. According to one former clerk, David Gee, Stewart gave them freedom to write and argue in their own way and to draw their own

[407] Blake, "Tribute: Justice I. Daniel Stewart."

[408] Gordon R. Hall, "Interview at His Salt Lake City Home," (Sept. 9, 2019).

[409] Stewart, "A Life: Dictated to Richard G. Ellis."

conclusions. When Stewart asked them to prepare a draft of a section of the brief, they knew he would provide a thorough critique of their work.[410]

After reviewing all the drafts and documents related to an assigned case, Stewart would put together a formal lead opinion and circulate it to the other justices. Dan quickly demonstrated the ability to make quick, resolute decisions. Then he would attach an "action slip" to his brief, giving each justice the opportunity to concur or reject it. Any of the four other justices could indicate their disapproval, but if they did so, they were expected to provide a written dissenting opinion. Some of these written dissents were as long and detailed as the lead brief.

Every second, third, and fourth Monday, when the court was in session, the justices would gather in the courtroom and hear oral arguments for four to eight cases. Both the lawyers for and against the plaintiffs were given a brief time, stipulated by court rules, to argue their side of the case. The justices would listen to the arguments and pose their own questions.

According to one of his former colleagues at the University of Utah, Dan quickly set an example for other justices, and became known "for being carefully prepared for oral argument, asking tough questions, writing thorough opinions, and ensuring that civil liberties and basic fairness were respected and honored."[411] It was not legal knowledge of Justice Stewart that sent shudders through the hearts of lawyers he faced, but "his piercing questions and grim facial expressions" during oral arguments.[412] Ultimately, the justices would decide on the case. If three or more voted one way, that was the decision of the court. Usually, the decision was unanimous.

In any new job, there is a learning curve. Stewart's curve was very steep, suggesting that he quickly figured out how the system worked. From the beginning, Stewart took seriously the smallest, most insignificant case and demanded of himself that he give it his serious consideration. Stewart realized that he had almost no information about the people involved in cases, but he went out of his way to learn about them and their situations.

---

[410] Gee, "Telephone Interview at His Home in Seattle, Washington."

[411] Flynn, "Isaac Daniel Stewart: 1932-2005."

[412] Rivera, "Robe Warriors Shaped a Golden Era."

He would strive to be the best that he could be, and he quickly began helping transform the Utah Supreme Court into an institution that was the best that it could be.

Whereas those in the political world are known for their hollow political dodges, sparse and misleading answers to questions, even spoken and written deceptions, the documents of lawyers and judges contain extensive, thorough written accounts of cases. Lead opinions are often thirty, forty or even fifty pages long. In every court case there is a disappointed party and a winning party.

Even though Dan Stewart was eminently qualified to serve on the Utah Supreme Court, his life was not without flaws. His first Supreme Court clerk, Anne Stirba, once suggested that Stewart was "neatness challenged."[413] Such a label came from someone, who was always perfectly well groomed, even fastidious. She took it on herself regularly to clean up his desk. She recalled a time, when she was putting piles of papers and books into some order that she found a two-month-old paycheck; he was using it as a bookmark in one of the texts on his desk. Elizabeth, his wife, was forever trying, sometimes without success, to find and deposit his paychecks.[414]

As a youth, Stewart had been physically active, engaged daily in sports and competition, but as a young man he had been forced to redirect his life toward reading, contemplation, and reflection. His colleagues on the supreme court often identified him as continuing the competitive spirit he exhibited as a youngster, and they even observed he showed a tendency to be argumentative. He was known for using colorful and blunt language, and verbally confronting his opponent.[415]

The transformation taking place in the court went beyond the quality of the new justices. It also had to do with structural issues, such as improving the poor pay of justices, reorganizing a terrible retirement apparatus,

---

[413] She would eventually serve as a Third District Court judge.

[414] Rivera, "Robe Warriors Shaped a Golden Era."

[415] Richard C. Howe, "Memorial to I. Daniel Stewart Upon His Retirement," (Salt Lake City1999); Durham, "Interview by Liz Stewart in Christine's Home in Salt Lake City."

and constructing a legal system that had been so disjointed that it was really no system at all. Under Governor Matheson, some of these issues were being addressed. For example, during the four years Dalin Oaks served on the bench the salaries of justices were doubled.[416]

A major issue that worried Dan Stewart was the growing number of cases coming before the court. In 1916, the Utah Supreme Court had only 116 filings. By 1976, the number had risen to 556, and the following year it rose again to 634.[417] Dan's work style was such that he demanded time and energy to do the most thorough job he could. Even though he worked far into the night and on weekends, he recognized that his thoroughness was being compromised, and the load threatened to impair the quality of his arguments. Before he finished writing an opinion, another was waiting for him, demanding his full attention, exhausting his limited energy.

In the spring of 1979, shortly after he had joined in court, Dan was invited to speak to the Young Lawyers Section of the Utah Bar Association. He told them: "The court is facing a genuine crisis." Whereas, nationally, in 1977, state justices averaged taking the lead in only 31.1 cases a year, Utah Supreme Court justices averaged 67.4 opinions, more than twice as many as in other states. Dan declared that such an overload, "will soon impair the quality of our work, if it already hasn't done so."[418]

There were various ways to deal with the overload problem. For example, additional justices might be added to the Utah Supreme Court. That would reduce the number of lead opinions a single justice would write. That option was rejected by the Constitutional Revision Commission. A few months before Dan was appointed, the Commission decided to recommend a constitutional amendment that would change the wording of Article XIII, Section 9 of the Utah Constitution. It would allow the state to create an additional appellate court.

At the time, the Commission had already prepared four amendments that were scheduled to appear on the November 1980, ballot, and it declared

[416] Oaks, "Interview in the Church Office Building in Salt Lake City."

[417] Penny Pusey, "Appelate Court Measure Advances," *Deseret News* Sept. 8, 1979.

[418] "Tribunal Faces 'Critical' Load," *Salt Lake Tribune* May 10, 1979.

that yet another amendment would represent an election overload.[419] The Commission decided to delay placing the intermediate appellate issue on the ballot. In the meantime, Justice Stewart was required to deal with the overload the best way he could.

In the 1984 election the Utah Constitution was amended. It allowed the Commission to create a new court, known as the Utah Court of Appeals. In 1986, it would be incorporated into the state's judicial system. The Utah Court of Appeals is intermediate-level, and an adjunct to the Utah Supreme Court. The Court of Appeals finally began giving relief to Utah's highest court by hearing appellate cases dealing with civil matters such as divorce, child custody, visitation, adoption, paternity, and other matters. The Utah Supreme Court retained jurisdiction over appellate cases of first degree and capitol felony convictions from the district courts.

Another structural problem had to do with the difference between the Utah Legislature and the Utah Supreme Court. Justice Stewart reminded himself that the Utah Legislature has a different role than the courts. Common wisdom mandated that the legislature makes law, while the courts are expected to interpret the law. That is why there was a formal separation between the two branches of government.

That separation often extended into the informal arena. Karl Swan, a missionary friend, who served with Dan in Freiburg at the time he contracted polio, was for many years in the Legislature at the time Dan was on the Supreme Court. They limited their meetings to a cordial greeting in the elevator or the hallways of the Capitol Building.[420]

A problem Dan recognized was that some laws made by legislatures are often so abstract and vague that it becomes necessary for the Utah Supreme Court to legislate. For example, laws on discrimination might demand: "Thou shalt not discriminate." It is only when a case claiming discrimination comes before the court that it takes on the burden of clarifying the vague law.[421]

---

[419] Pusey, "Appelate Court Measure Advances."

[420] Swan, "Interview at His Home in Roy, Utah, ."

[421] Linda Greenhouse, "Sure Justices Legislate. They Have To," *New York Times* July 5, 1998.

Dan Stewart took for granted that, at times, when the law was not clear, the Utah Supreme Court had to legislate. For example, in *Maryboy v. Utah State Tax Commission*,[422] Mark Maryboy and his wife petitioned the Utah Supreme Court to overrule the decision of the Utah State Tax Commission to tax his earnings as a county commissioner, and Mrs. Maryboy's job at the San Juan Mental Health Clinic. The Maryboys lived on the Navajo Indian Reservation, and most of their work involved the Navajo Nation, which the Maryboys claimed excluded them from paying taxes to the State of Utah.

The law was unclear about what jurisdiction applied to them. Justice Stewart was compelled to make crucial decisions about the couple. He decided that even though Roselyn Maryboy worked for a county health office, almost all her work was with people on the reservation, and she had good reason to claim an exemption. The case of Mark Maryboy was quite different. He was a publicly elected official, and even though he worked mainly on the reservation, he was doing so as an official of the state. If the legislation had been clear, it would not have been necessary for the Utah Supreme Court to craft a legislative decision.

From the beginning of his tenure as a justice, Dan Stewart introduced innovative ways to solve the problems and resolve disputes that the court faced. Dan believed judges should not allow past decisions to dictate, without reflection, what they decided. He once wrote: "One doesn't get a decision by putting a quarter in the judicial dispensing machine and pulling the lever. We must evaluate each case in the context of present circumstances."[423]

Dan believed that justice is hammered out in the conflict of ideas, and the supreme court provided a good forum for discussion and argument. He recognized that, all too often, federal and state courts supported regressive tendencies, such as the 1896 *Plessy v. Ferguson* case,[424] which defended segregation laws for public facilities; or the 1944 case of *Korematsu v. United*

---

[422] Utah Supreme Court, "Maryboy V. Utah State Tax Commission, 904 P.2d 662 " (Sept. 14, 1995).

[423] "Tribunal Faces 'Critical' Load."

[424] *Plessy v. Ferguson* 163 U.. 537 (1896).

States,[425] which upheld the establishment of Japanese Americans in internment camps during World War II. He expected the court system "to operate fairly for those who are despised by society as much as those who are the most eminent in society."[426] He was concerned that the system did not always do a good job in serving the disenfranchised.

Justice Stewart advocated that the court would accomplish its mission by focusing its decisions on justice, the cornerstone of all legal action. Dan recognized that legal scholars have moved slowly in defining what justice is, and the concept has remained evasive; it is "a slippery and elusive concept."[427] If they strive to maintain "sensitivity and fairness," then occasionally "they may succeed in adding a new story to a temple of justice."[428]

Justice Stewart clearly put the human element into the practice of the law. He often struggled with the issue of wide human variation. There was also a tendency of justices to judge everyone by some precedent set by a previous court. Dan rejected this tradition in that he recognized that judges must exercise discretion. According to Stewart:

The strength of the law is based on, I think, the humane judgment of many judges who have tried to apply the law so that it makes sense in the lives of people. For example—insane people. The legislature has passed a law that has abolished the insanity defense. Off the record, I think it [the abolishment] is a terrible law. But when you can, you modify it in a responsible way to make sense.[429]

Justice Stewart always asked himself how the law could be applied in such a way that it gives a person a good and proper result, rather than seriously damaging a person's life. Dan's first case as a supreme court justice allowed him to put his perspective into practice. The facts of the case were

---

[425] *Korematsu v. United States,* 323 U.S. 214 (1944).

[426] Stephanie Machlis, "Interview with Daniel Stewart in Salt Lake City," (1999).

[427] I. Daniel Stewart, "The Legacy and Challenge of the Law," in *Commencement Address, University of Utah, College of Law* (May 24, 1980).

[428] Clark Lobb, "U. Law Graduates Hear Justice Tell of Challenges," *Salt Lake Tribune* June 19, 1986.

[429] Ellis, "Interview of Dan Stewart at His Home in Salt Lake City, ."

not in dispute. A woman was an apartment tenant of the plaintiff. She entered an arrangement to pay $135 a month but came on hard times and fell into arrears in the payments; the plaintiff served her an eviction notice. She was to leave the apartment within three days, or he would commence civil action against her.

On the surface, the case was straightforward and ought to have been supported by the Court. However, Justice Stewart found a sensible and humane solution for the woman, who claimed she had never received the eviction notice until civil action had been taken. The Utah Supreme Court ruled against the plaintiff, because he could not prove that the notice had been delivered to the woman.[430] Consequently, compassion for the "victim" won the day.

Seven days after his first case was heard, Justice Stewart's second case came before the Court. West Coast Recovery Services was practicing in Utah without procuring a certificate to do business in the State. The court unanimously agreed with Justice Stewart, that the state has the right to regulate individual businesses. West Coast Recovery Services could not practice in Utah, without procuring a certificate to practice.[431] Thereafter, Dan lost track of the cases coming to him, and they just kept coming.

He saw the Utah Constitution as a living document, in the same way that English is a living language. The meanings of words are ever changing, and the meanings of the words of the U.S. Constitution are evolving and demanding new and nuanced interpretations. Dan saw it as a legal record meant to be interpreted according to the changing values and demands of society, often brought about by technology and science. It was not static; its interpretation changed as society changed.

While most Mormons felt, as did Dallin H. Oaks, such "judicial activism has worked far-reaching mischief in the law,"[432] Dan often recalled the powerful evidence that social scientists had given in cases, such as the 1954, *Brown v. Board of Education of Topeka* landmark,[433] showing that the separation of

---

[430] Utah Supreme Court, "Sovereen V. Meadows, 595 P.2d, 852," (Apr. 11, 1979).

[431] "Horton V. Richards, 594 P2d 891 " (Apr. 18, 1979).

[432] "Sovereen V. Meadows, 595 P.2d, 852."

[433] 347 U.S. 483 (1954).

races denied Blacks equal protection before the law. In 1983, before the graduating class of Brigham Young University Law School, Dan reminded the graduates that the legal, political, and moral forces behind this 1954 decision were still operative. The graduates must stand on the shoulders of those who produced that work and move forward with their own moral imperatives.[434]

The *Salt Lake Tribune* was delighted to declare that Dan's early decisions were neither progressive nor conservative. He took cases as they came in deciding on their individual merits. The *Tribune* cited two cases. In the first, in 1979 the state of Utah faced an embarrassingly large surplus of revenues. The State Legislature, dominated by Republicans, passed a bill to return part of that surplus to taxpayers. That bill was challenged in the courts by the State Treasurer, Linn C Baker, a Democrat. Justice Stewart, reflecting the classical belief that money ultimately belonged to the individual who earned it, wrote a majority opinion upholding the wisdom of the Legislature in returning as much of the money as possible to the people.[435]

The *Tribune* cited a second case involved a "building permit." Most states allowed the state to rezone property, even after a builder has received a permit to build. Dan and three other justices voted in favor of the builder. In this case, Justice Stewart argued that the state is limited in its ability to regulate individual interests.[436]

Justice Stewart's court victories were neither greeted by cheering crowds nor wide acclaim.[437] There was no eloquent rhetoric or collective fever of outcome, although some lauded Justice Stewart for his magniloquence while on the bench. Announcement of court decisions were quiet, isolated events, usually not even given notice in the *Deseret News* or *Salt Lake Tribune*. They were exactly as Justice Stewart wished. He saw them as quietly raising the legal standard he was setting. Elizabeth Stewart, Dan's wife, did develop a

---

[434] Stewart, "The Legacy and Challenge of the Law."

[435] Dave Jonnson, "Utah Court Clears Way for Tax Rebate," *Salt Lake Tribune* Nov. 1, 1979.

[436] Kent Shearer, "Pragmatic Dogmatics," ibid.

[437] Sheila R. McCann, "Utah Supreme Court Not Always in the Spotlight, but Its Decisions Have Wide-Ranging Effect," ibid. Feb. 11, 1996.

tradition of collecting newspaper notices of Utah Supreme Court decisions, and actively discussing them at the dinner table. The daughters were active participants in these discussions.[438]

Dan was fortunate to have friends who were always there for him. Through the time he was on the Utah Supreme Court, several times a year, during lunchtime, Don Stringham would show up at the Capitol Building, carrying a sack containing sandwiches and drinks. He had recently purchased the McCune Mansion located on North State Street, less than two blocks down the hill from Dan's office. It was one of the elegant and historical buildings in the city, filled with glittering silver faucets in the bathrooms, dark hardwood panels, and plush carpets, but Don had turned it into an office building to house his law firm.

The two men would escape the Capitol Building and settle on a small plot of grass, under a Green Ash or Sycamore tree on the capitol grounds. There Don would fill him in on who won the latest tennis match at Wimbledon, or whether the Giants or Dodgers took the latest baseball series, and what the impending football season looked like. They let their hair down and spoke as buddies discussing the latest gossip regarding who would replace the recently deceased N. Elden Tanner as an apostle, or local news items.[439]

The Utah Constitution required that all judges in Utah run for retention election at each general election. Article VIII, Section 9 stipulated that, after being elected, the Supreme Court judge would not have to run again for ten years. Judges running for election were non-partisan, suggesting that they not align themselves with a political party, and act in an even-handed, unbiased manner. In Dan's case, he was required to run for retention election within months after his appointment.

The election process allowed other candidates to run for that office. Stewart's predecessor on the bench, Albert H. Ellett, had tried to set himself up for a lucrative consultantship after he retired, but his Utah Supreme Court

---

[438] Clark, "Telephone Interview at Her Home in Corona Del Mar, Ca."

[439] Stringham, "Interview at His Home in Salt Lake City ".

colleagues would have nothing to do with that move. Besides that, Ellett was a strong conservative and he resented Dan Stewart taking his place, so he talked Earl Smith Spafford into running against Stewart.[440]

Earl was the son of Belle Spafford, who, from 1945 to 1974, had served as the LDS Relief Society President. Earl Smith Spafford set in motion a campaign to replace Justice Stewart. His campaign stressed that he was a public, religious figure, active in the church. His mother sent mailers on Relief Society stationery, telling people her son had served a mission to England, was a Navy Medical Corpsman, and she connected his name to church activities, such as the Boy Scouts, and the LDS Indian Placement Program.[441]

Smith's campaign placed Dan Stewart at a disadvantage. He had never engaged in personal political activity, and he detested turning the Supreme Court appointment into a political process. Dan Stewart initially refused to allow his name to be used as part of some public political spectacle. In 1980, he would say: "One of the most important points of the judicial process is that we be assured judges are impartial, neutral and beholden to no group of persons or interest group."[442]

The Utah Bar Association quickly responded. The lawyers of Utah were strongly in favor of retaining Dan Stewart as a justice; they considered his appointment a significant professional upgrade in the Utah Supreme Court. A delegation of the Bar approached Dan with the proposal that they form an election committee and run his campaign. Dan told them he was disturbed that there was active politicking, that he be expected to raise campaign money, debate with opponents, and put ads in newspapers and on television. The delegation assured him that he would remain outside the process. They would run the campaign, and would appoint a young lawyer, recently out of the University of Utah Law School, Randy Dryer, to chair the election committee.

During the campaign, Dryer never met with Dan. For his part, Dan said, "I knew who the chairman of my campaign was, but that was about all. I really do not know who contributed to my campaign. I was able to insulate

---

[440] Stewart, "A Life: Dictated to Richard G. Ellis."

[441] Clark, "Interview at Her Home in Corona Del Mar, California."

[442] "Justice Stewart Favors Yes-No," *Deseret News* Nov. 24, 1980.

myself to the extent possible."[443] Dryer found it rather easy, among lawyers, to raise money and obtain endorsements. The committee did not solicit support from corporate donors.

Their ads were tasteful and positive, stressing Dan's character and stature. The committee also published long lists of names of lawyers, who endorsed Dan. One ad appearing in the *Salt Lake Tribune*, gave the headline: "Vote for Competence." It stressed that 75.46% of the Utah Bar Association members supported Dan Stewart.[444] In fairness, Spafford's campaign was also measured, although he claimed he was running for the court because "It is far too liberal."[445]

The election gave Dan 244,000 votes as opposed to 193,000 for Earl Smith Spafford. The election committee that supported Dan felt the outcome was close, even though Dan garnered fifty-six percent of the vote. They were impressed that Dan won twenty-seven of the twenty-nine counties, and he lost Daggett County by a mere five votes.[446] In other words, Dan won in both rural and urban Utah. The victory celebration was low-key. There was no victory party.

The quality transformation of the Utah Supreme Court, that began with Dan's appointment, was well-grounded and moving forward. Ten years later, by law, he was again required to participate in another retention election. That time, eighty-six percent of the voters supported him, as high as any election outcome in recent memory.[447]

---

[443] Ibid.

[444] "Ad: Vote for Competence," *Salt Lake Tribune* Nov. 3, 1979.

[445] "Candidates Provide Positions, Ideas Prior to Election Day: Earl S. Spafford," *Price Sun Advocate* Oct. 29, 1980.

[446] Dryer, "Interview with the Author in His Law Office at the University of Utah."

[447] I. Daniel Stewart, "My Personal Journal " (Salt Lake City Undated). Jan. 2, 1989.

14. MATHESON'S LEGACY

From 1979 through 1984, Governor Scott Matheson made five appointments to the Utah Supreme Court. All of these were remarkable and defined Matheson's legacy. The 1984 members of the bench remained for at least another decade. This allowed the Court to solidify its stature and for the justices to become recognized as competent jurists and loyal Americans.

I. Daniel Stewart was the first major Matheson appointment. From the beginning, he had a clear perception of who he was. Occasionally, he reflected on his life, and he knew it had been fulfilled beyond his wildest dreams, at least after the period he was attempting to rehabilitate from polio. He had a wife, who loved him with all her heart. He had two daughters, who were beautiful, well behaved, and smart. He was a recognized and respected legal expert, who held an honorable position in society. Events in Dan's life had made him into a solitary figure, for the most part, with his own thoughts and designs. He seldom rested or took breaks. His stooped shoulders seemed ill fitted for sitting at his desk, thumbing through papers and books. However, his face indicated a contentment, a joy, as he labored with his tasks.

Justice Stewart knew there were restraints on his life. He must refrain from fraternizing with members of the other branches of Utah government. He would not cultivate close social relations with other justices. He was a member of the cultural elite of Utah and would smoothly mix with other elites, while interacting comfortably with all the people. He would dress conservatively. Dan had a confident and sure demeanor, wearing, as always, his dark suit, white shirt and tie. His was a lonely but dignified life.[448]

Within months after Dan joined the bench, Justice D. Frank Wilkins announced that he was retiring. Governor Matheson nominated Richard C. Howe to replace Wilkins. In some ways, that selection appeared to be unfortunate, in that it looked like Governor Matheson had made another "political appointment," much like so many in the previous decades. Howe was a staunch Republican from Murray, in south Salt Lake County. On two occasions, he had been a member of the Utah House of Representatives (1951-58 and 1969-72). He was then elected to the Utah State Senate (1972-78).

When Howe moved into his office at the state capitol, Justice Stewart sought him out, asking how he might help Howe settle in. They went on to establish a warm human relationship. Howe had a receding hairline and a friendly, bespectacled demeanor. He was pleasant and unassuming. The two men often talked and discussed issues of mutual concern. Even though there was political distance between them, Howe saw Justice Stewart as "always open-minded, affable, and willing to talk."[449] According to Howe, Stewart was a model legal scholar. When Justice Stewart was given a case, he would begin with a deliberate sense of objectivity and neutrality, but when he decided what his position would be, he became a forceful defender of the position he had adopted.[450]

Howe often chided Dan for loving to argue for his point of view. He claimed Dan would consistently give colleagues who differed from him, a "good fight." "I think he enjoys kind of a scrap. He has a competitive spirit in him." "Dan tended to treat his cases like an athletic contest. He gets right in there and goes toe to toe with you."[451]

---

[448] Clark, "Interview at Her Home in Corona Del Mar, California."

[449] Howe, "Memorial to I. Daniel Stewart Upon His Retirement."

[450] Ibid.

[451] Ibid.

It was a battle of words, objections, and challenges. And Dan could cut deep with razor-like jabs at the weaknesses of the other's argument. He was relentless, as if his opponent's defeat must be decisive and final.

Howe defied the "political appointment" label initially placed on him, and he distinguished himself as a major player in a transformed court. Toward the end of his career, Justice Howe spoke to the State Legislature. He emphasized the importance of building trust and support for the Utah Supreme Court and for the rule of law. "More than ever," Howe said, "our society needs the reassurance that comes with a reliable, fair judicial system grounded in the predictability of that rule of law."[452]

While Howe's appointment may have initially had political overtones, he recognized that the Supreme Court must be distinguished from politics. It had the charge of interpreting the Utah Constitution, within the framework of the U.S. Constitution and the laws of the land. Howe claimed the Utah Supreme Court justices must be guided by the law rather than contemporary political will.

The next three appointments Matheson made were politically varied and extraordinary in terms of quality and distinction. In 1981, when D. Frank Wilkins resigned his seat on the Utah Supreme Court, Scott Matheson invited Dallin H. Oaks to take his place. Oaks, a solid Republican, presented the fatherly presence of a scholar, having served for ten years as professor, acting dean, and associate dean at the University of Chicago Law School. He then served another ten years as President of Brigham Young University. While in Provo, Oaks oversaw the establishment of the J. Reuben Clark Law School, and he taught there in its early years.

Oaks was able to attract people of distinction to the law faculty, for instance, Carl S. Hawkins, from the University of Michigan, who was respected for "both his competence and personal integrity.[453] BYU's law school quickly rose in reputation and soon rivaled the University of Utah Law School. The *Deseret News* greeted Oaks' appointment with the accolade: "If

---

452 Angie Welling, "Howe Hails Gains by Utah Judiciary," *Deseret News* Jan. 25, 2002.

453 Brian Craig, *Latter Day Lawyers* (Kindle Direct Publishing, 2019). 85.

ever the man and the job were made for each other, that is certainly the case with the appointment of Dallin H. Oaks to the Utah Supreme Court."[454]

Despite deep ideological divisions between Oaks and Stewart regarding issues such as the civil rights movement, they held certain beliefs in common. They each possessed an impressive work ethic, which they applied to the cases they were assigned. Stewart and Oaks were both ardent defenders of the rule of U.S. law and the foundational significance of the U.S. Constitution.[455] However, they differed in the way they thought the U.S. Constitution ought to be interpreted. Oaks believed the U.S. Constitution was inspire of God,[456] while Stewart clearly stated: "The Constitution was not written by God."[457]

On the one hand, Oaks believed in "Originalism," or the claim that the Constitution be explained the way the founders wanted it to be. Consequently, it is sacrosanct and untouchable. On the other hand, Stewart held to the belief that the U.S. Constitution should be interpreted in the context of case law, history, legislative statutes, precedence, and practical considerations. It was not a perfect document but could be refined and perfected.

Both Stewart and Oaks were careful communicators, Oaks as a radio announcer,[458] and Stewart as a writer. Perhaps the best-known aspect of Stewart's written work has to do with revision and careful editing. In the days prior to the computer, every edit demanded a rewrite of a document, and his secretaries were not bashful about complaints about rewrites.

The two men also shared a desire to assist the "little guy." Both Stewart and Oaks lost their father when they were young boys. Oaks was seven years old when his dad died, and Stewart was twelve. Both families struggled to

---

[454] Dallin H. Oaks, "Thank You, Dr. Oaks," *Deseret News* Nov. 24-25, 1980.

[455] Dallin H. Oaks, "Law and Order — a Two Way Street," *Dialogue: A Journal of Mormon Thought* III, no. 4 (1968); Stewart, "The Rule of Law and the Dilemma of Minorities."

[456] Oaks even gave speeches in Mormon General Conference about it being inspired of God. See, for example, Oaks' speech at General Conference in the spring of 2021.

[457] I. Daniel Stewart, "The Framing of the Constitution," in *Monument Park Stake High Priest's Quorum* (Sept. 17, 1987).

[458] As an undergraduate student at BYU, Oaks announced local basketball games on a Provo radio station.

survive. While at the University of Chicago, Oaks took on an appeals case defending a poor Polish boy who had been convicted of armed robbery.

After consulting with the boy's family, Oaks took the case, even though he knew it was a "looser." First, he felt privileged to argue an appeals case in the Illinois Supreme Court, in the same building where Abraham Lincoln had argued at least 175 cases. Second, he felt honored to represent a working-class family with very few resources but much good will. After the trial, the convicted boy's brother came by Oaks' office to offer a token payment, which Oaks refused. Oaks asked the brother what he was now going to do with his money. The response was: "It means that my wife and I can use this money to buy a washer."[459]

Stewart took great interest in those less fortunate or who were unfairly treated in the economic and political system. We have examined elsewhere his efforts, while at Jones Waldo, to protect small egg producers in Utah and the endeavors of large dairy farmers to gang up on small independent dairy farms. They wished to force the small farmers out of business, so they could then set their own prices for milk products.[460]

The major characteristic Oaks and Stewart shared was they were both academics. Whereas almost all other previous justices were lawyers or politicians, these two were scholars, who thought abstractly and theoretically, rather than practically and politically. They were both interested in the sources of ideas and their intellectual consequences. Despite their political differences, their scholarly concerns brought them together. They spoke the same language and respected sound logic and reasoning.[461] In spite of their political differences, almost all the time, they agreed on the cases that came before the Utah Supreme Court.

In 1982, following the death of Justice Richard J. Maughan, Matheson appointed Christine M. Durham to the state's highest bench. Durham had a distinguished background. She was a native of California. Her mother had

---

[459] Craig, *Latter Day Lawyers.*

[460] See Chapter 12: Jones Waldo.

[461] Oaks, "Interview in the Church Office Building in Salt Lake City."

often visited Dan when her girl scout troop, including eleven-year-old Christine, visited *Rancho Los Amigos* in Downey. When Christine was a teenager, her adopted father worked for the Internal Revenue Service in Washington, D.C., and he later served as the Treasury *Attaché* in the French Embassy in Paris. Christine received a classical French secondary education and spoke fluent French.

Whereas the Utah Supreme Court members had traditionally consisted of practicing lawyers and politicians, Durham came at a time when two members, Stewart and Oaks, had the distinction of being academics. They were scholars who thought theoretically and abstractly, and Christine Durham felt comfortable with them, having received a classical education in Paris, and having attended Wellsley University and Boston College, as well as law school at Duke University. Early on in her career, she also established an academic identity. While her husband did his medical residency at the University of Utah, she taught at the BYU law school, and in the medical school at the University of Utah. Consequently, she was comfortable in the academic atmosphere that Stewart and Oaks had brought into the Utah Supreme Court. For her, the Utah Supreme Court was all "about the ideas and cases, not personalities and egos."[462]

Durham, gave the impression of a "confident, capable woman next door." As it happened, she was the wife of George Durham, who had grown up as Dan's neighbor on Butler Avenue. And she was a devoted mother of three children. Christine met George in Boston, where she was attending Wellesley College, and he was in medical school. She recalled that one of the first things George mentioned to her was the story of Dan Stewart. He remembered Dan as an incredible athlete and scholar, almost larger than life. This gave Christine a mixed impression of Dan. On the one hand, George "absolutely idolized him."[463]

On the other hand, her mother had told her of Dan as an immobile, feeble adult in an iron lung. When she was appointed to the Supreme Court,

[462] Christine M. Durham, "Note to Dan Stewart at the Time of His Award at the University of Utah Sesquintennial Founders' Day Celebration " (Salt Lake City, UtahFeb. 28, 2000).

[463] "Address to the University of Utah Law School, Honoring Dan Stewart," (May 16, 2000).

she was aware that Dan was on the bench, and she wondered how her mixed impression of him would turn out. In fact, she was surprised to discover that he was an able, intellectual giant, who loved to tell stories about what it was like growing up in Utah.[464]

Durham confessed to have been an aggressive professional climber, having applied to be on the Utah Supreme Court at the time D. Frank Wilkins retired. Even though she did not receive that appointment, members of the Nominating Commission encouraged her to keep applying.[465]

Durham became the first woman appointed to the Utah Supreme Court. Four years earlier, Matheson had appointed her to a judgeship at the Third District Court. That appointment also marked the first time a woman sat on the bench of a Utah district court. Most of the flack she received over getting a female appointment came at the district level. There she did not find a collegial atmosphere, and she was even told by one critical judge that he never thought he would see the day a woman would sit on the bench.[466] But, by the time of her Supreme Court appointment, the reality of a female judge had generally been accepted. She was grateful to be on the Utah Supreme Court.[467]

We have noted that Richard C. Howe, a Republican, saw Dan as an intimidating opponent on the bench, at least when they were on opposite sides of issues. Christine M. Durham was on the other side of the political spectrum from Howe, but she agreed that Dan was a "formidable adversary." When she opposed Dan, she recognized that she always needed "to be well prepared." She claimed his mind was so agile that she knew he would have thought any issue through and was prepared to confront her with difficult questions.[468]

When Justice Durham joined the Supreme Court, her relationship with Dan and the others on the bench was a little strained. She felt like she was

---

[464] Ibid.

[465] Christine M. Durham, "Women Trailblazers in the Law: ," (https://abawtp.law.stanford.edu/exhibits/show/christine-m-durham, June 1 to Oct. 20, 2009).

[466] Ibid.

[467] Christine M. Durham, "Interview at Her Salt Lake City Home " (June 16, 2021).

[468] "Address to the University of Utah Law School, Honoring Dan Stewart."

an "outsider," as well as "a person without power,"[469] Because Dallin Oaks had recently been appointed, she bonded with him as someone relatively new to the bench. He made a habit of giving her advice about how to succeed. She recalled that the best advice he gave her was: "Whatever you do, don't get behind."[470]

She eventually formed a relationship of trust with justices like Daniel Stewart, and she came to regard them as "a little bit like a family." And in families you have disagreements and see things from different vantage points, but you remain bound together as family members.[471] Christine Durham learned Dan Stewart turned out to be, not only a heroic legend, but a warm and generous colleague.[472]

Unfortunately, in 1984, after serving less than four years, Dallin Oaks stepped down from the Court. He had been called to be a member of the Quorum of the Twelve Apostles of the Church of Jesus Christ of Latter-day Saints. Matheson replaced Oaks with another outstanding young lawyer, Michael D. Zimmerman, who had been serving as a special counsel for the governor. Zimmerman had a thick head of dark hair and a well-trimmed beard. He was born in Chicago into a Presbyterian family.[473] His family moved west, where Michael attended the University of Arizona, Arizona State University, and the University of Utah.

Dan Stewart and Michael Zimmerman shared much in common. Both had graduated from the University of Utah Law School, edited its *Law Review*, and served for five or six years as a professor of law at the University of Utah. Just as Stewart's professors had said he was the best student they had worked with, Stewart maintained that Zimmerman was his best student in the five years he served as a professor.[474]

---

[469] "Women Trailblazers in the Law: ."

[470] "Interview at Her Salt Lake City Home ".

[471] "Address to the University of Utah Law School, Honoring Dan Stewart."

[472] Ibid.

[473] https://en.wikipedia.org/wiki/Michael_Zimmerman_(jurist)

[474] Rivera, "Robe Warriors Shaped a Golden Era."

Consequently, Zimmerman fit the mold of a retooled Utah Supreme Court. He was a scholar more than a practitioner. He loved to reflect and theorize, and his decisions on the Supreme Court moved left or right, depending on the issue. He became the fourth member of the Utah Supreme Court, who replaced the old, tired politically oriented justices of the past.

Both Stewart and Zimmerman were exercise freaks. Dan was constantly lifting light weights as he read briefs, while Zimmerman spent considerable time on his exercise bicycle. Such regimes resulted in appeals by both for colleagues to write clear briefs that could be understood with reading while exercising.

Both Stewart and Zimmerman were active in community affairs. Governor Matheson appointed Stewart to serve on the Utah State Board of Oil, Gas, and Mining, where he had confronted Kennecott Corporation over their failure to engage seriously in environmental management issues. He was also appointed to the Interstate Oil Commission Executive Committee, which met in various states.[475] He also took time to work with the ACLU; however, as a justice his physical limitations prevented him from contributing more extensively to community affairs.

In contrast, Zimmerman was deeply involved. Shortly after he was appointed to the bench, Zimmerman was selected to serve on the Federal Civil Rules Advisory Committee, where he remained for six years. In 1986, he began a long service on the Utah Judicial Council. In addition, he was active in the arts, serving on the board of the Ririe-Woodbury Dance Company and the Snowbird Institute for the Arts and Humanities. He also served for many years as a trustee of Roland Hall/St. Marks School.[476]

When Zimmerman was fifty, his first wife died of cancer. At about the same time, he converted to Zen Buddhism. He practiced meditation at the Kanzeon Zen Center and began to teach Zen Buddhism. He was the recipient of the "Excellence in Ethics Award" at Utah Valley University. His second wife, Diane Musho Hamilton, was a prominent, award-winning mediator and a teacher of integral spirituality.[477]

---

[475] Stewart, "A Life: Dictated to Richard G. Ellis."

[476] Magleby and Peterson, *Justices of the Utah Supreme Court: 1896 -1996.*

[477] Michael Zimmerman, "Interview in His Salt Lake City Home " (June 16, 2021).

From 1984 until 1994, the composition of the Supreme Court remained unchanged. Court watchers tend to characterize justices with political labels. They often describe them as "liberals" or "conservatives" or on the "right" or the "left." Greg Orme, an astute observer of the Court, was one of the original 1986 appointees to the Utah Court of Appeals. Orme said, "What you had on the Utah Supreme Court in 1985 were Christine Durham and Michael Zimmerman, who pushed a 'left' agenda. On the 'right' were Gordon Hall and Richard Howe. And Daniel Stewart was the swing vote."[478] There were some observers, who cast Stewart and Durham as justices who formed a liberal coalition.[479] Even then, it was clear that Stewart was an independent justice, who did not join with another justice simply because the two shared certain common values.

Such political characterizations might be useful for the media, but it obscures the most obvious tendency of the Utah Supreme Court in that day. Almost all its decisions were unanimous and consensual. In 1985, for example, of the 189 decisions recorded by *Justia*,[480] more than one fifth of all decisions were *per curium*, or were unanimous opinions made by the court acting collectively, with no one judge taking responsibility for the argument and action of the court. And of the remaining 150 cases, 123 were ultimately decided by a consensus decision. At least three concurring judges were required to obtain a majority decision. Richard Howe concurred with the majority an astounding ninety-four percent of the time; Hall and Stewart, ninety-three percent; Durham, ninety-two percent; and Zimmerman, eighty-seven percent.

The Utah Supreme Court acted as a unified body during the late eighties and early nineties. The critical question was whether the full Court was moving in a certain direction. For example, did the Utah Supreme Court align itself with federal constitutional law, or were its rulings only consistent with the Utah Constitution? In this regard, in the 1950s, 60s and 70s, members of the Utah Supreme Court claimed Utah was accountable only to the Utah Constitution.

---

[478] Orme, "Interview at the Sheraton Park Motel in Park City, Utah ".

[479] Rivera, "Robe Warriors Shaped a Golden Era."

[480] The website specializing in legal information retrieval.

Justices of that period even expressed open hostility toward the federal government and the U.S. Constitution. After Matheson began appointing legal scholars to the Court, these judges demanded that their decisions fall within the framework of the U.S. Constitution. Consequently, their attitude was much like the attitude of justices during the first half century of Utah statehood, who had relied on the U.S. Constitution; however, these early justices saw the federal government as "schoolmasters" helping those in Utah learn how to live within the American Union.[481]

In the 1980s and 90s, the Utah Supreme Court justices always formally worked within the framework of the Utah Constitution. Dan Stewart and Christine Durham strongly advocated independently analyzing the Utah Constitution, then if problems arose, they would reconcile their analysis with the U.S. Constitution.[482] From the beginning of his tenure as a justice, Dan Stewart consistently demanded that the Court decisions be based on the Utah Constitution. In a 1985 case, Berry v. Beech Aircraft.[483] Dan was the lead justice. He wrote a complicated and detailed twenty-three-page brief, citing no less than seventy court cases. In the brief, Justice Stewart gave great credence to the Utah Constitution and to common law.

The facts of Berry v. Beech Aircraft were not disputed. Alan Berry died in an airplane accident, and his wife sued the manufacturer, Beech Aircraft Corporation and the owner, Hercules Flyers, Inc. One of the Hercules employees, the pilot, also died at the time of the crash. At the district level, the court ruled that the manufacturer and owner were not liable, because the statutes of limitations had been exceeded.

Justice Stewart argued that the lower court decision be overruled and that statutes of limitations rulings were arbitrary and without merit. He demonstrated how the statutes of limitations violated the "Open Courts" Clause

---

[481] Thomas G. Alexander, "Utah's Constitution: A Reflection of the Territorial Experience," *Utah Historical Quarterly* 64, no. 3, Summer (1996).

[482] Katharine Biele, "Utah Supreme Court '96," *The Intermountain Commercial Record* 40, no. 5 (Jan. 31, 1997).

[483] Utah Supreme Court, "Berry by and through Berry V. Beech Aircraft 717 P.2d 670 " (1985).

of the Utah Constitution.[484] The Open Courts Clause mandated that all courts in the state be open, and an injury done to anyone "in his person, property, or reputation, shall have remedy by due course of law."

In other words, the section prevented the judicial system from closing the doors of its courts to any person, who had a legal right to its services. There is no such provision in the U.S. Constitution, and Justice Stewart forcefully demonstrated how the Utah Constitution can be instructive to other state constitutions, and even to the U.S. Constitution. In fact, after the *Berry v. Beech Aircraft* case, the "Open Court" clause of the Utah Constitution that Justice Stewart discussed was broadly cited, as were other sections and articles of the Utah Constitution,[485] and Governor Matheson's legacy had been secured.

---

[484] Article I, Section 11.

[485] These included the Due Process Clause of Article 1, section 7; the Equal Protection Provision of Article 1 section 24; and the prohibition against abrogation of wrongful death action in Article 16, section 5.

PART V:

The Justice and his Pen

15. U.S. Constitution

Devout Mormons believe that the U.S. Constitution was inspired by God and is "true."[486] Dan Stewart's colleagues on the Utah Supreme Court, almost all of whom were Mormons, took for granted that Dan believed the U.S. Constitution was "divinely inspired."[487] This is not the only time a people believed their constitution was given by God. The Japanese believed their 1889 constitution was, "heaven descended, divine, and sacred."[488]

It confirmed that the emperor was a living God. Early Americans believed their document to be so perfect that the procedure to change it was terribly difficult. It required two-thirds of both houses of congress, and three fourths of the legislatures of the various states of the union.[489] Consequently, almost no changes have been made to the original document. Dan's colleague on the Court, Michael Zimmerman, believes this is the greatest flaw in the document. We are unable to adjust it to conform with the requirements of today. Consequently, Zimmerman believes the U.S. Constitution is more a burden to us today than a helpmate.[490]

---

[486] *Doctrine and Covenants*, (Salt Lake City, Utah: Church of Jesus Christ of Latter-day Saints, 1969). 101: 77-80.

[487] Lockhart, "Interivew at His Home in Salt Lake City."

[488] Linda Colley, *The Gun, the Ship, and the Pen: Warfare, Constitutions, and the Making of the Modern World* (London: Profile Books, 2021).

[489] "Constitution of the United States," (Philadelphia, Penn.Sept. 17, 1787). Article V.

In 1987, Dan's Monument Park High Priest's Quorum invited him to address the issue related to the role of inspiration in framing the U.S. Constitution. He wrote a carefully crafted twelve-page paper addressing the issue, and he stated explicitly that "the Constitution was not written by God."[491] In other words, Mormons should not regard it as a document akin to the *Book of Mormon*, or the *Doctrine and Covenants*. Despite this, Dan examined how the Constitution was framed and the struggles the founding fathers went through. He finally concluded: "It is my belief that through all this, the Lord brought home to their minds in some fashion the nature and significance of the enterprise that they were about... ." Indeed, Dan Stewart often said that the U.S. Constitution was established by wise men whom God raised up to preserve the natural rights of man, create a system of checks and balances, and protect America's precious freedoms.[492]

In an interview late in 1999, Stewart said, "that the U.S. Constitution is the culmination of the entire Judeo-Christian tradition," and he never tired of searching out the origins of its various articles and amendments.[493] He found them in the Old and New Testaments, English common law, Roman law, and elsewhere. Indeed, he believed it was the "most remarkable constitution yet devised by the hand of man."[494]

In the spring of 1958, at the time Dan was testing the waters of the legal profession, he wrote a paper for Professor Wormuth's Public Law Seminar. In was a long thirty-six-page analysis concerning issues surrounding the U.S. Constitution and how it prohibits penalizing an individual from exercising a constitutional right. The seventy footnotes in the paper were all citations of court cases, indicating he was already, mentally, in law school, and in the paper Dan was beginning to test issues that were foundational for him in his

[490] Zimmerman, "Interview in His Salt Lake City Home ".

[491] Stewart, "The Framing of the Constitution."

[492] "Interview with Richard Ellis at Stewart's Home in Salt Lake City," (Salt Lake City, UtahDec. 8, 1999).

[493] Ibid.

[494] I. Daniel Stewart, "Speech Given at Swearing in of Admittees to the Utah State Bar," (Oct. 9, 1980).

later professional life, including free speech and the constitutional system on which our nation is constructed.[495] Then as a professor and instructor, Dan often said, "Constitutional Law remained my favorite subject."[496] Professor Stewart would take his students back with him as he expounded on one or another aspect of this profound document.

If there was a flaw in the U.S. Constitution, Dan Stewart believed it would be its ponderous, heavy language. He recognized it is not "an inspiring document," and he found it to be "very dull" to read. Even though its language didn't soar and motivate like the *Declaration of Independence*, Stewart recognized it to be a "living, vital document."[497]

Justice Stewart wrote precedent-setting opinions involving the U.S. Constitution. One had to do with the death penalty. In 1967, the U.S. Supreme Court ruled capital punishment to be unconstitutional, because it violates the Eighth Amendment, which protects citizens from "cruel and unusual punishments." Five years later, that same court struck down death penalties in thirty-five states, including Utah, sparing the lives of more than 600 inmates awaiting execution.

In 1976, after another five years, the Supreme Court reversed itself, ruling capital punishment to be constitutional.[498] Utah was the first state to resume executions. By the time Dan Stewart was appointed to the Utah Supreme Court in 1979, Gary Mark Gillmore had been executed, and Ogden Hi Fi murderers, Dale Pierre and William Andrews, had been sentenced to die.[499]

In 1982, Justice Stewart clarified the constitutional standard regarding the death penalty in Utah. In the early 1980s, Walter J. Wood was charged with robbing and murdering David Aasved. Shortly after midnight, on June 10, 1978, Joseph Johann and Wood were on Interstate Highway 80 in a

---

[495] "Unconstitutional Conditions."

[496] "A Life: Dictated to Richard G. Ellis."

[497] "The Framing of the Constitution."

[498] L. Kay Gillespie, *The Unforgiven: Utah's Executed Men* (Salt Lake City, Utah: Signature Books, 1997).

[499] "Court Upholds Death Penalty," *St. George Daily Spectrum* Nov. 27, 1977.

rented automobile traveling from California to Salt Lake City. Johann was driving. East of Wendover, the two stopped and picked up David Aasved, a hitchhiker, who was carrying a container of gasoline back to his van, parked some seven miles farther east, where he had left his wife and children. Aasved sat in the rear of the automobile, and Wood sat in the passenger seat in front. As they drew near Aasved's van, Wood, who had been dozing and "was half asleep and half awake," abruptly turned around and, without speaking a word, shot Aasved four or five times in the chest. Johann and Wood traveled further on the Interstate, and after arriving at Knolls, Utah, they dragged Aasved's body off the side of the frontage road and left it. They then continued east on the freeway.

The fact that Wood shot the man multiple times was not in dispute, but Wood claimed there were mitigating factors. He did not have a criminal record. He had been drinking, and he claimed there was "organic brain deterioration from prolonged and extensive alcohol abuse."[500] And he had recently experienced blackouts. In weighing the aggravating factors of Wood's murder, without provocation, the district judge determined that the mitigating circumstances did not outweigh the aggravating circumstances. The judge sentenced Wood to die.

When Wood's lawyers appealed the case to the Utah Supreme Court, Daniel Stewart became the lead justice. While he found Wood's murder difficult to digest, he argued that the Utah State Legislature had created its own restrictions regarding the death penalty. When Utah legislators wrote the new capital punishment law, they adopted language borrowed from the so-called Furman death penalty case in the state of Georgia,[501] which stated that the death penalty should not be imposed in an arbitrary or capricious manner. And so, Utah had naively included a "reasonable doubt" standard in its legislation. That is, the death penalty was such a severe action that, if there was any doubt as to its appropriateness, the state must temper its decision to impose it. Justice Stewart argued that, in the case of Walter J. Wood,

---

[500] Utah Supreme Court, "State V. Wood, 648 P.2d 71," (May 13, 1982).

[501] U.S. Supreme Court, "Furman V. Georgia, 408, U.S. 238, 92 S. Ct.. 2726, 33 L. Ed. 2d 346 " (1972).

the mitigating circumstances were enough to cause doubt about inflicting capital punishment. There was growing evidence, for example, that heavy drinking caused Wood's erratic behavior, blackouts, and loss of memory.[502]

In addition, Stewart reminded his colleagues that "The Eighth Amendment requires that the state not act in disregard of the humanity of every individual, no matter how far that person may have fallen from the norms of civilized conduct."[503] Justice Stewart acknowledged that Utah once again "has the power to impose the death penalty for those who commit murder;" however, the Eighth Amendment requires "recognition of the fact that even among murderers there are those who are less culpable than others and that the death penalty is not appropriate in all cases."[504] Justice Stewart argued that Wood not be condemned to death even when he was guilty of a terrible and gruesome act. The entire bench agreed with the argument of Justice Stewart, and Mr. Wood was not executed, instead, he was committed to prison.

There are several instances, when Justice Stewart's Supreme Court opinions clarified the Sixth Amendment rights related to criminal prosecutions. In *State v. Holland*,[505] for example, James Holland appealed to the Utah Supreme Court that Holland's assigned counsel had not acted in his best interests. Justice Stewart, who wrote the court brief, determined that the assigned counsel had apparently decided that his client was guilty, and his conduct was such that he failed to carry out any semblance of loyalty to Holland. Justice Stewart stressed that the man's counsel had abandoned the adversarial relationship upon which the court system is based, to the detriment of both the court system and Holland.

Stewart recognized that his stated position might be interpreted to mean it was the task of counsel to do whatever is necessary to get the client off, so he clarified in his brief where he stood and what he meant. In one of the few

---

[502] A contemporary book gives a summary of issues related with drinking. See Malcolm Gladwell, *Talking to Strangers* (New York City: Little, Brown and Company, 2019).

[503] Court, "State V. Wood, 648 P.2d 71."

[504] Ibid.

[505] Utah Supreme Court, "State V. Holland, 876 P.2d 357," (Jan. 13, 1994).

deeply personal instances one finds in his court briefs, Justice Stewart describes coming home late at night and finding his daughters watching *LA Law* on television.

So, he sits down with them, just as a woman on trial was explaining to the judge that she feels it was the attorney's job to do what he could to get her off. Justice Stewart writes in the brief that "getting her off" might be an accepted approach on a television show, but it was not his task as a defense attorney. Of course, they were obliged to do their job and do what they can for their client.[506] He then explains what he would do:

I talk to my client; I need to know whether they commit that crime. I also need to know whether in the processing of that criminal through the system their constitutional rights were protected. And if that's the case then I feel it's my obligation to get that person to take the first step, and that is to come forth, admit their wrong doing, then to get them through the system in a sense that the appropriate punishment is imposed and they live with that punishment.[507]

In the case of *State v. Holland*, Justice Stewart demonstrated what the relationship should be between a defendant and the client. It is to make certain the system treats the client with as much respect as possible, but that the defendant remains within the law. A second example of the Sixth Amendment right of effective assistance of council is found in *State v. Standiford*.[508] On an evening in the spring of 1984, Fred W. Standiford and Joey Granato went to the residence of Mrs. Hisae Wood, where they purchased some cocaine. They returned to Granato's garage. Later that evening, Standiford told Granato he was going to a convenience store to purchase cigarettes.

Instead, Standiford returned to Mrs. Woods residence. A struggle ensued and Standiford stabbed her multiple times. He cleaned the knife he used and left, taking a bag of cocaine, the knife, and a gun he later claimed she had brandished in front of him. He went to the convenience store and returned to his garage, where his friend, Joey Granato, was waiting. Granato asked Standiford if he had returned to Wood's house, and he denied doing so.

---

[506] Machlis, "Interview with Daniel Stewart in Salt Lake City."

[507] Court, "State V. Holland, 876 P.2d 357."

[508] "State V. Standiford, 769 P.2d 799," (1988).

The next day, Standiford contacted Granato and asked him if he was aware that Ms. Wood had been murdered. Police had questioned Standiford and he reported to Granato that they were both in trouble and that they should tell the police that neither of them had returned to Ms. Wood's residence. Granato, recognizing the gravity of the situation, contacted the police and volunteered to give them a statement. Afterwards, the police searched Standiford's house and found incriminating evidence.

In preparation for the trial, the defense council contacted Dr. Lincoln Clark, a psychiatrist, and asked him to evaluate their client. Council gave Clark some papers, including a transcript of Standiford's taped confession. After meeting with Standiford, Clark informed defense council that his professional opinion would not help their client. Subsequently, Clark testified, at trail, on behalf of the prosecution. Of importance here is the defense council's claim that the prosecution had violated Standiford's rights by using someone hired by the defense to testify against Standiford. Justice Stewart reviewed the process and decided that the prosecution had been careful in developing its case not to violate the rights of Standiford.

A third example of a Sixth Amendment right of effective assistance of counsel is found in *Dunn v. Cook*.[509] After being placed in prison, Dunn petitioned for a writ of *habeas corpus*, claiming he had been arrested and convicted on unlawful grounds. His petition was dismissed without a hearing on the ground that all the issues he raised were waved because they could or should have been raised on Dunn's prior direct appeal.

A jury convicted Dunn of second-degree murder and aggravated kidnapping. He was represented at trial by a court-appointed attorney. After the conviction, the attorney wrote to Dunn and advised against an appeal based on the attorney's belief that if the appeal were successful, Dunn could be resentenced to death at a retrial.

Believing his attorney's advice was without merit, Dunn insisted on appealing his case. After reviewing the case, Justice Stewart successfully argued that the attorney's advice had been incorrect. Dunn should have been able to appeal without fear of a more severe resentencing. The lawyer apparently

---

[509] "Dunn V. Cook, 791 P.2d 873," (April 2, 1990).

did not know that Utah law prohibits the imposition of a new sentence that is more severe than the original sentence.

Still another aspect of interpreting the U.S. Constitution has to do with the so-called Brady rule. In 1963, in *Brady v. Maryland*,[510] the U.S. Supreme Court ruled that the prosecution must turn over all evidence, that might absolve or be favorable to a person involved in a court case. About a year after Justice Stewart was appointed to the Utah Supreme Court, an appeals case came to the court of a Daniel Craig Jarrell, who had been convicted of an attempted criminal homicide.

On appeal, Jarrell claimed, among other things, that prosecutors suppressed evidence, in that they failed to make the police report of the incident available to his lawyers. His council claimed the report had important information in it that would have benefitted their client's case. When Justice Stewart reviewed the case, he concluded that the police report would not have raised reasonable doubt as to the case prosecution had made.[511]

During the next two decades several other cases came up related to the Brady rule. For example, in 1988, Justice Stewart, wrote a lead opinion regarding Scott G. Worthen, who was convicted by a jury of second-degree murder for the death of his stepdaughter, three-year-old Heidi Pavich. He appealed the verdict, asserting, in part, that the court had not allowed him to call the prosecutor as a witness, who could introduce into evidence a letter written by the prosecutor, that he had evidence that Worthen was not guilty of wrongdoing.

The Defendant claimed that, just eleven days after his request that the prosecutor act as a witness had been denied, that same prosecutor had served as a witness testifying that he had interviewed approximately fifty people related to the case. When Justice Stewart reviewed the case, he concluded that the exculpatory evidence sought by Worthen was not sufficient to overturn the jury's verdict, and the court did not err by refusing to dismiss the charge of second-degree murder.

---

[510] U.S. Supreme Court, "Brady V. Maryland, 373 U.S. 83," (1963).

[511] Utah Supreme Court, "State V. Jarrell, 608 P.2d 218," (Feb. 19, 1980).

The actions taken by state supreme court justices are based mainly on the constitutions of a state. At times, the justices draw on the U.S. Constitution in the decisions they are making. Among the many legal contributions Justice Stewart made had to do with clarifying the U.S. Constitution. The issues we have reviewed include restrictions on Utah's death penalty, clarifying the Sixth Amendment, and interpreting the Brady Rule.

16. Utah Constitution

U tah has a unique constitutional history. The first Mormons in the West wished to establish a state, so they could elect their own people to public office and manage their own affairs. In 1849, two years after the saints arrived in the mountains, church leaders sought statehood from federal officials. The state was to be called "Deseret." Brigham Young and some other Mormon leaders even drew up a constitution.[512]

Congress refused to recognize Deseret as a state. Early leaders ultimately attempted seven times to attain statehood. Each time they drafted a new constitution. The first three drafts, drawn up in 1849, 1856, and 1862, relied mainly on the Iowa Constitution, the state where the Mormon Church was headquartered, when the saints were beginning their trek West. The next three drafts, drawn up in 1872, 1882, and 1887, drew largely from the Nevada Constitution. It became a state in 1864.[513]

Neither the Iowa nor Nevada constitutions was equipped to support all the decisions made by the Utah Territorial Legislature. For example, in 1870, the Legislature gave women the right to vote, a provision, at the time, unique to the territories of Utah and Wyoming. The 1872 constitution not only contained a clause mandating women's suffrage. It also introduced a system of

---

[512] Dale L. Morgan, *The State of Deseret* (Logan, Utah: Utah State University Press, 1987).

[513] Alexander, "Utah's Constitution: A Reflection of the Territorial Experience."

proportional representation, and a provision that the U.S. Congress could regulate polygamy.[514]

The final 1896 Utah State Constitution was eclectic, drawing from states such as Washington, Colorado, New York, Wyoming, California, and Montana. Utahns saw their constitution as a living document, reflecting the changing needs of citizens. While it is difficult to amend the U.S. Constitution, it is relatively easy to amend the Utah Constitution. And over time the state has made a number of amendments.[515] We have seen that sometimes, as many as four amendments have been on the ballot in one election.[516]

State constitutions are usually much longer than the U.S. Constitution. This is because they are detailed regarding day-to-day relationships between a state and its citizens. Utah is no exception. Its constitution is more than twice as long as the U.S. Constitution.

Some observers might find it antithetical that Utah Mormons, with their theological commitment to a perfected community of Zion, could comfortably adopt a democracy-based constitution. However, there is a strong conviction among Mormon faithful that the restoration of Christ's original gospel had only been possible in a flourishing democracy. The Mormon Church was founded at the time Jacksonian democracy swept the country's political landscape, and this new church incorporated sentiments toward equality and power to the common man. For example, from the beginning, the church has insisted that every major decision in a ward, stake, or the whole church be sustained and ratified by all the members of that jurisdiction.

Recognizing that the church is filled with egalitarian sentiments, Dan Stewart, as a professor, lawyer, and justice, did not hesitate to espouse populist themes and behave as a dedicated political activist. He grounded his beliefs, in part, on the *Book of Mormon*. As Nathan O. Hatch, a professor at Notre Dame University, has noted: "It is a document of profound social pro-

---

[514] Ibid.

[515] Jean Bickmore White, *The Utah State Constitution: A Reference Guide* (Westport, Connecticut: Greenwood Press, 1998).

[516] Chapter 13.

test, an impassioned manifesto . . . against the smug complacency of those in power."[517] The *Book of Mormon* is particularly harsh against arrogant leaders, who "are puffed in the pride of their hearts," oppress the meek, and persecute the poor.[518] While Dan had never been poor in the way Nephi meant, he constantly recalled the days of his youth, when being poor was his private shame.

In terms of constitutional rights, the U.S. Constitution is explicit in assuring certain rights, including the freedom of speech, the press, and assembly. Article 1, Section 25, of the Utah Constitution holds that there are certain "rights retained by people," although it does not specify what these rights are. Over time, a number have been revealed, such as the right of parents to be with, and to raise their children. This was an issue of particular concern to Dan Stewart. He and Elizabeth were married in the Mormon temple for "time and eternity." Their children were sealed to them, meaning they and their children are forever bound together.

Within a year after Dan took his place on the bench, he was assigned a case dealing with the visitation rights of a divorced mother. In *Kallas v. Kallas*,[519] a father, Allen Glade Kallas, was the custodian of his three minor children, although his wife was given overnight visitation rights on a bi-monthly basis. After Kallas learned that his former wife was engaged in homosexual practices and drug use, he sought, in court, to revoke her visitation rights, claiming the two behaviors ruled out her ability to serve as a role model.

In the lower court case, the judge, having respect for the long local tradition of protecting the rights of a mother, discounted most of the evidence his lawyers brought before the court. The judge ruled that the mother should continue to have visitation rights with her children. His wife's lawyers had argued that the evidence presented by Allen Glade Kallas was faulty, in that it included, among other issues, hearsay evidence, and evidence that is given

---

[517] Nathan O. Hatch, *The Democratization of American Christianity* (New Haven: Yale University Press, 1989).

[518] Book of Mormon, Second Nephi, 28: 12-15.

[519] Utah Supreme Court, "Kallas V. Kallas, 614 P.2d 641," (June 23, 1980).

outside of court and not under oath. For example, the testimony of a BYU professor of psychology, Dr. Cundick, was discounted because his testimony was based on out-of-court statements by the children.[520]

On appeal, Justice Stewart wrote the lead opinion for the Utah Supreme Court, stressing that a child custody proceeding must place the highest priority on the welfare and interest of minor children. In addition, he discounted the claims of the defense about faulty evidence. Within the context of that day, Stewart observed that the behavior of a lesbian set a bad example for the children, at least, in-so-far as the wife had propositioned a thirteen-year-old neighbor girl. Justice Stewart also rebuked the wife for her dependence on drugs. That dependence had more to do with servitude than it had to do with love and affection. The majority of the other justices agreed with Stewart's opinion. Stewart's brief clarified limitations on the rights of a mother. Dan Stewart demanded that a child's welfare is paramount.

Another human right that has been identified, has to do with the use of water. It is one of the vital aspects of living in the desert. From Utah's beginnings, water has been the topic of local lore. Brigham Young's colonizing efforts centered on water in that he sent saints out to places where water was known to be available. The need for water inspired great rejoicing among the settlers, who often claimed the Lord's divine grace sometimes provided water to the thirsty settlers. At other times, the saints recognized that the Lord sometimes chastened His people by drying up springs and creeks.[521]

In 1982, Justice Stewart wrote a lead opinion having to do with a proposed private fishing installation. In *J.J.N.P. Company v. State*,[522] Stewart faced a difficult decision involving the use of water. J.J.N.P. was a limited partnership that owned about 1200 acres in Lake Canyon, Duchesne County, a remote region in Eastern Utah. A natural lake was on the site, surrounded by J.J.N.P. land. It was mainly fed by a natural stream. The Company made

---

[520] Ibid.

[521] Austin Fife and Alta Fife, *Saints of Sage and Saddle* (Bloomington, Indiana: Indiana University Press, 1956).

[522] Utah Supreme Court, "J.J.N.P. Company V. State, 655 P.2d 1133," (Sept. 22, 1982).

application with the Division of Wildlife Resources to create a private fish hatchery. The division denied this request, and J.J.N.P. appealed the decision to the Utah Supreme Court.

J.J.N.P. argued that, since the early days of settlement, private ownership of water rights had dominated the thinking of the state's leaders, many of whom were farmers and ranchers.[523] They insisted the state must preserve the sanctity of the private rights of the people, by allowing J.J.N.P. to control the use of the lake.

Dan Stewart, representing the Utah Supreme Court, argued that water was so important that Utah treated it as a scarce public good. He challenged the claim that water was a to be controlled by the private sector. He was explicit about who should control its use: "All waters in the state, whether above or under the ground are hereby declared to be the property of the public, subject to all existing rights to the use thereof."[524] It did not matter that J.J.N.P. owned the land around and underneath the water, the lake belonged to the public, and it was subject to state regulation, to be used for the benefit and well-being of all the people. Justice Stewart's argument carried the day in the Utah Supreme Court and set a standard for water use in the state.

Some of Justice Stewart's seminal opinions had to do with the "open courts clause," of the Utah Constitution.[525] Article I: Section 11 was in the original Utah Constitution, and it guaranteed the right of every individual in the state to have access to the state's court system. It states explicitly:

All Courts shall be open, and every person, for an injury done to him in his person, property or reputation, shall have remedy by due course of law, which shall be administered without denial of unnecessary delay... .

As a university professor, Stewart traced the origins of the open courts clause back to the *Magna Carta* of 1215, signed by King John. It recognized certain basic liberties, such as due process, or legal proceedings that follow

---

[523] White, *The Utah State Constitution: A Reference Guide.*

[524] Court, "J.J.N.P. Company V. State, 655 P.2d 1133."

[525] Article I, Section 11.

established rules and principles.[526] Even though the agreement was between the King and rebellious barons, its provisions were eventually extended to all people. Despite its long history, the open courts clause is not available in the U.S. Constitution but appears in one form or another in the constitutions of thirty-seven states.

Christine Durham claims Justice Stewart's opinions regarding the open courts clause have been seminal.[527] It was an important aspect of one of Justice Stewart's best known cases, *Berry v. Beech Aircraft Corporation.*[528] In 1985, Lorna J. Berry filed a wrongful death action on behalf of her family, for her husband, Alan Berry, who died, in 1979, in an airplane accident. The defendants were the owner of the airplane, Hercules Flyers. Inc., and the manufacturer, Beech Aircraft Corporation.

Both defendants rejected her action, claiming both the "statute of limitations" of ten years and the "statute of repose" of six years had been reached. The statute of limitations pertained to the owners of the aircraft, and the statute of repose with product liability. After a long legal battle, the lower court trial judge agreed with the defendants, recognizing that the airplane was twenty-three years old and Hercules had owned the plane for nine years, and the accident had occurred more than six years before Lorna J. Berry sued.

Having lost her District Court case, Lorna J. Berry and her lawyers appealed the decision to the Utah Supreme Court; Justice Stewart was assigned the case. He noted that the state courts have long been divided on the statutes of repose and limitations.[529] He then outlined the many time limitations typically placed on people and products; however, he determined that there is a two part test to determine if the open court provision had been violated: (1) An effective and reasonable alternative remedy must be provided by due course

---

[526] Utah Supreme Court, "Craftsman Builder's Supply, Inc. V. Butler Manufacturing Co., 974 P.2d 1194," (March 5, 1999).

[527] Durham, "Address to the University of Utah Law School, Honoring Dan Stewart."

[528] Court, "Berry by and through Berry V. Beech Aircraft 717 P.2d 670 ".

[529] Dave Jonnson, "Top Court Quashes Act on Product Liability," *Salt Lake Tribune* Jan. 3, 1986.

of the law; (2) If there is no alternative remedy, the action may still be justified if it eliminates a clear social or economic evil, and the legal remedy is not an arbitrary or unreasonable means for achieving the objective.[530]

Justice Stewart wrote that Lorna J. Berry faced two questions: Do statutes of limitations appear arbitrary? Do they provide Berry with the possibility of achieving justice for her husband's death? In a lengthy twenty-six-page rebuttal, Justice Stewart determined that the statutes of limitations and repose did not give her justice: The statutes are sweeping and absolute. They bar all legal actions for death, personal injury, or damage to property caused by a defective product.[531]

He maintained that recent legislation limiting or barring her access to the courts was arbitrary and did not conform with the Utah Constitution. In fact, the statute was unconstitutional and voided Lorna J. Berry's right to sue a manufacturer for a product defect. The other justices concurred, and the Court quashed the 1977 Utah legislation that barred product liability.[532]

In the following decade, several times, Justice Stewart reaffirmed his "open court" opinion. In one case, Craftsman Builders Supply sued Butler Manufacturing Company and U.S. Construction for damages arising out of the collapse of one of their buildings, after a hard winter storm placed too much snow on the roof.[533] The district court ruled that the Utah statute of repose and the statute of limitations had been exceeded and did not allow Craftsman to take such action. Butler Manufacturing appealed the decision to the Utah Supreme Court.

Justice Leonard H. Russon wrote the lead opinion for the Supreme Court, and he relied heavily on the arguments Justice Stewart had developed in *Berry v. Beech Aircraft Corporation*.[534] He argued that such limitations are arbitrary and could not be defended. At the end of that brief, Justice Stewart supported

---

[530] Court, "Berry by and through Berry V. Beech Aircraft 717 P.2d 670 ".

[531] Dave Jonsson, "Top Court Quashes Act on Product Liability," ed. Salt Lake Tribune (Jan.3, 1986).

[532] Jonnson, "Top Court Quashes Act on Product Liability."

[533] Court, "Craftsman Builder's Supply, Inc. V. Butler Manufacturing Co., 974 P.2d 1194."

[534] "Berry by and through Berry V. Beech Aircraft 717 P.2d 670 ".

Russon's argument and conclusion, and he lauded his colleague for his "carefully and correctly reasoned" opinion.

One aspect of the Utah Constitution that Justice Stewart worried about was the failure of the state to protect "due process of the law." He believed that Utah had often denied due process. This denial had nothing to do with Utah's recent attempts to separate itself from federal mandates.[535] In fact, the Utah Constitution had a provision (Article 1, Section 7) that guaranteed due process of the law. Justice Stewart considered one state law that was "outrageous." It dealt with a "tricky issue" involving guests in a car or an airplane, who were injured from an accident. A mother might give her daughter's friend a ride home after school, and she would get into an accident that injured the friend, but the friend had no recourse for the injury.

Dan had personal incentive to see that justice was served. He spent his entire adult life dependent on others to provide transportation for him. He was often a "guest" in the trips he took. He was fortunate never to have been seriously hurt in an auto accident, but the threat was always there.

Utah was one of the few states to have a so-called "guest statute." It had been passed by the Utah Legislature during the depression. At the time about thirty states had such a provision. It was an attempt to promote "hospitality" on the part of the host driver, but also to prevent collusion between driver and guest to gain unjust compensation.[536] The state had passed this statute at the time the auto industry was just getting started, and nobody had a clear picture what direction the transportation industry would go.

Over time, all but five states had done away with the law, and Utah was one of the states that had retained it. While other states had found the provision unconstitutional, the Utah Supreme Court had upheld its provisions, "almost in a mechanical manner." Justice Stewart felt the previous justices had abdicated their responsibility. He also observed that auto insurance companies had relied on the

---

[535] U.S. Constitution, Amendment 5.

[536] Dave Jonnson, "State Supreme Court Kills Auto "Guest Statute" Law," *Salt Lake Tribune* May 4, 1984.

law to deny claims on the part of auto owners.[537] Stewart observed that the state now requires drivers to carry no-fault insurance and liability coverage, so there is no reason for drivers and insurance companies to support guest statutes.

Finally, in 1984, a case came before the Utah Supreme Court that would allow Justice Stewart formally to make his case. In *Malan v. Lewis*,[538] Justice Stewart explained that Steven L. Malan was a guest in the automobile of James C. Lewis, who drove his car off the road and struck a guardrail. Malan suffered compound fractures of his right leg, which was thereafter shorter than the other leg and required a brace for the rest of his life. Malan sued Lewis, but the trial the judge sustained the constitutionality of the guest statute and ruled in favor of Lewis.

Malan appealed and Justice Stewart, who wrote the brief, explained there are two arguments for the statute. First, "If the Guest Statute promotes hospitality, the tendency is obscure and more fanciful than real." He noted a decision in Iowa, regarding its guest statute: "No matter how laudable the state's interest in promoting hospitality, it is irrational to reward generosity by allowing the host to abandon ordinary care and by denying to nonpaying guest the common law remedy for negligently inflicting injury." Justice Stewart continued: "Whatever minor effect the statute has in fostering hospitality is offset by the statute's tendency to discourage the acceptance of hospitality by a guest. In short, the objective of furthering hospitality does not justify the discrimination against nonpaying automobile guests.

Justice Stewart turned to the second argument for the statute: "It discourages collusion between driver and passenger." There may be an occasional person, who would resort to such a strategy, but "to cut off the protection of negligence law for a whole class of automobile accident victims because a few persons within the class may attempt to commit a fraud, which they could also attempt irrespective of the Guest Statute, is to discriminate invidiously."

Justice Stewart recommended striking down the terrible tradition of the hospitality statute. All of the other justices agreed with Stewart's recommendation. At the same time as the Malan v. Lewis case was under way, a case regarding

---

[537] Stewart, "A Life: Dictated to Richard G. Ellis."

[538] Utah Supreme Court, "Malan V. Lewis, 693 P2.D 661," (May 1, 1984).

guest passengers in airplanes was also under review.[539] All justices found that Utah's Aircraft Guest Statute was unconstitutional. They cited the automobile statute, indicating that the aircraft statute was similarly flawed.[540] And later, when Stewart wrote one of his best-known decisions, *Berry v. Beech Aircraft*, he again cited the Malan case in support of a decision that led to the Lorna Berry receiving $1.5 million for the death of her husband in an airplane crash.[541]

The final constitutional issue to be considered here has to do with situations where the U.S. Constitution and the Utah Constitution appear to conflict with each other. For more than thirty years, after the 1940's, Utah Supreme Court justices often complained that the U.S. Supreme Court had often wrongly interpreted the U.S. Constitution, and that these interpretations were so egregious that Utah did not have to abide by certain legal decisions made in Washington, D.C. With the appointments of Justices Stewart, Durham, Zimmerman and others, the Utah Supreme Court was able to re-establish a credible reputation in the eyes of the nation, by aligning themselves with the U.S. Constitution.

However, as the Utah Supreme Court neared the turn of the twenty-first century, its justices struggled with a slightly different problem. What happens when the two constitutions differ? In a formal sense, the Utah Supreme Court is beholden to the U.S. Constitution; however, Justice Stewart often explained the charge given to the Utah Supreme Court. Utah Supreme Court justices found it to be their "duty to independently analyze the Utah Constitution."[542] And one would occasionally find the same language in both constitutions. For example, Article I, Section 7, and the Fifth Amendment use identical language.[543]

An example of the potential conflict in the two constitutions was raised in *State v. Anderson*.[544] Contrary to the situation in most other states, Utah

---

[539] "Johnston V. Stoker, 685 P.2d 539 " (July 5, 1984).

[540] "Aircraft "Guest" Statute Ruled Unconstitutional," *Salt Lake Tribune* July 7, 1984.

[541] "Court Calls Law Unconstitutional," *Daily Spectrum (St. George, Utah)* Jan. 3, 1986.

[542] Biele, "Utah Supreme Court '96."

[543] Due process law: "No person shall be deprived of life, liberty, and property, without due process of the law."

[544] Utah Supreme Court, "State V. Anderson, 910 P.2d 1229," (Feb. 2, 1996).

had struggled with the issue of warrantless search and seizure issues. There was, for example, a case in 1993, when Lester Anderson, in Millard County, had been arrested for possession of marijuana and methamphetamines. Someone had alerted the police that Anderson might have the drugs in his possession, while he and a friend were returning home from Las Vegas in his Cadillac. The officers did not have time to obtain a search warrant, but they stopped the car as it was traveling along highway 257, just south of Delta. and found the two men had a good supply of marijuana and methamphetamines.[545]

The Anderson case raised issues related to the warrantless search of a car. Did "exigent circumstances" justify doing this? The lower court ruled there was sufficient cause to do so. However, that lower court relied on U.S. Supreme Court cases to justify doing so. On appeal to the Utah Supreme Court, Anderson's lawyer claimed that the Utah Constitution would deny such action. Article I, Section 14 forbids "unreasonable searches" without a warrant. When the justices reviewed Anderson's case, they chose to agree with the lower court decision and rule that the U.S. Constitution demanded that they approve the warrantless search of Anderson's car.[546]

After the decision, Justices Zimmerman, Stewart, and Durham all gave lip service to the need to follow the Utah Constitution, but they all admitted there had been a conflict in their minds, and a more careful analysis would likely have disclosed an unavoidable dispute between the two constitutions. Justice Stewart suggested that if he had analyzed the Utah Constitution, he would have found such a conflict between the two documents; however, he also declared that, when there is a clear conflict "the state had to follow federal precedent."[547] That declaration ended the longstanding temptation of supreme court justices in Utah to disregard the U.S. Constitution.

---

[545] Ted Cilwick, "Court Rules Search-Seizure Arrest Legal in Millard Drug Conviction," *Salt Lake Tribune* Feb. 7, 1996.

[546] Biele, "Utah Supreme Court '96."

[547] Ibid.

17. Common Law

Common law originated in England and was based on local traditions. Judges relied on customs as they ruled on disputes that flared up in their jurisdictions. When a magistrate faced a certain problem, he would generally try to find if some other magistrate had given a ruling on a similar case, and he would consider that ruling in his own decision. Despite this, common law has always had great flexibility, allowing judges' discretion as they interpret and craft decisions according to contemporary conditions.

Justice I. Daniel Stewart loved the common law.[548] His affection for it came, in part, from his awareness that it embodied the heritage of his ancestors, especially the rulings that had been established in the local church courts in Mormon country. Early leaders had determined that the adversarial court system, so characteristic of the legal traditions in North America and continental Europe, were antithetical to their vision of God's kingdom on earth. Consequently, they set up their own court system designed to resolve, in a Christ-like manner, conflicts and injustices occurring in Zion. This court system ran parallel with the secular courts that were set up in 1850 in the newly established Utah Territory.

Church courts managed issues such as the acquisition and transfer of land, the allocation of water, and domestic conflicts.[549] When the saints arrived in

---

[548] Blake, "Tribute: Justice I. Daniel Stewart."

[549] Firmage and Mangrum, *Zion in the Courts*.

Salt Lake Valley, there were no federal regulations concerning the distribution of lands, so Brigham Young established a way for the saints to settle in small communities and own land on the outskirts, where they might grow their crops. Brigham young set the policy that "no man could hold more land than he could cultivate."[550]

In terms of water regulation, no man owned his own water. It was defined as community property, and individual saints could buy shares. More than once, a church court ruled that a man had taken more water than was allocated to him. Men who refused to confess their sin of taking too much, were occasionally disfellowshipped.[551]

After Utah became a state, the decisions church courts made for half a century became a part of common law. Dan Stewart was a devoted student of Mormon history, and he was one of the few scholars to pay attention to the church courts of that early time. He scoured church records, finding multiple accounts of these court's dealing with, for example, domestic difficulties in Mormon homes.

Divorce in single-wife households occurred often enough that lawyers publicized in local newspapers that they specialized in divorce.[552] In 1883, a Fillmore woman sued for divorce, claiming she disliked her husband. The local church court granted her request, stating that "she does not now nor never did have any affections for him."[553] In 1881, a man sued for divorce from his wife, after he discovered she had committed adultery. The local bishop assigned their ward teachers to investigate. They found she was not very bright and did not realize that, in God's kingdom, sexual immorality stands next to murder as a sin. The church court recommended that the man continue taking care of his wife but have no further sexual intercourse with her.[554]

---

[550] Brigham H. Roberts, *Comprehensive History of the Church*, vol. Six Volumes (Salt Lake City, Utah: Church of Jesus Christ of Latter-day Saints, 1930).3: 269.

[551] Firmage and Mangrum, *Zion in the Courts*.

[552] "The Cheap Divorce Sharp," *Salt Lake Herald* Dec. 16, 1884.

[553] Firmage and Mangrum, *Zion in the Courts*.

Divorce was especially prevalent in polygamist families, notably in the 1880s, when some husbands succumbed to threats of legal prosecution for having a second or third wife. And these wives often sued for divorce. In Rexburg, Idaho, a polygamous woman told the church court that celestial marriage is "just not working here." Her husband had stopped paying attention to her and no longer showed her affection. The local church court granted her request.[555]

After the church manifesto, prohibiting polygamy, in 1894, a Payson polygamist petitioned the stake to divorce his second wife, because he desired to obey the law of the land. Stake authorities allowed him to do so, but they required him to continue supporting his former plural wife.[556] There were no Utah Supreme Court rulings that considered queer, trans, or polyamorous conditions, but rulings on polygamy opened the way for such relationships. There would always be discrepancies between a state's accounts and social reality.

British explorer, Richard Burton, who had observed many polygamous cultures, noted that plural marriage among Mormons was tightly regulated, almost puritanical in nature. Burton wrote: "All sensuality in the married state is strictly forbidden beyond the requisite for ensuring progeny."[557]

As a justice of the Utah Supreme Court, Dan Stewart relied on many early Utah common law rulings. Some of these rulings involved disputes between the rights of parents and children. There is a long tradition in Utah that the relationship between parents and children is sacred. However, that relationship has changed over time. In early England, the father had ultimate authority in parent/child relationships, mainly because inheritance was such a crucial issue. Over time, the male/female relationship changed. Men were increasingly seen as having a public, political and economic role, while the women were assigned a private, domestic, maternal role. The role of the

---

[554]

[555] Ibid.

[556] Ibid.

[557] Richard F. Burton, *The City of the Saints and across the Rocky Mountains to California* (London: Longman, 1861).

mother began to take precedence in domestic affairs, until every effort was made to protect her authority.[558]

What happens when the mother is unfit to carry out her role in the family? That was the issue the Utah Supreme Court faced in 1982. The Utah Division of Family Services, finding a mother unfit or incompetent to carry out her role, filed a petition to terminate the right of the mother to retain custody of her four-year-old child. The presiding judge allowed the mother to retain possession of her child; otherwise, he claimed he would have violated her right to "life, liberty, and property," the child being her property, as guaranteed in the Utah Constitution.[559]

When the case reached the Utah Supreme Court, Dallin Oaks was assigned the task of writing the lead opinion.[560] He agreed with the lower court decision to leave the child with the mother, because such a decision upheld state constitutional law and is rooted "in nature and instinct." Oaks argued that a 1980 Utah law protecting the right of a child from an abusive mother suffering from personality disturbances, and engaging in regular child abandonment, must be overthrown, so that the Utah Constitution might be sustained.[561] Oaks confessed that no child should be relegated to the status of a piece of property and should not be subjected to parental mistreatment. Nevertheless, he and the majority of the court ruled that the parental right to treat a child as property must be protected.

Justice Stewart was the lone justice to dissent. He stood for the common law rights of the child to be protected from a parent, who has failed to demonstrate parental fitness. He argued, when there is *prima facia* evidence that a parent has abandoned her right to maintain custody, the court must protect the child from irreparable harm. When the child's welfare is at stake, stated Justice Stewart, "The child's welfare must prevail over the

---

[558] Val D. Rust, "Male and Female Teachers in Early Utah and the West," *Utah Historical Quarterly* 82, no. 2 Spring (2014).

[559] Article 1: Section 7.

[560] Utah Supreme Court, "In Re Jp, 648 P.2d 1364," (June 9, 1982).

[561] "Utah Court Rejects Children's Rights Bill," *Provo Daily Herald* June 13, 1982.

right of the parent."[562] Unfortunately, Justice Dallin Oaks and his colleagues, steeped in Mormon and American history, disagreed.

Norton v. Macfarlane is one of the important Utah Supreme Court decisions regarding a marriage relationship.[563] In that case Justice Stewart discussed two well-known and similar common law tort concepts: "alienation of affections," and "criminal conversation." Alienation of affections is a broad, general action brought by a spouse against a third party alleged to have interfered with a marriage relationship. Criminal conversation is a legal concept for adultery, or a term one uses when a person seeks damages from someone accused of sexual intercourse outside of marriage.

Both concepts are closely related and come out of old English common law, when men held rights to his wife's body in the way he held land or a machine. The concepts are now seen as so out-of-date that most states have abolished them. At the time Justice Stewart wrote his brief, the concepts were only continued in Hawaii, North Carolina, Mississippi, New Mexico, and Utah.

In *Norton v. Macfarlane*, Greg Norton alleged that he and his wife, Sherry Norton, lived a happy and contented life. She bore him three children. Sherry visited a medical doctor, J. Ralph Macfarlane, and he eventually exercised improper and undue influence over her until she was enticed to engage in adulterous sex with him. Dan Stewart pointed out that there are special groups of people, such as professors, physicians, psychiatrists, and employers, who take advantage of their position of power to obtain sexual favors. This was the claim Greg Norton was making. He claimed Dr. Ralph Macfarlane used his position to exercise undue influence over Sherry Norton.

After Greg Norton filed a claim against Macfarlane, the doctor reciprocated with a claim of his own, asking the lower court to dismiss Norton's case. Instead, the court dismissed Macfarlane's claim, suggesting he had taken advantage of Sherry Norton. He appealed his case to the Utah Supreme Court.

Justice Stewart wrote the opinion. Even though "alienation of affections," and "criminal conversation" are closely related, Justice Stewart

---

[562] Roger Pusey, "Utah Justices Reinforce Parental Rights," *Deseret News* June 11, 1982.

[563] Utah Supreme Court, "Norton V. Macfarlane, 818 P.2d 8," (Sept. 12, 1991).

treated them separately. In terms of alienation of affections, Stewart examined why the concept remains in force in Utah. When it is found there is almost always a loss of love, companionship, protection, and affection. The injured third party may demand compensation for the loss. Justice Stewart declared that, even today, at least in Utah, the marriage relationship is deserving of the strongest possible protection.

He was aware of some prior Utah cases. They typically follow a prescribed script. In 1936, for example, Delbert Smith Whipple filed suit against Roy Cowan of Clearfield charging him with alienation of affection of Whipple's wife. Whipple said that for three years Cowen had been seeking her affections. Whipple also requested custody of their child.[564]

There are some unusual cases, such as a suit filed by an American Fork man against his in-laws, whom he claimed had alienated his wife.[565] Justice Stewart believed these and other cases in Utah were sufficient to retain the concept.[566] Justice Stewart then turns to "criminal conversation." He reminded the court that the concept came into being in feudal society and was related to rights to inherit property. At the time, only legitimate children could inherit property. This concept was eventually abolished in England but has been retained in some form in places like Utah. It holds that adultery was actionable as a trespass on a man's wife. And the man who violates this right is liable for damages to the innocent spouse.

However, the assumption of this argument is that the third party damaged the marriage contract. Macfarlane disputed this claim, and Justice Stewart agreed with him. Justice Stewart pointed out that before Greg Norton's wife had established a relationship with Macfarlane, Norton's marriage was already on the rocks. Stewart was successful in overturning the Utah law that allowed Greg Norton to sue Ralph Macfarlane for having sex with his

---

[564] "Alienation Suit Requests Damages," *Salt Lake Telegram* March 25, 1936.

[565] "Utahn Sues in-Laws for Alienation of Wife's Affections," *Salt Lake Telegram* Dec. 27, 1949.

[566] Paul Rolly, "Court Abolishes Provision Allowing Lawsuits against Spouse's Lover," *Salt Lake Tribune* Sept. 17, 1991.

wife.[567] Justice Stewart pointed out that the law would have had some validity, if Macfarlane had caused the breakup between Norton and his wife, but that was simply not the case. The *Nortan v. Macfarlane* case was groundbreaking in that it allowed a person to file a lawsuit for damages against another person, including a spouse's lover, who breaks up a marriage.[568]

Many common laws in Utah deal with land and water issues. One version of the common law is known as "stigma damages." Rather late in his tenure as a justice Dan Stewart introduced the notion of stigma damages to the Utah Supreme Court. In *Walker Drug Company, Inc. v. La Sal Oil Co.*, a case in Southern Utah,[569] Justice Stewart laid out the case. The Jack Walker family owned three properties on a city block along Main Street of Moab, including a drugstore and a liquor store. There was also a gas station on the block, which leaked significant quantities of gasoline into the ground, apparently contaminating the properties owned by the Walkers. In 1990, Jack Walker tore the building down containing the liquor store and sold the land.

Subsequently, Greg Walker and his family sued the owners of the gasoline station, alleging that gasoline had leaked from its underground tank and had contaminated the groundwater and soil in the properties. They had been forced to sell their property at a rate far below market value. At the Seventh District Court trial the Walkers sought to introduce evidence detailing the damages they had sustained. The judge placed such strict limits on the evidence presented by the Walkers that the family was unable to convince the jury of the damages they claimed.

On appeal to the Utah Supreme Court, the Walkers challenged the lower trial-court process, particularly the judge's ruling that they could not introduce evidence related to what justice Stewart called "stigma damages." They claimed the property's market value was depressed and had remained so, in

---

[567] "Utah Statute on Adultery Lawsuits Overturned," *Deseret News* Sept. 19, 1991.

[568] Doug Smeath, "Alienated Spouses Can Sue," ibid. Sept. 26, 2004.

[569] Utah Supreme Court, "Walker Drug Co. V. La Sal Oil Company, 902 P.2d 1229 " (Dec. 22, 1998).

that there had been a long-term negative perception that the property was permanently devalued.

Dan Stewart wrote the lead opinion for the appeal. He explained that, among many other issues, no trial court in Utah had previously ruled on stigma damages. Stewart noted that the concept was common in other states, and the damages were real and evident. He argued that the public perception of lasting contamination had affected the property's value. For example, he allowed the Walkers to enter evidence from a real estate agent, who knew about the contaminated property and that its value had been permanently depressed. Justice Stewart recommended that the district court ruling be reversed. The other justices agreed. Consequently, stigma damages became a part of Utah tort law.

Another common law issue is found in *Robbins v. Finlay*.[570] Richard Blake points out that, in this case, Justice Stewart introduced the contract concept of "reasonability" into modern contract development.[571] That is, any covenant not to compete, must be reasonably framed and not extend to the point that it reflects competitive unfairness. In 1971, Douglas A. Finlay joined Beltone Utah, a hearing aid company, as a salesman. The company was the primary distributor of Beltone Brand Hearing Aids.

In 1975, Finlay left the company and set up his own hearing aid business. Beltone thereafter sued Finlay, claiming he had taken advantage of Beltone Utah for customer leads and business contacts. Beltone claimed he had signed a contract, when he joined their company, that he would not use his contacts for his own business interests. A jury for the district court agreed with Beltone, finding Finlay guilty of breaching a covenant he had signed with them.

Finlay appealed the case to the Utah Supreme Court, and Justice Stewart wrote the lead opinion. He noted that Finlay's case rested on his argument that Beltone had suffered no business loss from his departure, and any non-competition clause the company forced him to sign was unreasonable and

[570] "Robbins V. Finlay, 645 P.2d 623," (Mar. 23, 1982).

[571] Blake, "Tribute: Justice I. Daniel Stewart."

could not be enforced. Stewart noted that Finlay's subsequent business contacts went far beyond his Beltone connections. Beltone had provided no evidence that Finlay had relied heavily on their contact list.

In addition, Beltone argued that they had taught Finlay what he knew about selling hearing aids, and he had used that knowledge against them. Justice Stewart pointed out that Beltone had never claimed that they had any trade secrets. They were simply engaged in well-known and successful business practices. Their claim that Finlay should not be able to compete with them was unreasonable and unenforceable. The other justices agreed with his recommendation.

About a year later, the Justices again split in their opinions about another case, *State v. Mace*.[572] Aaron G. Mace, of Taylorsville, appealed his conviction and sentence for rape and aggravated robbery. Mace had gone to a woman's apartment in his housing complex, and he told her he saw someone trying to break into her car. She recognized him as a neighbor and invited him in. At knifepoint, he then threatened the woman, tied her hands and repeatedly raped her. He demanded money, but she only had $60, so they drove to her bank, and she withdrew $100. Mace noticed a sheriff's deputy watching them, so he let her drive away. She then called the police, and they arrested him at his apartment.[573]

Mace contended that when he committed these crimes, he had been insane, but the Utah Supreme Court rejected that claim, in spite of psychiatric reports that he had a terrible early life. At the age of fourteen he tried to kill himself by jumping off a cliff. He had also slashed his chest and stomach with raiser-blades. His mother's boyfriend had physically abused him, and a neighbor had sexually abused him.[574]

Both Justices Stewart and Durham, who had objected to the Herrera decision, again in the Mace case, voted against the majority decision. These repeated dissenting decisions on the part of Stewart and Durham, cast them,

---

[572] Utah Supreme Court, "State V. Mace, 921 P.2d 1372," (July 26, 1996).

[573] "Court Calls Law Unconstitutional."

[574] "Aaron Mace Sentenced for Rape of Neighbor," *Daily Spectrum* Sept. 15, 1993.

in the eyes of some observers, as a liberal coalition on the court.[575] In fact, in this case, Justice Stewart was the conservative, in that he wished to preserve a longstanding tradition in the courts. Utah held to its new position for several decades, and dozens of people with mental illnesses ended up in a justice system not equipped to handle them. Utah soon became one of only a few states that did not permit an insanity plea.[576]

---

[575] Biele, "Utah Supreme Court '96."

[576] Annie Knox, "Will Utah Alter Its Insanity Defense?," *Deseret News* Sept. 29, 2019.

18. EXPERT WITNESSES

Before Dan Stewart graduated from college and before he met Elizabeth, he rarely gave psychology a thought. He had never bothered to enroll in a psychology course, even one that would satisfy a general education requirement. But after Dan married Elizabeth and entered law school, he recognized that Elizabeth might know things that would help him deal with topics in law courses, such as torts, equity, conflicts, and evidence. They all required a considerable understanding of emotional and behavioral processes of individuals and groups.

Elizabeth subscribed to several professional journals. When an edition of *Psychology Today* arrived in the mail, Dan would read through it hoping it might assist him to understand her field. She also subscribed to *The American Journal of Forensic Psychology,* intended for psychologists who appear in court as specialized witnesses. The journals provided him with valuable insights into the way social scientists think about laws and the courts. By the time Dan was appointed to the Utah Supreme Court, he was somewhat versed in the field of psychology and became a strong advocate of its potential in assisting lawyers, juries, and judges.

The girls noticed he was often chatting with their mother about her profession. One day Liz asked her, "Mom, why did you become a psychologist?" "Oh I just fell into it." "You what?" "When I was in high school, I thought

I might like to be a fashion designer, so after I graduated I went back East and enrolled in the *New York Traphagen School of Fashion* and studied how to design clothes. I was there for nine months, and I decided it was a cut-throat business, and besides, I wasn't good at it."

"But you were good enough to win a scholarship." "I had no imagination, no creativity at all. I could not compete with the talent in the New York design world." After arriving back in Salt Lake City, Elizabeth kept asking herself: "What am I going to do?" Nothing came to mind.

She enrolled again at the University of Utah, and had about finished her general education requirements, but she needed a five-hour course. "The only thing I could find was Introduction to Psychology. I took it and liked it, so I took another class, then another, and soon I was majoring in psychology."[577] The girls also knew that Elizabeth had gone to law school. One day Liz again asked, "Mom, why did you study law?"

"I never wanted to practice law, but I thought it might be the best general education program I could take. And I took my time. It took me six years to complete the three-year program." "What did dad say about that?" "Oh, I never asked!"[578]

Psychologists serving as expert witnesses were quite new in the court system. In fact, in 1958, when Elizabeth received her PhD, social scientists of any kind rarely appeared in court. There had been an occasional court case involving psychologists as specialized witnesses. After World War I, for example, scientific management swept the consciousness of the world, spawning attempts to measure everything. Two French scientists proclaimed that they had created a machine that would determine how to separate truth from falsehood by calibrating people's involuntary body responses to questions they were asked. The machine was billed a "lie detector," or a "polygraph" test. In 1923, the results of a lie detector test were first included as evidence in an American court case.

---

[577] Stewart, "Interview at the Home of Shannon Stewart Clark in Newport Beach, California."

[578] "Interview at Her Home in Salt Lake City, Utah," (Feb. 25, 2020).

Lawyers challenged these test results, but the District of Columbia Circuit Court ruled, in *U.S. v. Frye*, that this polygraph evidence met acceptable standards set by the American Psychological Association. It was known as the "Frye test."

Before lie detector tests were generally used in the courts, lawyers and physicians were two of the few professionals, who claimed to be able to divorce themselves from their peculiar circumstances and look at psychological evidence with a critical, unbiased eye. Psychologists were still deemed unworthy of serving as specialized witnesses, because they were members of the "soft" social sciences and the legal profession believed they were not yet able to look objectively at evidence.

One factor that complicated the issue was the fact that many psychologists were women. In contrast, judges and physicians in Utah were men. In the late 1950s, there had never been a female Utah Supreme Court justice nor a district court judge. Even though the social boundary between men and women was beginning to blur, men's public political, and economic role and women's private, domestic, and maternal role continued to dominate the scene in Mormon Utah. Dr. Elizabeth Bryan, Dan Stewart's future wife, was an exception. When Elizabeth met Dan, she was serving as chief psychologist at the rehabilitation center of the University of Utah College of Medicine. Nevertheless, she would not have been allowed into a court room as an expert witness, and she continued to act as a responsible homemaker in the Stewart house.

In April 1959, shortly after she had become engaged to Dan, Elizabeth Bryan was invited to travel to Ogden to attend an annual meeting of the Rocky Mountain Regional Convention of the Soroptomist Society, a group of well-educated women. An attractive, slender woman, Elizabeth was dressed in a trim, formal black, long-sleeved skirt suit. Her keynote address in the Hotel Ben Lomond was titled: "Life is Meant to Have Spiritual Values." She explained to the 300 Soroptimists that the field of psychology had not yet attained the status of an objective science, but it was doing what it could to achieve that standing. She confessed that she worried that the emphasis was so strong, problems were being created:

Sometimes we leave the most vital things out when we strive to be too ob-jective. The extra something, quite unmeasurable, but nonetheless vital element, seems to be the incorporation into the personality of spiritual values. This de-termines the person's behavior and feelings.

This was not quite the kind of speech that the feminists in the audience wanted to hear. An observer could imagine someone asking: "Don't you think your perspective is preventing professionals like psychologists from serving as credible witnesses in the courts of our land?"

By the time Elizabeth received her law degree in 1976, psychologists were becoming common place in the courts. Elizabeth specialized in forensic psychology and began serving as an expert witness in courts regarding child custody. Nevertheless, social scientists sometimes created unique problems. In a 1982 Utah Supreme Court case, Dan found himself facing a difficult sit-uation regarding two psychologists who were giving testimony. In *Sessions v. State*,[579] William Thomas Sessions was convicted of forcible sexual abuse, and his lawyer appealed the case to the Utah Supreme Court, claiming that the lower court had failed to give Sessions' jury appropriate instructions on his diminished mental capacity.

The facts of the case were not in dispute. Sessions entered an elevator in a parking lot, and he found a young woman on her way to the fifth floor, where her car was parked, When the elevator doors closed, Ses-sions exposed his genitals, touched her breasts and vagina area, and forced her hand to his genitals. He was physically aroused, but later argued that he had smoked ten marijuana cigarettes, and he had drunk several cans of beer. He confessed that he had succumbed to the urge to expose himself, in part, because of his anger toward his father, who had often abused him.

Justice Stewart faced a difficult choice. Both psychologists agreed that Sessions had a deficient mental condition; however, the one claimed he had no control over himself when he attacked the young woman, while the other determined that, despite Sessions' mental incapacity, he remained capable of conforming his behavior to the law. In other words, the psychological ev-

[579] Utah Supreme Court, "State V. Sessions, 645 P.2d 643," (Mar. 30, 1982).

idence gave little help to Justice Stewart as he attempted to decide on the outcome of the case.

At the dinner table, Dan mentioned the Sessions case to Elizabeth and his daughters and outlined his dilemma. Shannon asked, "Mom, what would you suggest?" In her guarded, professional manner, Elizabeth responded: "I would not draw any conclusions until I had engaged in my own psychological assessment of the man."

Elizabeth's response was sound, but it did not help Justice Stewart. In his lead opinion, Stewart stated that Sessions exposed himself and performed other acts of lewdness, and that he did so, knowing his action would cause alarm, and that he acted intentionally and knowingly. He noted the lower court refused to provide elaborate instructions on Session's diminished mental capacity. He wrote that was a proper decision. The other members of the bench agreed with Justice Stewart.

In 1982, Dan Stewart's efforts to ensure that psychology had a place in the courts was rewarded by being invited by Central Washington University to attend a two-week institute sponsored by the American Board of Professional Psychology. Dan told participants: "the role of mental health professionals in the courtroom will become even more important in the next few years than it is today."

"You have to know psychology to sift reliable evidence from the unreliable."[580] He was especially critical of the dominant hold medical doctors had in helping judges and juries make decisions involving insanity, sexual abuse, or physical violence.

"At one time," Dan Stewart told the audience: "The issue of insanity was being decided because of a physicians' testimony. The doctor, many times a general practitioner, was the ultimate authority." Dan noted that "those venerable physicians were still using leeches at the time our constitution was framed."[581]

---

[580] "Courtroom Role of Mental Health Professionals Deemed Vital," *Ellensburg Daily Record* August 2, 1982.

[581] Ibid.

Fortunately, times had changed and now psychology had finally begun to help judges make appropriate decisions in the courtroom. The field was becoming a part of the judicial system. Dan Stewart then sent a genuine warning to the group gathered at Central Washington University. There are great potential benefits that social scientists can make in court cases. However, "the psychological community must carefully screen and certify those who will represent it in court. Only with complete public accountability will the public confidence be maintained."[582]

Dan would clearly have his wife in mind as he considered the kind of qualifications a specialized witness should have. She not only had her PhD in psychology, but she had received a law degree. Elizabeth knew how to talk in a court of law and lawyers considered her a prize witness.

By the time Dan Stewart became a justice, judges and juries generally took for granted that psychologists and social workers could give valuable testimony in trials. For example, in 1987, Justice Stewart was assigned to write the lead opinion on a Third District Court case, *State v. DePlonty*.[583] Three years earlier, Michael Anthony DePlonty attacked and sexually assaulted a nine-year old girl. When originally convicted, the judge sentenced him to an indeterminate term of ten years to life imprisonment, and his lawyers appealed the case, claiming the sentence for assault lacked appropriate evidence, and his claim of being mentally ill had been erroneously dismissed.

At the appeal, Justice Stewart agreed with the findings of the lower court, except that he concluded that the man was, indeed, mentally ill. The court had appointed two mental health experts, including Dr. Breck Jon Lebegue, a psychiatrist from Tacoma, Washington, who recommended that DePlonty be convicted, and that he be committed to the Utah State Hospital in Provo for treatment. Justice Stewart supported that recommendation.

Even after Dan joined the Utah Supreme Court, there were times when prejudice against psychologists appeared. As late as 1985, the testimony of prominent BYU professor of psychology, Robert J. Howell, who appeared

---

[582] Ibid.

[583] Utah Supreme Court, "State V. Deplonty, 749 P.2d 621," (Dec. 31, 1987).

over 1,000 times in court, was denied. In *State v. Miller*,[584] Howell's testimony included a psychological profile of individuals who sexually abuse children. This profile was excluded. The judge concluded that Howell's profiling activities would confuse the jury.[585]

---

[584] "State V. Miller, 709 P.2d 350 " (Oct. 29, 1985).

[585] Howell happened to be a scholar, who agreed with Justice Stewart's claim that the insane should not be judged with the same measuring stick as normal people. He showed evidence that very few people in trouble with the law, successfully claimed to be insane. He even published research showing that the percentage of people successful in using the insanity defense was approximately one-tenth of one percent. See Tad Walch, "In Defense of the Insanity Plea," *BYU Magazine* (1997).

19. EVIDENCE

There are several kinds of evidence in a court of law, the most common relating to testimony, documents, scientific data, and other means intending to convince a judge or jury those certain facts are true or false, and to tear down the opposition's case.[586] During each of the five years Dan Stewart was a law professor, he taught an evidence course.

As a new Utah Supreme Court justice, he knew that he would not be rehashing the exemplary issues he had raised in his classes. He was no longer dealing with theory and precedent but with real human beings, whose lives depended on the decisions he was making. Fortunately for these people, Justice Stewart refused to let past decisions define where he would take a case. For him, life was ever changing, and, as a justice, he recognized he was ever confronting new and challenging situations and insights.

As a professor and justice Dan made significant contributions regarding evidence. For example, he provided new insights into evidence regarding children acting as witnesses. One case involved Stanley Allen Smith, who was eventually convicted of aggravated kidnapping, raping a child, and two

---

[586] There were several valuable books that frame the evidence issues, including Brian Siegel, *How to Succeed in Law School* (Woodbury, N.Y.: Barron's Educational Series, 1975).

counts of sodomy.[587] On May 8, 1993, Smith abducted a six-year-old child from a schoolyard in her neighborhood in the tiny village of Corinne, Utah, forced her into his car, and drove to a remote area of Box Elder County.

After about an hour, Smith drove the child back to Corinne, where neighbors found her. She showed signs of terrible physical injury. The neighbors took her to the local hospital, where she was examined by a physician, while being questioned by LuEllen Brown, a child-abuse investigator. The child described the man's clothing and car. She also told them what was in the car. The physician took more than an hour to repair and bandage her frail body.

Two days later, Keith Brady, a family friend, and police officer, interviewed the child. He described her to be detached and in a dissociative state, suffering from psychic shock. However, she gave corroborative evidence of the incident. Based on the information the child gave, police apprehended Smith and found DNA evidence in his car, as well as the child's hair and clothing fibers. He was later convicted of kidnapping, rape, and sodomy, and was sentenced on four counts, each running consecutively for at least fifteen years. His attorneys had considered requesting that he was mentally not competent to stand trial. He had twice tried to kill himself,[588] and was also observed "hearing voices, swatting at unseen objects, and has no recollections of that day... ."[589]

Smith's appeal to the Utah Supreme Court involved several issues, such as his claim that the sentences essentially relegated him to prison for life. Justice Stewart, who wrote the lead opinion, rightly admonished the First District Court that in Utah a person can only be given a life sentence for murder. The night after news of the trial appeared in the newspapers, at the dinner table, over hamburger patties and boiled string beans, Elizabeth pulled up the newspaper clip she had cut from the afternoon *Deseret News*. It indicated that the Utah Supreme Court was giving Smith's lawyers the right to request resentencing.[590]

---

[587] Utah Supreme Court, "State V. Smith, 909 P.2d 236," (Dec. 20, 1995).

[588] "Lawyer for Accused Rapist May Use Insanity Defense," *Salt Lake Tribune* Aug. 19, 1993.

[589] "Accused Kidnapper Files Motions for Exams," *Daily Spectrum* 30 Sept 1993.

[590] "Child Rapist Entitled to Resentencing," *Deseret News* Jan. 1, 1996.

Liz asked her father: "What do you think about this guy being given permission to request a reduced sentence?" "I wrote the lead opinion, and that is what I recommended. The guy is in his thirties and should not be given a sixty-year sentence, even if he is a child rapist." Smith's sentence was later reduced. In addition, while in the courtroom for resentencing, Smith was able publicly to confess his sins and apologize to the family for the harm he inflicted on the child.[591]

The Smith case raises an issue related to children who are, for one reason or another, expected to give testimony. The issue of children serving as witnesses and giving evidence has long been difficult. They are so easily swayed by others and are not always clear between fantasy and reality. When the appeal reached the Utah Supreme Court, Justice Stewart wrote the lead opinion. He pointed out that there is an "excited utterance" rule that assumes a person, even a six-year-old girl, telling her about an event that is so startling that it elicits a spontaneous reaction rather than being the result of reflective thought or borrowed from someone else.

Justice Stewart claimed that the utterance of the girl to LuEllen Brown was so close to the actual event that her utterances could be seen as spontaneous and not fabricated by reflection. In contrast, her discussion with Keith Brady two days later was too distant from the event to be seen as unprompted. Justice Stewart's argument was sufficient to persuade his colleagues, Howe and Durham, that Smith was guilty.[592]

Justice Stewart wrote opinions involving children perpetrating evils on other children. *State v. Bullock* is a case in point.[593] It began with charges of aggravated sexual assault and sodomy on a four-year old, on the part of three boys and the father of one of the boys. Eventually, it extended to harm done to all the boys. At issue here is the claim by the defense that the evidence was so tainted that it had been rendered inadmissible. The four boys involved

---

[591] Tom Quinn, "Child Kidnapper Wins Reduced Prison Term," *Salt Lake Tribune* Jan. 27, 1996.

[592] Utah Supreme Court, "State of Utah V. Smith, 909 P.2d 236," (Dec. 20, 1995).

[593] "State V. Bullock, 791 P.2d 155," (Oct. 18, 1989).

in the case provided most of the evidence, and the lawyers claimed the way it was collected was not trustworthy. Justice Hall wrote the lead opinion. He recognized that the evidence was tainted, but the evidence was so clear that he recommended conviction. Justices Billings and Zimmerman concurred. Justice Stewart dissented.

This dissent gets to the heart of Justice Stewart's concerns about evidence. One of the parents learned that her son had been involved in sexual activity, and she took the boy to the Intermountain Sexual Abuse Center, where Dr. Barbara Snow, a social worker, began working with him. The boy had told his mother that three other boys had touched and sucked on his penis. After contacting the Bountiful Police Department, Snow eventually interviewed the boys identified by the youngster. The boys confirmed that they had engaged in the sexual activities. Ultimately, the boys also indicated that the father of one of the boys had engaged in aggravated sexual abuse of all four boys.

The three older boys were then interviewed by Dr. Ann Tyler, a psychologist, and the executive director of the Family Support Center. These interviews confirmed the information gathered by Barbara Snow, although the defense claimed the information Tyler had gathered was so tainted that its value was suspect.[594]

Later, the three older boys, their parents, and the local police met with county attorneys, where the boys recounted what they claimed had happened. Weeks prior to the trial, the testimonies of the three boys were videotaped for use at the trial, so that none of the children appeared in the courtroom.

All the interviews and the video itself appear straight forward and reasonable, but upon further review, problems appear. A major complaint Justice Stewart made in his dissent was that Dr. Barbara Snow, a therapist, claimed her interview approach was therapeutic in nature. She was not interested in collecting evidence of a crime, but in treating children in a way that "helps them heal." In addition, Snow did not tape her initial interviews, and by the time tapes were made, nobody could be certain the taped interviews had anything to do with facts.

---

[594] Dave Jonsson, "Laws Work Only If Bullock Is Guilty," *Salt Lake Tribune* Dec. 29, 1989.

Finally, Stewart questioned the qualifications of Snow and Tyler. They may have been therapists, but that does not necessarily qualify them to serve as witnesses to events experienced by their clients, especially if the clients are young children. Barbara Snow was notorious for manipulating the stories of youngsters so that they coincided with her preconceived notions. In addition, she was actively involved in dredging up memories of children who confessed to having molested other kids and who admitted they had been molested.[595] Such an approach may have therapeutic value, but Snow's allegations were often so bizarre they had gone beyond common belief. She claimed to have uncovered Satanic Mormon child abuse rings and other conspiratorial delusions. Her license to practice was even suspended for a time. The license was eventually restored after she agreed not to engage in therapy of preteen children.[596]

The Bullock case ran over several years and became a news spectacle. Each year, dozens of letters were written in support of Bullock and complaining about issues such as the lack of adequate representation he had received.[597] Dave Jonnson's articles in the *Salt Lake Tribune* were cited in many of the letters.[598] Petitions were circulated claiming the father had been unjustly convicted.[599]

Justice Stewart challenged Snow's approach to gathering evidence, suggesting that she "tainted" the evidence by persuading, cajoling, and maneuvering the children to "confess to unspeakable acts." To add complexity to the case, the court-appointed attorney for the accused father, failed to object to anything.[600] Nevertheless, the defense did find their own expert witnesses,

---

[595] Grey Faction, "Barbara Snow Dsw Lcsw," *https://greyfaction.org/resources/proponents/snow-barbara/*.

[596] https://swallowingthecamel.me/2018/10/07/satanic-panic-and-recovered-memory-in-the-news/

[597] Anita Walker, "Letter to Justice Zimmerman," (Nov. 3, 1989).

[598] E.g., Dave Jonnson, "Testimony in Sex-Abuse Case Called Unconstitutional," *Salt Lake Tribune* Mar. 16, 1988.

[599] Signed Petition by 16 People, "Subject: The Arden Brett Bullock Case," (Oct. 31, 1989).

[600] "Therapist Denies Interviews Tainted Evidence," *Daily Spectrum* Oct 24, 1989.

who questioned the therapeutic approach taken by Dr. Snow and the information gathered by Dr. Tyler. The expert witnesses of the defense were particularly critical of the use made of the videos. In fact, they maintained that the way the evidence was gathered deviated so much from standard procedure that it was of little value and certainly not admissible. According to the *Salt Lake Tribune*, the procedure stretched credulity beyond the breaking point.[601] Justice Stewart noted that the children's preparation for trial amounted to "brainwashing" the boys.[602]

By putting those presenting the state's evidence on trial, the defense tried to show the evidence was so obscured that the actual facts could not be determined.[603] While the majority of the Utah Supreme Court accepted the tainted evidence, Justice Stewart claimed that the adult defendant, one of the fathers of the children, an architect in Salt Lake City, was tried and convicted on "an avalanche of hearsay."[604] From the time Justice Stewart had been a law professor, he had attempted to clarify the reliability of hearsay evidence.

As early as 1970, he made a major contribution to the legal literature with an article, "Perception, Memory, and Hearsay," published in the *Utah Law Review*.[605] In the article, Professor Stewart points out that the U.S. Judicial Conference had recently issued a draft of new rules of evidence that would be admitted for District Courts and magistrates. Stewart claimed that such rules would have a dramatic effect in "redeeming an important area of procedure from the chaotic and sometimes unknowable domain of trial-judge law."[606] Of particular concern was hearsay evidence.

Hearsay evidence comes in many forms. It might be written statements, something someone told a person, or even gestures by someone. A person

---

[601] Jonsson, "Laws Work Only If Bullock Is Guilty."

[602] Court, "State V. Bullock, 791 P.2d 155."

[603] Dave Jonnson, "Utah Supreme Court Upholds Architect's Sex Convictions," *Salt Lake Tribune* Oct. 20, 1989.

[604] Court, "State V. Bullock, 791 P.2d 155."

[605] I. Daniel Stewart, "Perception, Memory, and Hearsay: A Criticism of Present Law and the Proposed Federal Rules of Evidence," *Utah Law Review*, no. January (1970).

[606] Ibid.

giving hearsay evidence in a court has no direct knowledge or experience of an incident. Professor Stewart pointed out that hearsay evidence is fraught with difficulties and is not reliable. A tradition has been established to restrict the use of hearsay, and Dan, as a professor, had proposed in his *Utah Law Review* article, a standard, requiring that someone providing hearsay evidence be required to testify in court. This would allow the other side to question and cross-examine that person. Stewart admitted that confronting a witness might not be foolproof, but it would promote greater accuracy in judicial factfinding. That recommendation was later adopted by the U.S. Judicial Conference.

In *State v. Bullock*, according to Justice Stewart, the prosecution had missed the mark at every turn. Not once was the accused architect "allowed to confront the primary accusers face to face, nor was he able to cross examine them at trial. The accusations were also presented at trial through the testimony of a social worker and a psychologist who had repeatedly interrogated, in private, the four young complainants and then acted as conduits for the admission of more of the boy's hearsay evidence."[607]

As was so often the case, Justice Stewart's dissent represented a long, detailed forty-four-page argument that was far more persuasive than the original relatively short lead opinion by Gordon R. Hall. And Stewart's argument was enough to persuade Justice Hall, who wrote the lead opinion, that he should change his vote and concur with Justice Stewart's dissent. Nevertheless, Bullock was found guilty and sent to prison for a minimum of fifteen years.

There is a sequel to the case. After Arden Brett Bullock was in the Utah State Prison for more than a decade, the time approached when he be granted a release date, Dan Stewart, now retired, took the unusual step of writing a long letter to Michael Sibbett of the Utah Board of Pardons and Parole, outlining why he believed Bullock ought to be given a release date.[608]

A condition of such a date was that Bullock undergo therapy, but an unfortunate condition of being admitted to therapy was that he confess his

---

[607] Court, "State V. Bullock, 791 P.2d 155." P. 165.

[608] I. Daniel Stewart, "Letter to Michael Sibbett Regarding Arden Brett Bullock," (Nov. 19, 2000).

crime. Bullock refused to make such a confession, so he had not received the therapy. Stewart noted that he did not know Bullock but found it prudent to excuse him from this precondition rather than force him to lie just to gain his freedom.

In 2001, about a year later, Bullock sent Dan a hand-written note. He had written Dan a more formal letter to the previous year outlining his case and thanking Dan for his support. In the note, Bullock wrote: "I am also going to be so bold as to ask that you attend my actual hearing."[609] He did not ask Dan to say anything, but his presence would give his case "a tremendous boost." The hearing was held on Dec. 6, 2001.

Despite growing health issues, Dan attended and spoke on behalf of Bullock. This was likely the only time a Utah Supreme Court justice had ever appeared at a prison hearing. After seven long weeks, the Parole Board determined that Bullock would not be required to subject himself to sex-offender therapy, the first time that had ever happened, and he would be released from prison in November 2004.[610]

Some evidence included awakened forgotten events. For example, in 1993, he was chosen to write the lead opinion in *Olsen v. Hooley*,[611] a case that involved a woman, Lisa Hooley. She claimed that from the time she was admitted to kindergarten until she left home at the age of nineteen, she had been sexually abused by her father. However, she said she had repressed any memory of the abuses. She claimed recollection of these abuses began to occur as nightmares and flashbacks. They were so severe that, on three occasions, she was hospitalized. The matter eventually ended up in court, and the defense claimed the time lapse had been too great to make such claims. The basic defense was that the statute of limitations had expired, and the lower court agreed.

When the appeal came before the Utah Supreme Court, Justice Stewart, who wrote the lead opinion, argued that the statute of limitations does not

---

[609] Arden Brett Bullock, "Letter to I. Daniel Stewart," (Nov. 11, 2001).

[610] Lynn J. Lund, "Letter to I. Daniel Stewart Regarding Arden Brett Bullock," (Aug. 12, 2002).

[611] Utah Supreme Court, "Olsen V. Hooley, 865 P.2d 1345," (Oct. 27, 1993).

begin until Lisa Hooley began to recall the facts about abuse. Her mistreatment continued until she left home at age nineteen, but she had completely repressed any memory even of the time, when she was legally an adult. This was the first court case to clarify the issue related to the statute of limitations concerning repressed memories.[612]

Justice Stewart recognized that research concerning the reliability and authenticity of revived memories remains an issue. He noted Lisa Hooley did not provide the case to resolve these larger issues. After the Hooley trial, Justice Stewart was careful to point out that this case did not prove that her repressed memory was correct, and it would have been necessary to provide corroborating evidence supporting her claim. Justice Stewart also said that the case did not deal with the therapeutic methods used to revive the memories, and whether the methods induced incorrect memories. His case only dealt with the issue of the statute of limitations, and other issues were left to be determined.[613] However; her account was sufficiently clear that she began to recall her memories in 1988 and by 1990 she had realized that they were real memories, which fell well within the statute of limitations. Justice Stewart recommended the earlier decision be reversed, and the other justices concurred.

Evidence studies related to memory studies were controversial. Cognitive psychologists, such as Elizabeth Loftus, an expert on human memory, found that events people remember are often inaccurate and highly malleable. The retention of information over time is affected by misinformation and memory loss. Loftus came to serve as a consultant and witness in court cases that relied heavily on the revived-memory testimony of witnesses. She was particularly known for questioning the claims women make about sexual encounters, when they were young, and Loftus showed how their recovered memories are not always accurate and can be easily manipulated.[614] In some respects, Justice Stewart agreed with Loftus. He once stated:

[612] "Court Clears Way for Repressed Memory Suit," *Provo Daily Herald* Oct. 30, 1993.

[613] "High Court: No Time Limit on Repressed Abuse Suit," *The Daily Spectrum* Oct 30, 1993.

[614] For example, Loftus, "Reconstructing Memory: The Incredible Eyewitness."; "Leading Questions and the Eyewitness Report," *Cognitive Psychology* 7, no. 4 (1975); "The Malleibility of Human Memory," *American Scientist* 67, no. 3 (1979).

We simply don't have the tools to adequately detect the truth in spoken tes-
timony. Polygraph tests and testimony based on information gained while a
subject was under hypnosis are not admissible in court, and competent research
shows how unreliable eyewitnesses' perception of recollection can be.[615]

Even though the rules of evidence are tough, Justice Stewart was a master
at developing an understanding of individual rules and how they have come to
form a coherent system. In addition, he was aware that these evidence rules
were ever evolving, and he worked to refine them in such a way that they constituted even greater coherence and assistance in the court of law.

Psychologists introduced novel ways to collect evidence. The lie detector
test illustrates one new means of evidence, although its value was constantly being questioned.[616] Within months after Dan Stewart was appointed
to the Utah Supreme Court, he wrote the lead opinion on a rape conviction
in the Second District Court, where the judge relied on the results of a polygraph. A young teenager from Brigham City was shopping with her friend
in Ogden and temporarily lost her keys. The girls met two young men, who
helped them find the keys, and the teenager agreed to drive them home.

After dropping her friend and one of the other men off, as she was driving the other young man home, she claimed he suddenly grabbed the steering
wheel, drove to a secluded spot, and raped her. Of course, he told quite a
different story. She filed a complaint against him in the Utah Second District
Court, and he later agreed to take a polygraph test.

In this instance, the court faced conflicting accounts. The young lady
claimed rape, the young man claimed consent. Everyone agrees that the results
of a polygraph must be seen in a larger context. It must align with additional
evidence presented by the defendant's lawyer. The young man's lawyer argued
that the judge had given too much credence to the results of the test.

On appeal to the Utah Supreme Court, in Justice Stewart's lead opinion,
he reviewed the long account of using polygraph tests and came to the decision

---

[615] "Courtroom Role of Mental Health Professionals Deemed Vital."

[616] *The Polygraph and Die Detection*, (Washington, D.C.: National Academies Press,
2003).

that there was not sufficient corroborating evidence to convict the young man. Justices Maughan and Wilkins agreed. The defendant went free.

Other novel approaches psychologists have introduced are found in *State v. Ramsey*,[617] where Justice Stewart wrote the brief. Robin Charles Ramsey was separated from his wife, who had legal custody of their five-year-old son and three-year-old daughter; however, the children were allowed to make overnight visits to their father. After one visit, the children's mother began to worry that the father was engaging in illicit behavior with the children. She found her daughter's vaginal area was inflamed. The girl told her mother that her father and brother had played with her "pee pee" during the recent visit. The mother issued a formal complaint, and the father was brought to trial.

In the courtroom, a psychologist gave testimony that she had worked with both Ramsey children. She informed the judge that she had engaged in a novel way to gathering evidence from the young three-year-old. She had presented the girl with an anatomically correct doll, and she asked her to show her how the father and brother had touched her. In addition, using dolls, she asked the children to show how the boy had lain on top of her, when the father was teaching them how babies are made.

The Ramsey case illustrates a third new source of evidence introduced by psychologists. Dr. Mercedes Reisinger, a psychologist, who treated both Ramsey children, introduced to the court a profile of abused children. Prior to this time psychological profiles had been rare in the courts. During the last half of the past century, profiling quickly became a major activity of the police, who created profiles of offenders by inspecting crime scenes where offenders had left evidence of their background. A similar approach was taken to create profiles of the victims of crime. Psychologists had determined that the victims of assault usually had common traits and personalities, and they attempted to lay out what these traits were. In the Ramsey case, Dr. Reisinger indicated that both children fit the profile of an abused child.

---

[617] Utah Supreme Court, "State V. Ramsey, 782 P.2d 480," (Oct. 19, 1989).

20. UTAH'S HERITAGE OF EVIL

W hen Daniel Stewart joined the Utah Supreme Court, he became a
part of an institution that is inextricably bound up with evil. Utah
was not immune from evil. In 1984, the *Salt Lake Tribune* drew up a
"time clock" of crime in the state, stating that a major crime occurred
every 6.4 minutes. A rape took place every 22 hours, murder every 6.8
days, and an aggravated assault every 3 hours.[618] As a justice, Stewart encountered the acts of rapists, murderers, addicts, thieves, gangsters, and
thugs, who accounted for large numbers of cases appearing before the
court. Justice Stewart was assigned to write the lead opinions on many
of these cases.

Fortunately, he was never required, as a justice, to deal with a broad
crime so vicious that it would have put the entire state of Utah to shame.
There were such historical cases. As a youngster in the social-studies class
at Bryant Junior High School, Danny had learned about one of the great
crimes of the early West, the Mountain Meadows Massacre. In 1857, saints
from Cedar City, in Southern Utah, attacked a group of belligerent Arkansas
travelers passing through the area, killing more than 120 men, women, and

---

[618] Dave Jonsson, "Utah Murder Rate at 6-Year Low," *Salt Lake Tribune* Aug. 29, 1984.

older children.[619] And then the perpetrators attempted to cover up their crimes by pretending they were Indians.[620]

Utahns today often think that Mormons were the exception in the Wild West, where lawlessness and chaotic violence were taken for granted. Smug Mormons too often assume that early Utah saints were well behaved and law abiding, but there is historical evidence, that moral depravity and physical violence were, at times, a part of some Mormon settlements.[621] If visitors to Salt Lake City are to be believed, even the streets of that city were filled with some of the most "filthy, miserable, neglected looking and disorderly rabble" that could be found.[622] And the courts, including church courts,[623] were given the task of adjudicating much of the resulting wickedness.

For young Danny, the case of the Mountain Meadows Massacre was an event he read about in a history book, but when he was entering adulthood, he faced a stark, personal, contemporary reality. As a missionary, he spent thirty months in West Germany, interacting with people, who were trying to reconcile their country's complicity with Adolf Hitler and National Socialism. Elder Stewart met many, who had actively supported the Nazi cause.

The Mormon Church was well-known by Nazi leaders, who had adopted some church practices, such as abstaining from smoking cigarettes and drinking alcohol, fasting one day a month, and engaging in genealogical research.[624] At the time Elder Stewart was in the country, most Germans, including local Mormons, were silent, if they had colluded with the Nazis in their persecution of the Jews, as if to speak of them was to confess their personal guilt. It was only after Elder Stewart had known certain German Mormons for some time and had gained their trust that some confessed to him

[619] Ronald W. Walker, Richard E. Turley, Jr., and Glen M. Leonard, *Massacre at Mountain Meadows* (New York: Oxford University Press, 2008).

[620] Juanita Brooks, *Mountain Meadows Massacre* (Norman, Oklahoma: University of Oklahoma Press, 1970).

[621] Davis Bitton, *The Ritualization of Mormon History and Other Essays* (Urbana, Illinois: University of Illinois Press, 1994).

[622] Benjamin Ferris, *Utah and the Mormons* (New York: Harper and Brothers, 1854).

[623] Firmage and Mangrum, *Zion in the Courts*.

[624] Clark, "Mormonism in the New Germany."

that they had cheered at the rallies of Hitler and had boasted publicly of their support of National Socialism.[625]

When Stewart was appointed to serve as a justice, one of the first major cases he heard dealt with a heinous crime. The so-called Hi-Fi murders in Ogden, Utah, were some of the worst acts of evil perpetrated, not only in Utah, but in America.[626] In 1974, five years before Dan joined the Utah Supreme Court, depraved brutes entered a Hi-Fi record shop in Ogden, bound the six occupants and took them to the basement. Three of the victims were less than twenty years of age. The thieves, who were unfortunately Black, forced four to drink Drano, while they shot two others. When the Drano victims screamed in pain, they attempted to tape their mouths shut but could not stop the pus oozing from their blistered mouths and throats. One of the shooting victims did not die, so the attackers shoved a pen into his ear and kicked it, all the while choking him with a wire. One of the girls was raped. [627]

The Hi-Fi break-in was so tumultuous that the city of Ogden was changed. People had been trusting and open in their behavior, and afterward they began locking their doors, even while at home, and were cautious around strangers. Another consequence on the city, which was almost all white, was that residents began to ostracize its few Black residents.

The murderers escaped but were eventually apprehended and identified as airmen stationed at Hill Air Force Base, located just south of Ogden. The court cases lasted for years.[628] Eventually, two of the men were convicted and sentenced by a jury to die.

Because the incident was so widely publicized, an international campaign was set off to commute the death sentences of Dale S. Pierre and William

[625] Stewart, "Missionary Journal ".

[626] Andreas Rivera, "Forty Years Later, Ogden Hi-Fi Murders Are Still the Worst," *Ogden Standard-Examiner* Apr. 22, 2014.

[627] DeVoy, "Hi Fi Evidence Unpacked."

[628] The Utah Supreme Court entered the picture in 1977 as both Pierre and Andrews appealed their 1974 case. See Utah Supreme Court, "State V. Pierre, 572 P.2d 1338," (Nov. 25, 1977); "State V. Andrews, 574 P.2d 709," (Nov. 25, 1977).

Andrews.[629] In 1988, Pierre was finally executed, but Andrew's case was submitted to the Inter-American Commission on Human Rights. Its lawyers drew on one of Justice Stewart's arguments in defending their client. In *State v. Wood*,[630] Stewart had argued effectively against the use of the death penalty, claiming that mitigating factors often outweighed aggravating factors to the point that it casts doubt on execution as an appropriate punishment. That argument temporarily won the day for Andrews, who was placed in prison. In July 1992, the case again came before the Utah Supreme Court. After eighteen years, the situation of Andrews finally came to light. In the 1974 trial, feelings had been so high that the court overlooked the fact that Andrews had not been present when Pierre murdered the victims. Despite this, the Utah Supreme Court affirmed the trial court decision that execution of Andrews was appropriate.[631]

Justice Stewart agreed with the court that Andrews was guilty of a great crime, but he challenged the court's decision to execute the man. In his rebuttal to Justice Hall's lead opinion, he wrote a stirring account of William Andrews early life, explaining that he had grown up in a terrible environment. His IQ tests suggested that he was mentally retarded, and in the basement of the Hi-Fi store, when Pierre insisted that Andrews assist him in the murders, he said, "I can't do it, I'm scared."

The prosecution argued that Andrews was a threat to society, in that he might one day be paroled, but Justice Stewart pointed out that Utah had enacted a new capital sentencing statute that allowed criminals to be sentenced to prison without the possibility of parole. In addition, Stewart later noted that the legal process had taken almost two decades. At the time of sentencing, he was a different person than he had been when the murders were committed.[632]

Dan Stewart noted that the recent legal provision was not applicable in Andrew's case, but he argued that the law suggested that the death penalty

---

[629] Pierre later changed his name to Pierre Dale Selby, hoping that his family would avoid further embarrassment.

[630] Court, "State V. Wood, 648 P.2d 71."

[631] "State V. Andrews, 843 P.2d 1027," (July 21, 1992).

[632] Machlis, "Interview with Daniel Stewart in Salt Lake City."

for people like Andrews was without merit. He reminded his colleagues that Utah society values life as much as any society, and it ought to refrain, if possible, from pushing the legal process to its ultimate end. In his rebuttal, Stewart argued that "formal justice must be tempered with mercy and compassion."[633]

Over the years, Andrews had attempted to change. His life's moto became "Where there's life, there's hope," and he had gained the reputation in prison for encouraging other inmates to gain self-control and maintain a sense of self-respect.[634] In spite of Stewart's appeal, on July 30,1992, Andrews was executed by lethal injection, eighteen years after the Hi-Fi incident, even though he had never killed anyone.[635]

Justice Stewart was aware that evil is found in every society, including his own. If one had asked him about wrongdoing and violence, he likely would have replied: "I wish they were not to be found, but that is not the case." In his first year on the Utah Supreme Court, about one fifth of the cases he and his fellow justices dealt with involved murder, sexual assault, possession of illegal drugs, or aggravated theft.[636] And some years, nearly half of all the cases coming before the court involved violent, pernicious crimes. In 1988, for example, 52 of the 106 Utah Supreme Court cases listed by *Justia* involved savage and barbarous behavior, and about a dozen of these had to do with aggravated sexual assault on small children and youth.[637]

Some of the most heinous and shockingly loathsome court cases involve little children. For example, in 1994, in *State v. Lowder*.[638] Jason Alan Lowder was brought to trial before the Utah Supreme Court for aggravated sexual

---

[633] Court, "State V. Andrews, 843 P.2d 1027." In a concurring statement.

[634] Gillespie, *The Unforgiven: Utah's Executed Men.* p. 163.

[635] The only other person condemned to be executed without killing someone was John D. Lee. See Robert Glass Cleland and Juanita Brooks, eds., *A Mormon Chronicle: The Diaries of John D. Lee: 1848-1876* (San Marino, CA: The Huntington Library, 1955).

[636] https://law.justia.com/cases/utah/supreme-court/1979/

[637] https://law.justia.com/cases/utah/supreme-court/1988/

[638] Utah Supreme Court, "State V. Lowder, 889 P.2d 412," (Dec. 16, 1994).

abuse of a baby less than two years of age. The baby suffered a dozen different severe injuries in her buttocks and genitalia. All justices, including Dan Stewart, agreed that the defendant took extended indecent liberties with the innocent creature and was guilty.

These types of cases were foreign to Dan's personal life. When he was young, Danny had little direct experience with such harsh reality of depraved behavior and wickedness. There were no cases known to Utahns like the French tradition of common and open sexual abuse of minors by well-known older men, or of fathers praying on their own children without public notice and prohibition. Dan had a temper that flared up when things didn't go his way, but whenever it erupted, he had long since learned to hold it in check, until he got control of himself. And Dan did not act in a hateful manner. He maintained self-control to a degree that hostile feelings did not dictate his behavior.

Dan's family was like most other families in Utah. They owned an old 30/30 Winchester, which they used in the fall to hunt deer. And they had a 22 Ruger handgun. During hunting season, Danny and his friends were often out near Redwood Road looking for pheasants. However, Danny's favorite weapon was an old mother of pearl handled jack-knife, which he and his school buddies called a toad-stabber.[639]

Dan's own participation in aggressive behavior would best be classified as pranks. Even though young Danny showed great respect for others, he was forever playing practical jokes on friends and family members. For example, when his older sister, Mary Louise, married, she and her new husband parked their car in front of the Stewart family home on Butler Avenue.

It was all packed and ready for their honeymoon getaway; however, when she and her new partner, LeGrand Holbrook, came out to drive away, they found the car was missing. Danny, barely out of high school, had put the car gear in neutral, and had coasted it down the hill, without a key, to University Street, then to South Temple, and thirteen blocks west, all the way past Temple Square, before it came to rest on the West side of town. LeGrand

---

[639] Holbrook, "Interview at the Dan Stewart Home in Salt Lake City."

and Mary Louise were in shock but managed to turn the event into a form of delayed marriage celebration.[640]

No behavior Dan engaged in ended up in any court of law, let alone, the Utah Supreme Court, so Justice Stewart struggled to understand how villainy occurs and he asked hard questions about how courts might wisely help resolve pernicious acts. It was not enough simply to execute people, or put them away in prison, where they would be invisible to society. He wondered about a person, who might be convicted of murder. How might that person's behavior have been changed?

Would it have been possible at some key point in the person's life, to help him experience things that most of us take for granted? He believed even the depraved and wicked have dreams and goals they wished to fulfill. Dan often asked: "How can we apply rules across the board to people with different experiences?"[641]

It was not enough to struggle with issues related to criminal behavior. Dan also wondered how it might be possible to make certain the victim of a crime feels justice is served. And how could he reconcile the consequences of a crime on the criminal and the victim? One of justice Stewart's many clerks on the Utah Supreme Court, David Gee, explained that Dan was often expected to make judgments on abhorrent and abominable crimes, but he insisted that he carefully and dispassionately looked at the many legal issues involved in each case, and ruled on the legal issues involved, rather than exclusively on the emotionally charged events themselves.[642]

Early in life, Dan had learned the concept that we are all equal before the law, but he found it difficult to explain what that means. There are so many inequalities in people, and they are far more evident than our equalities. There are old and young, tall and short, fat and skinny, smart and dumb, beautiful and ugly, rich and poor, good and bad, empathetic and small minded. Dan certainly had great empathy, but it is hard to say where Dan's empathy came from.[643]

---

[640] Ibid.

[641] Ellis, "Interview of Dan Stewart at His Home in Salt Lake City, ."

[642] Gee, "Telephone Interview at His Home in Seattle, Washington."

[643] Social scientists claim empathy is a major marker of modernity. See, for example,

While growing up, Dan had been in a family that experienced many hardships. In addition, Stewart family members were, at times, not sensitive to another family member's needs and desires. In fact, one of Dan's sisters felt her family was so dysfunctional and conflictual that, as soon as she graduated from high school, she left Utah and moved to Westwood, California.[644] Dan's response to tensions in the family was to express empathy for other family members and try to understand why they were acting the way they were. That empathy only increased while he was in an iron lung fighting for his life and while he was trying to adjust to living life in a wheelchair.

After joining the Supreme Court, Justice Stewart, tried to apply his empathic sense to the cases he reviewed. That first year on the court, Justice Stewart was given the task of writing lead opinions on almost half of all the violent crimes that came before the bench. The first seemed like so many cases. In cases of violent behavior, the lawyers usually turned to some technicality rather than the facts of the case itself. The case of defendant, Brent A. Carson was steeped in evil, and he was charged with "three first degree burglaries, aggravated sexual assault, and aggravated burglaries."[645]

After negotiating with Counsel, the defendant was ultimately charged with rape, and, prior to sentencing, the defendant was assigned to the Division of Corrections for a diagnostic evaluation. At the end of the evaluation, the defendant appeared before a different judge, who sentenced him, by law, for a second-degree felony, one-to-fifteen years. The defendant appealed the case claiming the judge should have ordered a second evaluation. In addition, his lawyers claimed the judge, being new, did not have a sufficient factual basis even to sentence him. It was here that Justice Stewart comes into the picture.

One of the advantages of an appellate court is the record from the earlier court case. It gives the justice a chance to review early evidence gathered from both sides. This evidence provides most of the information Justice Stewart needed to determine whether the second judge had been able to make

Daniel Lerner, *The Passing of Traditional Society* (New York: Free Press, 1958).

[644] Saundra Stewart, "Interview in Westwood, California," (Sept. 24, 2019).

[645] Utah Supreme Court, "State V. Carson, 597 P.2d 862," (June 18, 1979).

an appropriate evaluation of his case. The information provided enough evidence of the Brent A. Carson case, for example, that allowed Justice Stewart to conclude that each step was sufficiently thorough to ensure that the defendant's condition had been appropriately reviewed and a proper judgment rendered. The system justly placed Carson in prison for almost three years, then place him on parole. He soon again committed burglary. He was committed to prison for another four years, and shortly after he was released, he raped his employer's daughter, who was said to be permanently emotionally damaged from the attack.[646]

One category of evil that Justice Stewart regularly faced had to do with various aspects of sexual assault involving minors. Many of these cases were closely linked with family troubles and often involved child molestation and kidnapping, which were particularly difficult to deal with. Justice Stewart was personally invested in such cases; he had two daughters, who, as young girls, were vulnerable to such dangers.

In a single year, 1989, Justice Stewart was assigned two cases involving the sexual abuse of a child. One case, *State v. Ramsey*,[647] was of a father abusing his three-year-old daughter and five-year-old son. It is discussed elsewhere,[648] so we turn to the second case, *State v. Gibbons*. Bruce Gibbons was charged with two counts of sexual abuse of a child and one count of sodomy (anal sex). Gibbons initially pleaded guilty to all three counts and was convicted; however, he later appealed his case, asserting that he had not "knowingly and voluntarily made his confession."[649] He again went to court and the jury was unable to reach a verdict. At the sentencing hearing two witnesses testified that Gibbons was sincere in his desire to change and to undergo treatment.

This type of case appears to have been of behavior that is common in some cultures. That is, children throughout the world are exposed to various

[646] Ibid.

[647] Utah Supreme Court, "State V. Ramsey, 782 P.2d 480," (Oct. 19,1989).

[648] Chapter 23: Expert Witnesses.

[649] Utah Supreme Court, "State V. Gibbons, 779 P.2d 1133," (Sept. 13, 1989).

levels sexual stimulation as a matter of course; however, in America some of those behaviors are seen to violate moral boundaries.[650] And Utahns view sexual violation of children with no degree of compassion or forgiveness.

Gibbons did not use a weapon, inflict bodily injury, use pornography, or work in concert with anyone else. In addition, he had not been convicted of a previous public offense, so he claimed the verdict against him was too severe. The lower court had sentenced him to fifteen years for two counts of sexual abuse and for ten years to life for sodomy on a child. Gibbons appealed the case to the Utah Supreme Court.

Justice Stewart was chosen to write the brief. He reviewed the Utah Code and requirements for suspending the sentence and found the trial court had acted in accordance with the law. Gibbons further contended that the trial court abused its discretion by sentencing him to ten years rather than the lesser option of five. Justice Stewart outlined the formal procedure for determining if a sentence should have been five, ten, or fifteen years and he determined that the court had been careful to sentence him appropriately. He recommended that the previous decision be affirmed, and the other judges agreed with him.

A whole category of problems in modern society has to do with possessing, selling, and using drugs. The state of Utah is extremely puritanical regarding drugs of any kind, and its laws have usually been strict regarding their possession and use. In the 1980s, marijuana was treated as a toxic, addictive substance that had no place in society. The Mormon Church has even placed heavy restrictions on coffee, tea, and alcohol, and drugs are considered eviler and more insidious. In his personal life, Dan usually held to these religious restrictions. Occasionally, he would bend a bit, by accepting an alcoholic drink or a cup of coffee, when a social situation demanded some flexibility, or because his wife, a Mormon convert, had not grown up with church restrictions and she did not always include them as part of her lifestyle.

---

[650] E.g., Margaret Mead, *Coming of Age in Samoa* (New York: Morrow, 1928); E. E. Evans-Pritchard, "Sexual Inversion among the Azande," *American Anthropologist* 72, no. 6 (1970).

During Justice Stewart's tenure on the Court, there were recurring in-stances when cases involving drugs came before the court, and his name was, at times, drawn to review a case. For instance, in 1988, Danny Duane Buck was convicted of possessing and distributing about half a pound of mari-juana and a large quantity of amphetamines, a synthetic drug. These had been discovered when police obtained a search warrant authorizing them to enter Buck's residence. Even though the county deputy attorney agreed with the police officers that the warrant was to be no-knock, the county deputy attorney neglected to state that on the formal writ. And Buck appealed the case, claiming the police overstepped their authority by unlawfully breaking into his home, where they discovered the drugs. In reviewing the case, Justice Stewart noted that no-knock is applicable regarding a general warrant, when no one is present, as was the case with Buck, so Justice Stewart wrote that the state did not err, given the circumstances at play.[651]

While Justice Stewart sat on the bench of the Utah Supreme Court, each year there were several cases related to adultery. The Mormon church took a strong stand regarding sexual relations outside of marriage, claiming it opened the floodgates regarding any number of evils, including gonorrhea and syphilis, physical violence, divorce, broken homes. The church claimed adultery is "most abominable above all other sins, save it be the shedding of innocent blood or denying the Holy Ghost."[652]

Consequently, the Utah courts were often burdened with the con-sequences of spousal infidelity. Adultery was almost never the issue in the courts. This was handled, if it came to light, within the church courts, often leading to disfellowship and excommunication from the church in question. However, the consequences of infidelity led, at times, to divorce, legal sep-aration, and a host of violent and vicious crimes. These cases showed up sev-eral times a year on the Utah Supreme Court agenda, at least until 1987, when the Appellate Court came into the picture, which dealt with, among many other things, issues dealing with alimony, visitation rights, the division of property, medical expenses, ownership of property, etc.

---

[651] Utah Supreme Court, "State V. Buck, 756 P.2d 700," (June 6, 1988).

[652] Book of Mormon, Alma 39.5.

Of all the cases that came before the court, murder was the most difficult. Justice Stewart knew the Mormon Church took a strong stand regarding the conscious or premeditated killing of a human being "with malice aforethought." He learned, as a young man, that the church believed there was no forgiveness for murder, meaning a murderer could never gain salvation. Such a person could not even be baptized and join the Mormon Church. It proclaimed that a murderer should pay the price of an unlawful slaying by shedding his own blood.[653]

Early in life, Danny had accepted the church position on murder, but as he matured, he began to question the wisdom of such a doctrine. During the first year on the bench, Stewart was required to deal with a case of murder in *State v. Wells*.[654] However, the case in question was ruled to be manslaughter, and it was not necessary for him to confront the issue of capital punishment. In 1982, as a Utah Supreme Court justice, he found he must write a lead opinion on an appeals case related to the capital punishment of someone, who had shot a stranger several times without provocation. Stewart asked himself what kind of judgment he should make about the consequences of murder. In addition, the person he was passing judgment on claimed to be mentally impaired.[655]

Justice Stewart recognized that it was not enough to put a person away in prison, without making sure that the prisoner's life could continue and even thrive. He was involved in cases, where prisoners were subjected to inhuman injustices. Since childhood, Stewart had believed in the infinite worth of each human being. You could not subtract poor judgment or deficient mental capacity to get something less than the infinite worth of a human being, even if it involved a case of murder or aggravated sexual assault. Just because someone is convicted of a crime and placed in prison, that person should continue to be treated as a human being with infinite worth and worthy of the rights of a citizen. Dan once exclaimed, "a jail door does not close off all protections of the U.S. or the Utah Constitution."

---

[653] Bruce R. McConkie, *Mormon Doctrine* (Salt Lake City: Deseret Book Co., 1966).

[654] Utah Supreme Court, "State V. Wells, 603 P.2d 810 " (Nov. 13, 1979).

[655] "State V. Wood, 648 P.2d 71."

The case that gave rise to the above statement had to do with the Weber County Jail, north of Salt Lake and Davis Counties. It had such poor physical facilities it could not accommodate visitors. Justice Stewart did not mince words with Weber County. He noted that jails are not required to provide the comforts and amenities available to those in the outside world, "but neither is incarceration a justification for dissolving the protection of the Eighth Amendment of the United States Constitution, which prevents the inhumane treatment of prisoners... ."[656]

In 1996, the Utah Supreme Court made decisions related to medical treatment of prison inmates. In the first complaint, Albert L. Ross, a prison inmate, alleged that the prison physician misdiagnosed his leg fracture and ligament damage. Ross was later treated by the University of Utah Medical School, but he had already sustained permanent impairment from the prison physician. He sued the first physician, and the Utah Supreme Court ruled against Ross, claiming that the prison practices were not subject to conventional medical rules.

Justice Stewart was the lone justice to write a dissenting brief. In some of his most colorful language, Justice Stewart pointed out that medical professionals are not immune from liability when treating an incarcerated person, who is entitled to competent medical treatment. He wrote that in the penitentiary "prisoners are treated as a subspecies of the human race, who are not entitled to reasonable, competent medical care... . The majority's ruling is repugnant to fundamental legal precepts... ."[657]

Justice Stewart argued that most of the court claimed, "discipline will somehow be harmed." He rejected that extreme position, saying: "I find no Justification either as a practical or as a legal matter for allowing prison physicians to commit malpractice with impunity."[658] And the *Salt Lake Tribune* agreed with Stewart. It headlined the Supreme Court's decision: "Court Frees Prison Docs from Negligence Suits."[659]

---

[656] Ibid.

[657] Utah Supreme Court, "Ross V. Schackel, 920 P.2d 1159 " (July 12, 1996).

[658] Biele, "Utah Supreme Court '96."

[659] Sheila R. McCann, "Court Frees Prison Docs from Negligence Suits," *Salt Lake Tribune*

In his dissent, Stewart accepted the common-law principles of the past that have protected professionals under certain circumstances. Common law has come to distinguish between discretionary and ministerial acts, the main difference being that discretionary acts involve many personal judgments, while ministerial acts do not.[660] Professionals are liable when their acts are discretionary, but they have never protected government employees, who function in a ministerial capacity. Stewart challenged his colleagues for changing their definitions of these acts. They have decided that when physicians treat a patient at a state hospital, their acts are ministerial. When physicians treat a patient in prison, these same acts are somehow discretionary.[661]

July 13, 1996.

[660] Utah Supreme Court, "Frank V. State, 613 P.2d 517," (June 12, 1980).

[661] Biele, "Utah Supreme Court '96."

21. CHURCH AND STATE

When growing up, young Danny Stewart participated in religious-oriented activities that, today, would be prohibited, or at least frowned upon. He was a pupil at the "progressive" Stewart Laboratory School, technically a public school; but because it was affiliated with the University of Utah, the teachers chose not to begin the school day with prayer, as was the case in almost all of Utah's public primary schools. Danny would regularly go on excursions with his class to places like Temple Square, with its renowned Tabernacle; the Lion House, where Brigham Young made his home and established his administrative offices; the Zion House, where most of Young's many wives lived; and This Is the Place Monument, at the mouth of Emigration Canyon. There was always a ring of pride, as the teacher explained to the pupils the historical significance of the sites. Nobody gave a second thought to the possibility that a "gentile" parent, living in the school boundaries, might object to such religiously oriented field trips.

When Danny was in secondary school, most of his classmates requested "released time" to attend seminary and receive religious instruction. They were excused from one of their classes to walk across Eighth Street, on the north side of East High School, where a Mormon church was located. There they studied LDS church history, the *Bible,* or the *Book of Mormon.* Danny's friends were all athletes, who played football, basketball, and tennis. They were so busy, they chose not to attend seminary, and so young Danny also chose not to do so, even though his sisters enrolled in religious instruction. The credits earned in seminary classes counted toward graduation from high school.[662]

When Danny Stewart graduated from high school, commencement was held in Kingsbury Hall at the University of Utah. One of his teachers and coaches, Harold Johnson, began the graduation ceremony with an invocation. The program consisted of short talks by several graduating students, including one of Danny's best buddies, Ashby Decker. The theme of the talks was "Preservation of Our American Ideals," and their speeches sounded like a Sunday service in the church house. They orated on topics such as "Public Morals," "Religious Ideals," and "Home and Family." One of the Salt Lake City School District board members, LeGrand P. Backman, a former bishop and Mormon mission president, gave the benediction.[663]

In those days, in Salt Lake City, the issue of the separation of church and state rarely came up. School prayer, released time, and the *Book of Mormon*, were simply thought of as an integral part of educational life. In 1963, Dallin Oaks, a professor at the University of Chicago, edited a small volume titled: *The Wall between Church and State*.[664] Oaks stressed that no area of public life was more important than school, for that is where knowledge of, and respect for society, are taught. Oaks noted that there was great debate among scholars about whether the U.S. Constitution allowed school prayer and released time to take place in our public schools; however, in Utah the debate remained almost exclusively among scholars and failed to penetrate the public arena.

When Danny went to West Germany on a Mormon mission, he encountered quite a different church/state model. Protestants in the North, and Catholics in the South, enjoyed formal state recognition. Everyone contributed through taxes to the state church, where the person lived. Consequently,

---

[662] Mary Louise Holbrook, "Telephone Interview at Her Salt Lake City Home," (Jan. 15, 2020).

[663] East High School, "Fifty-Ninth Commencement of East High School," (June 7, 1951).

[664] Dallin H. Oaks, ed. *The Wall between Church and State* (Chicago: The University of Chicago Press, 1963).

Elder Stewart quickly learned what it was like to belong to a religious group that tried to survive in competition with state-sponsored religious institutions. Most of the European countries do not have a tradition of voluntary contributions to their church of choice, beyond the collection plate during Sunday service, and Elder Stewart came to understand the unique position the United States cultivated, as its churches relied almost entirely on donations by their members, while the state and federal governments avoided giving special status or recognition to any one of the hundreds of different religions.

By the time Oaks published his volume, Dan Stewart had contracted polio in Europe and had returned home to complete his bachelor's and law degrees. Dan had studied the U.S. Constitution in his political science classes and was aware that the First Amendment protects the right of freedom of religion and that the "due process clause" of the Fourteenth Amendment prohibits states from establishing or favoring specific religious institutions. Dan, on his own, had also studied the Utah Constitution, including Article 1, Section 4, a relatively long statement that outlined conditions related to religion. These included the sentences:

There shall be no union of church and state, nor shall any church dominate the state or interfere with its functions. No public money or property shall be appropriated for or applied to any religious worship, exercise, or instruction, or for the support of any religious establishment.

When Dan Stewart became a professor of law, he taught each year the mandatory course on the U.S. Constitution. His lectures included issues related to the separation of church and state. He discussed the U.S. Constitution provisions regarding religion and compared them with provisions of the Utah Constitution. He suggested that Article 1, Section 4 was more detailed and inclusive than the First and Fourteenth Amendments, at least as they were related to religion.

After Dan joined the Utah Supreme Court, he found that all the other justices accepted and even lauded the notion that that religion was central for most Utahns. Even justice Zimmerman, who was neither a native of Utah nor a Mormon, acknowledged that religion was important to the state's citizens. And Dallin Oaks changed his position regarding the "wall" between church and state. He decided a wall was an inappropriate metaphor. There must be separation, but Oaks declared it was more like a curtain than a wall.[665]

The highest court of Utah rarely struggled with issues falling under the state/church umbrella. These were usually handled in the federal courts. For example, reproductive rights were a polarizing issue. In 1990, the Utah Legislature passed a bill that aimed to protect the life of the unborn child and sharply curtail the effect of Roe vs. Wade. The Legislature, consisting almost entirely of Mormons, considered abortion as tantamount to killing an unborn child and was therefore akin to murder.[666] The ACLU sued in federal court, so Justice Stewart Dan was not able to express himself as a judge on the case. He had already expressed his positive position on Roe v. Wade: It was the law of the land and must be protected.

Yet another issue that captivated Utah society had to do with gays and others practicing alternative lifestyles. For example, gays fought for equal rights in the workplace, and they demanded that they be able to marry and raise children. In 1989, a Gay Liberation Front was organized in Salt Lake City.

One of the volatile court battles came about when Nebo School District, in South Utah County, imposed a gag order on a Spanish Fork High School gym teacher, Wendy Weaver, because school officials identified her as a lesbian. The Utah ACLU sued the school district, and she was reinstated.[667] That case went to the U.S. District Court, so an appeal would not have come to the Utah Supreme Court, where Justice Stewart could have acted on the case. It is reasonably clear that he would have sided with Weaver, just as people such as Stephen Drabner and Scott Carpenter did,[668] although there are always technical issues that may have intervened.

---

[665] "Interview in the Church Office Building in Salt Lake City."

[666] The legislation is discussed at length in Linda Sillitoe, *Friendly Fire: The Alcu in Utah* (Salt Lake City, Utah: Signature Books, 1996).

[667] U.S. District Court, "Weaver V. Nebo School District, 29 F. Supp. 2d 1279," (Nov. 25, 1998).

[668] Scott Carpenter, "Letter on "Losing Our Sense of Privacy"," *Salt Lake Tribune* Nov. 17, 1997; Stephen Curtis Drabner, "Letter to "Support Wendy Weaver","ibid. (Mar. 30, 2002).

The Weaver trial exemplifies the kind of cases that were raised in terms of religion in educational institutions. Perhaps this was because parochial schools were rare in Utah; however, the issue of school prayer and released time had been mainstays in Utah's public education enterprise.[669] Prayer was said in school, and the *Bible, Book of Mormon*, and *Doctrine and Covenants* were, historically, often mandated readings.[670] Nevertheless, church/state issues relating to schools were rare among Utah Supreme Court cases.

In the two decades that Justice Stewart sat on the bench, he never encountered a case related to the role of religion in educational institutions. The battle over school prayer, for example, had been played out in the U.S. Supreme Court,[671] and various state courts including Pennsylvania, Maryland, and Alabama.[672] Utah educators aligned their public-school policies with the mandates that were being defined elsewhere.

The one national organization that focused on court cases related to religion in Utah was the Society of Separationists. This was an atheist group, founded in 1963, headquartered in Maryland, and was the publisher of the *American Atheist Magazine*.[673] One target of the Separationists was the Salt Lake City Council that, they contended, violated the Utah Constitution by organizing prayer at the beginning of its City Council meetings. On September 26, 1991, the Separationists requested that they stop the practice. When the City Council refused, the Separationists filed an action against them in the Third District Court of Utah. It found that this prayer tradition was a

---

[669] In 1981, the Tenth Circuit Court of Appeals declared Utah's released time program to be constitutional. See Tenth Circuit U.S. Court of Appeals, "Lanner V. Wimmer, 662 F.2d 1349," (July 9, 1981).

[670] Andrew Love Neff, *History of Utah: 1847-1869* (Salt Lake City, Utah: Deseret News Press, 1940).

[671] For example, U.S. Supreme Court, "Engel V. Vitale " in *370 U.S. 421* (1962).

[672] Bruce J. Dierenfield, *The Battle over School Prayer: How Engel V. Vitale Changed America* (Lawrence, Kansas: University Press of Kansas, 2007).

[673] The Separationists dealt with issues other than religion. See, for example, Utah Supreme Court, "Society of Separationists V. Taggart, 862 P.2d 1339," (Oct. 12, 1993).

"religious exercise," in that public money and property were being used for these practices. The Court demanded that the City Council discontinue the prayers. The City Council appealed the case to the Utah Supreme Court.

Justice Michael Zimmerman was assigned to write the lead opinion for the Court. He began by composing a ten-page account of early Mormon history. In dramatic language, he argued that from the beginning of the early settlement the religiously cohesive nature of the settlers defined almost every aspect of their lives. They would kneel in prayer in the morning, bless their food at every meal, and kneel in prayer before retiring. The church hierarchy established a theocratic system of government. There was no "wall" between church and state. The ten pages on Utah history was not a legal document, but Zimmerman noted that, fifty years earlier, Justice Oliver Wendell Holmes had argued "a page of history is worth a volume of logic."[674]

Justice Zimmerman ended his fifty-two-page narrative with a description of how, when Utah prepared to become a state, leaders dealt with the issue of religion. In writing its provisional constitution, the leaders borrowed from other state constitutions to demand the separation of church and state.[675] After all, Utah was becoming part of the United States of America, and the U.S. Constitution required that there be separation; however, Zimmerman stressed that the disconnect was "soft and malleable" and admonished his fellow justices always to consider Utah's history and values. In fact, the Utah State Legislature was actively considering a constitutional amendment of the Utah Constitution so that such religious activities could be conducted in the state.[676]

Zimmerman recognized that the Separationists had a valid point, in that there might have been a religious intent in the City Council prayers, but he also acknowledged the City Council's argument that there was no religious intent, at least as it pertained to a specific church. In fact, clergy from Jewish, Protestant, and Catholic congregations had been invited to give the prayer. He concluded that some middle-ground must be reached, and he stressed the

---

[674] "Society of Separatists V. Whitehead, 870 P.2d 916."

[675] Ibid.

[676] Dan Harrie, "Legislators' Quest to Amend Constitution Grinds to Halt," *Salt Lake Tribune* Dec. 16, 1993.

necessity of strict neutrality on the part of the state. It can neither be an advocate of, nor show hostility, toward a particular religion. Zimmerman concluded that the City Council had achieved constitutional neutrality. Both justices Hall and Durham concurred with Zimmerman's argument, and Howe, after expressing some reservations, also concurred.

Daniel Stewart dissented, with an eight-page account of how the argument of the other justices had, in fact, eroded religious freedom and he indicated that his colleagues refused "to enforce the plain meaning of a constitutional provision."[677] Stewart reminded them of a 1973 decision former justice Utah Justices J. Allan Crockett, Albert Hayden Ellett, F. Henri Henriod had made. These justices were ardent advocates of Utah rights as opposed to federal rights, and they had often been severely rebuked for their anti-nationalism rhetoric. In *Manning v. Sevier County*, they argued that a case in Richfield had neither violated the First Amendment nor Article 1, Section 4 of the Utah constitution.[678]

The plaintiffs had argued that Sevier County had violated both by entering into an agreement with the Mormon Church, jointly to build a hospital in Richfield. After it was built, they had signed a contract for Church Health Services to lease and run the hospital for twenty-five years. The Utah Supreme Court had determined that appropriate safeguards had been made to protect the interests of the city, county, and public in general, so that separate church/state interests had been protected. Justice Stewart told his colleagues that, in this instance, the former justices had "got it right."[679]

Justice Stewart knew there were precedents in Zimmerman's middle-ground argument. In 1973, the Salt Lake City Council and Salt Lake County had erected a permanent granite monolith on City-County grounds, with the Ten Commandments, the All-Seeing Eye of God, the Star of David, the Order of Eagles, letters of the Hebraic alphabet, and an image of Christ inscribed on the granite. Certain residents and taxpayers sued. At the initial trial, the court

---

[677] "Utah Supreme Court Upholds Salt Lake City Council Prayer," *Times-News (Twin Falls, Idaho)* Dec. 11, 1993.

[678][678] Utah Supreme Court, "Manning V. Sevier County, 517 P.2d 549," (Dec. 21, 1973).

[679] "Society of Separatists V. Whitehead, 870 P.2d 916."

determined the monolith was clearly "religious in character," and ordered its removal. On appeal, the Tenth Circuit Court of Appeals reversed the decision. After reviewing the history of relevant cases, it claimed there is no wall between church and state; rather, it is a "blurred, indistinct, and variable barrier," and the court must strike a balance between what is primarily "religious," and what is primarily "secular."[680] The Court was clearly trying to tread a middle-ground in the church/state debate.

Justice Stewart was a child of the Mountain West and had spent his life as a committed member of the Church of Jesus Christ of Latter-day Saints. He was not rejecting religion by challenging Zimmerman's argument. In fact, he recounted another case involving the Mormon Daughters of Utah Pioneers, which had built a pioneer museum on land it had leased at the state Capitol grounds. Its intent was to house artifacts from early Utah pioneers.[681] In 1941, the State Legislature had appropriated funds for this joint effort. On the face of the issue, the museum was a clear breach of the separation of church and state; however, in 1948, when the issue came before the Utah Supreme Court, Justice Stewart noted it was clear that the museum would not be used for religious worship or instruction, but to celebrate the lives of the early residents of the state.

Justice Stewart rejected the middle-ground argument. He pointed out that even the *deist*, Thomas Jefferson, had figured out ways to keep religion separate from politics, when the two issues appeared to be about to clash. Jefferson advocated, for example, the use of public buildings for the use of religious services, when the government was not in session, and he allowed the use of the University of Virginia, without violating the separation clause. In the case before the Utah Supreme Court, Stewart claimed the other justice were "flatly wrong" that the Utah Supreme Court had "shirk[ed] from its duty" by failing to uphold the plain and simple language of the Utah Constitution, which prohibits the use of public money and property to engage in

---

[680] Tenth Circuit U.S. Court of Appeals, "Anderson V. Salt Lake City Corporation, 475 F.2d 29 " (Mar. 19, 1973).

[681] Utah Supreme Court, "Thomas V. Daughters of Utah Pioneers, 197 P.2d 477 108 " (July 14, 1948).

a religious exercise. He claimed the other justices had engaged in a "stunning and revolutionary change" in the meaning of Article 1, Section 4, that could lead to "tyranny."

A curious aspect of the separation issue is that it always involved what was considered improper religious behavior or programs being conducted in the public sector. The other side of the issue has never been a part of public discourse. There has never been a court case that attacked the secular, public intrusion into religious environments, even though, at least in Utah, these encroachments included Johnston's Army, which invaded Utah in the 1850s, or attempts to rid America of polygamy. From the 1860s through the 1880s the federal government did everything it could to destroy the practice of polygamy, and even went so far as to threaten the very existence of the Mormon Church.

After gaining statehood in 1896, church authorities have been left with the right to determine what is appropriate in terms of secular topics in the religious sphere. For example, the church sponsored many programs intending to expose adults and young people to the secular world and nobody objected to those initiatives. The church sponsored theatrical groups and the Seventies Council Hall held regular philosophical, historical, and scientific lectures. These activities were eventually taken over by secular groups, and the church was left to focus on religious issues. In the 1960s and 70s, a last vestige of the early tradition took place in the church. In the Women's Relief Society, once a month all the women were asked to read a prescribed text taken from classical literature, including essays, short stories, and poems from Aristotle, Thomas Aquinas, Frost, Thoreau, Dickinson, etc. Later, enterprising members often organized *Great Books of the Western World* discussions in various wards.

Unfortunately, in recent years church authorities have determined that the only appropriate topics for discussion in adult church classes were religious texts, particularly from Mormon scriptures. Dan Stewart spent almost his entire adult life teaching adult "gospel doctrine" classes in his own ward, but he quietly challenged the policy of focusing exclusively on religion in religious instruction. He accepted the prescribed topic sent to all the wards of the church, at least in America; however, he refused to restrict himself to the messages that came from church headquarters.

For example, if the topic was faith, Dan would not settle for such a discussion as found in Alma of the *Book of Mormon*, but he would explore how, for instance, William James considered faith in his essay, *The Will to Believe*, where James discusses the importance of conviction in accomplishing tasks that require confidence or achieving scientific breakthroughs.[682] If he was assigned the topic of purity, Dan would, of course, discuss instances of purity in the *New Testament*, but he would also explore how the early English founders of America dealt with the issue and why they were called Puritans.

There have always been watchdogs in every congregation of the LDS church, who would look out for deviants, who fail to follow the guidelines sent out to instructors. If someone deviated too much, the watchdog would report them to the leaders of the ward, who would then then face the task of calling the person to repentance or releasing the person from the position of teacher. That never happened to Dan Stewart. He knew and respected the boundaries of deviance, and was able to be thoughtful, critical, and questioning, even though he knew there were limits. Dan would never suggest, for example, that there was not a living prophet at the head of the church, even though the issue of what a prophet is was open for debate.

Through his entire post-mission life, Dan never accepted a calling in the church beyond being a teacher. He possessed values somewhat distinct from those of most Mormons, who, all too often define their relationship with God in terms of the status of their "callings" in the church. The higher the calling the greater their sense of their relationship with God. Dan aspired to be the best possible person he could be, but he measured his value solely in terms of his relationship with God. His feeling of being a complete and full human being had little to do with the status of his calling in the church.

---

[682] William James, *Will to Believe and Other Essays* (New York: Longmans, 1897).

22. Dissent

From the time Dan was an undergraduate one of his central beliefs had been the importance of dissent. He had titled his valedictory address when he graduated from the university, "The Right to Dissent." He told his classmates that one of their vital interests was to encourage dissent. It had utilitarian value. It was the hallmark of an educated man.[683] He had often cited John Stuart Mill, *On Liberty*, who stressed the ability to dissent in a free society.[684]

As a Utah Supreme Court justice, Dan Stewart had a reputation for dissenting. Dan would have claimed his dissents were, objectively speaking, obvious and necessary. He challenged the decision of his fellow justices to allow a mother to have custody over her child even when the woman was not worthy of that custody.[685] He dissented when the other justices chose to take a "middle-ground" approach to the separation of church and state in Utah, arguing that complete separation is the only constitutional alternative.[686] Justice Stewart claimed he had no alternative but to dissent, when his fellow justices refused to acknowledge that a

---

[683] Stewart, "The Right to Dissent."

[684] Mill, *On Liberty*.

[685] Discussed in Chapter 17. Common Law.

[686] Discussed in Chapter 21. Church and State.

medical doctor in the state prison had engaged in malpractice while treating a prisoner.[687]

Dissents are important parts of the legal process: they serve notice that legal decisions are not black and white. There are various sides to any issue; dissents often clarify what those differences are. Regarding supreme courts, a major argument against dissents is that they disrupt the harmony and collegiality among the justices.[688] This argument could have held, when the Utah Supreme Court consisted mainly of practicing lawyers and politicians. But the atmosphere changed after Dan Stewart and Dallin Oaks were appointed. They and those who followed were not practitioners, but scholars who thrived on argument and challenge.

They never took a challenge to their argument as something personal but as intellectually stimulating and energizing.[689] They recognized dissent as part of the process of clarifying and refining an argument. This atmosphere did not abate when Oaks resigned in 1984 to become a Mormon Church general authority, but it continued when Christine Durham and Michael Zimmerman, both steeped in academic traditions, were appointed to the Utah Supreme Court.

Even though other scholars were appointed as justices, Dan Stewart retained his reputation for dissenting. The reasons are many why he had such a reputation. Christine Durham believes Stewart held firmly to the curious claim that the dissenter in an argument always gets the last word, and she believed Dan always wanted to have the last word in any argument.[690] Or perhaps his reputation was partly because in the first two years he was on the bench he dissented seventeen times. At the time, the other justices chose to dissent about half as often.

Usually, the justices decide cases by unanimous consent. In 1985, for example, there were dissents in only 27 of the 189 (14%) lead opinions rendered

---

[687] Discussed in Chapter 20, Utah's Heritage of Evil.

[688] Iman Zekri, "Respectfully Dissenting: How Dissenting Opinions Shape the Law and Impact Collegiality among Judges," *Florida Bar Journal* 94, no. 5 (Sept./Oct. 2020).

[689] Oaks, "Interview in the Church Office Building in Salt Lake City."

[690] Durham, "Interview at Her Salt Lake City Home ".

by the Utah Supreme Court.[691] After the Utah Court of Appeals was established in 1986, and civil cases dealing with divorce, child custody, alimony, etc., shifted to that body, the number of cases the Utah Supreme Court justices considered was considerably reduced; however, the number of dissents increased, probably because justices could devote more attention to each case. In 1989, for example, of the 143 cases to come before the court, dissents occurred 38 times (26%). Justice Stewart dissented 15 times, which was more often than any of the other justices.[692]

If one were to ask Justice Stewart why he had a reputation for dissenting, he would likely have said that dissenting opinions are hard to write, mainly because there is little incentive to do so. "Dissents are extra work," he stated, "and you don't get paid for them."[693] In spite of this, he claimed he often dissented because he had a streak of stubbornness.[694] He believed it was his nature to buck the general sentiment; however, a fundamental conviction lay behind his tendency to challenge conventional thinking. He studied the lives of people who had gone against the tide, and he found they had often made all the difference. Some included the Founding Fathers of the United States, such as Thomas Jefferson and John Adams; leaders of the Protestant Reformation, like Martin Luther and John Calvin; and the Puritans of early New England, including Roger Williams, Anne Marbury Hutchinson, and John Wheelwright.

Stewart's reputation was likely related, in part, to the adamant nature of his dissents. Professor Richard Blake claimed that Stewart's dissents packed a "punch."[695] Justice Richard Howe used the same term, when speaking of Justice Stewart's arguments. Howe noted that when Stewart gets hold of a pen or pencil, he chooses words with a "punch."[696]

---

[691] Data calculated from: 1985 :: Utah Supreme Court Decisions :: Utah Case Law :: Utah Law :: US Law :: Justia

[692] Data calculated from: 1989 :: Utah Supreme Court Decisions :: Utah Case Law :: Utah Law :: US Law :: Justia

[693] Ellis, "Interview of Dan Stewart at His Home in Salt Lake City, ."

[694] Ibid.

[695] Blake, "Tribute: Justice I. Daniel Stewart."

Stewart's dissents were known for their relentless criticism of his colleagues and their majority opinions. He used terms such as "moral nonsense" or "repugnant." He would chide the majority for "shirking from its duty."[697] At other times Stewart would argue that the majority was adopting a "stunning and revolutionary change" that could lead to "tyranny."[698] In the case where he made that critique, he argued that the majority was "flatly wrong."[699] In a case regarding sexual abuse, Justice Stewart pointed out that a man was convicted "on an avalanche of hearsay." The procedures used against the defendant were converted into an "hysteria of overruns" that "trampled the rights" of the accused.[700]

Even though, at times, Justice Stewart agreed with the final decision of other justices, he sometimes dissented because he disagreed with a specific point in their argument. For example, Louis Fred Ireland was convicted of sodomy on a child by the Third District Court. Ireland's lawyers appealed the case to the Utah Supreme Court, and they made several claims about evidence being excluded by the lower court judge. Justice Christine Durham crafted the lead opinion and persuasively rejected all the lawyers' claims. She argued Ireland was clearly guilty, and three of her colleagues concurred.

Stewart dissented, not because he disagreed with the decision of his colleagues; however, he wished to clarify a language issue. Ireland's lawyers claimed the judge had rewritten the wording of his jury instructions related to "reasonable doubt." Durham had dismissed this claim, suggesting that the language was "almost identical" to the typical language given to juries.

Stewart took issue with Durham. On the surface, it was clear that the man was guilty. So why bother with a dissent about a linguistic flaw? Justice

[696] Howe, "Memorial to I. Daniel Stewart Upon His Retirement."

[697] Court, "Ross V. Schackel, 920 P.2d 1159 ". See also, Sheila R. McCann, "Justice Stewart Will Sheathe His Powerful Pen," *Salt Lake Tribune* Sept 1, 1999.

[698] Court, "Society of Separatists V. Whitehead, 870 P.2d 916." See also Flynn, "Isaac Daniel Stewart: 1932-2005."

[699] Court, "Society of Separatists V. Whitehead, 870 P.2d 916."

[700] "State V. Bullock, 791 P.2d 155."

Stewart recognized that the Utah Supreme Court was more than a body to make decisions about guilt or innocence. It was also a meeting ground to exchange ideas, to engage in dialogue, to clarify issues.

State v. Ireland provided an opportunity for Justice Stewart to make a point about language. The judge in the lower court had chosen to give the jury a set of instructions about "reasonable doubt" that deviated from the conventional instructions. The judge instructed the jury that the evidence should be so convincing that "there is no reasonable doubt." There would be an "abiding conviction to the truth of the charge."

Justice Stewart reminded his colleagues that such instructions may be clear, but "that is not the law." In fact, he said, the judge's instruction "misstates the law." There will always be doubt, but there must be no "reasonable doubt." It was crucial to Justice Stewart that processes always be correctly framed. A consequence of his dissent in the Ireland case took immediate effect on a different case being considered. Even though his dissent did not change the outcome of the Hererra case, at the time, the Utah Supreme Court was engaged in a case, *State v. Johnson*,[701] that relied on his dissenting opinion.

In his dictated life story, Justice Stewart commented that a particular dissent stood out for him. *Elks Lodges v. Alcohol Beverage Control*,[702] was one of the few cases ever to come up in Utah involving female discrimination. Elks and Moose Lodges in Utah were men's groups. They did not allow women to be members. In 1993, the Division of Alcoholic Beverage Control (DABC) served notice to twelve Elks Lodges and two Moose Lodges that their private club liquor license would be taken from them, because they did not comply with regulations prohibiting discrimination based on gender.

Upon receiving notice from DABC, ten of the Elks Lodges changed their policies claiming they were complying with the directive. The two other Elks Lodges, in Ogden and Moab, lodged a petition for a review by

---

[701] "State V. Johnson, 774 P.2d 1141," (May 11, 1989).

[702] "Elks Lodges No 719 (Ogden) an No. 2021 (Moab) V. Department of Alchoholic Beverage Control. Moose Lodges No. 259 (Salt Lake City) and No. 2031 (Tooele) V. Department of Alcoholic Beverage Control, 905 P.2d 1189 " (Oct. 23, 1995).

the Utah Supreme Court, the two Moose Lodges, in Salt Lake City and Tooele, also filed a separate petition for review. Because the claims made by both organizations were identical, they were thrown together as a single case.

The two groups are private, non-profit fraternal organizations. They belong to national organizations and abide by their rules and bylaws. Both groups prohibited women from membership, although women participated as guests in meetings, in sponsored activities like "demolition derbies, charity efforts, and several committees, and parties."[703] The four lodges claimed that they were private organizations, and the First Amendment gave them the right to choose the membership of their club.[704]

The argument against them was that the state-issued liquor license each of the lodges held made them subject to the Utah Civil Rights Act. By baring women from membership, the lodges were not living according to the demands of this act. The Court had ruled earlier that if a club bars women as members, it cannot serve alcohol.

Justice Durham wrote the lead opinion. She rejected all the arguments made by the lawyers for the lodges, and she recommended suspending their licenses to serve liquor. Justices Howe and Zimmerman concurred. Justice Stewart dissented.

Justice Stewart wrote that Justice Durham had made a strong case against the Elks and the Moose Lodges. The flaw in her argument was her assumption that the two different organizations were identical. In fact, Justice Stewart pointed out that her arguments only held for the Elks Lodges, which are quasi-public in nature. Elks Lodges operate public restaurants, make their facilities available for public meetings and social gatherings, and carry out extensive catering businesses, making them subject to state and local regulation in the way they dispense liquor.

The Moose Lodges are quite a different organization. They are strictly private. Their members and prospective members are the only people, who are allowed in their facilities. Prospective members must become a member

[703] "Court Calls Law Unconstitutional."

[704] Tricia Ciaravino, "Oh Brother, the Lady's an Elk," *The Daily Spectrum (St. George, Utah)* Dec. 21, 1995.

after the second visit, or they are not allowed further visits. It is a strictly private entity, and it is consequently entitled to constitutional rights of free association. Justice Stewart argued that the Moose Lodges in Salt Lake City and Tooele should have been able to keep their liquor licenses. Justice Russon agreed with Justice Stewart's argument.

The news media had a field day over the decision. Vern Anderson, an Associated Press writer, proclaimed that the case sharply divided the Utah Supreme Court on a 3-2 decision. Justice Durham, a strong advocate of women's rights, argued that Justice Stewart was conferring on a private club the right to "promote prejudice for profit," by suggesting that it be allowed to retain a license granted by the Department of Alcoholic Beverage Control. Justice Stewart recognized the difficulty his argument placed him in regarding women, but he was willing to let the chips fall where they would. In terms of the Moose Lodges, he said, "I didn't see how the courts could interfere."[705] The upshot of all this legal activity ultimately led to a surprising consequence. The fourteen Elks Lodges in Utah quickly began contemplating allowing women to become members,[706] which would solve the problem.

Specific types of cases raised Justice Stewart's ire. Lynn Eric Johnson, a former missionary companion, suggests that Stewart believed the most significant issue Stewart confronted as a justice, had to do with insanity.[707] Stewart believed that the insane, like children, don't realize the wrongfulness of their acts, and it was an injustice on the part of the legal system to determine that insane people could not be exempted from criminal punishment for the acts that they committed.[708] He knew that even before Utah became a state, it had been active in creating institutions and facilities to care for the

---

[705] Stewart, "A Life: Dictated to Richard G. Ellis."

[706] Lili Wright, "Elks Lodges May Buck Tradition: Accept Women," *Salt Lake Tribune* Sept. 23, 1995.

[707] Eric Johnson, "Note to Stewart in Preparation for His Award by the Alumni Association," (Dec. 1999).

[708] Ibid.

insane. Early Utah's Territorial Law prohibited harsh treatment of people, who were insane.[709]

On March 30, 1981, John Hinkley Jr. shot and seriously wounded U.S. President Ronald Reagan outside the Hilton Hotel in Washington D.C. At his trail, Hinkley successfully pleaded innocence because of insanity. There was such outrage throughout the country that several state legislatures, including Utah's, chose to restrict the insanity defense. A crucial decision was the Utah Supreme Court ruling in 1995, *State v. Herrera*.[710]

In 1991, Tomas R. Herrera shot his ex-girlfriend, Claudia Martinez, twice in the head. He thought she was a mannequin and an evil spirit had come to possess her. He attempted to get rid of the spirit. When Claudia's mother and brother confronted him, Herrera unsuccessfully tried to shoot them. In court, the judge charged Herrera with murder and attempted murder. Herrera pleaded not guilty because of insanity. The judge made a curious decision to withdraw the charge of killing Claudia, mainly because insanity rulings in murder cases were still in flux, but the judge pushed to convict him for the attempted killings of her family members. After being sentenced to fifteen years in prison, Herrera's attorneys appealed the case to the Utah Supreme Court.

That case was combined with a second attempted murder by a homeless schizophrenic, Mikell Sweezey, who had attacked a California visitor to Salt Lake City outside the Marriott Hotel. By all accounts, at the time he shot Steven Mathews, Sweezey was hallucinating and hearing voices.[711] He later claimed he was angry because somebody had torn down the shanty he had constructed.[712]

In his lead opinion on the case, Justice Howe noted the long-standing tradition in Utah of compassion regarding cases involving insanity. Despite this tradition, Howe, certainly reflecting on the attempted murder

[709] Charles R. McKell, "History of the Utah State Hospital" (University of Utah, 1948).

[710] Utah Supreme Court, "State V. Herrera, 895 P.2d 359," (April 21, 1995).

[711] E.g., Stephen Hunt, "Homeless Man Gets Prison for Shooting While Hallucinating," *Salt Lake Tribune* Dec. 20 1995.

[712] "A Quick Reaction May Have Saved His Life," *Provo Daily Herald* Nov. 19, 1991.

of President Reagan, argued that insanity defenses now require a "realistic appreciation" of the relationship between mental impairment and murder. Justice Howe agreed that the District Courts were able to deny Herrera's and Sweezey's insanity pleas. Justices Zimmerman and Russon agreed with Howe, and the two parties that had attempted murder were convicted. Justice Stewart dissented.

Stewart's dissent began with a quote from Justice Felix Frankfurter: "Ever since our ancestral common law emerged out of the darkness of its early barbaric days, it has been a postulate of Western civilization that the taking of life by the hand of an insane person is not murder."[713] Stewart noted that the Utah court's decision represented a "monumental departure" from one of the most fundamental principles of Anglo-American criminal law. Stewart noted the court had decided that an insane person, who commits a crime, is as guilty as a sane person despite the longstanding common law tradition that "an act does not make one guilty unless his mind is guilty."

Justice Stewart noted that Howe's decision had eliminated any notion that the mind plays a part in a crime, even though every civilized social system of law recognizes that insanity is a reasonable principle that must be considered. Now, according to Justice Stewart, the Utah Supreme Court justices were sinking back into the "darkness" of the nation's "early barbaric days" by the delusional belief that they should refuse to entertain the possibility that someone may be insane.[714] Stewart indicated that prior to the new law on insanity in Utah, mentally ill defendants had to prove they did not understand that their crime was wrong. Under the new law, the defendant had the burden of proving that they did not understand their victim was a human being.[715]

---

[713] U.S. v. Baldi, 344 U.S. 561, 570, 73 S. Ct. 391, 396, 97 L. Ed. 549 (1953).

[714] McCann, "Utah Supreme Court Not Always in the Spotlight, but Its Decisions Have Wide-Ranging Effect."

[715] Brian Maffly, "Insanity Plea Bargain: Court Finds Defendant Innocent in Wife's Death," ibid. Oct 21, 1996.

Justice Stewart did not dissent merely to vent his ire against a decision his colleagues had made. He usually wished to persuade his fellow justices to reverse their opinion. Such reversals are rare. Less than five months after he joined the Utah Supreme Court. Justice Stewart had been successful. Uranium Services, Inc. had filed on a uranium claim that they believed Torval Albrecht and Sons had abandoned in 1966. When the case reached the Utah Supreme Court, Justice Maughan wrote the lead opinion arguing that the Albrechts had long since given up the uranium site in Southern Utah. Consequently, Uranium Services had a right to take over the claim. He was supported by Justices Wilkins and Hall. Justice Stewart dissented.[716]

His argument was simple and straightforward. The majority in the court had misapplied a rule stating that a litigant has a constitutional right to have issues of fact in a common law action reviewed before a jury of his peers. If disputed affidavits are at play, no judge can take the place of a jury. This had been the case in the Albrecht case. It is likely that his fellow justices were a bit embarrassed to be reminded by a brand-new fellow justice that they were not following prescribed procedure. Nevertheless, two justices reversed their decision.

Just two years after the Uranium Services trial, Justice Stewart's dissent was again successful in persuading at least one of his fellow justices to change her decision. In 1982, Donald Leon Malmrose appealed his conviction by a jury at the Second Judicial District Court of the crime of forcible sexual abuse. The assault victim, an Ogden resident, was jogging on a Weber State University track, when she was met and overwhelmed by a stranger.

Over a period of several weeks, she reviewed pictures from various sources, and eventually identified the assailant from a picture in a school yearbook. The man was a teacher and track coach at a local junior high school. The man testified that, at the time, he was not at the Weber State track and was attending to duties at his school. Eleven witnesses claimed he was at the school when the attack took place. They said they were all waiting

---

[716] Utah Supreme Court, "Albrecht V. Uranium Services, Inc., 596 P.2d 1025 " (May 29, 1979).

for a storm to subside. Weather reports indicated it was a clear day, so their testimonies were dismissed.[717]

Malmrose appealed the case to the Utah Supreme Court, and Justice Howe wrote the lead opinion. He agreed with the original conviction, and Justices Hall and Oaks concurred. Stewart dissented.[718] Justice Stewart had long struggled with issues surrounding eyewitnesses and their memories. In fact, as a professor, he had published research concerning rules of evidence.[719] Eyewitness accounts have, historically, been the most damning of evidence. When a witness says, "I saw him," or makes a claim, "I will never forget his face," the case is often as good as finished. In the Malmrose case, the victim had said there was "no doubt in her mind" that the defendant was the man who had assaulted her.

Despite the respect people show for eye-witness accounts, researchers of that time were beginning to question such evidence. Elizabeth Loftus, for one, showed that recall changes over time, and perception of events can be manipulated.[720] In his rebuttal to Justice Howe's brief, Justice Stewart emphasized that the abused woman was the only eyewitness of the event. And such accounts are shaky, at best. In the aftermath of a traumatic experience, her memory of events was easily distorted and emotionally disturbed.[721] In his dissent, Justice Stewart indicated that the woman's description of the man had many discrepancies, and there was a lengthy time between the event and her identification. In addition, the way pictures of the man were presented to the victim was questionable.

However persuasive Stewart's argument was, it was not enough to overturn the verdict, even though Justice Durham chose to change her opinion. She agreed with Stewart's argument. More importantly, the dissent penned

---

[717] "Jurors Find Coach Guilty of Assault," *Salt Lake Tribune* Feb. 13 1981.

[718] Utah Supreme Court, "State V. Malmrose, 649 P.2d 56," (June 22, 1982).

[719] Stewart, "Perception, Memory, and Hearsay: A Criticism of Present Law and the Proposed Federal Rules of Evidence."

[720] Elizabeth Loftus, *Eyewitness Testimony* (Cambridge, Mass.: Harvard University Press, 1979).

[721] "The Malleabiility of Human Memory."

by Stewart was cited in later cases as providing valuable insights into the gathering and presentation of evidence and the requirement of eyewitness jury instruction.[722]

There were other times when he was successful. For example, in 1984. Jerry Lee Velarde was convicted of murder in the second degree, and through the efforts of Justice Stewart, the judgment of the court was later reversed.[723] In that same year, David M Hansen was also convicted of murder, and Justice Stewart again persuaded his colleagues to reverse their decision.[724]

In the 1980s, a different kind of dissent took place. In *State v. Webb* Justice Stewart did not feel that Michael Zimmerman had gone far enough in his lead opinion about a sexual abuse case.[725] He was able to persuade all his colleagues, including Zimmerman, to change their decisions.

Daniel Webb was convicted of sexually abusing his eighteen-month-old daughter. Zimmerman had been assigned to write the lead opinion for the Utah Supreme Court and accepted as evidence the cry of his baby daughter, "ow, bum, daddy," as her mother lowered her into her bath water. Zimmerman wrote that Webb was denied a fair trial, because the lower court had admitted his daughter's statement as hearsay evidence and Webb's lawyers did not have an opportunity to cross-examine the child. Zimmerman wanted to send the case back to the Seventh District Court, so they could clear the air regarding the evidence and Webb's conviction.[726]

Justice Stewart agreed with Zimmerman's judgment that the lower court trial had not been fair, but he said that Zimmerman's decision did not go far enough. Stewart argued that the lower court could not cross-examine the child in an effective manner. In addition, the hearsay evidence, "ow, bum, daddy" could have meant any number of things and did not necessarily point to the father.

---

[722] E.g., Utah Supreme Court, "State V. Long, 721 P.2d 483," (June 20, 1986).

[723] "State V. Velarde, 734 P.2d 449," (Dec. 4, 1986).

[724] "State V. Hansen, 734 P.2d 421," (Nov. 5, 1986).

[725] "State V. Webb, 779 P.2d 1108 " (July 21, 1989).

[726] "Supreme Court Overturns Sexual Abuse Conviction," *Provo Herald* July 26, 1989.

Justice Stewart stated that the lower court could not have effectively cross-examined the baby. He claimed, "it is beyond credulity that the law could allow a conviction to stand on such evidence."[727] The baby could not even speak in sentences, and was unable to carry out a conversation, let alone serve as a witness to a horrible crime. Stewart's colleagues agreed with his argument that the Utah Supreme Court reverse the conviction of the lower court and allowed Webb to go free.

---

[727] Paul Rolly, "Father's Sex Conviction Overturned," *Salt Lake Tribune* July 26, 1989.

PART VI:

LIFE SPACE

23. Mountain of the Lord's House

When Dan Stewart's daughters were growing up, on most weekends during the summer, his wife drove him and their two daughters up one of the canyons along the Wasatch Front. The car was Dan's freedom. It represented movement and liberty that his wheelchair failed to provide. Their usual weekend destination was Millcreek Canyon, just south of Parley's Canyon, especially known for its hiking trails. There were also picnic facilities available at Church Fork, Pipeline Trail, Winter Gate, or Gobbler's Knob.

The road was nestled in the bottom of a narrow, undeveloped, tree-lined gorge cutting through cliffs rising on both sides. At the picnic stops along the way, Dan could lounge while the girls explored the rough trails leading off into the mountains. They always had to select a spot to park where Elizabeth could unload the wheelchair and help Dan wheel himself into the area. At times, they would take along their small charcoal grill, so they could barbeque hamburgers and eat on permanent, concrete picnic tables, but more often, on the way home, they would stop at a McDonalds for hamburgers or some other take-out.[728]

The Stewart home was close to the mouth of Emigration Canyon, and across the road from *This Is the Place Monument*, signaling where the early pioneers first entered Salt Lake Valley, and Brigham young rose from his

---

[728] Clark, "Interview at Her Home in Corona Del Mar, California."

wagon sick bed to utter the famous words, "This is the place. Go on." Whereas most canyons are rough and craggy, Emigration Canyon is moderately smooth and gentle, though it is heavily wooded. It allowed the early pioneers a relatively easy pathway through the mountains. Dan often went with his family up to a campground or picnic area, with an exotic name, such as Rattlesnake Point, Strong's Fork, or Big Jensen Hollow.

Dan was sensitive of the need to be ever watchful that a stopping place was clean and in order. At the end of their stay in a picnic area, he would organize Elizabeth, Liz, and Shannon in military fashion, to "police the area," marching them through the grounds making sure they picked up all the paper and garbage. His purpose was that they leave the place cleaner than before they arrived and to clear away stray beer cans, napkins, or ketchup bottles that were left by previous visitors.

Dan often recalled his school days when he and his buddies would head for Little or Big Cottonwood Canyon. Toward the end of his life, Dan and his family were especially fond of the Silver Lake area at the head of Big Cottonwood Canyon. The lake is flanked by exquisite mountain summits, with almost one hundred different species of wildflowers, including Colorado columbine, elephant heads, shooting stars, and geraniums, always bursting in bright bloom. There is now a boardwalk around much of the clear, blue lake, which is less than half a mile in circumference, and it forms part of a smooth walking trail all the way around the shallow waters. Toward the end of his life, in his wheelchair, Dan was able to travel the entire distance along the boardwalk and trail surrounding Silver Lake, his travel interrupted only by an occasional large pine tree root spanning across the trail.

Since his youth, Dan had been a lover of the Wasatch mountains. The Stewart weekend drives also included visits to Sundance Ski Resort in Provo Canyon and Weber Canyon. Albian Basin was a favorite site. Located at an altitude of almost 10,000 feet and just above Alta Ski Resort in Little Cottonwood Canyon, Albian's Basin was covered with vibrant wildflowers, including Indian paintbrush, sunflowers, and fireweed. Its massive cliffs and valleys abounded with white pine and quaking aspen groves.

Dan and Elizabeth would occasionally take off with the girls for the weekend, and stay at the old Homestead Resort at Midway, near Heber. They would occasionally travel along the pony express trail all the way to Wendover. Their favorite short vacation spot remained Hot Lava Springs, Idaho. They had gone there for their honeymoon, and they loved to lounge in the hot water that bubbled up from its source deep underground. These weekend excursions were made during the summer months, but occasionally during the winter months they would drive up to Park City, where there were abundant places to stay overnight.[729]

As a practicing Latter-day Saint, Dan had always taken a keen interest in the American Indian. The *Book of Mormon* claims to be an early record of Utah's original inhabitants, including the Ute, Paiute, Goshute, Shoshone, and Navajo. On the many excursions Dan and his family made, they were always keen to check the calendar to see if a Pow Wow was scheduled where they were going. When the girls were pre-teens, more than once the family visited the Uinta Basin, where Bottle Hollow Indian Reservation is located, and the girls played with young Native Americans. At one Pow Wow, Liz and Shannon even participated in gunny sack races and other competitive games with young Ute Indians.[730]

Soon after the pioneers landed in Salt Lake Valley, Brigham Young sent small groups in every direction to colonize the region. Some were sent to the "red rock" region, which has often been called the most spectacular land in the world, filled with colorful and unique geologic formations "characterized by an aloof, seemingly super-terrestrial grandeur."[731] Various tributaries often cut through layers of sedimentary rocks, creating enchanting valleys and gorges.

Those early settlers, who went to Southern Utah, were expected to live off the parched, barren, unproductive wilderness. They did everything they could, but when summer storms filled the rivers to overflowing, settlers

---

[729] "Interview at Her Corona Del Mar, Ca Home," (Feb. 15, 2020).

[730] Ibid.

[731] Stephen C. Jett, "The Canyons of Zion," *Plateau* 51, no. 2 (1979).

would see their entire farms flooded, and their gardens washed away. Or their crops would be scorched and destroyed by the relentless desert sun. And at other times, their canals and irrigation ditches would fill with silt and sand, making it impossible to deliver water to their crops.

Juanita Brooks, Mormon historian, writes that, to the early settlers, Southern Utah looked like "the land that God forgot." To them, it certainly was not something to appreciate and admire. It "spoke to them more of sterility than beauty."[732] While the region would one day be considered a scenic treasure "more beautiful than anything in human art,"[733] most early settlers could see only a barren desolation, promising hardship and suffering. George A. Smith, after whom St. George was named, once said: "If I had a lot here and one in Hell, I'd sell the one in St. George."[734]

These pioneers did not have the time nor inclination to enjoy the spectacular beauty. They were working hard at the business of serving God, surviving, and setting up communities that would be part of God's Kingdom. They did not have the time or energy to sit back and look upon the fragile ecology. They did not even ask whether their efforts preserved or destroyed the native environment. State leaders often decried attempts on the part of the federal government to protect the environment. Land management actions were inevitably seen as "done to us rather than with us." In 1961, at the height of the Utah-federal government conflict, Governor George Clyde, whose family owned a large road construction company, rejected attempts to protect the land, saying, "We are a mining state. We might need this as building stone."[735]

While most settlers would have agreed with Brooks that the red rock area was a land that God forgot, in contrast, Dan Stewart argued that it was a land where God himself would walk. He often thought of Isaiah 2:2 that

[732] Juanita Brooks, "The Land That God Forgot," *Utah Historical Quarterly* 26, no. summer (1958). 207.

[733] Dutton, *Tertiary History of the Grand Canyon District.*

[734] Melvin T. Smith, "Forces That Shaped Utah's Dixie: Another Look," *Utah Historical Quarterly* 47, no. 2 (1979).

[735] Stephen Trimble, "Restore Utah's National Monuments," *Los Angeles Times* Feb. 14, 2021.

suggested this was the "mountain of the Lord's house," and during the summers, he regularly took his family to visit. There he found Zion National Park and Bryce Canyon National Park. Oddly, the family never ventured into the Kaibab National Forest to the North Rim of the Grand Canyon, although they did travel as far South as Jacob Lake. A total of eight national parks were in the region, each unique and incredibly beautiful. Dan also insisted that the family be exposed to the areas that are not tourist spots. The Capitol Reef area is not as accessible as other national parks, and he especially liked to take them to small villages, such as Torrey, where apple, peach, and apricot trees grow along the highway, just like shade trees in other parts of the country.[736]

The Stewarts were regular visitors to Zion National Park, the oldest of all the parks. Its soft sandstone formations had been cut by the Virgin River, creating deep gorges and byways, forming the spectacular Zion Narrows, the Patriarchs, and the Great White Throne. The main reason Zion was their favorite, had to do with the fact that they had a friend and client from the days at Jones Waldo. Robert Brown owned a house in Springdale, on the south edge of the park. It was available to them for free.

The girls were particularly fond of the Moab area, where Arches National Park and Canyonlands National Park are located. Their favorite spots included Dead Horse Point, where, far below, the Colorado River makes an abrupt U-turn, and Gooseneck State Park where the San Juan River twists through several buttes.[737] When Christine Durham joined the Utah Supreme Court, she quickly learned that Dan had the greatest possible affection for the scenic wonders of the state. Christine claimed Dan knew every byway, important fork in the road, and place one could not turn around.[738]

One of the Stewart's memorable trips was to what they called "Hell's Backbone," near Escalante and Boulder, where they were able to visit Anasazi Indian remains. At the time, the roads were almost impossible to navigate.

---

[736] Elizabeth Neff, "Daniel Stewart, Former Utah High Court Justice, Dies," *Salt Lake Tribune* June 25, 2005.

[737] Clark, "Interview at Her Home in Corona Del Mar, California."

[738] Durham, "Interview by Liz Stewart in Christine's Home in Salt Lake City."

They were often not paved, and the car got stuck in deep sand that ground it to a stop. Thereafter, Elizabeth insisted that they always have provisions in the trunk of the car, including food and blankets, as well as a well-stocked first-aid kit.[739]

On these regular excursions, the topics of conversation centered on the mundane things going on and on having fun. The kids, sweet, wholesome and beautiful, were always "messing around," talking and laughing. Dan occasionally indicated a pedagogical bent. "Look at all the colors no matter how subtle." Or he would say: "Look at the green leaf over there and how different and beautiful it is." Or he might ask: "What do you find beautiful?" "Look at those ancient, scraggly Bristlecone Pines. How many different shapes do you see?"

On those long trips, Dan would often remind his daughters that most people only see "a dry, dead landscape," but he constantly pointed out to them the multiple colors of purple, blue, green, brown. "See if you can find five different shades of blue." "Which is your favorite color off in the distance?"

He wanted them to appreciate the region and encouraged them to wander around in the mountains and the desert brush. He especially liked the springtime, when the prickly poppy, blue larkspurs, and woolly locoweed were in bloom. At that time, his daughters were in school, so they could usually only venture south during the hot summer months, when the Utah Supreme Court was not in session. The early mornings were especially attractive. They could stand on a ridge and look onto the seemingly limitless and endless horizon of the desert, interrupted here and there by a lonely mesa or pinnacle that seemed like a painting, shrouded in warm, balmy, hazy air. When the girls saw something of interest, they would exclaim to each other, "Yaba Daba Doo!" It meant a delightful, self-serving "hooray, and here I am," all at once.[740] The fact that Dan was in a wheelchair only entered the equation in that he depended on Elizabeth to drive the car.

The region spawned more than one hundred art studios featuring photos and paintings of the red rock area. Dan's friend and architect, Ron Molen,

---

[739] Clark, "Interview at Her Corona Del Mar, Ca Home."

[740] "Retirement Celebration for Daniel Stewart," (Jan. 7, 2000).

enjoyed the relaxation that sketching the desert scenes provided, and his home was adorned with many such paintings. He enjoyed the "priceless sense of place" the paintings provided, and he occasionally even sold one to a client.[741]

Dan's love of the Four Corners area impelled him to acquire paintings of the region and place them in his home. The predictable themes of these paintings were of mesas standing alone in the desert; pinnacles, such as one would find at Bryce Canyon; or a sandstone arch across a ravine. Two favorites that he owned were painted by an old Sigma Chi brother, Ed. Moreton. He constantly reminded his daughters of the region's importance and the beauty it brought to his life. His keen interest in the red rock area also led him to invest in a collection of rugs, sand paintings, and jewelry, usually made by Navajos or Paiutes; these he gave to Elizabeth when she celebrated a birthday or an anniversary.[742]

Dan recognized that the red rock region is one of the most ecologically sensitive areas in the world, and he worried that unwary residents and enterprising entrepreneurs would take advantage of its fragile landscape for immediate financial gain. In the mid-1960s, after Dan had arrived back in Utah to be a law professor, he became alarmed that another power plant, known as the Kaiparowits Power Project, was under consideration. It had already received the endorsement of Secretary of Interior, Stewart Udall, and Utah Senator Frank Moss. As the project moved forward, it became clear that California Edison, the primary sponsor, envisioned a huge plant that would burn approximately 23,000 tons of locally mined coal a day, and produce 3,500 megawatts of electricity a year. It would, consequently, become "the largest coal-fired power generating station in North America." In addition, it would daily belch tons of black smoke into the air.[743]

---

[741] Helen Forsberg, "Visual Art," *Salt Lake Tribune* May 31, 1998.

[742] Clark, "Retirement Celebration for Daniel Stewart."

[743] David Kent Sproul, "Environmentalism and the Kaiparowitz Power Project, 1964-76," *Utah Historical Quarterly* 70, no. 4, Fall (2002).

Environmentalists quickly mounted an active, vociferous campaign against Edison. Utah, and particularly Mormons, had recently stiffened their political posture toward the conservationists. Indeed, they rejected any intrusion of the federal government and other national entities on their sovereignty, and special place in the world.

The rejection of national norms was expressed in various ways. In terms of conservation, in 1975, Senator Moss conducted a survey in Utah and found that 82.1 percent of the 85,374 responses supported the project.[744] When Robert Redford, a local movie hero and owner of Sundance Ski Resort, located in Provo Canyon, Utah, showed support for the environmentalists, the residents of Kanab, the closest town to the proposed project, burned Redford in effigy in front of the church house on main street. At the time, John Nelson said, ". . . the people of Kane County have put a torch to skunkman Redford, a self-proclaimed voice of the hypocritical obstructionists."[745] In spite of this attitude, and in the face of mounting negative consequences, Edison chose to shut the Kaiparowits Power Project down.[746]

There were times when Dan found himself in strong agreement with popular environmental sentiment of Utahns. The MX project is a case in point. In the 1970s and 80s, the federal government owned more than half the land in the Great Basin. During the Carter and Reagan administrations, the Defense Department proposed establishing a fifteen-thousand-square-mile MX missile base in Western Utah and Eastern Nevada. It promised thousands of local jobs and the infusion of millions of dollars into the local economy, but it would also disrupt the local ecology and further degrade an area that many already thought was almost useless.[747]

[744] Ibid.

[745] "Angry Band of South Utahns Burns Actor, Others in Effigy," *Ogden Standard Examiner* Apr. 19, 1976.

[746] Jack McClellan, "Kaiparowits Coal Power Plans Scuttled," *High Country News* April 23, 1976.

[747] Matthew Glass, *Citizens against the Mx: Public Languages in the Nuclear Age* (Urbana, Illinois: University of Illinois Press, 1993).

Dan was an early opponent of the project, simply because the hundreds of thermonuclear warheads to be buried in silos would be so detrimental to the world he loved. Dan's wife was particularly concerned. She had lived much of her youth in Pioche, Nevada, which, should the project be approved, would be surrounded by silos. Also, she had spent time in Southern Utah near the Utah/Arizona border, while researching her PhD dissertation, and had come to love and appreciate the people there, even though, at the time, she was not yet a member of the church. In her dissertation, she exclaimed that the communal social environment was a major factor in helping young people with muscular dystrophy successfully adjust.[748] She did not want their lives to be placed in harm's way by the Defense Department.

The President of the Church, Spencer W. Kimball, harbored sentiments against the federal government. As did Dan, President Kimball loved America and the choice land the Lord had given us, but he found the federal government was acting in ways that are contrary to the wishes of the Lord. In 1976, he wrote a passionate essay in the *Ensign Magazine*, with the title: "The False God's We Worship." In that essay, he suggested that the federal government's infatuation with military might was taking the country in a direction God did not like, and he declared that we must repent.[749]

Dan's old law school colleague, Professor Edwin Firmage, took advantage of such sentiment and persuaded the Mormon leadership that the local population would share a "highly disproportionate share of the burden," should their lives one day be lost, and property destroyed.[750] Consequently, the MX project was tabled.

After Dan Stewart joined the Utah Supreme Court, he was constantly reminded of the red rock region. A huge 1905 painting of a sandstone

---

[748] Bryan, "Psychological Characteristics of Adolescents in a Kindred Known to Have Facio-Scapula-Humeral Muscular Dystrophy."

[749] Spencer W. Kimball, "The False Gods We Worship," *Ensign Magazine* June (1976).

[750] Jacob W. Olmstead, "Educating the Mormon Hierarchy: The Grassroots Opposition to the Mx in Utah," in *Utah in the Twentieth Century*, ed. Brian Q. Cannon and Jessie L. Embry (Logan, Utah: Utah State University Press, 2009).

arch, by artist H.L.A. Culmer, named *Caroline Bridge*,[751] was placed on the wall behind the bench at the capitol building. It was a geological picture of a magnificent natural bridge that appeared to span across all the natural world. Two people on horses at the edge of the river running under the bridge, were barely visible and certainly not the center of attention. But they suggested the justices were in the wilds of Southern Utah, making decisions about the state that might be light years beyond our understanding, but which were indistinguishable from the broader truths that dominate our stage in life. The Supreme Court bench was lit by a curved overhead skylight that spanned above the entire front of the chamber, and the arch in the painting could have accommodated a sports stadium.

Two years before Dan Stewart retired as a Justice of the Utah Supreme Court, the justices left the capitol building and moved to the Scott Matheson Court Building on Fourth South and State Street. It was a difficult move for all. The building housed the Third District Court, and the justices complained that they were moving down to a lower court setting. They believed the highest court in Utah belonged in the Capitol Building.

When the Utah Supreme Court did move, they discovered Chief Justice Michael Zimmerman, as formal head of the court, had commissioned a new painting, costing $75,000, to be placed behind the new bench.[752] It was named *Capitol Reef* by painter Doug Snow, a prominent Utah artist, known for creating large abstract murals. The painting at the new Utah Supreme Court stood almost twenty feet high and was an abstract creation that only confused and distracted the lawyers facing the bench.[753] Its name suggested something related to the red rock region, but even one with a good imagination could see nothing related to Southern Utah. Fortunately for all, a gray curtain was pulled over the painting during court sessions, but it only reinforced the opinion of the justices that the move to the Matheson Building had not been made in their best interests.

---

[751] Now known as Kachina Bridge.

[752] Ron Molen, "Telephone Interview with Molen at His Salt Lake City Home," (July 20, 2020).

[753] Clark, "Interview at Her Corona Del Mar, Ca Home."

24. Dinner and Discussion

There is a tradition in Utah, thought by locals to be unique and special, that people regularly gather for group discussion. Grethe Peterson, wife of a former University of Utah President, calls this "a Mormon thing."[754] From their beginnings, Mormons would assemble in someone's home for "fireside chats." In the early days of the church, these discussions usually focused on religious doctrine and standards, but people organized into small groups to explore more general issues.

Discussion groups were an important part of Dan Stewart's adult social existence. Don Stringham has suggested these events had become so important to Dan that toward the end of his life they were keeping him alive.[755] Dan's participation in discussion groups began shortly after he was released from the ward of the LDS Hospital. Dan suggested to friends, Ken Handley and Bruce Robinson, that they organize a conversation each Thursday at Dan's home on Butler Avenue.[756]

They responded positively. Each week they identified a familiar *Bible* story. A session began by reading a story, such as the Tower of Babel, Noah in the belly of a whale, the Samaritan woman at the well, or Jesus walking

---

[754] Grethe Peterson, "Interview at Her Home in Salt Lake City," (Sept. 25, 2018).

[755] Stringham, "Interview at His Home in Salt Lake City ".

[756] Stewart, *Addendum.*

on water. The basic question they asked was: "What lessons can we learn from this story?"[757]

The group lasted only a matter of months but provided valuable stimulation at a time when Dan was trying to adjust to a world outside the hospital. Every person in the group was a gifted speaker. Each had his say, and the various points of view were framed and developed. The time was not wasted. Dan was engaged, connecting again with his social world, and discussion groups became a regular part of Dan's life.

Even before Dan Stewart returned home from *Rancho Los Amigos*, a discussion group was meeting at the home of Lowell L. Bennion, the director of the University of Utah Institute of Religion. Several members of this group were former missionaries from the West German mission, including John Bennion, Don Stringham, Val Rust, Dale Larsen, and Eric Pollei. Bennion created the forum, in part, so he could get feedback and clarification on church issues he was writing about. At the time, he was writing a book that discussed the different ways of knowing, and how each way might assist someone seeking religious knowledge.[758] The students and their wives and dates, met at Bennion's home at least one Sunday evening each month.

Several members of that discussion group eventually decided that the group meeting was getting too large and unwieldy, so a small contingent, including John Bennion, Don Stringham, Dean Larson, Jim Clayton, and Ron Molen, broke away from the larger body, and set up a smaller group. Because so many of these friends had been missionaries in West Germany, they were generally described as the "German group," and they soon invited others to join them, including Dan Stewart.

The German Group always discussed topics of pressing personal concern. The most explosive issue at the time, at least for thoughtful, young Mormons, was church policy to exclude Blacks from holding the priesthood. This policy arose in the 1830s, during the time the Mormons had located in

---

[757] Handley, "Interview at Their Home in Salt Lake City, ."

[758] Lowell L. Bennion, *Religion and the Pursuit of Truth* (Salt Lake City, Utah: Deseret Book, 1959).

Missouri. There was great tension between the locals and the Mormons. One source of stress was the fact that the Mormons were, by and large, New England abolitionists, while the Missourians were Southern defenders of slavery. In fact, Joseph Smith had received a revelation telling him: "Therefore, it is not right that any man should be in bondage one to another."[759] There were already Black members of the church, who were being given "callings" in congregations, but Mormon leaders were pressured by Missourians to keep Blacks in their place. They attempted to placate the locals by assuring them that they would no longer give Blacks leadership roles. In 1835, the policy became codified in Mormon scripture by the following *Doctrine and Covenants* verse:

...we do not believe it right to interfere with bond-servants, neither preach the gospel to, nor baptize them contrary to the will and wish of their masters, nor to meddle with or influence in the least to cause them to be dissatisfied with their situations in this life....[760]

Mormons stopped ordaining Blacks as priesthood holders. In 1852, Brigham Young declared that Blacks could neither hold the priesthood nor participate in temple ordinances.[761] This policy lay dormant for a century, although there were explanations circulating among the saints connecting Blacks with the curse of Ham or suggesting that in their pre-mortal life Blacks were fence-sitters during the war in heaven.[762]

In the 1950s, the issue finally came to the fore. As racial tensions arose in America, some church leaders began questioning the policy. Lowell Bennion was known to meet regularly with various General Authorities, such as Joseph Fielding Smith, trying to convince them to change this policy. However, church leaders argued to Bennion that the rules relating to Blacks were codified in Mormon scriptures, and a policy-change required God's intervention, by way of revelation to the prophet.

---

[759] D&C 101:79

[760] Doctrine and Covenants 134: 12.

[761] Bowman, *The Mormon People: The Making of an American Faith.*

[762] Claudia L. Bushman, *Contemporary Mormonism: Latter-Day Saints in Modern America* (Westport, Connecticut: Praeger Publishers, 2006).

Dan Stewart and his young friends wanted to explore various mechanisms to ensure that their voices be heard. Others advised them that a policy to begin giving Black men the priesthood was a church matter, and they must wait until the church acted. They argued that God told them: "it is not meet that I should command in all things; for he that is compelled in all things, the same is a slothful and not a wise servant."[763]

Dan and his friends believed they should take action. They believed God would not give a new commandment until his people were ready to receive it. In other words, these young men believed a change in church policy toward Blacks would not occur until Mormons generally believed their prophet ought to receive a new revelation. So, they held meetings, wrote letters, and openly discussed their displeasure. The letters went to Dan's neighbor, President David O. McKay, or apostles, who might be receptive to their message, including Hugh B. Brown, Spencer W. Kimball, or Adam S. Bennion. Letter-writing was not Dan Stewart's style. Instead, he joined the American Civil Liberties Union (ACLU). In 1979, LDS President, Spencer W. Kimball, announced that he had received a revelation that every male member in the church was eligible to be ordained to the priesthood.

The German Group moved from home to home, and the responsibility fell on the shoulders of the host to decide what members would read to be discussed. They might discuss immigration one month and the atonement the next, or the homeless in March then tithing in April. Dan was always in attendance, but he usually played a relatively passive role. Even as a teacher, he had never been feisty and discordant, but quietly and gently moved a discussion forward.

In the beginning of the Stewart's involvement with the group, he was sensitive to the fact that his wife, Elizabeth, was new to the gospel and needed nurturing much more than testing. She was usually relatively quiet, but was self-possessed, and the others recognized there was steel in her.[764] Having studied at a clothing design school, she knew how to dress her model

---

[763] Doctrine and Covenants 58:26.

[764] James Clayton, "Interview in His Home in Salt Lake City," (On File with the Author Sept. 28, 2018).

figure. She moved in an elegant manner. She had big brown eyes, full lips, and medium brown hair cut shoulder length.[765]

She was proud not only of being a woman but of being the wife of Dan Stewart. She regularly, openly said to him, in public, "I love you," and "was totally focused on him and his welfare."[766] Some in the group felt she was not as open as Dan, but she was respected for making an occasional thoughtful comment or observation.[767] Dan would sit back and listen to various comments, then he would quietly offer his opinion. He neither invited debate nor worried about the possibility that someone in the group might have a different opinion.[768]

One of Dan's gifts was his ability to synthesize an issue. After listening to various opinions about a topic being discussed, he would often frame the arguments for and against an initiative or action. Of course, many people possess such a skill, but his gift was his ability to outline an issue without alienating people or making them feel he was accusing them of being guilty of poor judgment. He appeared always to be open and sympathetic to various points of view.[769] Dan and his colleagues recognized that the church has, since its beginnings, held to claims of having a prophet who speaks for Christ on earth and demands obedience of religious adherents, but they recognized there was a difference between the "office" and the man.

Early Mormons were part of a general religious movement that included several new churches, including Campbellites, Millerites, Seventh Day Adventists, Christian Scientists, and Jehovah's Witnesses. They all attempted to rid themselves of stark divisions between common believers and an elitist clergy by creating unpaid, lay leaders, who possessed no more formal authority than anyone else. However, Mormons differed from these other religions. While these other churches eliminated the basic dualism between elites

[765] Clark, "Interview at Her Home in Corona Del Mar, California."

[766] Donna Smart, "Interview at Her Home in Salt Lake City," (Sept. 24, 2018).

[767] Peterson, "Interview at Her Home in Salt Lake City."

[768] Ron Molen, "Interview at His Home in Salt Lake City, ," (June 6, 2018).

[769] Smart, "Interview at Her Home in Salt Lake City."

and commoners by doing away with the professional clergy, Mormons elevated all men to the station of a priest.

The prophet was just the ranking member of the priesthood. Those in the German group certainly believed that while Mormon prophets possessed the authority of God, they are neither learned theologians nor professional clergy, but ordinary people like themselves, who are called by God to serve as His spokesperson here on earth. These prophets neither demand nor expect reverence, let alone unquestioned allegiance, because they are simple, ordinary human beings, just like all the other Mormon subjects of God.

By any measure, these young men, including Dan, were the elites of Utah society. They were articulate, well educated, and well-connected; however, they were also young, inexperienced, and innocent. Even Dan, who had suffered so much through his struggle with polio, was just beginning his journey through life. Of course, the Mormon leaders were not those "that preach false doctrines. . . and commit whoredoms," but these young Mormons felt that their leaders were, at times, guilty of making ill-advised choices.

For example, General Authorities often appeared to be insensitive to the populist-driven Preservation Movement of the twentieth century, which focused on protecting and maintaining their buildings of religious historical value. For example, in 1962 the church announced it was going to raze the old, beautiful Salt Lake Temple annex on Temple Square, and replace it with a new building. For years this annex served as the entrance to the Temple, where all those preparing to attend Temple sessions, could meet and dress appropriately.

For many, the old annex stood as a wonderful symbol with artistic charm. Dan and Elizabeth Stewart, who had first visited the Salt Lake Temple by way of that annex, objected to the destruction of one of the city's few Victorian versions of a Byzantine style. It was designed by Brigham Young's architect son, Joseph Don Carlos Young. The Stewarts were convinced that the destruction of this annex was a "wart on the symbol of the church,"[770] and vigorously opposed it, but to no avail. The old annex was replaced by a building that had a vague and distasteful resemblance to the temple.

---

[770] Peterson, "Interview at Her Home in Salt Lake City."

The German group also opposed the razing of the ninety-three-year-old Coleville Tabernacle, although in 1970 it had been placed on the Utah State Register of Historic Sites and in 1971 on the National Register of Historic Places. Its gothic-style architecture was accented by striking and elaborately designed stain-class windows imported from Belgium. The activists in the discussion group joined with others in focusing media attention on the issue, and the lawyers in the group supported locals by helping to place a restraining order on the church. Eventually, to the dismay of Dan and his friends, a judge struck down the order and the building, so beautiful in the eyes of so many Mormons, was torn down. Some of the women spoke of the event as "the rape of the Coleville Tabernacle."[771]

The activism, so prevalent in the early years of the discussion groups, continued throughout Dan's life; however, the issues shifted over time. In the early 1990s, Ron Molen's son was a graduate student at the University of Indiana. He investigated a fight between a female student living next door and her German boyfriend, who had recently arrived from Stanford. The German student shot and killed him, then shot his girlfriend and finally killed himself.

The incident had a dramatic effect on Molen's attitude toward gun control. He joined "Utahns against Gun Violence" and eventually became its president.[772] When it was his turn to host the discussion group, he asked group members to read literature that supported gun control. Almost all the male members had hunted deer, pheasants, or ducks, and each usually had a rifle and/or a shotgun in the house. However, through Ron's urging, they became sensitized to the dangers of a society filled with weapons.

A particular concern was that young people were beginning to hunt without any instruction as to the proper and restricted use of firearms. Molen wanted the state to go beyond "educating the youth about guns" and adopt measures that would prevent others from experiencing what had happened to his son. The discussion group advocated a state law that would ensure

---

[771] Renee C. Nelson, "Arguing Added 12 Years to His Life," *Provo Daily Herald* Feb. 16, 1982.

[772] "Task Force Recommends Restrictions on Gun Laws," *Salt Lake Tribune* Nov. 18, 1994.

safety for everyone by restricting the purchase and use of firearms.[773] Dan was particularly supportive of Ron's attempt to enlighten people about the misuse of firearms.[774]

From time to time the group would invite a guest to discuss a specific topic. Neal A. Maxwell, who would eventually be called to the Quorum of the Twelve Apostles in the church, spent an evening with the group discussing the topic: "How to Be a Change Agent in the Church." Not all guests were religious leaders. Calvin Rampton, Utah governor from Davis County from 1965 until 1977, was a close friend of Don Stringham, who was also from Davis County; Don invited him to talk with the group about "How to Be a Successful Politician."

Members of the group included Chase and Grethe Peterson. Chase was eventually chosen to be the President of the University of Utah, and when it came time for them be the host, Grethe was the one who selected the readings and prepared for the group. Chase had studied medicine at Harvard, while Grethe had attended Radcliffe, next door to Harvard. While in the East they subscribed to the *New York Times* and the *New Yorker,* and their reading selections were always taken from these sources. Their affiliation with the church remained strong. He had served as Bishop while he was in Cambridge and shared Dan's values.

Jim Clayton, distinguished professor of history at the University of Utah, was an active member of the group, which he often hosted in his home, located on what some people call "the nicest street in Utah," East Arlington Drive, just a few minutes from the old Stewart home on Butler Avenue. Dan usually attended the meetings Clayton hosted, although it was very difficult for him to get into the house. The driveway was a long slopping divided track down to the street, and the steps between the two tracks were difficult for an ordinary person to manage, and especially challenging for Dan. He had to rely on several people to lift his wheelchair up the hill and into the house.

Clayton was somewhat confrontational in nature, and the readings he recommended usually sparked controversy and criticism. For example, one

---

[773] Smart, "Interview at Her Home in Salt Lake City."

[774] Ron Molen, "Telephone Interview at His Home in Salt Lake City," (Nov. 9, 2018).

month he had the group read a paper that was a precursor to the book, "Bell Shaped Curve," by conservatives Richard Herrnstein and Charles Murray, who maintained that American policies regarding Blacks were misguided.[775] Based on "objective" test scores they pointed out that Blacks were always, on average, far below Whites. They claimed it was a disservice to Blacks, placing them in the same academic groups with Whites. On this discussion evening, Clayton extended a special invitation to David Gardner, President of the University of Utah, assuming Gardner would explain why the university policy was not in accord with "objective evidence." Clayton was dismayed that Gardner didn't take the bait dangling in front of his eyes.

Clayton complained, "He said nothing."[776] Dan was rarely argumentative and confrontational, but he was always prepared and well-informed. On the evening at Clayton's home, Dan confessed to the group that he was deeply committed to "objective" data, but he wondered aloud how one should respond to the data Herrnstein and Murray were presenting.[777]

The particular discussion assemblage that sustained itself through most of Dan's adult life, was known as the Dinner and Discussion (D&D) group. The label D&D was so ubiquitous that it was used by many groups in Utah,[778] and was likely attached to more than one group to which Dan belonged. Certainly, the German Group, and others connected with Dan Stewart, were so known. The host prepared the "dinner," usually with care, but it rarely consisted of no more than a soup or casserole, with cheeses and cold cuts on the side, along with a non-alcoholic drink. More than a dozen people were usually in attendance on a given evening, so it was rarely possible to sit at a table. Everyone usually held a tray on his lap. Desert consisted of ice cream, with a cookie or brownie.

---

[775] Richard Herrnstein and Charles Murray, *The Bell Curve: Intelligence and Class Structure in American Life* (New York: Simon and Schuster, 1996).

[776] Clayton, "Interview in His Home in Salt Lake City."

[777] Ibid.

[778] See, for example, "Calendar of Music and Events," *Park Record* June 5-7, 2002; "Civic Clubs to Hear Resource Discussion," *Tremonton Garland Times* Nov. 12, 1964.

One of the D&Ds lasting many decades, was initiated by Bob and Dixie Huefner. In 1971/72, they were in Massachusetts, where Bob was attending the Massachusetts Institute of Technology. In fact, Boston provided a common connection for the Huefner D&D group. The Handleys, Petersons, and Huefners met while they were all in the East doing graduate studies. And the issues they discussed were often personal and intimate to the life of one or another member of the group. The Molen experience with the murder of their son, noted above, is instructive.

In 1966, Dan's classmate at East High, Eugene England, started publication of what was to become a prominent, independent quarterly, known as *Dialogue: A Journal of Mormon Thought.* England had gathered several young scholars at Stanford, where they were all graduate students, and they collectively acted as the editorial staff. Its articles were peer-reviewed and ran the gamut of academic disciplines, from sociology to geography, history, and the physical sciences. Dan, wishing to keep abreast of his friend's work, and thinking the journal might provide valuable readings for the discussion group, decided to subscribe.

He asked Ken Handley to do the paperwork for him. The subscription was a mere six dollars for four issues per year. Dan had loaned Ken some money the previous week, and he assumed Ken would pay it back by helping to pay for the subscription, so he sent Ken five dollars, thinking Ken would make up the difference. Ken didn't realize why Dan was sending him less than the subscription price, so when Dan's first *Dialogue* arrived, he tore out half the pages and forwarded the rest of the copy to Dan with the following note: "Welcome to *Dialogue*, you stingy bastard."[779]

The monthly papers the members chose to read would have likely been selected by any similar group. They included titles, such as Daniel P. Moynihan's "Defining Deviancy Down," Peter Drucker's "The Age of Social Transformation," Cornel West's "Race Matters," James Fallow's "Breaking the News, How the Media Undermines American Democracy, or Wilfred M. McClay's "Do Ideas Matter in America?" There were topics that Mormon intellectuals would gravitate toward, such as a discussion of a Sunstone Sym-

---

779 Handley, "Interview at Their Home in Salt Lake City, ."

posium on "Why We Stay," or issues that thoughtful Mormons would be curious to know, such as a discussion on "Significant Changes in the Book of Mormon," or a general topic on "Mormonism and Politics: Are They Compatible?"[780]

Of significance would be the topics that Dan chose. Through his adult life, he had subscribed to many journals, including *Foreign Policy*, *The American Scholar*, *New Yorker*, *Atlantic Monthly*, *Dialogue*, and *Sunstone*. For example, in 2003, toward the end of his life, he selected a newspaper editorial of Serge Schmemann, editorial page editor of the *Paris Herald Tribune*, titled: "The Burden of Tolerance in a World of Division."[781]

Some of the discussion groups that Dan was a part of, met on a regular schedule for more than sixty years. The membership shifted through the years, but Dan and his wife's involvement was a constant. Toward the end of Dan's life, his daughter, Liz, began to attend, mainly because she could drive her mother to the event. John Bennion called Liz one day and told her he had polled every member of the group, and they had all agreed, it would be a privilege if she were to become a formal member. I asked her once what a young woman found stimulating in such a gathering, and she said, "They all relate these large issues being discussed to their own personal lives."

Dan's participation was somewhat Socratic in that he raised issues more than he resolved them. John Bennion found him to be "one of the profound thinkers I have ever known."[782] Finally, in 2005, his participation was cut short by his failing health and death.

---

[780] Shannon Stewart Clark possesses a collection of the papers read by the group.

[781] Serge Schmemann, "The Burden of Tolerance in a World of Division," *International Herald Tribune* Dec. 20, 2002.

[782] John Bennion, "Funeral Oration at the Time of Dan Stewart's Death," (Salt Lake City, Utah June 23, 2005).

25. Legacy and Death

Political observers consider the 1980s and 90s to have been the "golden period for the Utah Supreme Court."[783] All sitting justices, including Dan Stewart, were among the best the state had produced. Dan's was the first of a series of outstanding appointments, which included Richard C. Howe, Dallin H. Oaks, Christine M. Durham, and Michael D. Zimmerman.

Dan Stewart's major legacy was his role in helping to restore the quality of the Utah Supreme Court and turning it into a model institution. His appointment signaled the end of a brief but difficult time in the state. Since the end of the 1940s, the state government, particularly the Utah Supreme Court, had been ladened with crisis, bickering, and ineptitude. The crisis was brought about mainly because the leaders of Utah, including members of the Utah Supreme Court, and the Utah Legislature consciously and intentionally separated themselves from the central government of the United States.

Utah's attempts to withdraw from the American mainstream were burdened with mistakes, misrepresentations, and ridicule. For example, Justice Albert H. Ellett, Dan's immediate predecessor on the Utah Supreme Court, claimed that the Bill of Rights had no place in the state.[784] He believed it was only valid in Washington, D.C. Both the Utah Legislature and the Utah

---

[783] Rivera, "Robe Warriors Shaped a Golden Era."

[784] Court, "Dyett V. Turner."

Supreme Court came under criticism so severe that Utah's government fell into crisis. And the state became a source of scorn in America. Law professors at the University of Utah felt the contempt was well earned. Dan's former colleague, Professor Arlo van Alstyne, would write: "By any objective standard, the Utah Legislature is the worst legislature in the world, but compared to the Utah Supreme Court, it is a crown jewel of institutions."[785]

The Utah Supreme Court suffered ridicule. One of Stewart's colleagues on the bench and former law professor from the University of Chicago, Dallin H. Oaks, who had grown up in Utah and would become a Mormon apostle, suggests that prior to the appointment of Dan Stewart, the Utah Supreme Court had been held in such low regard, that it had become a "hiss and a byword" among legal scholars.[786]

Utahn's contempt for the federal government was rather recent, and it represented a sharp departure of attitude from the first half of the twentieth century. After 1896, when Utah became a state, both its political and religious leaders attempted to draw the state into a closer alliance with the United States. At first, the U.S. Congress, claiming the Utah representatives, such as Reed Smoot, still practiced polygamy and refused to acknowledge the elected Utah representatives in Washington, D.C. Eventually, Utah was able to establish its legitimacy, and Mormons achieved respectability by becoming models of patriotism and citizenship.

In addition, their religious and political values shifted in that they tended to become similar to those of the general population. Sociologist Armand Mauss suggests that Mormons assimilated so thoroughly that they seemed to "out American" other Americans.[787] The LDS Church even became involved in American capitalism, with extensive investments in businesses and corporations.[788] By the middle of the twentieth century, Utah Mormons had

---

[785] Aaron, "Interview at the College of Law, University of Utah, in Salt Lake City."

[786] Oaks, "Interview in the Church Office Building in Salt Lake City." The phrase is taken from the *Book of Mormon*, I Nephi 19, 14.

[787] Mauss, *The Angel and the Beehive: The Mormon Struggle with Assimilation.*

[788] Stephen Mansfield, *The Mormon Ethic and the Spirit of Capitalism* (Washington, D.C.: Worthy Publishing, 1990).

become fully assimilated, not only in secular, social, and political matters but, ominously, in most of their religious practices and beliefs.[789]

After World War II, Utahns finally began to question whether their decision to assimilate had been a good one, and they chose to begin withdrawing their allegiance to federal mandates. To Dan Stewart's chagrin, Utah leaders blamed the federal government for the state's lack of support, claiming those in Washington, D.C. had abandoned the basic precepts of the U.S. Constitution and had coopted local state independence.[790] During the 1950s, the *Deseret News,* the Mormon Church newspaper, ran a weekly editorial, critical of the federal government. It had a subtitle: "We stand for the Constitution of the United States as having been divinely inspired," suggesting that the federal government had abandoned God's chosen land.

Dan Stewart recognized that Mormons had an additional incentive to pull back from federal influence. Mormons believed they were becoming so Americanized that they were forsaking their "uniqueness." From the beginning of the LDS Church in 1830, Mormons claimed they were a special people with distinct practices and beliefs, including possessing a variety of spiritual gifts, wearing unique clothes, as well as practicing special eating and drinking traditions. They thrived in their sense of being different.

After all, they believed they were God's chosen, deserving of special status and recognition. But now Mormons worried that they were melding with America to the point that they were losing that reputation of being distinct. Mormons appreciated and enjoyed any opportunity to be seen as outsiders. Their peculiarity often made them appear, in the eyes of the world, curious and odd, like the naive, inadequate, and hilarious American Mormon missionaries in Africa found in the contemporary Broadway hit, *The Book of Mormon.*[791]

---

[789] Yorgason, *Transformation of the Mormon Culture Region.*

[790] Editorial, "Why Businessmen Go Home," *Deseret News* Dec. 29, 1955; "No Wonder Our Cities Lack So Much," *Deseret News* May 18, 1952.

[791] https://thebookofmormonmusical.com/

Even as most Utahns were distancing themselves from the country's mainstream, some citizens remained committed to being fully American. Dan Stewart was one of these people. He knew that American democracy was a fragile thing. It would only be safeguarded by what lies in the hearts of the men and women of the country. And Utah's democratic principles would, likewise, only be protected and nourished by the spiritual safeguards that have always protected the state's democracy and freedoms. [792]

We have always turned to the country's foundational documents, in time of need, for they certify people's rights and beliefs. Dan Stewart was adamant that documents, including the constitutions, ensure the continuation of the rights of all Americans. He was fully and unconditionally committed both to the U.S. Constitution, the Utah Constitution, and the various branches of the federal government. To the uninformed, such a constitutional relationship seems self-evident; indeed, the Utah Constitution stipulates that "the State of Utah is an inseparable part of the Federal Union, and the Constitution of the United States is the supreme law of the land."[793]

Toward the end of the twentieth century, the transformation of the court was a remarkable development. Even those law professors at the University of Utah, who had been so critical of the Utah Supreme Court, began to boast of its present quality shift. Professor Edward Firmage, one of the earlier court's sharpest critics, remarked that Dan Stewart and his colleagues on the bench created a court that was "the equal of the national court." He claimed the Utah justices were certainly "as articulate and intellectually able as the [U.S.] Supreme Court."[794]

Justice Stewart's place on the Utah Supreme Court was seminal and groundbreaking. Christine Durham, a colleague on the Utah Supreme Court, says Justice Stewart saw the world through a unique lens.[795] He had a distinctive perspective of the Utah Constitution, one that was quite different

---

[792] Stewart, "Speech Given at Swearing in of Admittees to the Utah State Bar."

[793] Article 1, Section 3.

[794] Edwin B. Firmage, "Note to Stewart at the Time of His Award by the Founder's Day Commission," (Feb. 23, 2000).

[795] Durham, "Address to the University of Utah Law School, Honoring Dan Stewart."

from any of her other colleagues on the bench. For example, Justice Stewart was the only justice of his time to insist that Article I, Section 4 of the Utah Constitution meant what is stated: There must be a distinct separation of church and state. All the other justices of his time were melioristic in their attitude, taking a middle-ground approach in the relationship that should exist between church and state. Dan believed the Mormon Church was stronger when separation was maintained.[796]

Richard Blake, a colleague at the University of Utah law school, also suggested Justice Stewart's notions were "praiseworthy and distinct, regarding the rights and liberties protected by the Utah Constitution."[797] Stewart had studied other state constitutions and knew what was unique and what was conventional. He paid particular attention to the inalienable rights of women, children, criminals, and the mentally ill. And Justice Stewart differed from the other justices, for example, in that he placed a higher priority on the rights of a child over the rights of an abusive mother.[798]

Dan's intellectual and spiritual underpinnings did not originate exclusively through his Mormon heritage. He had steeped himself in classical Western literature, and he became an avid student, for example, of the German Shakespeare, Johann Wolfgang von Goethe (1749-1832). This is likely because Goethe's spiritual beliefs were, in many ways, consistent with Dan's religious faith. Goethe rejected the claim that all science is mathematics based and objective. He held to the idea that there is spirit in all things, including natural science, that cannot be objectified.[799]

Dan's belief in a spiritual element of reality extended to his conviction that the basic documents of America and Utah have a spiritual origin. Certainly, Dan did not think these documents were the word of God in the same way he believed the *Bible* was the word of God;[800] however, he often cited Mormon scripture that claimed the Lord himself had established the

---

[796] Court, "Society of Separatists V. Whitehead, 870 P.2d 916."

[797] Blake, "Tribute: Justice I. Daniel Stewart."

[798] Court, "In Re Jp, 648 P.2d 1364."

[799] Cassirer, "Goethe and the Kantian Philosophy."

[800] Stewart, "The Framing of the Constitution."

U.S. Constitution by raising up wise men for that purpose.[801] That document codified our fundamental human beliefs and protected our fundamental human rights.

Through his entire professional life, Dan Stewart claimed: "Working with the U.S. Constitution is the most thrilling thing anyone can do." He believed that "for the first time in the history of mankind the U.S. Constitution brought together basic principles that are the warp and woof of human freedom." He believed that the U.S. Constitution was so important that without it "our society could not exist."[802]

Dan insisted that there be coordination and harmonization of the U.S. and Utah Constitutions. His judicial decisions reflected that allegiance. For example, in the 1970s, after Utah established, once again, the death penalty for murder, Justice Stewart correctly pointed out that Utah had naively included a "reasonable doubt" clause in its legislation, and in a case of a particularly gruesome murder, the perpetrator had such deficient mental capacities that any reasonable person would wonder if the felon ought to be held accountable for his actions.[803] In other words, Stewart found yet another way to align Utah with the U.S. Constitution.

And Stewart was a strong supporter of the Bill of Rights, particularly as it has been applied to our basic freedoms, including speech, search and seizure, abortion, the separation of church and state, sexual preferences, and race. We recall that Justice Albert H. Ellett, whom Dan replaced on the Utah Supreme Court, did not belief the Bill of Rights was relevant to the state of Utah. Dan Stewart recognized that the courts are flawed, in that they do not always reach the ideal or best result; nevertheless, they "provide a forum for making issues concerning the application of our fundamental liberties a key part of our national agenda."[804]

Stewart was also a strong defender of the rule of law. For example, he defended Roe v. Wade (1973), not because he held a strong commitment to

---

[801] Doctrine and Covenants: 101: 80.

[802] Ellis, "Interview of Dan Stewart at His Home in Salt Lake City, ."

[803] Court, "State V. Wood, 648 P.2d 71."

[804] Stewart, "Speech Given at Swearing in of Admittees to the Utah State Bar."

abortion, but because it was the law of the land. Even though he had little personal experience with minority groups, he stood on the forefront of the national struggles regarding race, ethnicity, and gender.[805] He argued forcefully for the right of anyone to engage in civil disobedience in order to rectify an injustice, such as racial discrimination, or an unfairness leveled against a woman in the workplace,[806] even though a legitimate consequence of that civil disobedience might be incarceration or something worse.

Even while aligning himself with the basic documents of the United States and of Utah, Dan remained committed to applying the law in such a way that "it makes sense in the lives of the people."[807] He was known for going beyond his traditional role as a justice, for seeking creative ways to achieving desired goals. He became a referee for social justice.[808] In his judicial rulings, he tried to raise the awareness of people, to help them see that they have a chance to make something of their lives.

He believed a judge's commitment to precedence has limits. One cannot simply plug in a situation into a vender and expect a standardized script to come up that tells a judge what to do. He believed that good judges exercise their own wisdom and discretion, so that their decisions are ultimately in the best interests of society and its people. In addition, holding firmly to his German literary background, he believed the law ought to emulate, as far as possible, spiritual principles.

Dan believed: "The ideal of justice is usually at best approximated, rarely if ever totally achieved."[809] Dan emphasized that justices "shouldn't be timid in exercising judicial powers."[810] If judges strive to develop a sensitivity and fairness in the rule of law, Stewart believed they may occasionally be able to

---

[805] Edwin B. Firmage, "Note on Dan Stewart for the University of Utah Sesquicentennial Founders' Day Celebration," (Salt Lake City, UtahFeb. 24, 2000).

[806] Stewart, "The Rule of Law and the Dilemma of Minorities."

[807] "Interview with Richard Ellis at Stewart's Home in Salt Lake City."

[808] Ray Rivera, "Utah's Courts Are Changing, Says Howe," *Salt Lake Tribune* Jan. 18, 2000.

[809] I. Daniel Stewart, "The Law as a Value-Added Profession," in *Speech at the Utah Bar Swearing In* (Salt Lake City, Utah Oct. 15, 1997).

[810] Ellis, "Interview of Dan Stewart at His Home in Salt Lake City, ."

add a new story to the temple of justice.[811] For example, Utah passed a law that abolished the insanity defense. Justice Stewart believed the Utah Legislature had done a terrible thing, and in his decisions on the bench, he found a way to reconcile what he believed was sound judgment with a terrible law.[812]

For Dan Stewart, the significance of the U.S. Constitution was neither just the interpretations of its founders nor the judgments contemporary society makes about it, but how it can help us human beings see a better way, a more just and beautiful world in which to live. One of his old missionary friends, Lynn Eric Johnson, explains that Dan wrote his court drafts not only to make a narrow court decision. Johnson believed Dan wrote drafts "for the eternities." He attempted to reach verdicts that "contained the wisdom of Solomon."[813]

Dan's tendency to "think otherwise" was reflected in his relationship to the Mormon Church. He never hesitated to challenge, when necessary, a decision made by the Church. For example, his friend, Dick Ellis, had a sister who was excommunicated. He was so enraged that he became inactive in the church. Dan challenged his friend, saying, "it is your church too, and you have a duty to speak up about what bothers you."[814] So Dick went back to church and spoke up when he found it necessary.

Dan rarely directly challenged LDS doctrines, except when the policies were blatantly hurtful, such as the policy of depriving Blacks of the priesthood. His legacy in the Mormon church was marginal. He never held a high position. He rarely mixed with church leaders. He was a thoughtful critic of religion. Prior to the time when the Church changed its policy regarding Blacks and the priesthood, Dan wrote a profound essay about the Mormon church and its tenuous relationship with racial issues.[815] Even though the

---

[811] Stewart, "The Law as a Value-Added Profession."

[812] "Interview with Richard Ellis at Stewart's Home in Salt Lake City."

[813] Lynn Eric Johnson, "Note to Dan Stewart at the Time of His Award at the University of Utah Sesquintennial Founders' Day Celebration," (Salt Lake City, Utah Feb. 24, 2000).

[814] Stewart, "A Life: Dictated to Richard G. Ellis."

[815] "The Rule of Law and the Dilemma of Minorities." The Mormon Church relationship with racial groups is framed by Armand L. Mauss, *All Abraham's Children: Changing Mormon Conceptions of Race and Lineage* (Urbana, Illinois: University of Illinois Press, 2003).

church stressed missionary work, after his mission to West Germany and his marriage, Dan never again attempted to convert anyone. His "calling" in the church was as a teacher, and he was satisfied with that role.

Dan's legacy was to be contemplative and reflective, never to intrude on someone else's religious point of view. Through his life he retained a gentle but clear sense of religious restraint. He rarely spoke with others about his religious beliefs, and Mormon colleagues often wondered where he stood in terms of his faith.[816]

Dan's legacy was that of a true, productive Utahn. He adhered to the expected local standards of conduct. He was always courteous, though a bit aloof. He was a devoted friend and visitor of the local mountains and red rock area. And he committed himself to the virtues of the local Utah aesthetic environment. Classical music, ballet, and theater were not just free-time diversions. They played a constant and central role in his life.

Dan often proudly declared he was a family man. His wife and daughters were his lifeblood, his ultimate responsibility. He recognized that his wife, Elizabeth, was a "remarkable woman." She had a profound insight into people and a sensitivity for their feelings and desires. He knew she loved him with all her heart. She claimed he was never a burden to her. She accepted with equanimity his physical limitations and dedicated herself to do everything necessary to help him fulfill his dreams and ambitions.

He accepted, with great appreciation, everything Elizabeth did for him. He recognized that she took great risks with him and encouraged him to take risks that he otherwise would have passed up. Dan wished her to be, not just a partner, but the fullest and most productive woman she could be. Dan believed that, together, they created an "amazing relationship."[817] Elizabeth agreed.

Dan Stewart was a loving father, but he recognized his role was complex. He never felt comfortable acting as the head of the household and family. As a young man, he was always told that God had ordained a patriarchal

---

[816] For example, Bohling, "Interview in Downtown Salt Lake City."

[817] Stewart, "A Life: Dictated to Richard G. Ellis."

order.[818] This meant that the man should preside over the family. Dan rejected such a relationship. His was a family that he expected to be as democratic as possible, where the authority was shared.

As Liz and Shannon grew and became more and more independent, he felt increasingly relaxed in his role. His daughters were becoming his equal. They both married, raised families, and established their own professional identities as lawyers. Dan believed such equality represented the highest form of human experience.[819]

To his friends, Dan Stewart's legacy was as a teacher, the person who brought them together. They all considered him to be one of the profoundest thinkers they had ever known.[820] One friend would say he exemplified the saying: "It's not the hand you are dealt, but the way you play the cards."[821]

On Feb. 24-25, 2000, the University of Utah conducted its Sesquicentennial Founders Day Celebration. It was a two-day affair and Dan Stewart was the special guest of honor.[822] This is usually seen as the premier honors event of the year, but this year was more eventful. Special people wrote laudatory notes to the organizers praising them for selecting Dan for the award. Dan was gracious in receiving the recognition it offered.

We are fortunate to have several pages of notes he composed as he attempted to put together a brief speech. In typical fashion, his infatuation with revision came to the fore, as he refined his thinking until he got his comments exactly right. The night of the ceremony, Dan told those in attendance that most people begin their association with a university when they enter it as a freshman. In Dan's case, his association began at the age of six, when he became a pupil at the Stewart Laboratory School. Because he lived close

[818] Church of Jesus Christ of Latter-day Saints, "Proclamation to the World," (Sept. 23, 1995).

[819] Stewart, "A Life: Dictated to Richard G. Ellis."

[820] Bennion, "Funeral Oration at the Time of Dan Stewart's Death."

[821] Thomas Greene, "Funeral Oration at the Time of Daniel Stewart's Death," (Salt Lake City, Utah June 23, 2005).

[822] I. Daniel Stewart, "University of Utah Sesquicentennial Founders' Day Celebration," (Salt Lake City, Utah Feb. 24, 2000).

to campus, each day, he would twice walk across the President's Circle to and from school. He noted, "The campus was my playground."[823]

Each year the University of Utah College of Law holds an Annual Alumni Event, where it gives special recognition to those in political and legal fields. Award winners are not necessarily former students and faculty. On May 16, 2000, ten weeks after his Founders' Day Celebration, Daniel Stewart received another "special recognition" award, this time by the College of Law.[824] This was the second time the awards committee had given him the award, and he received dozens of laudatory notes from prominent folks expressing the highest possible praise for Stewart's quality of life and for his contribution to society. John Flynn, Dan's old colleague at the College of Law, made the formal presentation. In his concluding remarks about Dan, he wrote the following:

Dan, your College of Law recognizes you this day as a "Distinguished Alumnus." I think it should be the other way around: we all recognize you this day for what you have done for the College of Law, its students, its faculty and its alumni by your distinguished career.... . You have brought us even greater distinction by the example you have set for us all in the way you have lived your private and public life, and the example of how a person of unflinching commitment to excellence and his ideals can make a difference.[825]

As Dan's health declined, he was less and less able to keep up with his court assignments. Sometimes he would take more than a year to finish writing his assigned case. One of Dan's legacies was clearly that he took little notice of time in terms of his Supreme Court tasks. It was as if he was not aware that time was an essential part of his court responsibilities.

For Dan, time was almost incidental, when compared to the quality of argument. He was so uncompromising in terms of quality, that all else became a non-factor. Consequently, toward the end of his tenure as a justice he became increasingly inflexible in working with the other justices. Michael

---

[823] Ibid.

[824] College of Law, "Annual Alumni Event, Doubletree Hotel, Salt Lake City," ed. University of Utah (May 16, 2000).

[825] John J. Flynn, "Isaac Daniel Stewart," in *Alumni Luncheon* (May 16, 2000).

Zimmerman explained: "The longer you are on the court the more brittle you become. You write opinions based on prior opinions."[826]

Time became such a critical issue, regarding Dan Stewart, that Justice Michael Zimmerman, who was the Chief Justice during most of the 1990s, began breaking a sacred rule in the court procedure. We recall that justices were assigned cases on a rotating basis; however, Zimmerman recognized that Dan's tardiness during the last years of his tenure so impeded the work of the court, that he decided to skip over Justice Stewart, when his turn came up to review a new case. Zimmerman's argument was that it was simply silly to assign a new case to a justice, if he was already several months delinquent in submitting his assigned lead opinion.[827]

Regarding Dan Stewart's declining health, as he began his tenure as a justice of the Utah Supreme Court, specialists concentrating on polio victims were discovering what they termed post-polio syndrome (PPS). In 1984, the first international conference was organized that paid attention to PPS.[828] At the time, Justice Stewart was fifty-four years old. He had been on the Utah Supreme Court for five years, and he was already experiencing some PPS symptoms, which usually begin with middle age.[829] There was speculation that, over time, the tissues and nervous system of the body of polio victims would simply begin to wear out.

Dan did what he could to slow the development of his own PPS symptoms. His home began to take on the appearance of a gym, with bar bells, floor mats, and conditioning equipment.[830] He had always had a primitive weight pulling machine that allowed him to exercise his upper body. He eventually installed a stationary bicycle. It was light and compact, so that it could be set up anywhere, although it was usually in the space near the extended

---

[826] Zimmerman, "Interview in His Salt Lake City Home ".

[827] Ibid.

[828] Halstead and Grimby, *Post-Polio Syndrome*.

[829] Anne Nixon, *Post-Polio Syndrome* (Self Published, 2017).

[830] This account comes from Stewart's younger daughter. See Clark, "Interview at Her Home in Corona Del Mar, California."

kitchen, close to the garage door. Usually, one of the girls would help him strap his legs to the bike pedals. His legs were useless, but he would push them with his arms so that the pedals provided a full-body exercise.

The most elaborate piece of equipment Dan had was his stretch or slant board. The family usually set it up next to his bicycle. A family member would strap him to a long board that would rotate Dan's body until he was upside down and his body stretched by the force of gravity. After sitting all day in his wheelchair, inversion therapy allowed Dan's body to relax and extend his neck, back, and hips, giving him much needed comfort and relaxation.

Through his adult life, one of the major problems Dan experienced was a weakened condition of his lungs. After polio struck, he had always found it difficult to breathe, and was often told that he only had about thirty percent use of his lungs. By the time he was on the bench of the supreme court, the percentage of lung use was declining, and he was experiencing increasing difficulty breathing.

Twice during his tenure on the Supreme Court, he caught pneumonia, and the weak air sacs in his lungs filled with phlegm. Dan suggested it felt almost like he was reliving his days back at *Rancho Los Amigos*. His first bout with pneumonia took place in the early 1980s and the second late in the same decade. After the 1989 case, he was required to remain home for about three weeks, before returning to the court.[831]

Technology had improved to the point that respirators completely replaced the iron lung, and he rarely found it necessary even to use these machines to help him take in oxygen and expel carbon dioxide. In June 1985, he collapsed, and everyone thought he had suffered a heart attack. He stayed in the hospital two days, but he was released after they decided it had been a false alarm.[832]

As he battled with his health, he quipped about his "dumb old body."[833] In spite of health struggles, Justice Stewart maintained an exceptional record of participation in the Utah Supreme Court.[834] The court justices usually met

[831] Stewart, "My Personal Journal ". Jan. 17, 1989.

[832] Ibid. June 21, 1985.

[833] Neff, "Daniel Stewart, Former Utah High Court Justice, Dies."

about once a week to review and decide on cases. In his first three years on the court, he missed only three court sessions. In 1983, when the first case of pneumonia hit, justice Stewart only missed two court sessions. In the next three years, he did not miss a single court session. [835]

In 1989, when pneumonia hit a second time, he missed six of eleven sessions during late October to the first half of November, but during the 1990s he was almost always able to attend. Occasionally, his compulsion to revise and edit got the best of him. At times, wishing to make yet another revision, he requested that the justices delay a decision on a case. If the other justices could muster at least three votes on a case, now and again, they would inform Justice Stewart that he was signed off as "not participating in the case," so they could move it forward.[836]

One of the major physical complaints Dan made in his journal had to do with his not being able to sleep. In August 1990, he found it necessary to spend time at the University of Utah Sleep Lab. Dr. Jones, told him the tests indicated his condition was "life threatening." Jones told him something serious could happen any night, and even sometimes during the day.[837] In 1994, Dan began to find blood in his stools. Tests indicated there was a precancerous tumor and it was removed. Doctors told him the colon was generally healthy, but a full colonoscopy was impossible.[838]

The most serious incident, in terms of Dan's declining physical well-being, occurred in the late summer of 1998. Dan and Elizabeth were invited to the home of Ron Molen for a quiet evening with himself and John Bennion. On the appointed evening, Elizabeth pulled the van up to the curb just below Foothill Drive on Hubbard Avenue. She parked across the street from the Molen house and efficiently got Dan out of the vehicle on the van elevator. As she was raising the ramp up to fold it back into the van, Dan suddenly

---

[834] There are various listings of these sessions. The most accessible is: Utah Supreme Court Decisions :: Utah Case Law :: Utah Law :: US Law :: Justia

[835] 1984, 1985, 1986.

[836] Orme, "Interview at the Sheraton Park Motel in Park City, Utah ".

[837] Stewart, "My Personal Journal ". Aug. 13,1990.

[838] Ibid. Mar. 1994.

pulled his electric wheelchair away from the van and started across the street toward the intersection of 1900 East and Hubbard. He relished every chance he found to be independent, but Elizabeth was alarmed at his action. She rarely raised her voice, and she was almost always an angel in her relationship with Dan, at least in public, but this time she began to call and "chew him out" for not waiting for her.[839]

There was a slight incline in the street, and Dan suddenly lost control of his wheelchair. It skidded and tipped over; Dan tumbled out onto the street. Fortunately, Ron was waiting at the other side of the street. Seeing Dan fall, Ron ran to him and found him crumpled on the pavement, his arms thrown out as if attempting to grasp something solid on the road. Sensing that Dan was injured, Ron yelled to Elizabeth: "Call the medics. The phone is in my house. My front door is open. Quick — run." Elizabeth soon yelled, "I reached the hospital at the U. They are on their way."

Ron's neighbor was interning at the university medical school. Ron rushed to his house. The neighbor grabbed a blanket on his way out of the house and quickly covered Dan on the street. The paramedics showed up just a few minutes later and they took Dan to the University of Utah Hospital, the setting for the next debacle. Dan needed an X-ray.

The technicians wouldn't let Elizabeth accompany Dan to the X-ray room. She carefully and insistently instructed them: "Dan is paralyzed from his waist down and has no control over his lanky legs. Please, hold his legs or they will fall off the gurney or the X-ray table."

The technicians paid no attention, and his left leg predictably fell off the table, breaking his upper femur, and requiring a high-risk surgery to implant a steel rod. He experienced a painful recovery,[840] and from that point his neck and lower body were in constant pain. He also wrote in his journal that since the accident he had much greater difficulty breathing. He then began to take oxygen from artificial means.[841]

---

[839] Shannon Stewart Clark, "Molen's Story About Dan Falling out of His Wheelchair," (G-mail note, July 18, 2020).

[840] Liz Stewart Whitney, "E-Mail Message to Author: Https://Mail.Google.Com/Mail/U/0/#Inbox/Fmfcgxwjwrclwcvsrxpjxkqbxfbzdqcv," (July 20, 2020).

In the new century, Dan's health continued to decline. He was not afraid of death. His faith promised him that dying is but a transition from one condition to another. And that new place was a step forward in his eternal progression. He was losing his strength, but the ever-present sweetness and meaning of family provided a tranquility of feeling and joy. His wife prayed continually for his life.

And in the few moments when nobody was near, he acknowledged the joy of occasional solitude What made him happy? He enjoyed holding a pen in his hand. He celebrated reading a brief to its end, and, yet again, doing a bit of editing. He often blissfully shared dinner with his two bright, beautiful daughters. He felt privileged to lie beside a loving wife each night.

There was comfort in those silent moments. He recalled his existence here on earth. It filled his soul with sad, sweet, and comforting memories. There had been moments of tragedy and sorrow. There had been times of great accomplishment and fulfillment. His life had not been in vain. He was content but did not want to die in despair. According to his daughter, Liz, a few days before he died, he exclaimed, "I am not yet ready to move on."[842]

In 1998, Dan had written in his journal that his uncle, Grant Iverson, who had died several years earlier, came to him in a dream, knelt by his bed, put his hands on his head, and gave him a blessing. Iverson, a well-known physician, told his nephew that he would walk again. Dan was not a mystical person, and he did not know what to make of the dream. He speculated that his uncle might have come to him from a distant world, telling him, not that he would walk in this mortal world, but "in a later time." Dan confessed, "I have never had anything like that dream before."[843]

As he approached the end of his life, it seems that every physical problem he had suffered through began again to appear. Post-polio syndrome was ever present. He suffered from hypertension, as his blood pressure shot up to dramatic levels. Both lungs filled with fluid. He was always hooked up to

---

[841] Stewart, "My Personal Journal ". Sept 13, 1998.

[842] Liz Stewart Whitney, "Interview at the Home of Val Rust in Irvine, California," (May 7, 2021).

[843] Stewart, "My Personal Journal ". Sept. 5, 1998

the Bird Respirator that enabled him to exhale carbon dioxide and breath in fresh oxygen. These were all physical issues that were ever present in those last years. And he was occasionally in the hospital, where the medical staff knew he was on his way out. Their behavior spoke loud and clear. "Here is this old guy, who is just a tax on the medical system. Let him go. To keep him alive is just a waste."[844]

Every time Dan was in the hospital, all he wanted was to go home. Even that was asking too much. One time, he was released from the hospital, but before he arrived home, the ambulance turned around and brought him back. Dan's most valuable asset, his brain, functioned fully until near the end of life. Then even it began to die. At the very end, Shannon implored her mother to sing to him, touch him, kiss him. "Mom, this is the last chance you will ever have. Hold him close." And she did.

---

[844] Shannon Stewart Clark, "Interview at Her Corona Del Mar Home," (Mar. 26, 2021).

Bibliography

"8 Students Lead on Red Cross Trip." *Deseret News*, 1946.

"16-Inch Snow Hits State, Snarls Traffic." *The Glens Falls Post-Star*, March 17, 1956.

"Aaron Mace Sentenced for Rape of Neighbor." *Daily Spectrum*, Sept. 15, 1993.

Aaron, Richard. "Interview at the College of Law,, in Salt Lake City." Feb. 1, 2019

"Accused Kidnapper Files Motions for Exams." *Daily Spectrum*, 30 Sept 1993.

"Ad: Vote for Competence." *Salt Lake Tribune*, Nov. 3, 1979.

"Aircraft "Guest" Statute Ruled Unconstitutional." *Salt Lake Tribune*, July 7, 1984.

Albrecht, Stan L., and Tim B. Heaton. "Secularization, Higher Education, and Religiosity." In *Latter-day Saint Social Life: Social Research on the LDS Church and Its Members* Provo, Utah: Brigham Young University Press, 1998.

Alexander, Thomas G. "Utah's Constitution: A Reflection of the Territorial Experience." *Utah Historical Quarterly* 64, no. 3, Summer (1996).

"Alienation Suit Requests Damages." *Salt Lake Telegram*, March 25, 1936.

Andrews, Charles H. *No Time for Tears*. Garden City, New York: Doubleday and Co., 1951.

"Angry Band of South Utahns Burns Actor, Others in Effigy." *Ogden Standard Examiner*, Apr. 19, 1976.

Bates, John. "Interview at the Stewart Home in Salt Lake City." Jan. 30, 2019

Bean, Lawrence. "Missionary Journal." West German Mission: Hand Written Diary, 1954-1956.

Bennett, Joyce. "Interview at Her Home in Salt Lake City,." June 6, 2018.

Bennion, John. "Funeral Oration at the Time of Dan Stewart's Death." Salt Lake City, Utah June 23, 2005

———. "Interview at His Home in Salt Lake City, ." Oct. 25, 2017.

———. "Interview in His Salt Lake City, Utah, Home." June 6, 2018.

Bennion, Lowell L. *Religion and the Pursuit of Truth*. Salt Lake City, Utah: Deseret Book, 1959.

Bennion, Lowell L. (Ben). "Interview at His Home in Salt Lake City." Sept. 9, 2019.

Benson, George S. "Protecting Our Freedom." *Helper Utah Journal*, Mar. 24, 1960.

Bentley, Anthony I. jr. "Interview in His Salt Lake City Home." (June 5, 2019).

Berg, Roland H. *Polio and Its Problems*. Philadelphia: J. B. Lippincott Co., 1948.

Biele, Katharine. "Utah Supreme Court '96." *The Intermountain Commercial Record* 40, no. 5 (Jan. 31, 1997).

Bitton, Davis. *The Ritualization of Mormon History and Other Essays*. Urbana, Illinois: University of Illinois Press, 1994.

Blake, Richard Cameron. "Tribute: Justice I. Daniel Stewart." *Utah Law Review* 2000, no. 1 (2000).

Bloom, Harold. *The American Religion: The Emergence of a Post-Christian Nation*. New York: Simon and Schuster, 1992.

Bodenheimer, Edgar. "Reflections on the Rule of Law." *Utah Law Review* 8, no. 1 (1962).

Bohling, William. "Interview in Downtown Salt Lake City." Feb 1, 2019.

Bowman, Matthew. *The Mormon People: The Making of an American Faith*. New York: Random House, 2012.

Bradford, Mary. "Telephone Interview at Her Arlington, Virginia, Home ", Feb. 1, 2019

Brooks, Juanita. "The Land That God Forgot." *Utah Historical Quarterly* 26, no. summer (1958): 207-19.

———. *Mountain Meadows Massacre.* Norman, Oklahoma: University of Oklahoma Press, 1970.

Bryan, Don. "Interview at the Little America Hotel in Salt Lake City, ." Sept. 27, 2018.

Bryan, Elizabeth. "Psychological Characteristics of Adolescents in a Kindred Known to Have Facio-Scapula-Humeral Muscular Dystrophy." University of Utah, 1958.

"Bulletin of the College of Law." edited by University of Utah. Salt Lake City, Utah: University of Utah, 1977-78.

Bulletin of the University of Utah College of Law. Salt Lake City, Utah: University of Utah, 1962.

Bullock, Arden Brett. "Letter to I. Daniel Stewart." Nov. 11, 2001.

Burton, Christopher "Kit". "Interview at His Home in Salt Lake City." June 4, 2019.

Burton, Richard F. *The City of the Saints and across the Rocky Mountains to California.* London: Longman, 1861.

Bushman, Claudia L. *Contemporary Mormonism: Latter-Day Saints in Modern America.* Westport, Connecticut: Praeger Publishers, 2006.

Bushman, Richard. "Mormonism and Politics: Are They Compatible?". Key West, Florida: Biannual Faith Angle Conference on Religion, May 4, 2007.

"Cacklling Acres, Inc, Et Al. V. Olson Farms, Inc.". In *541 F. 2d 242:* U.S. Court of Appeals, Tenth Circuit.

"Calendar of Music and Events." *Park Record*, June 5-7, 2002.

Campbell, Eugene E. "Pioneers and Patriotism; Conflicting Loyalties." In *New Views of Mormon History*, edited by Davis Bitton and Maureen Ursenbach Beecher. Salt Lake City, Utah: University of Utah Press, 1987.

"Candidates Provide Positions, Ideas Prior to Election Day: Earl S. Spafford." *Price Sun Advocate*, Oct. 29, 1980.

Cannon, Elaine. "Teensters Discuss World Peace Problems." *Deseret News*, Jan. 2, 1049.

Carpenter, Scott. "Letter on "Losing Our Sense of Privacy"." *Salt Lake Tribune*, Nov. 17, 1997.

Cassirer, Ernst. "Goethe and the Kantian Philosophy." In *Rousseau, Kant and Goethe*. New York: Harper and Row Publishers, 1945.

———. *The Problem of Knowledge*. New Haven, Conn.: Yale University Press, 1950.

Center, Rancho Los Amigos Medical. "Outpatient Progress Notes on Issac Daniel Stewart ". Downey, California August 29, 1995.

"The Cheap Divorce Sharp." *Salt Lake Herald*, Dec. 16, 1884.

"Child Rapist Entitled to Resentencing." *Deseret News*, Jan. 1, 1996.

Ciaravino, Tricia. "Oh Brother, the Lady's an Elk." *The Daily Spectrum (St. George, Utah)*, Dec. 21, 1995.

Cilwick, Ted. "Court Rules Search-Seizure Arrest Legal in Millard Drug Conviction." *Salt Lake Tribune*, Feb. 7, 1996.

Circuit, US Court of Appeals Tenth. "Mchanical Contractors Bid Depository V. Christiansen, 352 F2d 817." Nov. 15, 1965.

"Civic Clubs to Hear Resource Discussion." *Tremonton Garland Times*, Nov. 12, 1964.

Clark, Dale. "Mormonism in the New Germany." *Deseret News: Church Section*, Dec. 9, 1933, 3+7.

Clark, Shannon Stewart. "Handwritten Note to Val Rust." Feb. 15, 2021.

———. "Interview at Her Corona Del Mar Home." Mar. 26, 2021.

———. "Interview at Her Corona Del Mar, Ca Home." Feb. 15, 2020.

———. "Interview at Her Home in Corona Del Mar, California." May 22, 2019.

———. "Molen's Story About Dan Falling out of His Wheelchair." G-mail note, July 18, 2020.

———. "Retirement Celebration for Daniel Stewart." Jan. 7, 2000.

———. "Telephone Interview at Her Home in Corona Del Mar, Ca." Sept. 18, 2020.

———. "Telephone Interview at Her Home in Corona Del Mar, Ca." August 21,2018.

Clark, Shannon Stewart, and Liz Stewart Whitney. "Conversation with Val Rust at the Family Home on Millicent Drive in Salt Lake City." Sept. 4, 2019.

Clayton, James. "Interview in His Home in Salt Lake City." On File with the Author Sept. 28, 2018.

Cleland, Robert Glass, and Juanita Brooks, eds. *A Mormon Chronicle: The Diaries of John D. Lee: 1848-1876.* San Marino, CA: The Huntington Library, 1955.

Colley, Linda. *The Gun, the Ship, and the Pen: Warfare, Constitutions, and the Making of the Modern World.* London: Profile Books, 2021.

"Constitution of the United States." Philadelphia, Penn., Sept. 17, 1787.

Costanzo, Joe. "Court Rules on Jail Rights." *Deseret News,*, April 24, 1981.

"Court Calls Law Unconstitutional." *Daily Spectrum (St. George, Utah)*, Jan. 3, 1986.

"Court Clears Way for Repressed Memory Suit." *Provo Daily Herald*, Oct. 30, 1993.

Court, U.S. Supreme. "Furman V. Georgia, 408, U.S. 238, 92 S. Ct.. 2726, 33 L. Ed. 2d 346 ", 1972.

Court, U.S. District. "Weaver V. Nebo School District, 29 F. Supp. 2d 1279." Nov. 25, 1998.

Court, U.S. Supreme. "Brady V. Maryland, 373 U.S. 83." 1963.

———. "Engel V. Vitale " In *370 U.S. 421*, 1962.

———. "Metromedia Vs. American Society of Composers, Authors, and Publishers 382 U.S. 38." 1965.

———. "Rowe V. Wade, 410 U.S. 113." Jan. 22, 1973.

———. "United States V. National Dairy Products Corp. 372 U.S. 29 ", 1963.

"Court Upholds Death Penalty." *St. George Daily Spectrum*, Nov. 27, 1977.

Court, Utah Supreme. "Albrecht V. Uranium Services, Inc., 596 P.2d 1025 ", May 29, 1979.

———. "Berry by and through Berry V. Beech Aircraft 717 P.2d 670 ", 1985.

———. "Craftsman Builder's Supply, Inc. V. Butler Manufacturing Co., 974 P.2d 1194." March 5, 1999.

———. "Dunn V. Cook, 791 P.2d 873." April 2, 1990.

———. "Dyett V. Turner." In *439 P2d 266* 1968.

———. "Elks Lodges No 719 (Ogden) an No. 2021 (Moab) V. Department of Alchoholic Beverage Control. Moose Lodges No. 259 (Salt Lake City) and No. 2031 (Tooele) V. Department of Alcoholic Beverage Control, 905 P.2d 1189 ", Oct. 23, 1995.

———. "Frank V. State, 613 P.2d 517." June 12, 1980.

———. "Horton V. Richards, 594 P2d 891 ", Apr. 18, 1979.

———. "In Re Jp, 648 P.2d 1364." June 9, 1982.

———. "J.J.N.P. Company V. State, 655 P.2d 1133." Sept. 22, 1982.

———. "Johnston V. Stoker, 685 P.2d 539 ", July 5, 1984.

———. "Kallas V. Kallas, 614 P.2d 641." June 23, 1980.

———. "Malan V. Lewis, 693 P2.D 661." May 1, 1984.

———. "Manning V. Sevier County, 517 P.2d 549." Dec. 21, 1973.

———. "Maryboy V. Utah State Tax Commission, 904 P.2d 662 ", Sept. 14, 1995.

———. "Norton V. Macfarlane, 818 P.2d 8." Sept. 12, 1991.

———. "Olsen V. Hooley, 865 P.2d 1345." Oct. 27, 1993.

———. "Prows V. Industrial Commission of Utah 610 P.2d 1362." 1980.

———. "Robbins V. Finlay, 645 P.2d 623." (Mar. 23, 1982).

———. "Ross V. Schackel, 920 P.2d 1159 ", July 12, 1996.

———. "Society of Separationists V. Taggart, 862 P.2d 1339." (Oct. 12, 1993).

———. "Society of Separatists V. Whitehead, 870 P.2d 916." Dec. 10, 1993.

———. "Sovereen V. Meadows, 595 P.2d, 852." Apr. 11, 1979.

———. "State of Utah V. Smith, 909 P.2d 236." Dec. 20, 1995.

———. "State V. Anderson, 910 P.2d 1229." Feb. 2, 1996.

———. "State V. Andrews, 574 P.2d 709." (Nov. 25, 1977).

———. "State V. Andrews, 843 P.2d 1027." July 21, 1992.

———. "State V. Buck, 756 P.2d 700." June 6, 1988.

———. "State V. Bullock, 791 P.2d 155." Oct. 18, 1989.

———. "State V. Carson, 597 P.2d 862." June 18, 1979.

———. "State V. Deplonty, 749 P.2d 621." Dec. 31, 1987.

———. "State V. Gibbons, 779 P.2d 1133." Sept. 13, 1989.

———. "State V. Hansen, 734 P.2d 421." (Nov. 5, 1986).

———. "State V. Herrera, 895 P.2d 359." April 21, 1995.

———. "State V. Holland, 876 P.2d 357." Jan. 13, 1994.

———. "State V. Jarrell, 608 P.2d 218." Feb. 19, 1980.

———. "State V. Johnson, 774 P.2d 1141." May 11, 1989.

———. "State V. Long, 721 P.2d 483." (June 20, 1986).

———. "State V. Lowder, 889 P.2d 412." Dec. 16, 1994.

———. "State V. Mace, 921 P.2d 1372." (July 26, 1996).

———. "State V. Malmrose, 649 P.2d 56." June 22, 1982.

———. "State V. Miller, 709 P.2d 350 ", Oct. 29, 1985.

———. "State V. Pierre, 572 P.2d 1338." Nov. 25, 1977.

———. "State V. Ramsey, 782 P.2d 480." Oct. 19,1989.

———. "State V. Ramsey, 782 P.2d 480." Oct. 19, 1989.

———. "State V. Sessions, 645 P.2d 643." Mar. 30, 1982.

———. "State V. Smith, 909 P.2d 236." Dec. 20, 1995.

———. "State V. Standiford, 769 P.2d 799." 1988.

———. "State V. Velarde, 734 P.2d 449." Dec. 4, 1986.

———. "State V. Webb, 779 P.2d 1108 ", July 21, 1989.

———. "State V. Wells, 603 P.2d 810 ", Nov. 13, 1979.

———. "State V. Wood, 648 P.2d 71." May 13, 1982.

———. "Thomas V. Daughters of Utah Pioneers, 197 P.2d 477 108 ", July 14, 1948.

———. "Walker Drug Co. V. La Sal Oil Company, 902 P.2d 1229 ", Dec. 22, 1998.

"Courtroom Role of Mental Health Professionals Deemed Vital." *Ellensburg Daily Record*, August 2, 1982.

Craig, Brian. *Latter Day Lawyers*. Kindle Direct Publishing, 2019.

Crockett, J. Alen. "Remembering Justice A.H. Ellett." *Utah Historical Quarterly* 61, no. 3, Summer (1993).

Davis, Frances Gilroy. "A History of the William M. Stewart School: 1890-1940." University of Utah, 1940.

Davis, Fred. *Passage through Crisis: Polio Victims and Their Families*. Indianapolis, Indiana: Bobbs-Merrill Co., 1963.

Davis, Margaret Leslie. *The Culture Broker: Franklyn D. Murphy and the Transformation of Los Angeles.* Berkeley, CA: University of California Press, 2007.

Decker, Ashby. "Interview at His Home in Salt Lake City," October 25, 2017.

———. "Interview at His Home in Salt Lake City," Sept. 27, 2018.

———. "Telephone Interview at His Home in Salt Lake City," April 14, 2018.

Decker, Harold A. "Everett L. Cooley Oral History Project, 1983-2014." edited by America West Center University of Utah. Salt Lake City, Utah: Special Collections Library, June 26, 2010.

Degnan, Ronan. "Everett L. Cooley Oral History Project, 1983-2014." edited by Edited by the University of Utah America West Center. Salt Lake City, Utah: Special Collections Library, March 1, 1983.

DeVoy, Beverly. "Hi Fi Evidence Unpacked." *Deseret News*, Aug. 9, 1992.

Dierenfield, Bruce J. *The Battle over School Prayer: How Engel V. Vitale Changed America.* Lawrence, Kansas: University Press of Kansas, 2007.

"Distinguished Alumni Banquet." Salt Lake City Ft. Douglas Country Club: Sigma Chi Fraternity, May 12, 1994.

Doctrine and Covenants. Salt Lake City, Utah: Church of Jesus Christ of Latter-day Saints, 1969.

Drabner, Stephen Curtis. "Letter to "Support Wendy Weaver." In *Salt Lake Tribune*, Mar. 30, 2002.

Dryer, Randy. "Interview with the Author in His Law Office at the University of Utah." Sept. 9, 2019.

Duckworth, Angela. *Grit: The Power of Passion and Perserverance.* New York: Scribner, 2016.

Durham, Christine M. "Interview by Liz Stewart in Christine's Home in Salt Lake City." June 7, 2017.

Durham, Christine M. "Address to the University of Utah Law School, Honoring Dan Stewart." May 16, 2000.

———. "Interview at Her Salt Lake City Home ", June 16, 2021

———. "Interview by Liz Stewart in Christine's Home in Salt Lake City." June 7, 2017.

———. "Note to Dan Stewart at the Time of His Award at the University of Utah Sesquintennial Founders' Day Celebration ". Salt Lake City, Utah, Feb. 28, 2000

———. "Women Trailblazers in the Law: ." https://abawtp.law.stanford.edu /exhibits/show/christine-m-durham, June 1 to Oct. 20, 2009.

Durham, George. "Interview by Liz Stewart Whitney at His Home in Salt Lake City." June 7, 2018.

Dutton, Clarence E. *Tertiary History of the Grand Canyon District.* Tucson, AZ: University of Arizona Press, 2001.

Dyer, Kenneth B. "West German Mission Quarterly Report." Salt Lake City: Church History Library, Dec. 30, 1955.

———. "West German Mission Records." Church History Library: West German Mission Headquarters, 1955-1956.

Dykstra, Daniel. "Everett L. Cooley Oral History Project, 1983-2014." In *University of Utah, America West Center.* Salt Lake City, Utah: Special Collections Library, February 23, 1983.

Editorial. "No Wonder Our Cities Lack So Much." *Deseret News*, May 18, 1952.

———. "Why Businessmen Go Home." *Deseret News*, Dec. 29, 1955.

Edwards, Geraldine B., William H. Clark, and Robert M. Drake. *Polyomyelitis in California During the Pre-Vaccine Period.* Sacramento, CA: California State Department of Public Health, 198.

Ellis, Dick. "Interview at the Ellis Home in Salt Lake City." sept. 21, 2018.

Ellis, Richard. "Interview of Dan Stewart at His Home in Salt Lake City, ." Dec. 8, 1999.

Evans-Pritchard, E. E. "Sexual Inversion among the Azande." *American Anthropologist* 72, no. 6 (1970): 1428-34.

"F.D. Wormuth, U. Scholar, Dies." *Salt Lake Tribune*, June 2, 1981.

Faction, Grey. "Barbara Snow Dsw Lcsw." *https://greyfaction.org/resources/proponents/snow-barbara/.*

Faerber, LeRoy. "Interview at His Home in Murray, Utah," Feb. 20, 2018

Ferris, Benjamin. *Utah and the Mormons.* New York: Harper and Brothers, 1854.

Fetzer, Leland A. "Tolstoy and Mormonism." *Dialogue: A Journal of Mormon Thought* 6, no. 1 (1971).

Fife, Austin, and Alta Fife. *Saints of Sage and Saddle.* Bloomington, Indiana: Indiana University Press, 1956.

Firmage, Edwin B. *An Abundant Life: The Memoirs of Hugh B. Brown.* Salt Lake City, Utah: Signature Books, 1988.

———. *Ends and Means in Conflict.* Salt Lake City, Utah: Frederick William Reynolds Association, 1987.

———. "Everett L. Cooley Oral History Project, 1983-2014." Salt Lake City, Utah: University of Utah America West Center, 2010.

———. "Note on Dan Stewart for the University of Utah Sesquicentennial Founders' Day Celebration." Salt Lake City, Utah, Feb. 24, 2000.

Firmage, Edwin B. . "Note to Stewart at the Time of His Award by the Founder's Day Commission." Feb. 23, 2000.

Firmage, Edwin B., and Richard C. Mangrum. *Zion in the Courts.* Champaign/Urbana, Illinois: University of Illinois Press, 2001.

Firmage, Edwin B., Bernard G. Weiss, and John W. Welch. *Religion and Law: Biblical-Judaic and Islamic Perspectives.* Winona Lake: Eisenbrauns, 1990.

Fliedner, Colleen Aair. *Centennial: Rancho Los Amigos Medical Center: 1888-1988.* Downey, CA: Rancho Los Amogos Medical Center, 1990.

Flynn, John J. "Isaac Daniel Stewart." In *Alumni Luncheon,* May 16, 2000.

———. "Isaac Daniel Stewart: 1932-2005." In *Funeral Eulogy,* June 29,2005.

———. "Note to Dan Stewart at the Time of His Award at the University of Utah Sesquicentennial Founders' Day Celebration ". Salt Lake City, Utah, Feb 24, 2000

Fogg, Gary. "Missionary Journal." West German Mission: Hand-Written Diary, 1955-1958.

Forsberg, Helen. "Visual Art." *Salt Lake Tribune,* May 31, 1998.

Galbraith, John Kenneth. "Writing, Typing, and Economics." In *Writing in the Social Sciences*, edited by Joyce S. Steward and Marjorie Smelstor. Glenview, Ill.: Scott, Foresman and Co, 1984.

Garrett, Alice L., Jacquelin Perry, and V. L. Nickel. "Stabilization of the Collapsing Spine." *Journal of Bone and Neck Surgery* 43-A, no. 4 (1961): 474-84.

Gawne, Anne Carrington. "Strategies for Exercise Prescription in Post-Polio Patients," *Post-Polio Syndrome*(1995).

Gee, David. "Telephone Interview at His Home in Seattle, Washington." July 16, 2020.

Gillespie, L. Kay. *The Unforgiven: Utah's Executed Men*. Salt Lake City, Utah: Signature Books, 1997.

Gladwell, Malcolm. *Talking to Strangers*. New York City: Little, Brown and Company, 2019.

Glass, Matthew. *Citizens against the Mx: Public Languages in the Nuclear Age*. Urbana, Illinois: University of Illinois Press, 1993.

Glock, Charles Y., and Rodney Stark. *A Study of Religion in American Life* Berkeley, California: Survey Research Center, University of California, 1964.

"A Great Jurist." *Salt Lake Tribune*, May 2, 2000.

Greene, Thomas. "Funeral Oration at the Time of Daniel Stewart's Death." Salt Lake City, Utah June 23, 2005

———. "Funeral Oration for I. Daniel Stewart." June 23, 2005.

Greenhouse, Linda. "Sure Justices Legislate. They Have To." *New York Times*, July 5, 1998.

Griffin, Paul. "Interview at His Home in Salt Lake City, ." October, 25, 1017.

Grotegut, David. "Interview at His Home in Springville, Utah, ." Feb. 22, 2018.

Hall, Gordon R. "Interview at His Salt Lake City Home." Sept. 9, 2019.

Halstead, Lauro S., and Gunnar Grimby, eds. *Post-Polio Syndrome*. Philadelphia: Hanley and Belfus, Inc., 1995.

Handley, Ken and Kate. "Interview at Their Home in Salt Lake City, ." Sept. 24, 2018

Hanks, Nedra Taylor. "Telephone Interview at Her Home in Salem, Utah."

Oct. 2, 2018.

Harrie, Dan. "Legislators' Quest to Amend Constitution Grinds to Halt." *Salt Lake Tribune*, Dec. 16, 1993.

Hatch, Nathan O. *The Democratization of American Christianity.* New Haven: Yale University Press, 1989.

Herrnstein, Richard, and Charles Murray. *The Bell Curve: Intelligence and Class Structure in American Life.* New York: Simon and Schuster, 1996.

"High Court: No Time Limit on Repressed Abuse Suit." *The Daily Spectrum*, Oct 30, 1993.

Hoffman, Joel. "Telephone Interview at His Home in New York City." Sept. 19, 2018.

Holbrook, Mary Louise. "Interview at Her Home in Salt Lake City,." June 5, 2018.

———. "Interview at Her Home in Salt Lake City,." Feb. 22, 2018.

———. "Interview at the Dan Stewart Family Home in Salt Lake City." June 7, 2019.

———. "Telephone Interview at Her Salt Lake City Home." Jan. 15, 2020.

Holbrook, Mary Louise Stewart. "Interview at the Dan Stewart Family Home in Salt Lake City." June 7, 2019.

Holbrook, Steve. "Interview at the Dan Stewart Home in Salt Lake City." June 7, 2019.

Hospital, LDS. *A Tradition of Excellence.* Salt Lake City, Utah: LDS Hospital, 1980.

Hospital, Shrine. "All Star Football and Basketball." edited by Shrine Hospital. Salt Lake City, Utah August 15, 17, 18, 1951.

Howe, Richard C. "Memorial to I. Daniel Stewart Upon His Retirement." Salt Lake City, 1999.

Huefner, Robert and Dixie. "Interview in Their Home in Salt Lake City, ." On File with the Author Sept. 24, 2018.

"Huey to Appeal Decision." *The Daily Utah Chronicle*, March 4, 1968

Hummel, Robert B. "Personal Letter to Dan Stewart." Nov. 9, 1978.

"Hundreds Die as 2 Storms Cripple East." *Deseret News*, March 19, 1956.

Hunt, Stephen. "Homeless Man Gets Prison for Shooting While Hallucinating." *Salt Lake Tribune*, Dec. 20 1995.

Hutchins, Robert, and Mortimer Adler, eds. *Great Books of the Western World*. New York: Encyclopedia Britannica, 1952.

"An Ideal Choice." *Salt Lake Tribune*, Nov. 6, 1978.

Imwinkelried, Edward, James Hogan, and Kevin Johnson. "In Memoriam: Daniel J. Dykstra." Davis, California: UC Davis, 2000.

James, William. *Will to Believe and Other Essays*. New York: Longmans, 1897.

Jarvis, George. "Interview at the Church History Library in Salt Lake City, ." January 28, 2019.

Jenkins, Bruce S. "Everett L. Cooley Oral History Project, 1983-2014.", edited by America West Center University of Utah. Salt Lake City, Utah: Special Collections Library, June 15, 1993.

Jensen, Kennard. "Letter to the Editor: 'Raps Wilkins Decisions'." *Deseret News*, July 28, 1981.

Jett, Stephen C. "The Canyons of Zion." *Plateau* 51, no. 2 (1979): 3-10.

Johnson, Eric. "Note to Stewart in Preparation for His Award by the Alumni Association." Dec. 1999

Johnson, Lynn Eric. "Note to Dan Stewart at the Time of His Award at the University of Utah Sesquintennial Founders' Day Celebration." Salt Lake City, Utah Feb. 24, 2000.

Jonnson, Dave. "State Supreme Court Kills Auto "Guest Statute" Law." *Salt Lake Tribune*, May 4, 1984.

———. "Testimony in Sex-Abuse Case Called Unconstitutional." *Salt Lake Tribune*, Mar. 16, 1988.

———. "Top Court Quashes Act on Product Liability." *Salt Lake Tribune*, Jan. 3, 1986.

———. "Utah Court Clears Way for Tax Rebate." *Salt Lake Tribune*, Nov. 1, 1979.

Jonnson, Dave "Utah Supreme Court Upholds Architect's Sex Convictions." *Salt Lake Tribune*, Oct. 20, 1989.

Jonsson, Dave. "Laws Work Only If Bullock Is Guilty." *Salt Lake Tribune*, Dec. 29, 1989.

———. "Top Court Quashes Act on Product Liability." edited by Salt Lake

Tribune, Jan.3, 1986.

———. "Utah Murder Rate at 6-Year Low." *Salt Lake Tribune*, Aug. 29, 1984.

Julien, Stephen W. "The Utah Supreme Court and Its Justices." *Utah Historical Quarterly* 44, no. 3, Summer (1976).

"Jurors Find Coach Guilty of Assault." *Salt Lake Tribune*, Feb. 13 1981.

"Justice Stewart Favors Yes-No." *Deseret News*, Nov. 24, 1980.

Kehret, Peg. *Small Steps: The Year I Got Polio.* Chicago: Albert Whitman & Co., 1996.

Kenny, Elizabeth. *Infantile Paralysis and Cerebral Diplegia.* Sydney, Australia: Angus & Robertson Limited, 1937.

Kimball, Spencer W. . "The False Gods We Worship." *Ensign Magazine* June (1976).

Kirchhoefer, Erich. "Interview at His Syracuse, Utah Home." Feb. 21, 2018.

Knox, Annie. "Will Utah Alter Its Insanity Defense?" *Deseret News*, Sept. 29, 2019.

Krohn, Katherine. *Jonas Salk and the Polio Vaccine.* Mankato, Minn.: Capstone Press, 2007.

Kuehne, Wayne. "Interview at His Home in Orem, Utah, ." Feb. 22, 2018.

Lambert, Verl. "Everett L. Cooley Oral History Proect, 1983-2014." edited by America West Center The University of Utah. Salt Lake City, Utah: special Collections Library, Nov. 27, 2010.

Larsen, C. Dean. "Interview at His Home in Salt Lake City, ." June 6, 2018.

Larson, Dale. "Interview at His Cottonwood, Utah Home." Feb. 20, 2018.

Law, College of. "Annual Alumni Event, Doubletree Hotel, Salt Lake City." edited by University of Utah, May 16, 2000.

———. "The University of Utah College of Law Introduces Its 1962 Graduating Class." (Undated).

"Lawyer for Accused Rapist May Use Insanity Defense." *Salt Lake Tribune*, Aug. 19, 1993.

Lee, James B. "Interview in His Home in Salt Lake City." (June 6, 2019).

Lerner, Daniel. *The Passing of Traditional Society.* New York: Free Press, 1958.

Lichtenstein, Grace "Utah's Conservative Court Is Center of Duspute over

Rulings." *The New York Times* (Nov. 30, 1975).

Liechty, Janet M. "Psychosocial Issues and Post-Polio: A Literature Review of the Past Thirteen Years." In *Post Polio Syndrome*, edited by Lauro S. Halstead and Gunnar Grimby. Philadelphia: Hanley and Belfus, Inc., 1995.

Linduska, Noreen. *My Polio Past.* Chicago, Illinois: Pelligrini & Cudahy, 1947.

Lobb, Clark. "U. Law Graduates Hear Justice Tell of Challenges." *Salt Lake Tribune*, June 19, 1986.

Lockhart, William. "Interivew at His Home in Salt Lake City." Sept. 26, 2018.

Loftus, Elizabeth. *Eyewitness Testimony.* Cambridge, Mass.: Harvard University Press, 1979.

———. "Leading Questions and the Eyewitness Report." *Cognitive Psychology* 7, no. 4 (1975): 560-72.

———. "The Malleabiility of Human Memory." *American Scientist* 67, no. 3 (1979): 312-20.

———. "Reconstructing Memory: The Incredible Eyewitness." *Psychology Today* 8 (1974): 116-19.

Lowrie, James. "E-Mail to Shannon Stewart.", June 12, 2019.

Lund, Lynn J. "Letter to I. Daniel Stewart Regarding Arden Brett Bullock." Aug. 12, 2002.

Machlis, Stephanie. "Interview with Daniel Stewart in Salt Lake City." 1999.

Maffly, Brian. "Insanity Plea Bargain: Court Finds Defendant Innocent in Wife's Death." *Salt Lake Tribune*, Oct 21, 1996.

Magleby, James E., and John M. Peterson. *Justices of the Utah Supreme Court: 1896 -1996.* Salt Lake City, Utah: Quality Press, Inc. , 1997.

Mansfield, Stephen. *The Mormon Ethic and the Spirit of Capitalism.* Washington, D.C.: Worthy Publishing, 1990.

Mauss, Armand L. *All Abraham's Children: Changing Mormon Conceptions of Race and Lineage.* Urbana, Illinois: University of Illinois Press, 2003.

———. *The Angel and the Beehive: The Mormon Struggle with Assimilation.*

Urbana and Chicago: University of Illinois Press, 1994.

———. "Priesthood Ban against Blacks in the Mormon Church." *Dialogue: A Journal of Mormon Thought* 14, no. 3 (1983): 10-45.

May, Cheryll L. *Utah Judicial Council History*. Salt Lake City, Utah: Utah Judicial Council, March, 1998.

McCann, Sheila R. "Court Frees Prison Docs from Negligence Suits." *Salt Lake Tribune*, July 13, 1996.

———. "Justice Stewart Will Sheathe His Powerful Pen." *Salt Lake Tribune*, Sept 1, 1999.

———. "Utah Supreme Court Not Always in the Spotlight, but Its Decisions Have Wide-Ranging Effect." *Salt Lake Tribune*, Feb. 11, 1996.

McClellan, Jack. "Kaiparowits Coal Power Plans Scuttled." *High Country News*, April 23, 1976.

McConkie, Bruce R. *Mormon Doctrine*. Salt Lake City: Deseret Book Co., 1966.

McKell, Charles R. "History of the Utah State Hospital." University of Utah, 1948.

Mead, Margaret. *Coming of Age in Samoa*. New York: Morrow, 1928.

Mill, John Stewart. *On Liberty*. London: John S. Parker and Soy, West Strand, 1859.

"Miss Bryan Reveals Troth." *Salt Lake Tribune* August 9, 1959

Molen, Ron. "Interview at His Home in Salt Lake City, ." June 6, 2018

———. "Telephone Interview at His Home in Salt Lake City." Nov. 9, 2018.

———. "Telephone Interview with Molen at His Salt Lake City Home." July 20, 2020.

Morgan, Dale L. *The State of Deseret*. Logan, Utah: Utah State University Press, 1987.

Murphy, Michael. "Interview at the U.S. Court of Appeals in Pasedina, California." Feb. 1, 2018.

Neff, Andrew Love. *History of Utah: 1847-1869*. Salt Lake City, Utah: Deseret News Press, 1940.

Neff, Elizabeth. "Daniel Stewart, Former Utah High Court Justice, Dies." *Salt Lake Tribune*, June 25, 2005.

Nelson, David Conley. *Moroni and the Swastika: Mormons in Nazi Ger-

many. Norman, Oklahoma: University of Oklahoma Press, 2015.

Nelson, Renee C. "Arguing Added 12 Years to His Life." *Provo Daily Herald*, Feb. 16, 1982.

"New Utah Justice Takes Oath ". *Salt Lake Tribune*, January 9, 1979.

Nixon, Anne. *Post-Polio Syndrome*. Self Published, 2017.

Oaks, Dallin H. "The Beginning and the End of a Lawyer." *BYU Law Digital Commons* 2 (12.15.2009).

———. "Interview in the Church Office Building in Salt Lake City." June 15, 2021.

———. "Thank You, Dr. Oaks." *Deseret News*, Nov. 24-25, 1980.

———, ed. *The Wall between Church and State*. Chicago: The University of Chicago Press, 1963.

Oaks, Dallin H. . "Law and Order — a Two Way Street." *Dialogue: A Journal of Mormon Thought* III, no. 4 (1968): 59-69.

Ockey, Ronald J. "Letter to I. Daniel Stewart." Jan. 11, 2000.

Olmstead, Jacob W. "Educating the Mormon Hierarchy: The Grassroots Opposition to the Mx in Utah." In *Utah in the Twentieth Century*, edited by Brian Q. Cannon and Jessie L. Embry. Logan, Utah: Utah State University Press, 2009.

Olpin, A. Ray. "Letter from the Office of the President." Salt Lake City: University of Utah, June 24, 1952.

Orme, Greg. "Interview at the Sheraton Park Motel in Park City, Utah ", Sept. 10, 2019.

Oshinsky, David M. *Polio: An American Story*. New York: Oxford University Press, 2005.

People, Signed Petition by 16. "Subject: The Arden Brett Bullock Case." Oct. 31, 1989.

Perry, Jacquelin. "The Contribution of the Physical Therapist to Medicine." *Journal of American Physical Therapy Association* 45, no. 11 (November, 1965).

———. "Responsibilities in Patient Care: The Need for Nonprofessional Assistants in Physical Therapy." *Journal of American Physical Therapy Association* 46, no. 3 (1966).

Perry, Jacquelin, and V. L. Nickel. "Total Cervical-Spine Fusion for Neck

Paralysis." *Journal of Bone and Neck Surgery* 41, no. A (1959): 37-60.

Peterson, Grethe. "Interview at Her Home in Salt Lake City." Sept. 25, 2018.

Pinegar, Bonnie Lee Crabb. "Interview in Her Salt Lake City Home." On File with the Author Sept. 26, 2018.

"Pioche ". http://ghosttowns.com/states/nv/pioche.html June 18, 2018.

"Polio Cases, Deaths, and Vaccination Rates." *ProCon.org* (1917).

Poll, Richard. "Utah and the Mormons: A Symbiotic Relationship." In *New Views of Mormon History*, edited by Davis Bitton and Maureen Ursenbach Beecher. Salt Lake City, Utah: University of Utah Press, 1987.

———. "What the Church Means to People Like Me." *Dialogue: A Journal of Mormon Thought* 2, no. 4 (1967).

The Polygraph and Die Detection. Washington, D.C.: National Academies Press, 2003.

"Protestors Sue to Block Hershey's Draft Directive." *Civil Liberties, Monthly Publication of the American Civil Liberties Union*, Jan., 1968.

"Protestors Sue to Block Hershey's Draft Directive." *Civil Liberties*, Jan. 1968.

Pusey, Penny. "Appelate Court Measure Advances." *Deseret News*, Sept. 8, 1979.

Pusey, Roger. "Utah Justices Reinforce Parental Rights." *Deseret News*, June 11, 1982.

"A Quick Reaction May Have Saved His Life." *Provo Daily Herald*, Nov. 19, 1991.

Quinn, Tom. "Child Kidnapper Wins Reduced Prison Term." *Salt Lake Tribune*, Jan. 27, 1996.

Reilly, Daniel L. "Everett L. Cooley Oral History Project, 1983-2014." edited by America West Center University of Utah. Salt Lake City, Utah: Special Collections Library, Feb. 13, 2010.

Rentzsch, K.-J. "Incidence Rates of Poliomyelitis in Germany." *Post-Polio Health International* (2017).

Richards, LeGrand L. "Letter to Dan Stewart and His Wife." August 27, 1982.

———. *A Marvelous Work and a Wonder*. Salt Lake City: Deseret Book,

1960.

Rigtrup, Ken. "Interview at His Home in Salt Lake City ", Sept. 28, 2018

Rivera, Andreas. "Forty Years Later, Ogden Hi-Fi Murders Are Still the Worst." *Ogden Standard-Examiner*, Apr. 22, 2014.

Rivera, Ray. "Robe Warriors Shaped a Golden Era." *Salt Lake Tribune*, Jan. 31, 2000.

———. "Utah's Courts Are Changing, Says Howe." *Salt Lake Tribune*, Jan. 18, 2000.

Roberts, Brigham H. *Comprehensive History of the Church*. Vol. Six Volumes, Salt Lake City, Utah: Church of Jesus Christ of Latter-day Saints, 1930.

Rolly, Paul. "Court Abolishes Provision Allowing Lawsuits against Spouse's Lover." *Salt Lake Tribune*, Sept. 17, 1991.

———. "Father's Sex Conviction Overturned." *Salt Lake Tribune*, July 26, 1989.

Rowe, Lynn. "Interview in His Home in Orem, Utah ", June 8, 2018.

Rust, Val D. "Male and Female Teachers in Early Utah and the West." *Utah Historical Quarterly* 82, no. 2 Spring (2014): 151-66.

"S.L. Lawyer Named to Utah Top Court." *Deseret News,*, Nov. 4, 1978.

Sabin, Neil. "Interview at His Home in Lehi, Utah, ." June 8, 2018.

Saints, Church of Jesus Christ of Latter-day. "Proclamation to the World." Sept. 23, 1995.

Scharffs, Gilbert. *Mormonism in Germany*. Salt Lake City, Utah: Deseret Book Company, 1970.

Schiel, Lilo. "Interview at Her Home in St. George, Utah, ." August 14, 2018.

Schmemann, Serge. "The Burden of Tolerance in a World of Division." *International Herald Tribune*, Dec. 20, 2002.

School, East High. "Fifty-Ninth Commencement of East High School." June 7, 1951.

Selective Service Local Board, Number 22 "Minutes of Selective Service Local Board ". State of Utah Dec. 14, 1967

Shearer, Kent. "Pragmatic Dogmatics." *Salt Lake Tribune*, Nov. 1, 1979.

Shipp, Royal. "Telephone Interview at His Washington, D.C. Home ", Nov. 7, 2018

Siegel, Brian. *How to Succeed in Law School.* Woodbury, N.Y.: Barron's Educational Series, 1975.

Sillitoe, Linda. *Friendly Fire: The Alcu in Utah.* Salt Lake City, Utah: Signature Books, 1996.

Smart, Donna. "Interview at Her Home in Salt Lake City." Sept. 24, 2018.

Smeath, Doug. "Alienated Spouses Can Sue." *Deseret News,* Sept. 26, 2004.

Smith, Barbara B. "Frequently Asked Questions About the Proposed Equal Rights Amendment: A Closer Look." *Ensign* March (1980).

Smith, Joe "Telephone Interview at His Home in Portland, Oregon ", August 30, 2018

Smith, Joseph F. "Congress and the Mormons." *Improvement Era* (1903): 469-73.

Smith, Melvin T. "Forces That Shaped Utah's Dixie: Another Look." *Utah Historical Quarterly* 47, no. 2 (1979): 110-30.

Snyder, Richard C., and Richard Carlton. *Roots of Political Behavior.* New York: American Book Co., 1949.

Sproul, David Kent. "Environmentalism and the Kaiparowitz Power Project, 1964-76." *Utah Historical Quarterly* 70, no. 4, Fall (2002).

Stark, Rodney, and Charles Y. Glock. *American Piety: The Nature of Religious Commitment.* Berkeley, California: University of California Press, 1968.

"State V. Winkle, 528 P.2d 467." edited by Supreme Court of Utah, 1974.

Stewart, Elizabeth Bryan. "Commencement Address." Unpublished, Undated.

———. "Interview at Her Home in Salt Lake City, Utah." Feb. 25, 2020.

———. "Interview at the Home of Shannon Stewart Clark in Newport Beach, California." Sept. 18, 2017.

———. "Interview at the Home of Shannon Stewart Clark in Newport Beach, California, ." Sept. 17, 2017.

Stewart, I. Daniel, ed. *Addendum,* Missionary Journal. Salt Lake City, Utah: Handwritten undated.

———. "Burden of Proof in Summary Judgment Left Uncertain in Utah."

Utah Law Review 6, no. 3 (1960).

———. "Christmas Postcard to Edward Moreton ", December, 1955.

———. "The Framing of the Constitution." In *Monument Park Stake High Priest's Quorum*, Sept. 17, 1987.

———. "Handwritten Diary." Salt Lake City, Utah: Personal, undated.

———. "Interview at His Home in Salt Lake City, ." Dec. 8, 1999.

———. "Interview at His Salt Lake City Home." Dec. 8, 1999.

———. "Interview with Richard Ellis at Stewart's Home in Salt Lake City." Salt Lake City, Utah, Dec. 8, 1999.

———. "The Law as a Value-Added Profession." In *Speech at the Utah Bar Swearing In*. Salt Lake City, Utah Oct. 15, 1997.

———. "The Legacy and Challenge of the Law." In *Commencement Address, University of Utah, College of Law*, May 24, 1980.

———. "Letter Home to His Mother." Moers, West Germany: Handwritten, Sept. 1, 1954.

———. "Letter to Edward Moreton ", May 21, 1955.

———. "Letter to His Mother." Moers, West Germany: Personally written, August 1, 1954.

———. "Letter to His Mother." Munich, West Germany: Personally written, Oct. 10, 1955.

———. "Letter to His Mother." Moers, West Germany: Handwritten, April 14, 1954.

———. "Letter to Michael Sibbett Regarding Arden Brett Bullock." Nov. 19, 2000.

———. "Letter to Mr. Morris Sorenson, Reno, Nevada." Aug. 31. 1967.

———. "A Life: Dictated to Richard G. Ellis." Salt Lake City, Utah: Draft Manuscript, 2002.

———. "Limited Appearances." *Utah Law Review* 7 (1961).

———. "Missionary Journal ". Hand-written in West Germany 1953-1955.

———. "My Personal Journal ". Salt Lake City Undated

———. "Perception, Memory, and Hearsay: A Criticism of Present Law and the Proposed Federal Rules of Evidence." *Utah Law Review*, no. January (1970).

———. "Republican Institutions in the Twentieth Century." Salt Lake City,

Utah: Political Science Department, 1959.

———. "The Right to Dissent." Salt Lake City, Utah: Graduating Class of 1959 Valedictory Address, 1959.

———. "The Rule of Law and the Dilemma of Minorities." *Dialogue: A Journal of Mormon Thought* III, no. 4 (1968): 70-76.

———. "Speech Given at Swearing in of Admittees to the Utah State Bar." Oct. 9, 1980.

———. "Unconstitutional Conditions." edited by Instructor: F. W. Wormuth. Salt Lake City, Utah: University of Utah, Political Science Course 140, Spring, 1958.

———. "University of Utah Sesquicentennial Founders' Day Celebration." Salt Lake City, Utah Feb. 24, 2000

Stewart, I. Daniel "Letter to the Utah College of Law Alma Mater Office ". Salt Lake City, Utah June 2, 1963.

Stewart, Issac Daniel. "Interview at His Home in Salt Lake City, ." Dec. 8, 1999.

Stewart, Liz. "Interview at Her Mother's Home in Salt Lake City, ." June 6, 2018.

Stewart, Orabelle Iverson. "Memories of Orabelle Iverson Stewart." Salt Lake City: Private manuscript, Dec. 5, 1966.

Stewart, Saundra. "Interview at the Home of Marijana Benesh in Westwood, Ca." Sept. 21, 2019.

———. "Interview in Westwood, California." Sept. 24, 2019.

———. "Letter to Edward Moreton." July 16, 1956.

———. "Telephone Interview with Her in Los Angeles." Oct. 16, 2019

Stranquist, Ruth "Teenagers Can Share the Household Load." *Salt Lake Tribune*, Feb. 2, 1951.

Strauss, Feuerlicht Roberta. *Joe Mccarthy and Mccarthyism: The Hate That Haunts America.* New York: McGraw Hill, 1972.

Stringham, Don. "Interview at His Home in Salt Lake City ", June 4, 2018.

———. "Interview at His Home in Salt Lake City, ." Sept. 29, 2018.

———. "Interview at His Home in Salt Lake City, ." Oct. 27, 2017.

Sullivan, Alan. "Interview in His Salt Lake City Law Office." June 6, 2019.

"Supreme Court Overturns Sexual Abuse Conviction." *Provo Herald*, July 26, 1989.

Swan, Karl. "Interview at His Home in Roy, Utah, ." Feb. 21, 2018.

———. *Missionary Journal*. West German Mission: Hand Written Diary, 1953-1955.

"Talking It Over." *Deseret News*, Oct.2, 11950.

"Task Force Recommends Restrictions on Gun Laws." *Salt Lake Tribune*, Nov. 18, 1994.

"Therapist Denies Interviews Tainted Evidence." *Daily Spectrum*, Oct 24, 1989.

Tobin, James. *The Man He Became: How Fdr Defied Polio to Win the Presidency*. New York: Simon & Schuster, 2013.

"Tribunal Faces 'Critical' Load." *Salt Lake Tribune*, May 10, 1979.

Trimble, Stephen. "Restore Utah's National Monuments." *Los Angeles Times*, Feb. 14, 2021.

"Troubles Also Produce Good, Conference Hears." *Ogden Standard-Examiner*, April 25, 1959.

Turner, Friedrich Jackson. *The Frontier in American History*. New York: Holt, 1920.

U.S. Court of Appeals, Tenth Circuit. "Anderson V. Salt Lake City Corporation, 475 F.2d 29 ", Mar. 19, 1973

———. "Lanner V. Wimmer, 662 F.2d 1349." July 9, 1981.

———. "Pax Company of Utah V. United States, 454 F2d 93." Jan. 26, 1972.

Ulstein, Herbert. "Interview at His Bountiful, Utah Home." Feb. 19, 2018.

"Utah Court Rejects Children's Rights Bill." *Provo Daily Herald*, June 13, 1982.

"Utah Statute on Adultery Lawsuits Overturned." *Deseret News*, Sept. 19, 1991.

"Utah Supreme Court Upholds Salt Lake City Council Prayer." *Times-News (Twin Falls, Idaho)*, Dec. 11, 1993.

"Utahn Sues in-Laws for Alienation of Wife's Affections." *Salt Lake Telegram*, Dec. 27, 1949.

Van Buren, Jessica c., Mari J. F. Cheney, and Marsha C. Thomas. *Utah Legal Research*. Buffalo, New York: William S. Hein & Co., 2011.

Wahlquist, John T. *The Activity School*. Salt Lake City: University of Utah, Department of Elementary Education, 1936.

Walch, Tad. "In Defense of the Insanity Plea." *BYU Magazine* (1997).

Walker, Anita. "Letter to Justice Zimmerman." Nov. 3, 1989.

Walker, Ronald W., Richard E. Turley, Jr., and Glen M. Leonard. *Massacre at Mountain Meadows*. New York: Oxford University Press, 2008.

Walker, Turnley. *Rise up and Walk*. New York: E. P. Dutton & Co., 1950.

Welling, Angie. "Howe Hails Gains by Utah Judiciary." *Deseret News*, Jan. 25, 2002.

White, Jean Bickmore. *The Utah State Constitution: A Reference Guide*. Westport, Connecticut: Greenwood Press, 1998.

Whitney, Liz Stewart. "Interview at the Home of Val Rust in Irvine, California." May 7, 2021.

Whitney, Liz Stewart "E-Mail Message to Author: https://Mail.Google.Com/Mail/U/0/#Inbox/Fmfcgxwjwrclwcvsrxpjxkqbxfbzdqcv." July 20, 2020.

Williams, J. D. "Everett L. Cooley Oral History Project, 1983-2014." edited by University of Utah America West Center. Salt Lake City, Utah: Special Collections Library, October 22, 1984.

Wilson, Randon W. "Interview at the Jones Waldo Law Firm in Salt Lake City." Feb. 1, 2018.

Woodward, John D. "Letter to Orabelle Stewart ". Frankfurt a/M, West Germany March 16, 1957

Wright, Lili. "Elks Lodges May Buck Tradition: Accept Women." *Salt Lake Tribune*, Sept. 23, 1995.

Yorgason, Ethan R. *Transformation of the Mormon Culture Region*. Urbana, Illinois: University of Illinois Press, 2003.

York, U.S. District Court S.D. New. "United States V. Atlantic Richfield Company and Sinclair Oil Corporation, 297 F. Supp. 1061." 1969.

Zekri, Iman. "Respectfully Dissenting: How Dissenting Opinions Shape the Law and Impact Collegiality among Judges." *Florida Bar Journal* 94, no. 5 (Sept./Oct. 2020).

Zimmerman, Michael. "Interview in His Salt Lake City Home," June 16, 2021

INDEX

Aaron, Richard, 163, 171, 172

ACLU, 169, 170, 235, 314, 315, 352

aggravated theft, 300

Albert-Ludwig's University Medical Center, 32

American Atheist Magazine, 316

Amerikahaus, 21

Andrews, William, 245, 299

Antitrust Division, 172, 176

antitrust laws, 180

Appellate Judicial Nominating Commission, 207

Bachman, Gus, 113

Backman, LeGrand P., 312

Baden Württemberg, 16, 24, 32

Baertle, Lilo and Roswitte, 50, 51

basketball, 64, 67, 230, 311

Bates, John, 172

Be Mean to Girls, 68

Bean, Lawrence, 13, 17, 19

Becker, Karl, 14, 15, 17, 18, 19

Beltone, 273

Bennett, Bob and Joyce, 144, 148

Bennett, Robert, 34, 43, 64, 146

Bennett, Wallace F., 34, 102, 144

Bennion Jewelers, 39, 43

Bennion, Ben, 39, 43, 90, 91, 101, 351, 352

Bennion, John, 63, 97, 101, 350, 360, 377

Bennion, Lowell L., 350

Bern Mormon temple, 10

Bern Temple, 18

Berry v. Beech Aircraft, 238, 239, 257, 259, 262

Berry, Lorna J., 257, 258, 259

Beverly Hills, 182

Bill of Rights, 1, 362, 368

Blake, Richard, 183, 273, 325, 366

Bloom, Harold, 86

Board of Education of Topeka, 220

Bodenheimer, Edgar, 136

Book of Mormon, 85, 87, 102, 243,

253, 254, 307, 311, 312, 315, 321, 360, 363

Bowring, Benjamin L., 42

Boyd Park Jewelers, 26, 27, 29, 39, 62

Bradford, Chick and Mary, 145, 149

Brady v. Maryland, 250

Brigham Young University, 34, 117, 132, 140, 205, 221, 229

Brooks, Juanita, 341

Brown, Moroni, 114, 116, 117, 119, 128, 141, 220, 283, 285, 352

Bryan, Elizabeth, 116, 278

Bryant Junior High, 63, 64, 296

Bullock, Arden Brett, 290

Burton, Kit, 189, 191, 192

Cackling Acres Case, 178

Callister, Richard, 141

capital punishment, 4, 244, 246, 308

Caroline Bridge, 347

Castleton, Barbara, 68, 81, 82, 83, 91, 93, 94, 103, 104, 107

Chicago, 114, 144, 150, 151, 153, 166, 229, 230, 235, 312, 363

Christensen, Harold G., 181

civil disobedience, 3

Clayton, Jim, 350, 357

Coleville Tabernacle, 355

Collins, Michael P., 52, 58

common law, 4, 238, 243, 261, 265,

266, 267, 269, 271, 273, 332, 333

Constitutional Law, 133, 161, 208, 212, 237, 268

cornet, 42, 54

Couch, Larry, 67

Court of Appeals, 154, 207, 216, 236, 315, 319, 324

Crabb, Bonnie Lee, 30

Crockett, Allan, 206, 318

Dear John letter, 93

Decker, Ashby, 49, 63, 66, 67, 312

Degnan, Ronan, 131, 135, 147

democracy, 21, 77, 78, 123, 124, 137, 253, 365

Deseret, 28, 65, 67, 130, 222, 229, 252, 284, 364

Deseret News, 28, 65, 67, 222, 229, 284, 364

Dickens, Charles, 116

Dinner and Discussion, 198, 349, 358

dissent, 125, 269, 286, 290, 310, 323, 324, 327, 332, 333, 334, 335

Divorce, 266, 267

Downey, 35, 40, 43, 49, 50, 51, 53, 54, 56, 94, 95, 231

Dryer, Randy, 224

Dunn v. Cook, 249

Durham, Christine, 2, 209, 232, 234, 236, 238, 257, 324, 326, 342, 366

Durham, Christine M., 231, 233, 362

Durham, G. Homer, 62

Durham, George, 53, 96, 97, 232

Dyer, Kenneth B., 10, 11, 20, 23, 29, 30, 33, 34, 36, 73, 83, 86, 88, 91

Dyett v. Turner, 200

Dykstra, Daniel, 115, 131, 136, 164

East High School, 1, 148, 165, 196, 311

Editor-in-Chief, 5, 137, 175

electives, 162

Ellet, Albert H., 1, 196, 205, 206, 223

Ellett, Albert H., 1, 199, 362, 368

Ellis, Dick, 51, 67, 69, 370

Emery, Fred, 136

England, Eugene, 64, 165, 359

Equal Rights Amendment, 149, 197, 198

ERA, 198, 199

eye-witness testimony, 4

Eyring, Henry, 195

Faerber, LeRoy, 85

Federal Heights, 28, 48, 62, 63, 72, 90, 127, 128, 148

Firmage, Edwin B., 164, 201, 347, 365

First Amendment, 184, 200, 313, 318, 328

Flynn, John, 159, 160, 165, 172, 176, 181, 183, 201, 373

Fogg, Gary, 10, 11, 17, 18, 19, 20

football, 5, 11, 42, 64, 65, 66, 67, 98, 182, 222, 311

Fort Ord, 149

Founders' Day Celebration, 373

Fourteenth Amendment, 200, 205, 313

Freeman, Peter, 10, 14, 18, 21, 23

Freiburg, 10, 11, 13, 15, 16, 17, 20, 22, 26, 29, 32, 33, 36, 38, 91, 217

gamma globulin, 22

Garland, Judy, 35

Garn, Jake, 1, 64, 195

Gee, David, 153, 213, 303

George Washington University, 148, 202

German Group, 350, 352, 358

Gisseman, Ralph, 86

God's chosen, 197, 364

Goethe, Johann Wolfgang von, 88, 89, 367

Great Books of the Western World, 107, 114, 321

Griffin, Paul, 67, 69

Groscost, John P., 85

Grotegut, David, 30, 79

Gun Violence, 356

Hall, Gordan R., 2, 212, 236, 237, 286, 290, 299, 318, 333, 334

Handley, Ken and Kate, 127, 170, 349, 359

Hawkins, Carl S., 229

Heine, Heinrich, 88

Hi Fi, 4

Hi-Fi, 298, 299, 300

Highland Dairy, 179

Hoffman, Joel, 145, 146

Holbrook, Don, 174, 177, 178, 185

Holbrook, LeGrand, 29, 103, 158, 174, 184, 302

Holbrook, Mary Louise Stewart, 29, 54, 100, 103, 104, 108, 110, 158, 302

Homer Durham, 112, 132

Horne, Jonathan, 52, 58

Hot Lava Springs, 127, 340

Howe,, 233, 318, 331, 362

Howe, Richard C., 2, 227, 233, 362

Huefner, Bob and Dixie, 358

Hymns, 59

illegal drugs, 300

infantile paralysis, 21

Ingram, Denny, 163

Iverson, Preston, 28, 32, 33, 42, 136, 195, 379

J.J.N.P. Company v. State, 256

Jarvis, George, 36

Jenkins, Bruce, 125, 131, 132

Jerominski, Ellen, 52, 58

Johnson, Lynn Eric, 330, 370

Jones Waldo, 141, 174, 175, 177, 178, 183, 184, 185, 186, 190, 192, 193, 195, 196, 197, 204, 206, 210, 231, 342

Jones, Waldo, 174

Joseph, Utah, 166

Justice Department, 3, 141, 142, 144, 145, 150, 156, 157, 158, 172, 176, 177

Kaiparowits Power Project, 345, 346

Kaiserslautern, 35, 36

Kallas v. Kallas, 254

Kanab, 1, 345

Karpowitz, John, 84

Kennedy, John F., 115, 146, 149

Kenny method, 46, 47

Kenny, Elizabeth, 45

Kimball, Spencer W., 347, 352

Kingsbury Hall, 61, 118, 312

Kirchhoefer, Erich, 10, 19

Kletting, Richard K., 210

Korean War, 149

Korematsu v. United States, 218

Kraft Foods, 153

Kucik, George, 145

Kuehne, Wayne, 81

Lake, Louise, 96

Landstuhl Military Air Base, 34, 38

Larsen, C. Dean, 36, 70

LDS Hospital, 52, 58, 92, 94, 95, 96, 97, 99, 105, 349

Lee, J. Bracken, 114, 206, 300

legacy, 226, 239, 362, 370, 371, 372

Lichtenstein, Grace, 200, 201, 202

lie detector test, 278, 293

Lockhart, Bill, 170, 171

Loftus, Elizabeth, 292, 334

Magna Carta, 116, 257

Malan v. Lewis, 261

March of Dimes, 34, 35

Maryboy v. Utah State Tax Commission, 217

Masheter, Jean, 52, 58

Matheson, Scott, 196, 199, 208, 210, 215, 226, 227, 228, 235, 239, 348

Maughan, Richard J., 203, 231

Mauss, Armand, 363

McGuire Air Force Base, 39

McKay, David O., 28, 29, 59, 352

Meaders, Sister, 53

Mill, John Stewart, 116, 125, 167, 323

Millcreek Canyon, 338

Miller, Michael, 145

Millicent Drive, 186

Missionary Journal, 92

Molen, Ron, 344, 350, 355, 377

Moreton, Ed, 48, 51, 90, 344

mother's rights, 4

Mountain Meadows Massacre, 296, 297

Munich, 12, 16, 22, 26, 50, 86, 88, 90, 91

murder, 203, 245, 246, 249, 250, 266, 284, 296, 300, 302, 308, 314, 331, 332, 335, 359, 367

Murphy, Arthur, 145, 146, 147

Murphy, Michael, 178

Muscular dystrophy, 121, 346

MX project, 346, 347

National Foundation for Infantile Paralysis, 44, 108

National Heart Association, 181

National Socialism, 297

Native Americans, 340

Nazi period, 33

Nazis, 86, 297

New York Traphagen School of Fashion, 276

Nortan v. Macfarlane, 271

Oaks, Dallin, 2, 166, 167, 168, 195, 205, 209, 215, 220, 228, 229, 230, 231, 232, 234, 268, 269, 312, 313, 314, 324, 334, 362, 363

Ogden, 4, 31, 206, 244, 278, 293, 298, 328, 333

Olsen v. Hooley, 291

Olson Farms, 178, 179, 180

Olson, Clarence Dean, 181, 182

On Liberty, 125, 167, 323

Orme, Greg, 202, 236

Orson Spencer Hall, 111, 116

Osborne, Elsie and Evva, 50

Oswald, McKinley, 65

Park, John R., 39, 130

Parley's Canyon, 158, 338

Payson, 31, 267

People's Party, 197

Perry, Geraldine, 44

Peterson, Grethe, 349, 356

Peterson, Winfried, 11, 13, 15, 19, 20, 23, 24, 38
Pierre, Dale S., 299
Pioche, Nevada, 122, 346
Plato, 134
pneumonia, 375, 376
Pocatello, Idaho, 122
polygamy, 168, 197, 252, 267, 320, 363
Polygamy, 267
Polygraph tests, 293
post-polio syndrome, 30, 94, 374
Prows, Michael, 203
psychologists, 4, 45, 276, 277, 278, 279, 280, 282, 292, 294
Psychology, 116, 117, 142, 255, 276, 277, 279, 280, 281, 282
Psychology Today, 276
Rancho Los Amigos, 35, 40, 41, 43, 45, 46, 49, 51, 54, 55, 58, 92, 94, 96, 231, 350, 376
Randolph Air Force Base, 40
Reagan, Ronald, 330
Redford, Robert, 345
released time, 4, 311, 312, 315
Reservoir Park, 66
Richards, Le Grand, 106
Right to Dissent, 171, 323
Rigtrip, Ken, 52, 58
Ritter, Willis, 62, 175
Robbins v. Finlay, 273
Robinson, Preston, 28, 180, 349
Rocky Mountains, 158, 197

Roe v. Wade, 198, 199, 314, 368
Roe vs. Wade, 314
Romney, Vernon B., 202
Roosevelt, Franklyn Delano, 35, 45, 55, 115, 139
Rowe, Lynn, 30
rule of law, 3, 116, 137, 166, 167, 199, 228, 368, 369
Ryan, Patrick, 145
Sabin, Neil, 164
Salk, Jonas, 22, 30
Salt Lake Tribune, 1, 64, 66, 67, 100, 108, 175, 208, 221, 222, 224, 287, 288, 296, 310
Schiller, Friedrich, 88
Schiller, Herbert M., 125, 131
school prayer, 312, 315, 316
Selective Service, 170
Senior Thesis, 123
Sessions v. State, 279
Sevier County, 31, 318
sexual assault, 285, 300, 304, 305, 308
Shakespeare, 149, 367
Sherman, John, 67
Shipp, Royal, 166, 168
Sinatra, Frank, 35
Smith Stewart, Emily, 27, 34, 35, 43, 95
Smith, Barbara B., 198
Smith, Emily Stewart, 92
Smith, George A., 341
Smith, Joe, 148, 158

Snow, Barbara, 286, 287

Snow, Doug, 348

social workers, 4, 282

Society of Separationists, 316

Socratic method, 134

Soroptomist Society, 278

Spafford, Belle, 223

Spafford, Earl Smith, 223, 225

Spanish Fork, 30, 31, 69, 79, 315

St. Joseph's Hospital, 14, 15, 36

State v. Anderson, 263

State v. Bullock, 285, 289

State v. Gibbons, 305

State v. Herrera, 331

State v. Holland, 247, 248

State v. Lowder, 301

State v. Mace, 274

State v. Ramsey, 294, 305

State v. Standiford, 248

State v. Webb, 335

State v. Winkle, 199

Stegmann, Erich, 54

Stewart Lab School, 51, 63

Stewart Laboratory School, 62, 63, 311, 373

Stewart, Carolyn, 26, 27, 108, 109

Stewart, Daniel Sr., 59, 60, 61, 62

Stewart, Elizabeth, 222, 355

Stewart, Isaac Mitton, 130

Stewart, Orabelle, 26, 27, 28, 29, 32, 39, 40, 41, 42, 43, 60, 61, 62, 119, 201

Stewart, Saundra, 48, 50, 108

Stewart, Shannon, 360

stigma damages, 271, 272

Stirba, Anne, 214

Stringham, Don A., 88, 89, 90, 98, 111, 127, 132, 222, 349, 350, 356

Swan, Karl, 10, 14, 18, 21, 217

Swenson, Bob, 131, 136

Switzerland, 10, 16

Taylor, Kenneth, 31

tennis, 42, 64, 66, 222, 311

Texas, 40, 146, 174

The Book of Mormon, 253, 340, 365

Thomas, Robert, 43, 44

Truman, Harry S., 150

Tuckett, Robert LeRoy, 199

University of Utah, 5, 11, 52, 58, 59, 61, 62

Utah Bar Association, 196, 215, 224

Utah Law Review, 5, 136, 137, 175, 289

Utah State University, 117, 174

Utah Symphony, 27, 28, 174

Utah vernacular, 140

Utah Wilderness Act, 139

valedictory address, 5, 124, 323

van Pelt, Marion, 65

Vietnam war, 170

Walker Drug Company, Inc. v. La Sal Oil Co, 272

Watkins, David, 165

Weber State University, 333

Whitcomb, Hazel, 65, 115

Wilkins, D. Frank, 203, 227, 228, 233

Williams, J. D., 84, 113, 141, 325

Wilson, Randon, 179, 183

Wood, Steven A., 245, 246, 247, 248, 249, 299

Wood, Steven G., 162

Woodward, John D., 43

World War II, 3, 35, 46, 54, 60, 73, 76, 78, 139, 218, 364

Wormuth, Francis, 5, 111, 112, 113, 114, 243

Xenophon, 134

Zander, Ingo, 85

Zen Buddhism, 236

Zimmerman, Michael, 2

Zimmerman, Michael D., 234, 362

Zion National Park, 342